원서 읽는 단어장

new moon

Long tail Books

Contents

원서 읽는 단어장 소개 · 6
이 책의 구성 · 8
영어원서 읽기 전문가가 대답해주는 FAQ · 11

PREFACE
Vocabulary in New Moon · 16

1. PARTY
Comprehension Quiz · 18
Vocabulary in New Moon · 20

2. STITCHES
Comprehension Quiz · 46
Vocabulary in New Moon · 48

3. THE END
Comprehension Quiz · 66
Vocabulary in New Moon · 68

4. WAKING UP
Comprehension Quiz · 86
Vocabulary in New Moon · 88

5. CHEATER
Comprehension Quiz 108
Vocabulary in New Moon 110

6. FRIENDS
Comprehension Quiz 122
Vocabulary in New Moon 124

7. REPETITION
Comprehension Quiz 138
Vocabulary in New Moon 140

8. ADRENALINE
Comprehension Quiz 154
Vocabulary in New Moon 156

9. THIRD WHEEL
Comprehension Quiz 170
Vocabulary in New Moon 172

10. THE MEADOW
Comprehension Quiz 186
Vocabulary in New Moon 188

11. CULT
Comprehension Quiz	208
Vocabulary in New Moon	210

12. INTRUDER
Comprehension Quiz	226
Vocabulary in New Moon	228

13. KILLER
Comprehension Quiz	242
Vocabulary in New Moon	244

14. FAMILY
Comprehension Quiz	256
Vocabulary in New Moon	258

15. PRESSURE
Comprehension Quiz	270
Vocabulary in New Moon	272

16. PARIS
Comprehension Quiz	284
Vocabulary in New Moon	286

17. VISITOR
Comprehension Quiz	298
Vocabulary in New Moon	290

18. THE FUNERAL
Comprehension Quiz	314
Vocabulary in New Moon	316

19. RACE
Comprehension Quiz 330
Vocabulary in New Moon 332

20. VOLTERRA
Comprehension Quiz 342
Vocabulary in New Moon 344

21. VERDICT
Comprehension Quiz 356
Vocabulary in New Moon 358

22. FLIGHT
Comprehension Quiz 374
Vocabulary in New Moon 376

23. THE TRUTH
Comprehension Quiz 386
Vocabulary in New Moon 388

24. VOTE
Comprehension Quiz 398
Vocabulary in New Moon 400

EPILOGUE: TREATY
Comprehension Quiz 412
Vocabulary in New Moon 414

Answers 426
Index 428
영어원서 읽기 Tips 454

원서 읽는 단어장 소개

누구나 추천하는 최고의 영어 공부법, 영어원서 읽기!

최근 영어원서 읽기가 영어 공부법으로 주목받고 있습니다. 영어를 많이 접하는 것이 영어 실력을 향상시키는 가장 바람직한 방법이라는 공감대가 형성되면서, 쉽고 저렴하게 영어를 접할 수 있는 '원서 읽기'가 그 대안으로 각광받고 있는 것이지요.

실제로도 영어 좀 한다는 사람들이 원서 읽기를 추천하거나, 어린 아이들이 엄마표 영어 연수 등을 통해 원서를 읽는 많은 사례들을 인터넷 상에서 쉽게 찾아볼 수 있습니다.

원서 읽기를 위한 최고의 친구, 『원서 읽는 단어장』!

원서 읽기가 영어 공부를 하는 좋은 수단이긴 하지만, 한 번쯤 원서를 읽어본 독자들은 대부분 다음과 같은 고민을 하곤 합니다.

> 누가 여기 나오는 단어 좀 찾아주면 안 되나?
> 모르는 단어가 나올 때마다 사전을 찾을 수도 없고,
> 그렇다고 그냥 지나치자니 뭔가 찜찜한데...
>
> 지금 내가 제대로 읽고 이해하고 있는 걸까?
> 번역된 책을 찾아서 일일이 대조할 수도 없고,
> 뭔가 확인할 방법이 있었으면 좋겠는데...

이런 문제를 해결해주고자, 여기 『원서 읽는 단어장』이 왔습니다!
원서 읽는 단어장은, 영어원서에 나온 어려운 어휘들을 완벽히 정리해서 원

서 읽기의 부담감을 줄이고 보다 효과적으로 영어 실력을 쌓을 수 있도록 도와주는 책입니다. 또한 이해력을 점검하는 Comprehension Quiz를 통해 내가 원서를 정확히 읽고 있는지 확인해볼 수 있습니다.

『원서 읽는 단어장』시리즈를 통해 영어원서를 보다 쉽고 재미있게 읽고, 영어 실력도 쑥쑥 향상시켜보세요.

이 책은 Stephenie Meyer(스테프니 메이어)의 대표작 The Twilight #2:New Moon(뉴문) 독자들을 위해 만들어졌습니다. 위 영어원서는 시중 서점 및 인터넷 서점에서 쉽게 구입할 수 있습니다.

이 책의 구성

Comprehension Quiz

원서를 제대로 읽고 이해하고 있는지 측정해보는 간단한 퀴즈입니다.
원어민 Extensive Reading 전문가가 출제한 쉽고 재미있는 문제들로 구성되어 있습니다. 퀴즈를 풀어보고 틀린 부분이 있다면, 제대로 이해한 것이 맞는지 해당 내용을 다시 한 번 점검해봐야겠죠?

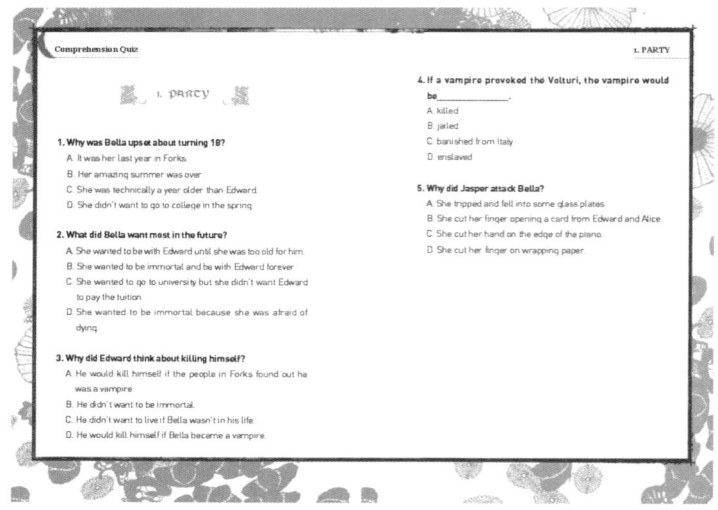

퀴즈는 각 챕터별로 약 5개 안팎의 문제가 출제되어 있습니다.
각 챕터를 읽고 바로 문제를 풀어보는 것도 좋고, 혹은 시간이 되는 대로 쭉 읽은 후 해당 부분만큼 문제를 풀어보는 것도 좋은 방법입니다. 자신의 상황과 스타일에 맞게 적절히 활용하세요!

정답은 426페이지에 있습니다.

Vocabulary in New Moon

원서에 등장하는 어려운 어휘가 정리되어 있습니다.

단어는 각 챕터별로, 원서에서 단어가 등장하는 순서 그대로 정리되어 있으며, [빈도-스펠링-발음기호-한글 뜻-영어 뜻] 순으로 표기되어 있습니다.

별표(★)가 많을수록 필수 어휘입니다. 또 이전 챕터에서 등장한 중요 어휘가 반복해서 나올 때는 '**복습**'이라고 표시해서 정리했습니다.

어휘 목록 중에 아주 기초적인 어휘는 제외되어 있습니다. 원서를 읽을 때 여기 나와 있는 단어 외에도 모르는 어휘가 너무 많다면, '내 영어 수준보다 지나치게 어려운 책을 골랐다'는 의미가 됩니다. 이런 경우에는 일단 더 쉬운 원서에 도전하는 것이 좋은 방법입니다.

여기 정리된 단어를 일일이 손으로 쓰면서 '암기'하려고 하지는 마세요! 실질적인 어휘 암기는 원서를 읽으면서 문맥 속에서 단어와 자주 마주칠 때 이루어집니다!

단어 리스트는 원서를 읽기 전, 후에 눈으로 쭉 살피면서 '단어와 익숙해지도록' 만드는 데 활용하세요. 원서를 읽을 때 단어에서 오는 부담감이 줄어들고, 매우 효율적으로 어휘 실력을 향상시킬 수 있습니다.

영어 원서 읽기 전문가가 대답해주는 FAQ

Q. New Moon은 어떤 책인지 알려주세요.

A. New Moon은 미국 소설가 스테프니 메이어(Stephenie Meyer)가 쓴 판타지 로맨스 소설 Twilight 시리즈의 두 번째 책입니다. #1 Twilight에서 서로 사랑을 확인한 벨라와 에드워드. 벨라를 죽이려는 악한 뱀파이어의 위협을 겪으며 더 깊어진 둘의 사랑은 #2 New Moon에서도 이어지는데요. 뱀파이어라는 이색적인 소재와 십 대 남녀의 사랑과 삼각관계라는 클래식한 스토리로 주로 여성 독자들에게 폭발적인 사랑을 받고 있습니다.

New Moon은 전편인 Twilight, 그리고 New Moon, Eclipse, Breaking Dawn과 함께 Twilight Series 혹은 Twilight Saga라고 불립니다. Twilight 시리즈는 여자 주인공인 Bella의 관점에서 서술하고 있는데, 같은 내용을 남자 주인공인 Edward의 관점에서 서술한 번외편 Midnight Sun도 있습니다. (2010년 현재 Midnight Sun은 아직 출간되지는 않은 상태입니다.)

New Moon Series는 2005년 출간된 이래 전 세계 38개 이상의 언어로 번역되어 8천 5백만 부 이상이 팔렸으며, 2008년부터 파라마운트 영화사에 의해 영화화되기 시작하여 2008년에 #1 Twilight이, 2009년에는 #2 New Moon이, 2010년에는 #3 Eclipse가 영화로 개봉되어 엄청난 흥행 성적을 거뒀습니다. 이 덕분에 국내에서도 번역판과 영어 원서 모두 큰 사랑을 받고 있습니다.

Q. New Moon이 제게 맞는 영어 원서인지 모르겠어요. 어떤 사람들이 이 책을 원서로 읽으면 좋을까요?

A. 무엇보다 이 책은 사람에 따라서 호불호가 갈리는 책이라는 점을 알아둬야 하겠습니다. 이 책을 가장 좋아할 만한 독자는 10대~20대의 여성들이라고 할 수 있습니다. (미국에서 처음 출간될 때에도 성인용 소설이 아닌 Children's Series Books로 분류되어 있었습니다.) 또한 평소에 로맨스 소설을 즐겨 읽지 않던 독자라면 유명하다는 이유만으로 이 책을 선택해서는 완독하기가 쉽지 않을 것입니다.

이 책의 영어 수준 역시 상당한 편입니다. 일단 분량이 많고, 사용된 어휘 역시 수준이 높습니다. (이 단어장만 훑어 봐도 책에 사용된 어휘 수준을 확인할 수 있습니다.) 따라서 처음 원서 읽기를 시작하는 초보자라면 완독에 어려움을 겪을 수 있습니다. 영어 수준만 생각해본다면 토익 점수 800점 이상 고득점자들에게 권할 만한 책입니다.

하지만 재미있는 사실은 이 책의 경우 호불호가 분명하게 갈리는 책이라 그런지 이 책의 내용을 얼마나 좋아하는지가 완독 여부를 많이 좌우한다는 것입니다. 원서를 선택할 때 자신의 영어 수준을 감안하는 것도 중요하지만, 그 책을 읽으려는 의지가 얼마나 큰지 여부 또한 매우 중요하다는 이야기입니다. 실제로 주변에서 이 책을 읽는 분들을 살펴봤을 때, 이 시리즈를 읽을 만큼 리딩에 능숙하지 않은 분들도 모든 시리즈를 별 어려움 없이 읽는 경우가 많았고, 반대로 영어에는 문제가 없지만 내용이 너무 맞지 않아서 몇 챕터를 읽기도 전에 포기하는 독자들도 많았습니다. 따라서 Twilight 시리즈의 열혈 팬이라면 영어 수준과 상관없이 원서로도 한번 읽어볼 것을 권합니다. 하지만 이 시리즈에 대해서 잘 모르고 있는 독자라면 우선 책에 대해서 더 알아본 뒤에 결정할 것을 권하겠습니다.

Q. 꼭 읽어보고 싶은데 책이 만만치가 않습니다. 좀 도와주세요!

A. 일단 모르는 단어와 문장이 나올 때마다 멈춰서 사전을 찾아보지 말고, 부분적으로 이해가 되지 않더라도 전체 스토리를 생각하면서 계속 읽어나가세요. 「원서 읽는 단어장」을 활용할 때에도 해당 챕터에 나오는 단어를 외우려고 하기보다, 어떤 단어들이 있는지 살펴본다는 기분으로 쭉 훑어보고 내가 모르는 단어들을 좀 더 주의 깊게 살펴본 뒤에 바로 리딩을 시작하세요.

분량이 상당한 책이기 때문에 하루에 1~2페이지씩 천천히 읽어서는 중간에 포기할 가능성이 아주 큽니다. 정확한 이해보다는 전체 스토리 맥락에 맞춰서 **빠르게 읽어나간다는** 생각으로 읽어보세요. 처음에는 힘들더라도 진도가 나갈수록 익숙해지는 단어가 많아지면서 자연히 이해도도 높아질 것입니다. 또 책을 읽기 전에 영화를 보고 읽어보시는 것도 도움이 될 것입니다.

    일단 #1 Twilight과 #2 New Moon의 내용이 자신에게 잘 맞고 완독에 별 어려움이 없었다면, 그 다음 책들인 Eclipse, Breaking Dawn도 읽어보세요. 유사한 어휘들이 반복적으로 사용되기 때문에 처음 읽을 때보다 훨씬 수월할 것입니다. 또한 Twilight Saga의 후속편들의 단어장들은 함께 모여 영어 원서를 읽는 스피드 리딩 카페(cafe.naver.com/readingtc)에 무료 PDF 파일로 올라와 있습니다. 이 PDF 파일을 활용하시면 시리즈의 다른 책들도 보다 부담 없이 읽으실 수 있을 것입니다.

Comprehension Quiz
Vocabulary in New Moon

Vocabulary in New Moon

* **terrify** [térəfài] vt. 무섭게[겁나게] 하다, 놀래다 (terrifying a. 놀라게 하는; 무서운)
  If something terrifies you, it makes you feel extremely frightened.

* **lung** [lʌŋ] n. [해부] 폐, 허파
  Your lungs are the two organs inside your chest which fill with air when you breathe in.

* **burst** [bə:rst] v. 파열하다, 터지다; 갑자기 …하다; n. 파열, 돌발
  To break open or apart suddenly.

* **callous** [kǽləs] a. 무감각한, 냉담한; 예사인; (피부가) 굳은, 못 박힌
  Not caring about other people's feelings or suffering.

* **relentless** [riléntlis] a. 냉혹한, 집요한
  Never stopping or getting any less extreme.

* **inexorable** [inéksərəbəl] a. 냉혹[무정]한; 굽힐 수 없는, 움직일 수 없는, 엄연한 (inexorably ad. 냉혹하게)
  Cannot be stopped or changed.

* **infinitely** [ínfənətli] ad. 무한히, 대단히, 몹시
  Used especially in comparisons very much.

* **extraordinary** [ikstrɔ́:rdənèri] a. 보통이 아닌, 비범[대단 · 비상]한 (extraordinarily ad. 비상하게, 엄청[유별]나게)
  Unexpected, surprising or strange.

* **toll** [toul] v. 울리다, 치다
  When a bell tolls or when someone tolls it, it rings slowly and repeatedly, often as a sign that someone has died.

* **vibrate** [vaibreit] v. 진동하다, (시계추처럼) 흔들리다
  If something vibrates or if you vibrate it, it shakes with repeated small, quick movements.

* **sole** [soul] ① n. 발바닥, 말굽 바닥; (구두 등의) 밑창 ② a. 단 하나의; 단독의
  The bottom surface of the foot.

PREFACE

* **sluggish** [slʌ́giʃ] a. 둔한, 활발하지 못한; 느린, 굼뜬; 부진한
  Moving, reacting or working more slowly than normal and in a way that seems lazy.

  bloodthirsty [blʌ́dθə̀ːrsti] a. 피에 굶주린, 잔인한, 흉악한
  Wanting to kill or wound; Enjoying seeing or hearing about killing and violence.

* **forfeit** [fɔ́ːrfit] vt. 상실하다, 몰수되다; n. 벌금, 과태료; 상실, 박탈
  To lose something or have something taken away from you because you have done something wrong.

※PREFACE는 Comprehension Quiz가 없습니다.

Comprehension Quiz

 1. PARTY

1. Why was Bella upset about turning 18?

   A. It was her last year in Forks.

   B. Her amazing summer was over.

   C. She was technically a year older than Edward.

   D. She didn't want to go to college in the spring.

2. What did Bella want most in the future?

   A. She wanted to be with Edward until she was too old for him.

   B. She wanted to be immortal and be with Edward forever.

   C. She wanted to go to university but she didn't want Edward to pay the tuition.

   D. She wanted to be immortal because she was afraid of dying.

3. Why did Edward think about killing himself?

   A. He would kill himself if the people in Forks found out he was a vampire.

   B. He didn't want to be immortal.

   C. He didn't want to live if Bella wasn't in his life.

   D. He would kill himself if Bella became a vampire.

1. PARTY

4. If a vampire provoked the Volturi, the vampire would be_____.

   A. killed
   B. jailed
   C. banished from Italy
   D. enslaved

5. Why did Jasper attack Bella?

   A. She tripped and fell into some glass plates.
   B. She cut her finger opening a card from Edward and Alice.
   C. She cut her hand on the edge of the piano.
   D. She cut her finger on wrapping paper.

Vocabulary in New Moon

* **shaft** [ʃæft] n. 자루, 손잡이; 한 줄기의 광선
  A narrow beam of light.

* **shone** [ʃoun] v. shine(빛나다, 비치다, 빛을 내다)의 과거·과거분사
  To produce or reflect light.

* **drizzle** [drizl] n. 이슬[가랑]비; vi. 이슬비[가랑비]가 내리다
  (drizzly a. 이슬비[가랑비] 내리는)
  Drizzle is light rain falling in fine drops.

* **wither** [wíðər] v. 시들다, 말라죽다
  To become weak and dry and decay.

* **bent** [bent] a. 굽은, 구부러진; 열중한, 결심한; n. 경향
  Not straight; Curved or having a bend.

  crease [kri:s] n. 주름, 구김살; v. 주름이 생기다, 주름투성이로 만들다, 구기다
  Creases are lines that are made in cloth or paper when it is crushed or folded.

* **cling** [kliŋ] vi. (clung-clung) 달라붙다, 매달리다
  If you cling to someone or something, you hold onto them tightly.

* **apricot** [éiprəkàt] n. [식물] 살구(열매); 살구나무
  An apricot is a small, soft, round fruit with yellowish-orange flesh and a stone inside.

  wizened [wi(:)znd] a. (사람·얼굴 등이) 시든, 쭈글쭈글한
  Looking smaller and having many folds and lines in the skin, because of being old.

  pucker [pʌ́kər] v. (입술 등을) 오므리다; 주름잡다, 구겨지다; n. 주름
  Something up to form or to make something form small folds or lines.

  awkwardness [ɔ́:kwərdnis] n. 어색함, 다루기 어려움; 거북함
  The quality of an embarrassing situation.

* **reunion** [ri:jú:niən] n. 재결합, 재회; 화해, 융화
  The act of people coming together after they have been apart for some time.

20

1. PARTY

slosh [slɑʃ] v. 절벅절벅 휘젓다, 물을 튀기다; n. (액체가) 튀어 흩어짐, 튀어 오름
To move around noisily in the bottom of a container, or to cause liquid to move around in this way by making rough movements.

‡ **thrill** [θril] v. 감동[감격·흥분]시키다; 오싹하다; n. 전율 (thrilled a. 흥분한, 감격한)
If something thrills you, it gives you a feeling of great pleasure and excitement.

‡ **shatter** [ʃǽtər] v. 산산조각이 나다; 파괴하다; n. 파편, 부서진 조각
If something shatters or is shattered, it breaks into a lot of small pieces.

shard [ʃɑːrd] n. (유리·금속 등의) 조각[파편]
A piece of broken glass, metal, etc.

‡ **glitter** [glítər] vi. 반짝반짝 빛나다, 반짝이다; n. 반짝거림, 광채
If something glitters, light comes from or is reflected off different parts of it.

‡ **stroll** [stroul] vi. 한가롭게 거닐다, 산책하다; n. 산책
If you stroll somewhere, you walk there in a slow, relaxed way.

★ **horrify** [hɔ́ːrəfài] vt. 소름끼치게 하다, 충격을 주다 (horrified a. 겁에 질린, 충격받은)
If someone is horrified, they feel shocked or disgusted, because of something that they have seen or heard.

sheepish [ʃíːpiʃ] a. 양 같은, 수줍어하는 (sheepishly ad. 수줍어하면서)
Slightly uncomfortable or embarrassed because you know that you have done something silly.

‡ **scold** [skould] v. 꾸짖다, 잔소리하다
If you scold someone, you speak angrily to them because they have done something wrong.

‡ **awkward** [ɔ́ːkwərd] a. 어색한, 불편한, 곤란한 (awkwardly ad. 어색하게, 거북하게)
An awkward situation is embarrassing and difficult to deal with.

‡ **enclose** [enklóuz] vt. 둘러싸다, 에워싸다; 넣다, 동봉하다
To build a wall, fence, etc. around something.

uncomprehending [ənkὰmprihéndiŋ] a. 잘 이해되지 않는, 이해력이 부족한
Not understanding a situation or what is happening.

Vocabulary in New Moon

- **mimic** [mímik] vt. 흉내 내다, 흉내 내어 조롱하다, 꼭 닮다
  If you mimic the actions or voice of a person or animal, you imitate them, usually in a way that is meant to be amusing or entertaining.

- **dizzy** [dízi] a. 현기증 나는, 아찔한
  If you feel dizzy, you feel as if everything is spinning round and being unable to balance.

- **jolt** [dʒoult] n. 충격, 급격한 동요; v. 덜컹거리다
  A sudden shock.

- **abrupt** [əbrʌ́pt] a. 갑작스러운, 뜻밖의 (abruptly ad. 갑자기)
  Sudden and unexpected.

- **reflection** [riflékʃən] n. (거울·물 등에 비친) 영상; 반사, 반영
  A reflection is an image that you can see in a mirror or in glass or water.

  excruciating [ikskrúːʃièitiŋ] a. 고문을 당하는 듯한; 몹시 마음을 아프게 하는 (excruciatingly ad. 괴롭게, 마음 아프게)
  Extremely painful or bad.

- **eyelid** [áilìd] n. (보통 pl.) 눈꺼풀(lid)
  Either of the two pieces of skin which can close over each eye.

- **pop** [pap] v. 갑자기 움직이다; 뻥 소리나다, 발포하다; n. 뻥[탁] 소리, 발포
  If you pop something somewhere, you put it there quickly.

  gasp [gæsp] v. (놀람 따위로) 숨이 막히다, 헐떡거리다; n. 헐떡거림
  When you gasp, you take a short quick breath through your mouth, especially when you are surprised, shocked, or in pain.

  dull [dʌl] a. 흐릿한, 따분한, 재미없는; 둔한, 활기 없는
  Not bright or shiny.

- **overcast** [òuvərkǽst] a. (하늘이) 흐린, 우중충한, 음울한
  Covered with clouds; Dull.

- **prophetic** [prəfétik] a. 예언의, 예언적인
  Correctly stating or showing what will happen in the future.

1. PARTY

* **bleak** [bli:k] a. 황폐한, 쓸쓸한, 냉혹한
  Without anything to make you feel happy or hopeful.

☆ **lurk** [lə:rk] vi. 숨다, 잠복하다; n. 잠복, 밀행
  If someone lurks somewhere, they wait there secretly so that they cannot be seen, usually because they intend to do something bad.

ambush [ǽmbuʃ] n. 매복[잠복]; 매복 공격; 복병; v. 매복하다; 매복하여 습격하다
  The act of hiding and waiting for somebody and then making a surprise attack on them.

quantify [kwάntəfài] v. 양을 나타내다, 수량화하다
  (quantifiable a. 수량화할 수 있는, 계량 가능한)
  To describe or express something as an amount or a number.

impend [impénd] vi. (위험·사건 따위가) 절박[임박]하다, 일어나려 하다
  Describes an event, usually something unpleasant or unwanted, that is going to happen soon.

☆ **wrinkle** [ríŋkəl] n. 주름, 잔주름; v. 주름살지게 하다, 구겨지다
  A line or small fold in your skin, especially on your face, that forms as you get older.

lodge in idiom …에 박히다
  To become fixed or stuck somewhere; To make something become fixed or stuck somewhere.

☆ **cheerful** [tʃíərfəl] a. 쾌활한, 명랑한
  Someone who is cheerful is happy and shows this in their behavior.

☆ **despair** [dispέər] n. 절망, 자포자기; vi. 절망하다, 체념하다
  Despair is the feeling that everything is wrong and that nothing will improve.

parking lot [pά:rkiŋ lὰt] n. 주차장
  An open area for cars to park in.

* **spot** [spɑt] vt. 발견[분별]하다; 더럽히다; n. 반점, 얼룩; 장소, 지점
  If you spot something or someone, you notice them.

Vocabulary in New Moon

‡ **polish** [páliʃ] v. 닦다, 윤내다; n. 광택; 세련
If you polish something, you rub it with a cloth to make it shine.

‡ **tribute** [tríbjuːt] n. 감사[칭찬·존경·애정]의 표시; 공물, 연공
A tribute is something that you say, do, or make to show your admiration and respect for someone.

pagan [péigən] n. 이교도
A person who holds religious beliefs that are not part of any of the world's main religions.

momentarily [mòuməntérəli] ad. 잠시, 잠깐
Momentarily means for a short time.

‡ **vanish** [væniʃ] v. 사라지다, 없어지다, 모습을 감추다
If someone or something vanishes, they disappear suddenly or in a way that cannot be explained.

sibling [síbliŋ] n. 형제, 자매
Your siblings are your brothers and sisters.

adopt [ədápt] vt. 입양하다; 채택하다; 선정하다
To take someone else's child into your home and legally become its parent.

‡ **precisely** [prisáisli] ad. 정밀하게, 정확히, 정확하게
Exactly.

‡ **bruise** [bruːz] n. 타박상, 멍; v. …에게 타박상을 주다, 멍들게 하다
A blue, brown or purple mark that appears on the skin after somebody has fallen, been hit, etc.

* **startling** [stáːrtliŋ] a. 놀라운, 깜짝 놀라게 하는 (startlingly ad. 놀랍도록, 놀랄 만큼)
Extremely unusual and surprising.

* **similarity** [sìməlǽrəti] n. 유사, 비슷함; 유사점
If there is a similarity between two or more things, they are similar to each other.

* **tawny** [tɔ́ːni] n. 황갈색; a. 황갈색의
Brownish-yellow in color.

1. PARTY

- **frown** [fraun] v. 눈살을 찌푸리다, 얼굴을 찡그리다; 찌푸린 얼굴
  To wrinkle the brow, as in thought or displeasure.

- **slam** [slæm] v. (문 따위를) 탕 닫다, 세게 치다; 털썩 내려놓다; n. 쾅 (하는 소리)
  If a door, gate etc. slams, or if someone slams it, it shuts with a loud noise.

  Chevy [ʃévi] n. (= Chevrolet) 시보레(미국 GM사가 제작한 자동차 이름) 애칭

- **speck** [spek] n. 작은 반점, 얼룩
  A speck is a very small stain, mark, or shape.

  flutter down phrasal v. 떨어지다; 흔들리다; 펄럭이다
  To move gently through the air to the ground.

  pixie [píksi:] a. 장난치는, 장난기 있는; n. 작은 요정; 장난꾸러기
  An imaginary little creature like a fairy.

- **hiss** [his] v. 쉿 하는 소리를 내다; n. 쉿 (제지·힐책의 소리)
  If people hiss at someone such as a performer or a person making a speech, they express their disapproval or dislike of that person.

- **eager** [í:gər] a. 열망하는, 간절히 하고 싶어 하는 (eagerly ad. 열망하여; 열심히; 간절히)
  If you are eager to do or have something, you want to do or have it very much.

- **protest** [prətést] v. 항의하다, 이의를 제기하다; 주장하다; n. 항의
  If you protest against something or about something, you say or show publicly that you object to it.

- **mumble** [mʌ́mbəl] n. 중얼거림; v. 중얼거리다, 웅얼거리다
  Speech or words that are spoken in a quiet voice in a way that is not clear.

- **senior** [sí:njər] n. (최)상급생; 연장자, 선배; a. 손위의; 선배의, 최고 학년의
  A student in the last year at a high school or college.

  glum [glʌm] a. 음울한, 시무룩한, 풀죽은
  Disappointed or unhappy, and quiet.

- **squeeze** [skwi:z] vt. 꽉 쥐다[죄다], 압착하다; n. 압착, 짜냄
  If you squeeze something, you press it firmly, usually with your hands.

Vocabulary in New Moon

stutter [stʌ́tər] n. 말 더듬기; v. 말을 더듬다, 더듬거리며 말하다
A speech problem in which a person finds it difficult to say the first sound of a word and repeats it several times.

articulation [ɑːrtìkjəléiʃən] n. 또렷한[명확한] 발음
The expression of an idea or a feeling in words.

tousle [táuzəl] vt. (머리카락을) 헝클어뜨리다; 마구 다루다 (tousled a. 헝클어진)
To make somebody's hair untidy.

※ **bronze** [brɑnz] n. 구릿빛; 청동
Dark reddish-brown in color.

※ **chime** [tʃaim] n. 차임, 종소리; v. (한 벌의 종·시계가) 울리다
A ringing sound, especially one that is made by a bell.

★ **rhetorical** [ritɔ́(ː)rikəl] a. 수사학의; 수사적인
(of a speech or piece of writing) Intended to influence people, but not completely honest or sincere.

preferable [préfərəbəl] a. 오히려 나은, 보다 바람직한
(preferably ad. 더 좋아하여, 가급적(이면))
If you say that one thing is preferable to another, you mean that it is more desirable or suitable.

★ **immortal** [imɔ́ːrtl] a. 불사의, 불멸의, 영원한; n. 영생하는 존재; 불멸의 인물
That lives or lasts for ever.

impasse [ímpæs] n. 막다른 골목; 난국, 곤경
If people are in a difficult position in which it is impossible to make any progress, you can refer to the situation as an impasse.

★ **mortality** [mɔːrtǽləti] n. 죽음을 면할 수 없음, 사망
The State of being human and not living for ever.

※ **complain** [kəmpléin] v. 불평하다, 투덜거리다
To say that something is wrong or not satisfactory.

1. PARTY

smug [smʌg] a. 잘난 체하는, 거만한 (smugly ad. 잘난 체하며)
Too pleased or satisfied about something you have achieved or something you know.

stammer [stǽmər] v. 말을 더듬다, 더듬으며 말하다
If you stammer, you speak with difficulty, hesitating and repeating words or sounds.

scramble for idiom …을 얻으려고 다투다
If a number of people scramble for something, they compete energetically with each other for it.

snort [snɔːrt] v. 콧김을 뿜다, (경멸·불찬성 등으로) 콧방귀 뀌다
To breathe air in a noisy way out through your nose to show that you are annoyed.

appreciate [əprí:ʃièit] vt. 진가를 인정하다; 평가하다, 감상하다; 고맙게 생각하다
To recognize the good qualities of something.

accuse [əkjú:z] v. 비난하다, 고발하다
To say that someone has done something morally wrong, illegal or unkind.

grin [grin] v. 이를 드러내고 싱긋 웃다; n. 싱긋 웃음
When you grin, you smile broadly.

glisten [glisn] vi. 반짝이다, 빛나다
If something glistens, it shines, usually because it is wet or oily.

peck [pek] vt. (구어) 인사치레로[마지못해·급히] 키스하다
If you peck someone on the cheek, you give them a quick, light kiss.

administrator [ædmínəstrèitər] n. 관리자, 행정인
A person whose job is to manage and organize the public or business affairs of a company or an institution.

cheekbone [tʃíːkbòun] n. 광대뼈
The bone below the eye.

Vocabulary in New Moon

prominent [prάmənənt] a. 현저한, 두드러진
Sticking out from something.

bristly [brísəli] a. 털이 억센; 빽빽이[꼿꼿이] 들어선; 화낸
Bristly hair is thick and rough.

disarray [dìsəréi] n. 혼란, 난잡; 단정치 못한 옷차림
A state of confusion and lack of organization in a situation or a place.

❉ **inspiration** [ìnspəréiʃən] n. 영감, 고취, 고무
A sudden good idea.

achieve [ətʃíːv] v. 이루다, 성취[완수]하다, 달성하다; (명성을) 얻다; 쟁취하다
To succeed in reaching a particular goal, status or standard, especially by making an effort for a long time.

❉ **imitation** [ìmitéiʃən] n. 모방, 흉내; 모조, 모사
An imitation of something is a copy of it.

❉ **mourn** [mɔːrn] v. 슬퍼하다, 한탄하다
If you mourn someone who has died or mourn for them, you are very sad that they have died and show your sorrow in the way that you behave.

accident-prone [ǽksidəntproun] a. (사람·차 등이) 사고를 많이 내기[당하기] 쉬운
If you describe someone or something as accident-prone, you mean that a lot of accidents or other unpleasant things happen to them.

klutz [klʌts] n. (미·속어) 손재주 없는 사람, 얼간이
A person who often drops things, is not good at sport(s), etc.

❉ **pointedly** [pɔ́intidli] ad. (말 등을) 날카롭게[비난하듯이]
In a way that is clearly intended to show what you mean or to express criticism.

✶ **kindergarten** [kíndərgὰːrtn] n. 유치원
A school or class for children aged five.

❉ **income** [ínkʌm] n. 수입, 소득
The money that a person, a region, a country, etc. earns from work, from investing money, from business, etc.

1. PARTY

- **microscopic** [màikrəskápik] a. 미세한, 현미경으로 봐야만 보이는; (구어) 극히 작은
  Extremely small and difficult or impossible to see without a microscope.

- **stubborn** [stʌ́bərn] a. 완고한, 고집 센
  Determined not to change your opinion or attitude.

- **accumulate** [əkjúːmjəlèit] vt. (돈 등을) (조금씩) 모으다, 축적하다; 쌓아올리다
  To gradually get more and more of something over a period of time.

  unlimited [ʌnlímitid] a. 끝없는, 무제한의, 무한정의
  If there is an unlimited quantity of something, you can have as much or as many of that thing as you want.

  uncanny [ʌnkǽni] a. 초인적인, 초자연적인; 이상한, 비정상적인
  Strange and difficult to explain.

- **predict** [pridíkt] v. 예언하다, 예상하다
  If you predict an event, you say that it will happen.

  tuition [tjuːíʃən] n. 교수, 수업; 수업료
  The money paid for this type of teaching.

- **ridiculous** [ridíkjələs] a. 웃기는, 우스꽝스러운; 터무니없는
  (ridiculously ad. 우스꽝스럽게; 터무니없이)
  If you say that something or someone is ridiculous, you mean that they are very foolish.

- **enthusiastic** [enθúːziǽstik] a. 열렬한, 열광적인
  If you are enthusiastic about something, you show how much you like or enjoy it by the way that you behave and talk.

  reciprocate with idiom …으로 보답하다
  To behave or feel towards somebody in the same way as they behave or feel towards you.

  unfathomable [ʌnfǽðəməbəl] a. 불가해한; 무슨 생각을 하는지 알 수 없는
  Too strange or difficult to be understood.

Vocabulary in New Moon

* **truce** [tru:s] n. 휴전(협정), 정전; v. 휴전하다
An agreement between enemies or opponents to stop fighting for an agreed period of time; The period of time that this lasts.

* **extreme** [ikstríːm] a. 극단의, 극도의
Very great in degree.

scary [skέəri] a. 놀라기 잘하는, 겁이 많은, 무서운
Something that is scary is rather frightening.

intimidate [intímədèit] vt. 겁주다, 소심하게 만들다 (intimidating a. 위협적인)
To frighten or threaten someone, usually in order to persuade them to do something that you want them to do.

* **phase** [feiz] n. 단계, 국면; v. (단계적으로) 실행하다
A particular stage in a process of development.

* **relationship** [riléiʃənʃìp] n. 관계, 관련
The way in which two people, groups or countries behave towards each other or deal with each other.

* **dissolve** [dizálv] v. 녹이다, 용해시키다
To break up and merge with a liquid.

ostracism [ástrəsìzəm] n. (격식) (사람에 대한) 외면[배척]
The act of deliberately not including somebody in a group or activity.

* **barely** [bέərli] ad. 간신히, 가까스로; 거의 …않다
Only with great difficulty or effort.

hazardous [hǽzərdəs] a. 모험적인, (특히 건강·안전에) 위험한
Something that is hazardous is dangerous, especially to people's health or safety.

* **vehement** [víːəmənt] a. 격렬한, 열렬한 (vehemently ad. 열정적으로; 격렬하게)
Showing very strong feelings, especially anger.

shush [ʃʌʃ] vt. 쉬잇 하여 입 다물게 하다; int. 쉿, 조용히
You say shush when you are telling someone to be quiet.

1. PARTY

halfhearted [hǽfhá:rtid] a. 마음이 내키지 않는 (halfheartedly ad. 어쩔 수 없이)
Showing a lack of enthusiasm and interest.

* **disapproval** [dìsəprú:vəl] n. 안 된다고 함, 불승인, 불찬성, 불만
A feeling of disliking something or what someone is doing.

‡ **reception** [risépʃən] n. [통신] 청취(상태), 수신(율); (호텔의) 프론트; 수령, 받아들임
The quality of radio and television signals that are broadcast.

sharp [ʃɑ:rp] a. 날카로운; 세련된, 이목을 끄는
Critical or severe.

‡ **temper** [témpər] n. 기질, 성질; 화, 노여움 (tempered a. (⋯한) 기질의; 조절된, 완화된)
If you refer to someone's temper, you mean that they become angry very easily.

* **temple** [témpəl] n. 관자놀이; 신전, 사원
Your temples are the flat parts on each side of the front part of your head, near your forehead.

jawline [dʒɔ́:lain] n. 아래턱의 선[윤곽]
The outline of the lower jaw.

‡ **fan** [fæn] vt. ⋯에 불다, (바람을) 부치다[보내다]; n. 부채, 선풍기
If something fans out, or if you fan it out, it spreads out or opens out into the shape of a circle or half circle.

smolder [smóuldər] vi. (감정이) 사무치다; 울적하다; 그을(리)다, 연기피우다
To be filled with a strong emotion that you do not fully express.

* **inhale** [inhéil] v. 들이쉬다, 흡입하다
To take air, smoke, gas, etc. into your lungs as you breathe.

* **exhale** [ekshéil] v. (숨 등을) 내쉬다; (증기·향기 등을) 발산[방출]하다
To breathe out the air or smoke, etc. in your lungs.

‡ **linger** [líŋgər] vi. 오래 머무르다, 떠나지 못하다
When something lingers, it continues to exist for a long time, often much longer than expected.

Vocabulary in New Moon

* **upward** [ʌ́pwərd] a. 위로 향한; 위쪽으로
Pointing towards or facing a higher place.

* **razor-sharp** [réizərʃɑ̀ːrp] a. 매우 날카로운; 매우 엄격한
Extremely sharp.

venom [vénəm] n. (독사 따위의) 독, 독액; 악의, 원한
The venom of a creature such as a snake or spider is the poison that it puts into your body when it bites or stings you.

* **coat** [kout] v. (막 같은 것을) 덮다[입히다]; n. 외투, 코트; 도금
(coated a. …을 입힌, …으로 덮인)
If you coat something with a substance or in a substance, you cover it with a thin layer of the substance.

* **trivial** [tríviəl] a. 하찮은, 사소한; n. 하찮은 일
If you describe something as trivial, you think that it is unimportant and not serious.

* **pulse** [pʌls] n. 맥박, 고동; v. 맥이 뛰다, 고동치다
Your pulse is the regular beating of blood through your body, which you can feel when you touch particular parts of your body, especially your wrist.

* **thud** [θʌd] v. 쿵[퍽·툭] 치다[떨어지다]; 쿵쿵거리다; n. 쿵[퍽·툭] (물건이 떨어지는 소리)
If something thuds somewhere, it makes a dull sound, usually when it falls onto or hits something else.

hyperactive [hàipəræktiv] a. 지나치게[비정상적으로] 활동적인[과민한]
(hyperactively ad. 지나치게, 비정상적으로)
Especially of children and their behavior too active and only able to keep quiet and still for short periods.

* **palm** [pɑːm] ① n. 손바닥 ② n. 종려나무, 야자나무
The palm of your hand is the inside part.

Capulets n. 〈로미오와 줄리엣〉에 나오는 줄리엣 가문

Montagues n. 〈로미오와 줄리엣〉에 나오는 로미오 가문

1. PARTY

something hack up phrasal v. 난도질하다, 산산조각 내다
To cut something roughly or violently.

★ **sprawl** [sprɔːl] v. 팔다리를 펴다[뻗다]; 불규칙하게 퍼지게 하다; n. 드러누움
If you sprawl somewhere, you sit or lie down with your legs and arms spread out in a careless way.

‡ **perch** [pəːrtʃ] v. 앉아 있다[쉬다]; 위치하다, 자리 잡다; (높은 곳에) 놓다, 앉히다
If you perch on something, you sit down lightly on the very edge or tip of it.

‡ **sculpture** [skʌ́lptʃər] n. 조각, 조각상; v. 조각하다
An object made out of stone, wood, clay etc. by an artist.

afghan [ǽfgæn] n. 모포[숄]의 일종
A blanket, wrap, or shawl of colored yarn.

‡ **offend** [əfénd] v. …의 감정을 상하게 하다; 위반하다; 죄를 범하다
To make someone upset or angry.

★ **fictional** [fíkʃənəl] a. 꾸며낸, 허구적인; 소설의
Not real or true; Existing only in stories; Connected with fiction.

Rosaline n. 〈로미오와 줄리엣〉에 나오는 캐릭터

fickle [fíkəl] a. 변하기 쉬운, 마음이 잘 변하는, 변덕스러운
Often changing their mind in an unreasonable way so that you cannot rely on them.

‡ **thoroughly** [θə́ːrouli] ad. 완전히, 철저히
Completely.

goose bumps [gúːsbʌ̀mps] n. (추위·공포로 인한) 소름
A condition in which there are raised spots on your skin because you feel cold, frightened or excited.

★ **distract** [distrǽkt] vt. (마음·주의를) 흐트러뜨리다, 딴 데로 돌리다
Nervous, anxious or confused because you are worried about something.

★ **irresistible** [ìrizístəbəl] a. 저항할 수 없는
Impossible to refuse or avoid because too pleasant, attractive or strong.

Vocabulary in New Moon

* **coarse** [kɔːrs] a. 거친, 올이 성긴; 야비한, 상스러운; 조잡한, 조악한; 열등한
  Rough and not smooth or soft, or not in very small pieces.

* **amusement** [əmjúːzmənt] n. 즐거움, 위안, 재미, 오락(물)
  The feeling that you have when something is funny or amusing, or it entertains you.

* **disgust** [disgʌ́st] vt. 역겹게 하다, 넌더리나게 하다; n. 싫음, 혐오감
  (disgusted a. 메스꺼운)
  To disgust someone means to make them feel a strong sense of dislike and disapproval.

* **suicide** [súːəsàid] n. 자살, 자해; v. 자살하다
  The act of killing yourself deliberately.

* **clarify** [klǽrəfài] v. (의미 등을) 뚜렷하게[명백하게] 하다; 명백하게 설명하다
  To make something clearer or easier to understand.

* **tease** [tiːz] v. 놀리다, 희롱하다 (teasing a. 놀리는, 짓궂게 괴롭히는)
  To laugh at or make fun of someone annoyingly.

  throw down phrasal v. 넘어뜨리다; 드러눕다; 퇴짜 놓다; 뿌리치다
  To send somebody/something from your hand suddenly and violently downwards.

  vial [váiəl] n. 유리병; 물약병
  A vial is a very small bottle which is used to hold something such as perfume or medicine.

* **extract** [ikstrǽkt] n. 추출물; v. (화학적 과정 등을 거쳐) 뽑다[얻다], 추출하다
  An extract is a substance that has been obtained from something else, for example by means of a chemical or industrial process.

  contingency [kəntíndʒənsi] n. 만일의 사태
  A contingency is something that might happen in the future.

* **concrete** [kánkriːt] n. 콘크리트; a. 유형의, 구체적인
  Concrete is a substance used for building which is made by mixing together cement, sand, small stones, and water.

1. PARTY

* **desperate** [déspərit] a. 필사적인; 절망적인, 자포자기의
  If you are desperate for something or desperate to do something, you want or need it very much indeed.

* **haste** [heist] n. 급함, 서두름, 신속함
  Speed, especially speed in an action.

  sadistic [sədístik] a. 사디스트적인
  Cruel and enjoying making other people suffer.

* **torture** [tɔ́ːrtʃər] vt. 고문하다, 고통을 주다; n. 고문, 고뇌
  To torture someone means to cause them to suffer mental pain or anxiety.

  hostage [hástidʒ] n. 인질
  A person who is captured and held prisoner by a person or group, and who may be injured or killed if people do not do what the person or group is asking.

  ruse [ruːz] n. 책략, 계략
  A way of doing something or of getting something by cheating somebody.

  unthinking [ʌnθíŋkiŋ] a. 생각 없는, 경솔한 (unthinkingly ad. 생각 없이)
  Not thinking about the effects of what you do or say.

★ **crescent** [krésənt] n. 초승달, 초승달 모양의 것; a. 초승달 모양의
  A curved shape that is wide in the middle and pointed at each end.

* **scar** [skɑːr] n. 흉터, (화상·부스럼의) 자국
  A mark that is left on the skin after a wound has healed.

* **grasp** [græsp] v. 완전히 이해하다; 붙잡다, 움켜쥐다; n. 움켜잡기
  If you grasp something that is complicated or difficult to understand, you understand it.

* **plunge** [plʌndʒ] v. 앞뒤로 흔들리다; 던져 넣다; 추락하다; 뛰어들다, 돌진하다; n. 돌진
  To move, fall, or be thrown suddenly forwards or downwards.

* **childish** [tʃáildiʃ] a. 어린이 같은, 유치한 (childishly ad. 유치하게, 애같이)
  Behaving in a stupid or silly way.

Vocabulary in New Moon

※ **provoke** [prəvóuk] vt. 화나게 하다, 도발하다; 일으키다, 유발시키다
If you provoke someone, you deliberately annoy them and try to make them behave aggressively.

brood [bru:d] vi. 수심에 잠기다, 곰곰이 생각하다; 알을 품다
To think anxiously or resentfully about it for a period of time.

※ **contemplate** [kántəmplèit] v. 깊이 생각하다, 응시하다, 찬찬히 보다
To think carefully about and accept the possibility of something happening.

※ **furious** [fjúəriəs] a. 성난, 격노한; 맹렬한, 왕성한
Someone who is furious is extremely angry.

※ **remote** [rimóut] a. 먼, 먼 곳의
Far away; Distant in time or place.

※ **vivid** [vívid] a. 선명한, 뚜렷한; 생생한, 발랄한
Produced very clear, powerful and detailed images in the mind.

★ **quartet** [kwɔːrtét] n. 4인조; 4중주
A group of four people.

※ **exquisite** [ikskwízit] a. 정교한, 절묘한; 우아한, 섬세한
Extremely beautiful or carefully made.

seraph [sérəf] n. 천사(인간과 닮은 모습으로 세 쌍의 날개가 있는 천사)
In the Bible, a seraph is a kind of angel.

★ **swirl** [swəːrl] vi. 소용돌이치다, 빙빙 돌다
If liquid or flowing swirls, it moves round and round quickly.

mayhem [méihem] n. 대혼란, 아수라장
Confusion and fear, usually caused by violent behavior or by some sudden shocking event.

※ **acquaintance** [əkwéintəns] n. 아는 사람(사이); 알고 있음, 면식, 지식
An acquaintance is someone who you have met and know slightly, but not well.

1. PARTY

☆ **patron** [péitrən] n. 보호자, 후원자; 고객, 단골손님
A person who gives money and support to artists and writers.

☆ **irritate** [írətèit] vt. 짜증나게[초조하게] 하다, 화나게 하다
If something irritates you, it keeps annoying you.

reverie [révəri] n. 공상, 환상, 몽상, 백일몽
A day-dream or absent-minded idea or thought.

moot [mu:t] a. 고려할 가치가 없는; vt. (의견 등을) 제기하다
If something is a moot point or question, people cannot agree about it.

☆ **cease** [si:s] v. 그만두다, 중지하다
If something ceases, it stops happening or existing.

☆ **chuckle** [tʃʌkl] vi. 낄낄 웃다; n. 낄낄 웃음
When you chuckle, you laugh quietly.

★ **blanch** [blæntʃ] vt. (공포·질병 등이) (얼굴 등을) 창백하게 하다
To become pale because you are shocked or frightened.

★ **complicate** [kámpləkèit] vt. 복잡하게 하다, 뒤얽히게 만들다
To complicate something means to make it more difficult to understand or deal with.

★ **posture** [pástʃər] n. (몸의) 자세, (모델 등의) 포즈; 몸가짐
The way one holds one's body while standing, sitting or walking.

cruiser [krú:zər] n. 크라이슬러 PT 크루저(Chrysler PT Cruiser), 스테이션 웨건 콤팩트 카

☆ **appetite** [ǽpitàit] n. 식욕, 욕구
Your appetite is your desire to eat.

Mariners n. 시애틀 매리너스(Seattle Mariners)
미국 메이저리그 야구 아메리칸리그에 소속된 프로 야구팀

Sox n. 보스턴 레드삭스(Boston Redsox)
미국 메이저리그 야구 아메리칸리그에 소속된 프로야구팀

Vocabulary in New Moon

- **scoop** [sku:p] vt. 퍼 올리다, 푸다, 뜨다; n. 국자, 주걱
  If you scoop a person or thing somewhere, you put your hands or arms under or round them and quickly move them there.

- **coordination** [kouɔ̀:rdənéiʃən] n. 조화; 조정; (근육 운동의) 공동 작업
  (coordinationally ad. 조직적으로, 조화롭게)
  The ability to control your movements well.

- **tumble** [tʌ́mbəl] v. 넘어지다; 굴리다; n. 추락, 전도
  If someone or something tumbles somewhere, they fall there with a rolling or bouncing movement.

- **snag** [snæg] v. (흔히 다른 사람보다 먼저) 잡아[낚아] 채다
  To succeed in getting something quickly, often before other people.

- **linoleum** [linóuliəm] n. 리놀륨(마루의 깔개)
  A stiff smooth material that is used for covering floors.

- **convalescence** [kànvəlésəns] n. 요양[회복] (기간)
  A period of time when you get well again after an illness or a medical operation.

- **dismissal** [dismísəl] n. 해산, 퇴거; 면직
  Permission to go.

- **triumphant** [traiʌ́mfənt] a. 승리를 한, 의기양양한
  Having achieved a great victory or success.

- **obscure** [əbskjúər] a. 어두운, 분명치 않은; 무명의, 눈에 띄지 않는
  Dark; Dim.

- **turnoff** [tə́:rnɔ̀(:)f] n. (간선 도로의) 지선 도로
  A place where a road leads away from another larger or more important road.

- **chafe at** idiom …에 짜증나다, 안달하다
  If you chafe at something such as a restriction, you feel annoyed about it.

- **enforce** [enfɔ́:rs] v. 집행[시행·실시]하다
  To enforce something means to force or cause it to be done or to happen.

1. PARTY

prehistoric [prìːhistɔ́ːrik] a. (경멸·익살) 아주 옛날의, 구식의, 고풍의; 선사 시대의
Prehistoric people and things existed at a time before information was written down.

‡ **groan** [groun] v. 신음하다, 끙끙거리다; n. 신음, 끙끙거리는 소리
If you groan, you make a long, low sound because you are in pain, or because you are upset or unhappy about something.

Audi n. 아우디 (독일 자동차 제조회사 브랜드)

coupe [kuːpéi] n. 쿠페형 자동차 (세단보다 작고 문이 두 개인 2–5인승); 쿠페형 마차 (2인승 4륜 유개 마차)
A car with two doors and usually a sloping back.

nonessential [nɑ̀nisénʃəl] a. 비본질적인, 중요치 않은
Not completely necessary.

★ **dime** [daim] n. 다임, 10센트 동전 ('잔돈'이라는 뜻이 내포됨)
A dime is an American coin worth ten cents.

★ **virtuous** [vɚ́ːrtʃuəs] a. 도덕적인, 고결한 (virtuously ad. 착하게; 절개 있게)
Behaving in a very good and moral way.

★ **slack** [slæk] n. 느슨함, 늘어짐; 한가로운 휴식; a. (로프·새끼 등이) 늘어진, 느슨한; 되는대로의; 꾸물거리는
Not stretched tight.

‡ **startle** [stáːrtl] v. 깜짝 놀라게 하다; 움찔하다; n. 깜짝 놀람
If something sudden and unexpected startles you, it surprises and frightens you slightly.

‡ **choke** [tʃouk] v. 숨 막히다[막히게 하다], 질식하다[시키다]
When you choke or something chokes you, you cannot breathe properly or get enough air into your lungs.

‡ **impression** [impréʃən] n. 인상, 감명, 느낌
An idea or opinion of what something is like.

Dartmouth [dáːrtməθ] n. 다트머스 (영국 Devon 주의 항구)

39

Vocabulary in New Moon

- **intruder** [intrúːdər] n. 침입자, 난입자; 훼방꾼, 방해자
  A person who enters a building or an area illegally.

- **prolong** [proulɔ́ːŋ] vt. 늘이다, 연장하다 (prolonged a. 오래 계속되는, 장기적인)
  To make something last longer.

  furtive [fə́ːrtiv] a. 몰래 하는, 내밀한, 은밀한 (furtively ad. 남몰래, 은밀히)
  Behaving in a way that shows that you want to keep something secret and do not want to be noticed.

- **playful** [pléifəl] a. 놀기 좋아하는; 장난의
  Very active, happy, and wanting to have fun.

- **carve** [kɑːrv] vt. 새기다, 조각하다
  To make something by cutting into especially wood or stone, or to cut into the surface of stone, wood, etc.

- **growl** [graul] v. 으르렁거리다, 고함치다; n. 으르렁거리는 소리
  To make a low rough sound, usually in anger.

  menacing [ménəsiŋ] a. 위협적인, 으르는
  If someone or something looks menacing, they give you a feeling that they are likely to cause you harm or put you in danger.

- **vow** [vau] v. 단언하다; 맹세하다, 서약하다; n. 맹세, 서약
  To make a formal and serious promise to do something or a formal statement that is true.

- **clench** [klentʃ] vt. (이를) 악물다, (손을) 꽉 쥐다
  To close one's teeth or one's fists tightly, especially in anger.

- **lantern** [læntərn] n. 랜턴, 초롱
  A lantern is a lamp in a metal frame with glass sides and with a handle on top so you can carry it.

- **porch** [pɔːrtʃ] n. (건물의 지붕 딸린) 현관, 포치
  A porch is a sheltered area at the entrance to a building. It has a roof and sometimes has walls.

1. PARTY

eave [i:v] n. (가옥의) 처마, 차양
The eaves of a house are the lower edges of its roof.

★ **radiance** [réidiəns] n. 광휘, 찬연히 빛남
Radiance is a glowing light shining from something.

★ **cedar** [síːdər] n. [식물] 히말라야삼목; 삼나무 목재; a. 삼나무로 만들어진
A cedar is a large evergreen tree with wide branches and small thin leaves called needles.

‡ **moan** [moun] v. 신음하다, 끙끙대다; n. 신음
If you moan, you make a low sound, usually because you are unhappy or in pain.

‡ **mutter** [mʌ́tər] v. 중얼거리다, 불평하다; n. 중얼거림, 불평
If you mutter, you speak very quietly so that you cannot easily be heard, often because you are complaining about something.

wary [wέəri] a. 조심하는, 경계하는 (warily ad. 조심하여, 방심 않고)
If you are wary of something or someone, you are cautious because you do not know much about them and you believe they may be dangerous or cause problems.

‡ **chorus** [kɔ́ːrəs] n. 합창; 일제히 내는 소리; v. 합창을 하다, 이구동성으로 말하다
A chorus is a part of a song which is repeated after each.

‡ **blush** [blʌʃ] v. 얼굴을 붉히다, (얼굴이) 빨개지다; n. 얼굴을 붉힘, 홍조
When you blush, your face becomes redder than usual because you are ashamed or embarrassed.

★ **stack** [stæk] n. 더미; 많음, 다량; v. 쌓다, 쌓아올리다
A stack of things is a pile of them.

‡ **encourage** [enkɔ́ːridʒ] vt. 용기를 북돋우다, 장려하다
(encouraging a. 격려하는, 힘을 북돋아 주는)
If you encourage someone, you give them confidence, hope, or support.

rein somebody/something in phrasal v. …의 고삐를 죄다, …을 억제하다
To control somebody or something more strictly.

Vocabulary in New Moon

- **glare** [glɛər] v. 노려보다; 번쩍번쩍 빛나다; n. 섬광; 노려봄
  If you glare at someone, you look at them with an angry expression on your face.

- **glorious** [glɔ́:riəs] a. 찬란한, 훌륭한, 영광스러운 (gloriously ad. 훌륭히; 멋지게, 근사하게)
  Something that is glorious is very beautiful and impressive.

- **mock** [mɑk] a. 가짜의, 모의의; vt. 조롱하다, 흉내 내며 놀리다; n. 조롱, 놀림감
  You use mock to describe something which is not real or genuine, but which is intended to be very similar to the real thing.

- **perceptible** [pərséptəbəl] a. 지각할 수 있는
  Great enough for you to notice it.

- **conspicuous** [kənspíkjuəs] a. 눈에 띄는, 현저한
  (conspicuously ad. 눈에 띄게, 두드러지게)
  Easy to see or notice.

- **sparkle** [spá:rkəl] v. 불꽃을 튀기다, 생기가 넘치다; n. 불꽃, 광채 (sparkling a. 반짝거리는)
  If something sparkles, it is clear and bright and shines with a lot of very small points of light.

- **coop** [ku(:)p] vt. 우리에 넣다; 비좁은 곳에 가두다; n. 닭장, 우리
  If you say that someone has flown the coop, you mean that they have left a place or situation that limits their freedom.

- **aversion** [əvə́:rʒən] n. 혐오, 싫음, 반감
  A strong feeling of not liking somebody/something.

- **obligation** [àbləgéiʃən] n. 의무, 책무; 은혜, 의리
  The state of being forced to do something because it is your duty, or because of a law.

- **precaution** [prikɔ́:ʃən] n. 조심, 경계; 예방책
  Something that is done in advance in order to prevent problems or to avoid danger.

- **scent** [sent] n. 냄새, 향기; v. 냄새 맡다; 냄새를 풍기다
  The scent of something is the pleasant smell that it has.

1. PARTY

- **elbow** [élbou] n. 팔꿈치
  The joint between the upper and lower parts of the arm where it bends in the middle.

- **tow** [tou] vt. 끌다, 밧줄[사슬]로 끌다, 견인하다; 끌고 가다
  To pull a car or boat behind another vehicle, using a rope or chain.

- **shiny** [ʃáini] a. 빛나는; 해가 비치는, 해가 쬐는, 청명한, 광택이 있는
  Smooth and bright; Reflecting the light.

- **martyr** [máːrtər] n. 순교자, 순난자, 희생자; (병 따위에) 늘 고통 받는 사람
  A person who suffers greatly or is killed because of their political or religious beliefs, and is often admired because of it.

- **replace** [ripléis] v. 대신하다, 제자리에 놓다
  If one thing or person replaces another, the first is used or acts instead of the second.

- **self-conscious** [sélfkánʃəs] a. 남의 이목을 의식하는; 자의식이 강한
  (self-consciously ad. 남의 시선을 의식하며, 수줍게)
  Someone who is self-conscious is easily embarrassed and nervous because they feel that everyone is looking at them and judging them.

- **tear** [tɛər] ① v. (tore-torn) 찢다, 찢어지다 ② n. 눈물
  To intentionally destroy a building because it is not being used any more.

- **conceal** [kənsíːl] vt. 숨기다, 감추다; 비밀로 하다, 내색하지 않다
  If you conceal something, you cover it or hide it carefully.

- **illumination** [ilùːmənéiʃən] v. 이해, 깨달음; 설명; (불)빛, 조명
  Understanding or explanation of something.

- **crack** [kræk] v. 날카로운 소리가 나(게 하)다; (소리를 내며) 부서지다; n. 갈라진 금, 갑작스런 날카로운 소리 (crack a smile : 방긋 웃다, 미소 짓다)
  To make a sudden, short noise, or to cause something to make this noise.

- **complaint** [kəmpléint] n. 불평, 불만, 푸념
  A statement in which you express your dissatisfaction with a particular situation.

Vocabulary in New Moon

apparently [əpǽrəntli] ad. 보기에, 외관상으로; 분명히, 명백히
Used to say that something seems to be true, although it is not certain; Used when the real situation is different from what you thought it was.

trill [tril] n. 떨리는 목소리; 지저귐; v. 떨리는 소리로 노래하다; 명랑하게 말하다
A repeated short high sound made, for example, by somebody's voice or by a bird.

basilisk [bǽsəlìsk] n. 바실리스크(쳐다보거나 입김을 부는 것만으로도 사람을 죽일 수 있다는, 뱀과 같이 생긴 전설상의 괴물 ≒ 메두사)
A creature like a snake, that can kill people by looking at them or breathing on them.

tingle [tíŋɡəl] v. 설레다; 따끔따끔 아프다; n. 설렘, 흥분; 따끔거림
If you tingle with a feeling such as excitement, you feel it very strongly.

jerk [dʒəːrk] v. 갑자기 움직이다; n. 갑자기 잡아당김; 바보
If you jerk something or someone in a particular direction, or they jerk in a particular direction, they move a short distance very suddenly and quickly.

ooze [uːz] v. 스며 나오다, 새어나오다; n. 보드라운 진흙, 습지
To flow slowly out of something through a small opening, or to slowly produce a thick sticky liquid.

fling [fliŋ] vt. (flung-flung) 던지다, 내던지다; (문 등을) 왈칵 열다
If you fling something somewhere, you throw it there using a lot of force.

scatter [skǽtər] v. 흩뿌리다, 뿔뿔이 흩어지다
To depart or send off in different directions.

slam into idiom …에 쾅 하고 충돌하다[충돌하게 하다]
If one thing slams into or against another, it crashes into it with great force.

boulder [bóuldər] n. 둥근 돌, 표석
A very large rock.

grisly [grízli] a. 섬뜩한, 소름끼치는
Extremely unpleasant, especially because death or blood is involved.

1. PARTY

* **snarl** [snɑːrl] v. 으르렁거리다; 고함[호통]치다; n. 으르렁거림
  If you snarl something, you say it in a fierce, angry way.

* **shove** [ʃʌv] v. 밀(치)다, 밀어내다; n. 밀치기
  If you shove something somewhere, you push it there quickly and carelessly.

* **grab** [græb] v. 부여잡다, 움켜쥐다; n. 부여잡기
  If you grab something, you take it or pick it up suddenly and roughly.

‡ **massive** [mǽsiv] a. 크고 무거운, 육중한; 굳센, 강력한
  Something that is massive is very large in size, quantity, or extent.

* **instinctive** [instíŋktiv] a. 본능적인, 직관적인; 무의식적인
  (instinctively ad. 본능적으로)
  Instinctive behavior or reactions are not thought about, planned or developed by training.

* **jagged** [dʒǽgid] a. 톱니 같은; 들쭉날쭉한; (목소리 등이) 귀에 거슬리는
  Rough and uneven, with sharp points.

  sear [siər] vt. 태우다, 그슬리다, (강한 통증 등이) 후끈 치밀다, 화끈거리게 하다; a. 시든, 마른
  To sear something means to burn its surface with a sudden intense heat.

‡ **sting** [stiŋ] vt. 찌르다, 쏘다; n. 찌르기, 쏘기; (동물의) 침; 고통
  If something stings you, a sharp part of it is pushed into your skin so that you feel a sharp pain.

‡ **daze** [deiz] vt. 멍하게 하다; 현혹시키다; n. 멍한 상태; 눈이 부심
  To stun, as with a heavy blow or shot.

  disorient [disɔ́ːriənt] vt. 길을 잃게 하다, 방향(감각)을 상실하게 하다
  To cause to lose orientation or direction.

  ravenous [rǽvənəs] a. 몹시 굶주린, 탐욕스러운; 게걸스럽게 먹는
  Extremely hungry.

Comprehension Quiz

 2. STITCHES

1. **Why did Edward leave the kitchen when Carlisle was fixing Bella's arm?**
   A. It was too difficult for him to be near Bella's blood.
   B. He didn't want to see Bella in pain.
   C. He left to find Jasper.
   D. He was angry with Carlisle and Alice.

2. **What did Carlisle like most about his job as a doctor?**
   A. He enjoyed being around human blood.
   B. He thought it was interesting watching humans suffer from different illnesses.
   C. Being a doctor wasn't boring for him.
   D. Sometimes his special abilities as a vampire could save a person's life.

2. STITCHES

3. In the four hundred years since Carlisle was born, he never _____.

　A. met the Volturi

　B. doubted if God existed

　C. had a real family

　D. believed in God

4. Edward believed _____.

　A. that changing Bella into a vampire would save her soul

　B. vampires had lost their souls

　C. vampires could go to heaven or hell

　D. there was an afterlife for vampires

5. Why did Mike Newton come up in Edward and Bella's conversation?

　A. Mike Newton was trying to copy how Edward looked and acted.

　B. Bella admitted that she wanted to date Mike Newton in the past.

　C. Edward thought that it would be healthier for Bella to date someone like Mike Newton.

　D. Bella thought it would be better if she dated someone like Mike Newton.

Vocabulary in New Moon

‡ **stitch** [stitʃ] n. [외과] (상처를 꿰매는) 한 바늘; v. 꿰매다; 바느질하다
A stitch is a piece of thread that has been used to sew the skin of a wound together.

‡ **emergency** [imə́ːrdʒənsi] n. 비상사태, 비상시, 위급, 급변
An unexpected and serious happening which calls for immediate and determined action.

‡ **evident** [évidənt] a. 분명한, 명백한, 뚜렷한
Easily seen or understood; Obvious.

★ **authoritative** [əθɔ́ːritèitiv] a. 권위적인, 권위 있는
Someone or something that is authoritative gives an impression of power and importance and is likely to be obeyed.

unbreakable [ʌ̀nbréikəbəl] a. 부술[깨뜨릴·꺾을] 수 없는
Impossible to break.

★ **crouch** [krautʃ] v. 몸을 구부리다, 쭈그리다, 웅크리다
To bend your knees and lower yourself so that you are close to the ground and leaning forward slightly.

‡ **defensive** [difénsiv] a. 방어적인, 방어의, 변호의
Behaving in a way that shows you protect yourself from being criticized.

‡ **divine** [diváin] a. 비범한, 아주 멋진; 신의, 신성한
Extremely good, pleasant or enjoyable.

‡ **ashamed** [əʃéimd] a. 부끄러운, 창피한, 수치스러운
Feeling shame or embarrassment about somebody/something or because of something you have done.

let by idiom …을 지나가게 하다; 통과시키다
If you let someone or something by, you allow them to leave or escape.

★ **murmur** [mə́ːrmər] v. 중얼거리다
To speak or say very quietly.

★ **stance** [stæns] n. [야구·골프] (공을 칠 때의) 발의 위치, 스탠스
A position in which you stand, especially when playing a sport.

2. STITCHES

* **kneel** [ni:l] vi. (knelt-knelt) 무릎 꿇다
  To lower oneself onto one's knees.

* **wound** [wu:nd] ① n. 상처, 부상, 상해; vt. 상처를 입히다 ② v. [waund] wind의 과거·과거분사
  A wound is damage to part of your body, especially a cut or a hole in your flesh, which is caused by a gun, knife, or other weapon.

* **rip** [rip] v. 벗겨내다, 찢다; 돌진하다; n. 잡아 찢음, 째진 틈
  If you rip something away, you remove it quickly and forcefully.

  tourniquet [túərnikit] n. 지혈대
  A tourniquet is a strip of cloth that is tied tightly round an injured arm or leg in order to stop it bleeding.

  plug into something idiom 접속하다, …에 연결되다
  To make something or someone fit well or have good connections with something.

* **protective** [prətéktiv] a. 보호하는, (위험에서) 지키는, 방어하는
  Protective means designed or intended to protect something or someone from harm.

* **rigid** [rídʒid] a. 굳은, 단단한; 엄격한, 완고한
  Stiff or fixed; Not able to be bent, moved, changed or persuaded.

* **intensity** [inténsəti] n. 강렬, 격렬; 집중, 전념
  The state or quality of being intense.

* **thirst** [θə:rst] n. 갈증, 갈망, 목마름; vi. 갈망하다
  A strong desire for something.

* **wince** [wins] vi. (아픔·무서움 때문에) 주춤하다, 움츠리다; n. 위축
  If you wince, you suddenly look as if you are suffering because you feel pain.

* **sting** [stiŋ] vt. (stung-stung) 찌르다, 쏘다; n. 찌르기, 쏘기, (동물의) 침, 고통
  If something stings you, a sharp part of it is pushed into your skin so that you feel a sharp pain.

Vocabulary in New Moon

masochistic [mæsəkístik] a. 자기학대 하는
If you describe someone's behavior as masochistic, you mean that they seem to be trying to get into a situation which causes them suffering or great difficulty.

intercede [ìntərsíːd] vi. 중재하다, 조정하다
If you intercede with someone, you try to persuade them to forgive someone or end their disagreement with them.

gang up idiom (구어) (…에) 단결하여 대항[반대]하다
To join together, especially to oppose, threaten, hurt or frighten somebody.

sprint [sprint] v. 역주하다, 달려가다
To run at full speed.

‡ **numb** [nʌm] a. 감각을 잃은; 멍한, 망연자실한; vt. 감각을 잃게 하다; 망연자실케 하다
If a part of your body is numb, you cannot feel anything there.

gash [gæʃ] n. 깊은 상처; (지면의) 갈라진 틈
A long deep cut in the surface of something, especially a person's skin.

‡ **gleam** [gliːm] vi. 환하다, 반짝이다; 어슴푸레 빛나다; n. 번득임; 어스레한 빛
If an object or a surface gleams, it reflects light because it is shiny and clean.

‡ **stirring** [stə́ːriŋ] n. (감정·생각 등이) 시작됨[일어남]; a. 감동시키는, 고무하는; 활발한
A stirring of a feeling or thought is the beginning of one.

unease [əníːz] n. 불안(감), 우려
If you have a feeling of unease, you feel rather anxious or afraid, because you think that something is wrong.

squeamishness [skwíːmiʃnis] n. 잘 토함; 메스꺼움; 까다로움; 신중함
When you've got over your squeamishness, there will be no stopping you.

‡ **tug** [tʌg] v. 당기다, 끌다; 노력하다; n. 힘껏 당김
If you tug something or tug at it, you give it a quick and usually strong pull.

2. STITCHES

- **apologetic** [əpɑ̀lədʒétik] a. 사죄의, 미안해하는
  Showing that you are sorry that something has happened, especially because you feel guilty or embarrassed about it.

  plink [pliŋk] n. 찌르릉 소리; v. 찌르릉 소리를 내다, 찌르릉 하고 울다[울리다]
  A short, high-pitched sound.

- **fragment** [frǽgmənt] n. 부서진 조각, 파편, 단편, 떨어져 나간 조각
  A fragment of something is a small piece or part of it.

  trail off idiom 말소리가 차츰 잦아들다
  If somebody's speech trails away/off, it gradually becomes quieter and then stops.

- **intense** [inténs] a. 강렬한, 격렬한, 심한
  Having a very strong effect or felt very strongly.

- **temptation** [temptéiʃən] n. 유혹, 유혹함[됨]; 유혹물
  The desire to do or have something that you know is bad or wrong.

- **shrug** [ʃrʌg] v. (양 손바닥을 내보이면서 어깨를) 으쓱하다; n. 으쓱하기
  If you shrug, you raise your shoulders to show that you are not interested in something or that you do not know or care about something.

- **tempt** [tempt] vt. 유혹하다, 부추기다
  Something that tempts you attracts you and makes you want it, even though it may be wrong or harmful.

- **vomit** [vɑ́mit] v. 토하다, 게우다 (vomiting n. 구토, 토하기)
  To empty the contents of the stomach through the mouth.

- **strategy** [strǽtədʒi] n. 전략, 작전
  A plan that is intended to achieve a particular purpose.

- **denial** [dináiəl] n. 부정, 부인, 거부
  A statement saying that something is not true.

- **endure** [endjúər] v. 참다, 견디다, 인내하다
  If you endure a painful or difficult situation, you experience it and do not avoid it or give up, usually because you cannot.

Vocabulary in New Moon

queasy [kwíːzi] a. 역겨운; 불안한, 소심한
(said of a person) Feeling slightly sick.

※ **thoughtful** [θɔ́ːtfəl] a. 생각이 깊은, 생각에 잠긴
Thinking deeply, or appearing to think deeply; Reflective.

★ **enhanced** [enhǽnst] a. (정도·가치·질 등을) 강화한, 높인
Improved or better.

diagnostic [dàiəgnǽstik] a. 진단의
Connected with identifying something, especially an illness.

mull [mʌl] v. 숙고하다, 엉망으로 만들다, 실패하다; n. 실수, 실패, 혼란
To think carefully about something for a long time.

★ **poke** [pouk] v. 쿡 찌르다; 밀다, 쑥 내밀다; n. 찌르기, 쑤시기
(poke around : …을 찾으려고 뒤지다, 캐다)
If you poke someone or something, you quickly push them with your finger or with a sharp object.

★ **splinter** [splíntər] n. 부서진 조각; v. 쪼개지다, 산산조각이 되다
A small thin sharp piece of wood, metal, glass, etc. that has broken off a larger piece.

rummage [rʌ́midʒ] v. 샅샅이 뒤지다, (찾기 위하여) 마구 뒤적거리다
To search for something by moving things around carelessly and looking into, under and behind them.

snip [snip] v. (가위로) 자르다, 싹둑 베다; n. 싹둑 자름, 가위질
To cut something with scissors, usually with small quick cuts.

※ **wipe** [waip] v. 훔치다, 씻다, 닦다, 비비다
To pass over, or rub on to.

Q-tip n. (상표) 큐팁 (미국의 면봉 (메이커))

복습 **thoroughly** [θɔ́ːrouli] ad. 완전히, 철저히
Completely.

2. STITCHES

- **gauze** [gɔːz] n. 가볍고 투명한 천; (상처에 붙이는) 거즈[가제]
  Gauze is a type of light, soft cloth with tiny holes in it.

- **clergyman** [klə́ːrdʒimən] n. 성직자, 영국 국교회의 주교 이하의 성직자

- **muse** [mjuːz] vi. 묵상하다, 곰곰이 생각하다
  To think about something carefully and for a long time.

- **harsh** [hɑːrʃ] a. 가혹한, 엄한; 잔인한, 무자비한, 무정한
  Unpleasant, unkind, cruel or unnecessarily severe.

- **soak** [souk] v. 적시다, 빨아들이다; 젖다, 스며들다; n. 적심
  If a liquid soaks something or if you soak something with a liquid, the liquid makes the thing very wet.

- **fiber** [fáibər] n. 섬유; 섬유질, 섬유 조직
  A material such as fabric or rope that is made from a mass of natural or artificial threads.

- **blaze** [bleiz] n. 불꽃, 화염, 섬광; vi. 타오르다
  Strong bright flames in a fire.

- **devoid** [divɔ́id] a. 결여된, …이 없는; vt. 빼앗다
  If you say that someone or something is devoid of a quality or thing, you are emphasizing that they have none of it.

- **Lutheran** [lúːθərən] a., n. 루터 교회의 (신자)
  A follower of Martin Luther or a member of a Lutheran Church.

- **pottery** [pátəri] n. 도기류, 도자기 제품
  Pots, dishes, etc. made with clay that is baked in an oven, especially when they are made by hand.

- **fad** [fæd] n. 일시적 유행; 변덕; 도락, 취미
  Something that people are interested in for only a short period of time.

- **bizarre** [bizɑ́ːr] a. 기괴한, 이상야릇한
  Something that is bizarre is very odd and strange.

Vocabulary in New Moon

offhand [ɔ́(:)fhǽnd] a. 무뚝뚝한, 퉁명스러운; ad. 즉석에서, 준비 없이; 아무렇게나
If you say that someone is being offhand, you are critical of them for being unfriendly or impolite, and not showing any interest in what other people are doing or saying.

by all accounts idiom 다른 사람들 말에 따르면
Used when the speaker does not have direct experience of the thing mentioned but is reporting the ideas, etc. of others.

※ **damn** [dæm] v. 저주[매도·욕설]하다; a. 빌어먹을, 우라질 (damned ad. 지독하게, 굉장히)
To criticize somebody/something very strongly.

regardless [rigá:rdlis] ad. 개의치[상관하지] 않고
Paying no attention, even if the situation is bad or there are difficulties.

deity [dí:əti] n. 신, 하느님
A god or goddess.

afterlife [ǽftərlàif] n. 내세, 사후; 여생
The afterlife is a life that some people believe begins when you die, for example a life in heaven or as another person or animal.

light bulb [láit bʌ́lb] n. 백열전구
A light bulb or bulb is the round glass part of an electric light or lamp which light shines from.

★ **flick** [flik] vt. 가볍게 치다, 튀기다; 휙 움직이다; (스위치 등을) 탁 누르다; n. 가볍게 치기
If you flick something away, or off something else, you remove it with a quick movement of your hand or finger.

※ **fuel** [fjú:əl] n. 연료; v. 연료를 공급하다
Any material that produces heat or power, usually when it is burnt.

★ **fervent** [fə́:rvənt] a. 열렬한; 강렬한, (감정 따위가) 격한; 뜨거운
Having or showing very strong and sincere feelings about something.

복습 **unfathomable** [ʌnfǽðəməbəl] a. 불가해한, 무슨 생각을 하는지 알 수 없는
Too strange or difficult to be understood.

2. STITCHES

- **thwart** [θwɔːrt] v. 의표[허]를 찌르다, 훼방 놓다; 반대하다; n. [항해] 보트 젓는 사람의 좌석
  If you thwart someone or thwart their plans, you prevent them from doing or getting what they want.

- **purse** [pəːrs] v. (불만 등의 표시로 입술을) 오므리다
  If you purse your lips, you move them into a small, rounded shape, usually because you disapprove of something or when you are thinking.

- **aware** [əwɛ́ər] a. 알고 있는, 의식하고 있는, 알아차린
  Knowing or realizing something.

- **stubborn** [stʌ́bərn] a. 완고한, 고집 센
  Determined not to change your opinion or attitude.

- **chin** [tʃin] n. 아래턱, 턱 끝; v. 턱걸이하다
  Your chin is the part of your face that is below your mouth and above your neck.

- **speculative** [spékjəlèitiv] a. 추측에 근거한; 사색적인, 명상적인
  (speculatively ad. 추측하여, 사색적으로)
  Based on guessing or on opinions that have been formed without knowing all the facts.

- **doom** [duːm] vt. 운명 짓다, 선고하다; n. 운명, 파멸
  If a fact or event dooms someone or something to a particular fate, it makes certain that they are going to suffer in some way.

- **shudder** [ʃʌ́dər] vi. 떨다, 몸서리치다; n. 몸이 떨림, 전율, 몸서리
  If you shudder, you shake with fear, horror, or cold.

- **unseeing** [ʌnsíːiŋ] a. 보고 있지 않는, 보려고 하지 않는
  (unseeingly ad. 보지 않고; 눈이 보이지 않게)
  Not noticing or really looking at anything although your eyes are open.

- **merely** [míərli] ad. 단지, 다만 (…에 불과한)
  Nothing more than; Just.

- **vague** [veig] a. 어렴풋한, 막연한
  Not clearly expressed, known, described or decided.

Vocabulary in New Moon

- **brevity** [brévəti] n. (시간·기간의) 간결, 짧음
  The brevity of something is the fact that it is short or lasts for only a short time.

- **regain** [rigéin] vt. (잃은 것을) 되찾다, 회복하다
  If you regain something that you have lost, you get it back again.

- **consciousness** [kánʃəsnis] n. 의식, 자각
  Your consciousness is your mind and your thoughts.

- **alert** [ələ́ːrt] a. 기민한; 정신이 초롱초롱한; n. 경보, 경계; v. 경고하다
  If you are alert, you are paying full attention to things around you and are able to deal with anything that might happen.

  ocher [óukər] n. 황토색, 오커색; 황토 (그림물감의 원료)
  A yellowish orange color.

  obsessive [əbsésiv] a. 강박적인, 사로잡혀 있는 (obsessively ad. 강박적으로)
  Thinking or worrying about something all the time.

- **relieve** [rilíːv] vt. 안도케 하다, (긴장·걱정 등을) 덜다, 구제하다
  To lessen or stop someone's pain, worry, boredom, etc.

- **fragile** [frǽdʒəl] a. 부서지기[깨지기] 쉬운
  Easily damaged, broken or harmed.

- **rage** [reidʒ] v. 맹렬히 계속되다; 격노하다[하게 하다]; n. 격노, 분노; 열광
  You say that something powerful or unpleasant rages when it continues with great force or violence.

- **cot** [kɑt] ① 소아용 침대; 간이침대 ② (양·비둘기 등의) 집, 우리
  A cot is a bed for a baby, with bars or panels round it so that the baby cannot fall out.

- **hoarse** [hɔːrs] a. 목쉰, 쉰 목소리의
  If your voice is hoarse, your voice sounds rough and unclear.

- **overwhelm** [òuvərhwélm] vt. 압도하다, 제압하다; 질리게 하다
  If you are overwhelmed by a feeling or event, it affects you very strongly, and you do not know how to deal with it.

2. STITCHES

★ **decade** [dékeid] n. 10년간
A decade is a period of ten years.

unblur [ʌnblə́:r] v. 흐린 것을 또렷이 떠올리는
un- (pre. 부정, 반대의 뜻을 나타냄) + blur (v. 흐릿해지다; 흐리다; 모호해지다)

intervening [ìntərví:niŋ] a. (명사 앞에만 씀) (두 사건·날짜 등의) 사이에 오는[있는]
An intervening period of time is one that separates two events or points in time.

indecision [ìndisíʒən] n. 우유부단, 주저
The state of being unable to decide.

★ **whim** [hwim] n. 변덕, 잘 변하는 마음; v. 일시적인 기분으로 바라다
A whim is a wish to do or have something which seems to have no serious reason or purpose behind it, and often occurs suddenly.

morgue [mɔ:rg] n. 시체 보관소; 음침한 장소; 자료집[실]; 조사부; 편집부[실]
A place where dead bodies that have been found are kept until they can be identified.

rooftop [rú:ftɑ̀p] n. 지붕, 옥상
A rooftop is the outside part of the roof of a building.

★ **shadowy** [ʃǽdoui] a. 그림자 같은; 흐릿한
A shadowy figure or shape is someone or something that you can hardly see because they are in a dark place.

unreadable [ʌnrí:dəbəl] a. 판독하기 어려운
If somebody's face or expression is unreadable, you cannot tell what they are thinking or feeling.

spasm [spǽzəm] n. 경련, 발작
A sudden and often painful contracting of a muscle, which you cannot control.

frosting [frɔ́:stiŋ] n. (케이크) 설탕을 입힘; (장식용) 유리가루
Frosting is a sweet substance made from powdered sugar that is used to decorate cakes.

Vocabulary in New Moon

‡ stride [straid] v. (strode–stridden) 큰 걸음으로 걷다; n. 큰 걸음, 활보
If you stride somewhere, you walk there with quick, long steps.

＊ mop [mɑp] v. 자루걸레로 닦다, 청소하다, (눈물·땀 등을) 닦다; n. 자루걸레
To use a stick with soft material fixed at one end for washing floors.

＊ bleach [bli:tʃ] n. 표백, 표백제; v. 표백하다, 희게 하다, 희어지다
Bleach is a chemical that is used to make cloth white, or to clean things thoroughly and kill germs.

‡ sew [sou] v. (sewed–sewn/sewed) 바느질하다, 꿰매다, 깁다
When you sew something such as clothes, you make them or repair them by joining pieces of cloth together by passing thread through them with a needle.

indecipherable [ìndisáifərəbəl] a. (암호 등이) 판독[해독]할 수 없는, 이해할 수 없는
Impossible to read or understand.

macabre [məkɑ́:brə] a. (죽음이나 다른 무서운 것과 관련되어) 섬뜩한[으스스한]
Unpleasant and strange because connected with death and frightening things.

‡ bandage [bǽndidʒ] n. 붕대, 안대; vt. …에 붕대를 감다
A bandage is a long strip of cloth which is wrapped around a wounded part of someone's body to protect or support it.

＊ spatter [spǽtər] v. 튀(기)다, 흩어지다; n. 튀김, 튀기는 소리, 후두두 하는 소리
If a liquid spatters a surface or you spatter a liquid over a surface, drops of the liquid fall on an area of the surface.

gore [gɔ:r] n. (특히 폭행당한 상처에서 흘러나오는 짙은) 피, 선혈
Gore is blood from a wound that has become thick.

＊ tense [tens] v. 팽팽하게 하다, 긴장시키다[하다]; a. 팽팽한, 긴장한, 긴박한
To make your muscles tight and stiff, or to become tight and stiff.

impassive [impǽsiv] a. 고통을 느끼지 않는, 무감각한
Not showing any feeling or emotion.

2. STITCHES

dashboard [dǽʃbɔ̀:rd] n. (자동차·비행기의) 계기판, 대시보드
The part of a car in front of the driver that has instruments and controls in it.

★ **intensify** [inténsəfài] v. 강렬하게 하다, 격렬하게 하다, 증강하다
To become greater, more serious or more extreme, or to make something do this.

serpentine [sə́:rpəntàin] a. 구불구불한
Bending and twisting like a snake.

‡ **lane** [lein] n. 좁은 길, 골목, 작은 길
A narrow road in the country.

‡ **insane** [inséin] a. 미친, 광기의
Someone who is insane is permanently and seriously mentally ill so that they cannot live in normal society.

★ **detached** [ditǽtʃt] a. 무심한, 거리를 두는; 사심 없는; 떨어져 있는
Someone who is detached is not personally involved in something or has no emotional interest in it.

cringe [krindʒ] vi. (겁이 나서) 움츠리다[움찔하다]
If you cringe at something, you feel embarrassed or disgusted, and making a slight movement.

remoteness [rimóutnis] n. 거리감, 아득함, 쌀쌀함
remote (a. 쌀쌀맞은; 동떨어진) + -ness (suf. 성질·상태·성격을 나타냄)

★ **flicker** [flíkər] n. (어떤 감정이 잠깐) 스침, 깜박임; v. (등불·희망·빛 등이) 깜박이다
If you experience a flicker of emotion, you feel that emotion only for a very short time, and not very strongly.

floodgate [flʌ́dgèit] n. 방조문, (수위 조절용) 수문
A gate that can be opened or closed to control the flow of water on a river.

end up idiom 끝나다; (구어) 마침내는 (…으로) 되다
To reach or come to a particular place or situation that you did not expect or intend to be in.

Vocabulary in New Moon

melodramatic [mèlo*u*drəmǽtik] a. 멜로드라마식의, 신파조의
Melodramatic behavior is behavior in which someone treats a situation as much more serious than it really is.

windshield [wíndʃìːld] n. (자동차 등의) 앞 유리
The windshield of a car or other vehicle is the glass window at the front through which the driver looks.

★ **salvage** [sǽlvidʒ] vt. 구출하다, (침몰선을) 인양하다
If something is salvaged, someone manages to save it, for example from a ship that has sunk, or from a building that has been damaged.

steer [stiər] v. 키를 잡다, 조종하다; 향하다 (steering wheel n. 핸들)
To control the direction a vehicle is going, for example by turning a wheel.

wallow [wálou] vi. 뒹굴다, 몸부림치다; 빠지다, 탐닉하다
Of large animals or people to lie and roll about in water or mud, to keep cool or for pleasure.

★ **remorse** [rimɔ́ːrs] n. 후회, 양심의 가책
A deep feeling of guilt, regret and bitterness for something wrong or bad which one has done.

‡ **stern** [stə́ːrn] a. 엄한, 단호한
Someone who is stern is very serious and strict.

hop out phrasal v. 차에서 뛰어내리다
To get out of quickly.

‡ **psychology** [saikálədʒi] n. 심리, 심리 상태
The psychology of a person is the kind of mind that they have, which makes them think or behave in the way that they do.

★ **tuck** [tʌk] v. 밀어 넣다, 쑤셔 넣다; n. 접어 넣은 단
If you tuck something somewhere, you put it there so that it is safe, comfortable, or neat.

★ **crook** [kruk] v. 구부리다, (활처럼) 굽히다; n. 구부러진 갈고리
(crooked a. 비뚤어진, 구부러진)
If you crook your arm or finger, you bend it.

2. STITCHES

* **ramble** [ræmbəl] vi. 횡설수설하다[지껄이다]; 거닐다; n. 횡설수설; 걷기, 긴 산책
  If you say that a person rambles in their speech or writing, you mean they do not make much sense because they keep going off the subject in a confused way.

* **babble** [bǽbəl] n. 재잘거림, 왁자지껄; v. 실없이 지껄이다, 쓸데없는 말을 하다
  The sound of many people speaking at the same time.

  anesthetic [ænəsθétik] n. 마취제; a. 마취의, 무감각한
  A drug that causes temporary loss of bodily sensations.

  effectiveness [iféktivnis] n. 유효(성), 효과적임
  Power to be effective; The quality of being able to bring about an effect.

* **lounge** [laundʒ] v. 느긋하게 서[앉아·누워] 있다
  If you lounge somewhere, you sit or lie there in a relaxed or lazy way.

* **prop** [prɑp] v. 받치다, 버티다; 기대 세우다; n. 지주, 버팀목, 소품
  If you prop an object on or against something, you support it by putting something underneath it or by resting it somewhere.

‡ **crush** [krʌʃ] v. 잔뜩 구겨지다[구기다], 밀어 넣다; 부서지다; 짓밟다; n. 눌러 터뜨림
  To crush something means to press it very hard so that its shape is destroyed or so that it breaks into pieces.

* **overboard** [óuvərbɔ̀:rd] a. 배 밖에[으로] (go overboard : 열중하다, 극단으로 나가다)
  If you say that someone goes overboard, you mean that they do something to a greater extent than is necessary or reasonable.

‡ **flush** [flʌʃ] v. (얼굴 등을) 붉히다
  When you flush, you become red in the face, especially as a result of strong emotions.

‡ **curse** [kə:rs] vt. 욕설을 퍼붓다; 저주하다; n. 저주, 악담
  To say a word or an expression which is not polite and shows that you are very angry.

  holey [houli] a. 구멍투성이의, 구멍 뚫린
  A holey piece of clothing or material has a lot of holes in it.

Vocabulary in New Moon

- **sweat** [swet] n. (pl.) 추리닝, 운동복 (= sweatsuit · sweatpants); 땀
  A loose top and trousers, worn either by people who are training for a sport or exercising, or as informal clothing.

- **idly** [áidli] ad. 하는 일 없이, 빈둥거려; 게으르게
  Without any particular reason, purpose or effort; Doing nothing.

  snuggle [snʌ́gəl] v. 달라붙다; 껴안다, 끌어안다; n. 다가붙음
  If you snuggle somewhere, you settle yourself into a warm, comfortable position, especially by moving closer to another person.

- **rectangle** [réktæ̀ŋgəl] n. 직사각형
  A rectangle is a four-sided shape whose corners are all ninety degree angles. Each side of a rectangle is the same length as the one opposite to it.

- **rectangular** [rektǽŋgjələr] a. 직사각형[장방형]의
  Something that is rectangular is shaped like a rectangle.

  voucher [váutʃər] n. 영수증(서); 증거(물); (보)증인; (현금 대용의) 상환[상품]권
  A voucher is a ticket or piece of paper that can be used instead of money to pay for something.

- **flip** [flip] v. (너무 흥분하여) 확 돌아 버리다; (책장 등을) 넘기다; 확 뒤집(히)다, 휙 젖히다
  To become very angry, excited or enthusiastic about something.

- **appropriate** [əpróuprièit] a. 적절한, 알맞은 (appropriately ad. 적절하게, 알맞게)
  Something that is appropriate is suitable or acceptable for a particular situation.

  rekindle [ri:kíndl] vt. (감정·생각 등을) 다시 불러일으키다[불붙이다]
  To make something become active again.

- **perplex** [pərpléks] vt. 당황하게 하다, 당혹스럽게 하다, 난처하게 하다
  To confuse and worry someone slightly by being difficult to understand or solve.

- **spill** [spil] v. 쏟아져 나오다
  If people or things spill out of a place, they come out of it in large numbers.

2. STITCHES

* **composition** [kàmpəzíʃən] n. 구성, 조립; 작곡
  The compositions of a composer, painter, or other artist are the works of art that they have produced.

* **lullaby** [lʌ́ləbài] n. 자장가
  A soft gentle song sung to make a child go to sleep.

* **swing** [swiŋ] v. (swang–swung) 흔들다; 매달리다; 빙 돌다
  If something swings or if you swing it, it moves repeatedly backwards and forwards or from side to side from a fixed point.

* **pill** [pil] n. 환약(丸藥), 알약
  A small solid piece of medicine which a person swallows without chewing.

* **chill** [tʃil] v. 춥게 하다, 오싹하다; a. 냉랭한, 차가운
  To lower its temperature so that it becomes colder but does not freeze.

* **tingle** [tíŋgəl] n. 설렘, 흥분; 따끔거림; v. 설레다; 따끔따끔 아프다
  A slight stinging or uncomfortable feeling in a part of your body.

* **spine** [spain] n. 등뼈, 척추
  Your spine is the row of bones down your back.

* **wary** [wɛ́əri] a. 경계하는, 조심하는
  Not completely trusting or certain about something or someone.

* **piqued** [piːkt] vt. …의 감정을 상하게 하다, 분개하게 하다, 애태우다
  To make somebody annoyed or upset.

* **forbid** [fərbíd] vt. (forbade–forbidden) 금하다, 허락하지 않다
  To refuse to allow something, especially officially, or to prevent a particular plan of action by making it impossible.

* **overreact** [òuvəriǽkt] vi. 지나치게 반응하다, 과잉 반응하다
  If you say that someone overreacts to something, you mean that they have and show more of an emotion than is necessary or appropriate.

* **urgent** [ə́ːrdʒənt] a. 긴급한, 절박한
  If something is urgent, it needs to be dealt with as soon as possible.

Vocabulary in New Moon

* **tangle** [tǽŋgəl] v. 얽히게 하다; 엉키다; n. 엉킴; 혼란
  If something is tangled or tangles, it becomes twisted together in an untidy way.

‡ **cautious** [kɔ́:ʃəs] a. 조심성 있는, 신중한
  Someone who is cautious acts very carefully in order to avoid possible danger.

* **quilt** [kwilt] n. (솜·털·깃털 따위를 둔) 누비이불; 누비 침대 커버
  A thin cover filled with feathers or some other warm, soft material, which you put over your blankets when you are in bed.

‡ **collapse** [kəlǽps] v. 무너지다, 붕괴하다; 쓰러지다; 맥없이 주저앉다; n. 무너짐, 붕괴
  If a building or other structure collapses, it falls down very suddenly.

elusive [ilú:siv] a. (뜻·성격이) 파악하기[알기] 어려운; 교묘히 피하는, 잡히지 않는
  Something or someone that is elusive is difficult to find, describe, remember, or achieve.

‡ **pant** [pænt] v. 헐떡거리다, 숨차다; 헐떡거리며 말하다
  To breathe quickly and loudly through your mouth, usually because you have been doing something very energetic.

overestimate [òuvəréstəmèit] v. (가치·능력을) 과대평가하다
  If you say that someone overestimates something, you mean that they think it is greater in amount or importance than it really is.

‡ **exhaust** [igzɔ́:st] vt. 다 써버리다, 소진시키다 (exhausted a. 지칠 대로 지친)
  If something exhausts you, it makes you so tired, either physically or mentally, that you have no energy left.

premonition [prì:məníʃən] n. (특히 불길한) 예감, 징후, 전조
  If you have a premonition, you have a feeling that something is going to happen, often something unpleasant.

sneaky [sní:ki] a. 교활한, 엉큼한
  If you describe someone as sneaky, you disapprove of them because they do things secretly rather than openly.

* **injure** [índʒər] vt. 상처를 입히다, 해치다
  To hurt a person, animal, or part of your body.

2. STITCHES

✱ **soothe** [suːð] v. (통증 등을) 완화시키다, 누그러뜨리다; 달래다, 진정시키다
Something that soothes a part of your body where there is pain or discomfort makes the pain or discomfort less severe.

unconsciousness [ʌ̀nkɑ́nʃəsnis] n. 의식 불명[인사불성] (상태)
A state like sleep caused by injury or illness, when you are unable to use your senses.

Comprehension Quiz

 3. THE END

1. Why did Bella take pictures of her friends?

   A. She wanted to make a scrapbook.

   B. She would send the pictures to her mother in the mail.

   C. She wanted to have pictures of her friends inside her room.

   D. Charlie wanted Bella to keep a record of her friends.

2. Edward said _____.

   A. Forks was no longer safe for his family

   B. he needed to leave Forks because Carlisle was offered a better job

   C. he never really loved Bella

   D. Bella wasn't good for him

3. Edward asked Bella _____.

   A. to never contact him again

   B. not to do anything reckless or stupid

   C. to take care of Charlie

   D. to throw away everything he ever gave to her

3. THE END

4. Who found Bella in the woods?
   A. Sam Uley
   B. Charlie Swan
   C. Dr. Gerandy
   D. Billy Black

5. Carlisle told Dr. Gerandy _____.
   A. he was offered a job teaching at a university
   B. he was offered a high paying job in Los Angeles
   C. he had to leave Forks because of a family emergency
   D. he was going back to Alaska

Vocabulary in New Moon

* **hideous** [hídiəs] a. 끔찍한, 오싹한, 흉측한, 극악무도한
  Extremely ugly or bad.

* **ache** [eik] vi. 아프다, 쑤시다
  To feel a continuous dull pain.

  duck out phrasal v. 도망치다; 탈옥하다
  To move somewhere very quickly, especially to avoid being seen or to get away from someone.

  ratchet up idiom 조금씩 증가하다[시키다]
  To make prices, etc. increase a little at a time.

* **imperfect** [impə́:rfikt] a. (지식·기능 등이) 불완전한, 불충분한; 결점[결함]이 있는
  Something that is imperfect has faults and is not exactly as you would like it to be.

  tenuous [ténjuəs] a. 박약한, 빈약한; 중요치 않은, 보잘것없는
  So weak or uncertain that it hardly exists.

* **impatient** [impéiʃənt] a. 성급한, 조급한, 몹시 …하고 싶어 하는
  Easily annoyed by someone's mistakes or because you have to wait.

* **aloof** [əlú:f] a. 서름서름한, 냉담한, 무관심한
  Unfriendly and distant.

* **occasionally** [əkéiʒənəli] ad. 때때로, 가끔
  Sometimes but not often.

* **sloth** [slouθ] n. [동물] 나무늘보
  American animal that lives in trees and moves very slowly.

* **tray** [trei] n. 쟁반, 음식 접시; 서류함
  A tray is a flat piece of wood, plastic, or metal, which usually has raised edges and which is used for carrying things, especially food and drinks.

  granola [grənóulə] n. 그라놀라 (곡물·견과류 등이 들어간 아침 식사용 시리얼의 일종)
  A type of breakfast cereal made of grains, nuts, etc. that have been toasted.

  pulverize [pʌ́lvəràiz] v. 가루로 만들다, 분쇄하다
  To crush something into a powder.

3. THE END

* **convince** [kənvíns] vt. 확신시키다; 설득하다
  To persuade someone or make them certain.

  Denali n. 데날리. 'The Great One'이란 뜻을 가진 알래스카 지역의 가장 높은 산

* **swallow** [swálou] vt. 들이켜다, 삼키다, 꿀꺽 삼키다; 마른침을 삼키다
  If you swallow something, you cause it to go from your mouth down into your stomach.

  dislodge [dislάdʒ] v. 이동시키다, 제거하다, 몰아내다; 숙소에서 나오다
  To force something out of a fixed or established position.

* **lump** [lʌmp] n. 덩어리, 한 조각; (구어) 땅딸보; 멍청이, 바보
  A piece of a solid substance, usually with no particular shape.

* **slump** [slʌmp] v. 쿵 떨어지다; 털썩 앉다; n. (활동·원기의) 슬럼프; 쿵 떨어짐
  To sit or fall heavily and suddenly.

* **plague** [pleig] n. 역병, 전염병; vt. 괴롭히다
  A plague is a very infectious disease that spreads quickly and kills large numbers of people.

  solicitous [səlísətəs] a. 걱정[염려]하는; 세심히 배려하는
  (solicitously ad. 걱정스럽게; 염려하여)
  A person who is solicitous shows anxious concern for someone or something.

* **indifferent** [indífərənt] a. 무관심한, 대수롭지 않은, 중요치 않은
  (indifferently ad. 무심하게)
  Having or showing no interest in somebody/something.

  lope [loup] v. 천천히 뛰다[뛰게 하다]; 성큼성큼 달리다[달리게 하다]
  To run with long bounding steps.

  hyperventilate [hàipərvéntəleit] v. (흥분·놀람으로) 숨을 크게 들이쉬다
  To breathe too quickly or too deeply, so that you get too much oxygen and feel dizzy.

  regularity [rèɡjəlǽrəti] n. 질서, 균형, 조화; 규칙[정기]적임
  A regularity is the fact that the same thing always happens in the same circumstances.

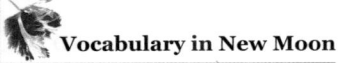

Vocabulary in New Moon

interminable [intə́:rmənəbəl] a. 끝없이 계속되는, 한없는, 지루하게 긴
Lasting a very long time and therefore boring or annoying endless.

uninterrupted [ʌ̀nintərʌ́ptid] a. 중단되지 않은, 연속된
Not stopped or blocked by anything.

immortal [imɔ́:rtl] n. 영생하는 존재; 불멸의 인물; a. 불사의, 불멸의, 영원한
A god or other being who is believed to live for ever.

composure [kəmpóuʒər] n. 침착, 냉정, 평정, 자제
Composure is the appearance or feeling of calm and the ability to control your feelings.

vaguely [véigli] ad. 모호하게, 막연히
In a way that is not detailed or exact.

scenario [sinɛ́əriòu] n. [연극] 대본; [영화] 시나리오, 영화 각본
A description of how things might happen in the future.

exotic [igzátik] a. 이국적인, 이국정서의; 색다른, 낭만적인
Something that is exotic is unusual and interesting, usually because it comes from or is related to a distant country.

locale [loukǽl] n. (사건 등의) 현장[무대], 장소
A locale is a small area, for example the place where something happens or where the action of a book or film is set.

ugh [u:x] int. 위, 액, 왜, 캑 (혐오·경멸·공포 또는 기침 소리를 나타냄)
The way of writing the sound that people make when they think that something is disgusting or unpleasant.

distinctive [distíŋktiv] a. 특유의, 특이한, 특색 있는
Easy to recognize because it is different from other things.

ESPN n. 미국의 오락·스포츠 전문의 유료 유선 텔레비전망(網)
Entertainment and Sports Programming Network.

weakly [wí:kli] ad. 약하게, 가냘프게; 무기력하게; a. 몸이 약한, 허약한; 가냘픈
In a weak way.

3. THE END

- **stray** [strei] vi. 길을 잃다; (옳은 길에서) 빗나가다; a. 길 잃은, 벗어난
  If your mind or your eyes stray, you do not concentrate on or look at one particular subject, but start thinking about or looking at other things.

- **banter** [bǽntər] n. (가벼운) 농담, 놀림; vi. (정감 어린) 농담을 주고 받다
  Friendly remarks and jokes.

  flinch [flintʃ] v. (고통·공포로) 주춤하다, 위축되다
  To make a small sudden movement, especially when something surprises someone.

- **permanent** [pə́:rmənənt] a. 영구적인, 영속하는, 변하지 않는
  Lasting for a long time or forever.

- **token** [tóukən] n. 표시, 징후, 증거
  Something that is a symbol of a feeling, a fact, an event, etc.

- **carefree** [kέərfrì:] a. 근심 걱정 없는 태평한
  care (n. 근심) + free (a. …에서 자유로운)

- **precipice** [présəpis] n. 절벽, 벼랑; 위기
  A very steep side of a cliff or a mountain.

- **crib** [krib] n. 유아용 침대; 구유, 여물통
  A small bed with high sides for a baby or young child.

  untidily [əntáidili] a. 단정치 못한, 어수선한, 흐트러진
  Not neat or well arranged; In a state of confusion.

- **regardless** [rigá:rdlis] ad. 개의치[상관하지] 않고
  Paying no attention, even if the situation is bad or there are difficulties.

- **compulsion** [kəmpʌ́lʃən] n. 강제, 강박(현상); 억제하기 어려운 욕망
  A compulsion is a strong desire to do something, which you find difficult to control.

- **meddle** [médl] vi. 쓸데없이 참견하다, 간섭하다
  To try to change or have an influence on things which are not your responsibility, especially in a critical, damaging or annoying way.

Vocabulary in New Moon

‡ **shiver** [ʃívər] n. 떨림, 전율; v. (추위·공포로) 후들후들 떨다; 전율하다
A sudden shaking movement of your body because you are cold, frightened, excited, etc.

복습 **lounge** [laundʒ] v. 느긋하게 세[앉아·누워] 있다
If you lounge somewhere, you sit or lie there in a relaxed or lazy way.

‡ **grumble** [grʌ́mbəl] v. 투덜거리다, 불평하다; n. 투덜댐, 불평
To complain about someone or something in an annoyed way.

obligate [άbləgèit] vt. 의무를 지우다; 강요하다
If something obligates you to do a particular thing, it creates a situation where you have to do it.

unintelligible [ənintélədʒəbəl] a. 이해할 수 없는, 난해한, 뚜렷하지 못한
Impossible to understand.

★ **admirable** [ǽdmərəbəl] a. 감탄[칭찬]할만한, 훌륭한
Deserving respect or approval.

‡ **indifference** [indífərəns] n. (…에 대한) 무관심, 냉담, 개의치 않음
If you accuse someone of indifference to something, you mean that they have a complete lack of interest in it.

‡ **arrangement** [əréindʒmənt] n. 정돈, 정리; 배열, 조정, 준비
A plan or preparation that you make so that something can happen.

★ **crevice** [krévis] n. 갈라진 틈, 균열
A small narrow crack or space, especially in the surface of rock.

‡ **commercial** [kəmə́ːrʃəl] n. (텔레비전·라디오의) 광고 (방송); a. 상업[통상·무역]의, 상업[무역]상의; 영리적인
A commercial is an advertisement that is broadcast on television or radio.

★ **trudge** [trʌdʒ] v. 터벅터벅 걷다; n. 터덕터덕 걸음
To walk slowly with a lot of effort, especially over a difficult surface or while carrying something heavy.

★ **sinister** [sínistər] a. 사악한, 음흉한; 불길한
Something that is sinister seems evil or harmful.

3. THE END

timeless [táimlis] a. 세월이 흘러도 변치 않는; 영원한 (timelessness n. 영원불멸)
Continuing forever.

impatience [impéiʃəns] n. 성급함, 초조, 조급함, 안달
Annoyance at having to accept delays, other people's weakness etc.

candid [kǽndid] a. 솔직한, 숨김없는, 거리낌 없는
Honest and open about what one thinks; Outspoken.

predictable [pridíktəbl] a. 예언[예상·예측]할 수 있는
If something is predictable, you know in advance that it will happen or what it will be like.

ensue [insúː] vi. (어떤 일·결과가) 뒤따르다, 뒤이어 일어나다, 후에 일어나다
To happen after or as a result of another event.

giggle [gígəl] v. 낄낄 웃다; n. 낄낄 웃음
If someone giggles, they laugh in a childlike way, because they are amused, nervous, or embarrassed.

flirt [fləːrt] vi. 이성과 시시덕거리다, 장난삼아 연애하다
If you flirt with someone, you behave as if you are sexually attracted to them, although not seriously.

apologetic [əpɑ̀lədʒétik] a. 미안해하는, 사과하는
(apologetically ad. 변명조로; 사과의 뜻으로)
Feeling or showing that you are sorry for doing something wrong or for causing a problem.

Thriftway n. 미국 내의 식료잡화 체인점

tuck [tʌk] v. 밀어 넣다, 쑤셔 넣다; n. 접어 넣은 단
If you tuck something somewhere, you put it there so that it is safe, comfortable, or neat.

uncanny [ʌnkǽni] a. 초인적인, 초자연적인; 이상한, 비정상적인
Strange and difficult to explain.

description [diskrípʃən] n. 기술, 서술, 설명서, 기재사항
An official list of the work and responsibilities that you have in your job.

Vocabulary in New Moon

- **tolerant** [tάlərənt] a. 관대한, 아량이 있는
  If you describe someone as tolerant, you approve of the fact that they allow other people to say and do as they like, even if they do not agree with or like it.

- **amusement** [əmjú:zmənt] n. 즐거움, 위안, 재미, 오락(물)
  The feeling that you have when something is funny or amusing, or it entertains you.

- **breathtaking** [bréθtèikiŋ] a. 깜짝 놀랄 만한, 아슬아슬한 (breathtakingly ad. 놀랍도록)
  Very exciting or impressive (usually in a pleasant way).

- **statue** [stǽtʃu:] n. 상(像), 조각상
  A statue is a large sculpture of a person or an animal, made of stone or metal.

- **shameful** [ʃéimfəl] a. 수치스러운, 창피한, 부끄러운
  (shamefully ad. 수치스럽게, 창피하게)
  If you describe a person's action or attitude as shameful, you think that it is so bad that the person ought to be ashamed.

- **scrawl** [skrɔ:l] vt. 휘갈겨 쓰다, 낙서하다
  To write something in a careless untidy way, making it difficult to read.

- **caption** [kǽpʃən] n. (신문·페이지 등의) 표제, 제목; (삽화의) 설명문
  Words that are printed underneath a picture, cartoon, etc. that explain or describe it.

- **frustrating** [frʌ́streitiŋ] a. 불만스러운, 좌절감을 주는
  Making you feeling annoyed, upset, or impatient because you cannot do what you want to do.

- **fade** [feid] vi. 바래다, 시들다, 희미해지다
  To disappear gradually.

- **urgency** [ə́:rdʒənsi] n. 긴급, 화급; 절박, 위급, 위기
  The state of being urgent.

- **snag** [snæg] v. (흔히 다른 사람보다 먼저) 잡아[낚아]채다
  To succeed in getting something quickly, often before other people.

3. THE END

crook [kruk] v. 구부리다, (갈고리처럼) 굽히다; n. 구부러진 갈고리
(crooked a. 비뚤어진, 구부러진)
If you crook your arm or finger, you bend it.

instantly [ínstəntli] ad. 즉각, 즉시
Immediately.

encroach [enkróutʃ] vi. 잠식하다, 침략하다, 침해하다
To gradually cover more and more land.

unwilling [ʌ̀nwíliŋ] a. 마음 내키지 않는, 마지못해 하는
(unwillingly ad. 마지못해, 본의 아니게)
Not wanting to do something and refusing to do it.

nausea [nɔ́ːziə] n. 메스꺼움, 욕지기; 뱃멀미
The feeling that you have when you want to vomit, for example because you are ill/sick or are disgusted by something.

distinct [distíŋkt] a. 별개의, 다른; 뚜렷한, 명백한
Clearly separate and different from something else.

grim [grim] a. 엄한, 엄격한; 험상스러운 (grimly ad. 잔인하게, 험악하게)
Looking or sounding very serious.

plea [pliː] n. 탄원, 청원; 간청; 기도
A plea is an appeal or request for something, made in an intense or emotional way.

unseeing [ʌ̀nsíːiŋ] a. 보고 있지 않는, 보려고 하지 않는
(unseeingly ad. 보지 않고; 눈이 보이지 않게)
Not noticing or really looking at anything although your eyes are open.

precisely [prisáisli] ad. 정밀하게, 정확히, 정확하게
Exactly.

absorb [əbsɔ́ːrb] vt. 받아들이다, 흡수하다; 열중시키다
If you absorb information, you learn and understand it.

uncomprehending [ənkʌ̀mprihéndiŋ] a. 잘 이해되지 않는, 이해력이 부족한
Not understanding a situation or what is happening.

Vocabulary in New Moon

* **apology** [əpάlədʒi] n. 사죄, 사과
  An act of saying sorry.

* **bottomless** [bάtəmlis] a. 밑바닥이 없는, 헤아릴 수 없는, 매우 깊은
  If you describe a supply of something as bottomless, you mean that it seems so large that it will never run out.

* **contradiction** [kὰntrədíkʃən] n. 부정, 부인; 반박, 반대
  If you describe an aspect of a situation as a contradiction, you mean that it is completely different from other aspects, and so makes the situation confused or difficult to understand.

* **awareness** [əwέərnis] n. 알아채고[깨닫고] 있음, 자각, 인식; 의식
  Knowing that something exists and is important; Being interested in something.

* **seep** [si:p] vi. 스며 나오다, 새다
  If something such as liquid or gas seeps somewhere, it flows slowly and in small amounts into a place where it should not go.

* **trickle** [tríkəl] vi. 똑똑 떨어지다, 졸졸 흐르다; (비밀 따위가) 조금씩 새어 나가다; n. 물방울, 실개울
  If liquid trickles somewhere, it flows slowly and without force in a thin line.

* **acid** [ǽsid] n. [화학] 산(酸); 매서움, 신랄함
  A chemical, usually a liquid, that contains hydrogen and has a pH of less than seven. The hydrogen can be replaced by a metal to form a salt.

* **vein** [vein] n. 혈관, 정맥, 광맥; 기질, 특질
  Any of the tubes that carry blood from all parts of the body towards the heart.

* **serene** [sirí:n] a. 고요한; 화창한; 침착한, 평온한
  Very calm or peaceful.

* **vow** [vau] v. 맹세하다, 서약하다; 단언하다; n. 맹세, 서약
  To make a formal and serious promise to do something or a formal statement that is true.

3. THE END

* **reckless** [réklis] a. 무모한, 분별없는
 Showing a lack of care about danger and the possible results of your actions.

* **helpless** [hélplis] a. 어찌할 수 없는, 주체 못하는
 (helplessly ad. 어찌해 볼 수도 없이, 의지할 데 없이)
 Unable to take care of yourself or do things without the help of other people.

* **interference** [ìntərfíərəns] n. 간섭, 방해, 참견
 Interference by a person or group is their unwanted or unnecessary involvement in something.

 wobble [wábəl] v. 흔들흔들하다, 비틀대다; 동요하다; n. 흔들림
 To shake or move from side to side in a way that shows a lack of balance.

 sieve [siv] n. 체 (가루・물 등을 거르는 데 쓰는 부엌 도구)
 (have a memory/mind like a sieve : 기억력이 아주 나쁘다; 건망증이 심하다)
 A sieve is a tool used for separating solids from liquids or larger pieces of something from smaller pieces.

* **tranquil** [trǽŋkwil] a. 조용한, 평온한, 평화로운
 Quiet and peaceful.

* **plural** [plúərəl] n. 복수형
 The plural of a noun is the form of it that is used to refer to more than one person or thing.

* **breeze** [bri:z] n. 산들바람, 미풍; v. (주어 it) 산들산들 불다
 A light and pleasant wind.

 undergrowth [ʌ́ndərgròuθ] n. 덤불, 풀숲
 Undergrowth consists of bushes and plants growing together under the trees in a forest.

* **stumble** [stʌ́mbəl] v. 비틀거리며 걷다, 발부리가 걸리다; n. 비틀거림
 If you stumble, you put your foot down awkwardly while you are walking or running and nearly fall over.

Vocabulary in New Moon

bracken [brǽkən] n. 고사리 (양치식물의 일종)
A large plant with leaves that are divided into many thin sections. It grows on hills and in woods.

★ **filter** [fíltər] v. 거르다, 통과하다, 여과하다; n. 여과기
To filter a substance means to pass it through a device which is designed to remove certain particles contained in it.

chink [tʃiŋk] n. 갈라진 틈, 균열; 좁은 틈새
A small slit or crack.

★ **canopy** [kǽnəpi] n. 숲의 우거진 윗부분; 덮개
A layer of something that spreads over an area like a roof, especially branches of trees in a forest.

★ **utterly** [ʌ́tərli] ad. 완전히, 순전히, 아주, 전혀
You use utterly to emphasize that something is very great in extent, degree, or amount.

★ **eclipse** [iklíps] n. [천문] (해·달의) 식 (lunar eclipse : 월식)
An eclipse of the sun is an occasion when the moon is between the earth and the sun, so that for a short time you cannot see part or all of the sun. An eclipse of the moon is an occasion when the earth is between the sun and the moon, so that for a short time you cannot see part or all of the moon.

✼ **mute** [mju:t] vt. …의 소리를 죽이다, …을 약하게 하다; a. 무언의, 말없는
To make the sound of something, especially a musical instrument, quieter or softer.

★ **muffle** [mʌ́fəl] vt. (덮어서 소리를) 지우다, 억제하다; 덮다, 목도리로 감싸다
If something muffles a sound, it makes it quieter and more difficult to hear.

복습 **unthinking** [ʌnθíŋkiŋ] a. 생각 없는, 경솔한
Not thinking about the effects of what you do or say.

stupor [stjú:pər] n. 인사불성; 무감각; 마비, 혼수
Someone who is in a stupor is almost unconscious and is unable to act or think normally, especially as a result of drink or drugs.

3. THE END

numbness [nʌ́mnis] n. 무감각
Partial or total lack of sensation in a part of the body.

startling [stáːrtliŋ] a. 놀라운, 깜짝 놀라게 하는 (startlingly ad. 놀랍도록, 놀랄 만큼)
Something that is startling is so different, unexpected, or remarkable that people react to it with surprise.

snuffle [snʌ́fəl] v. 코를 킁킁거리다, 코가 막히다, 콧물을 훌쩍거리다
If a person or an animal snuffles, they breathe in noisily through their nose, for example because they have a cold.

dim [dim] a. 어둑한, 흐릿한, 희미한; v. 어둑하게 하다, 흐려지다
Dim light is not bright.

illuminate [ilúːmənèit] vt. 밝게 하다, 비추다; 계발[계몽]하다
To illuminate something means to shine light on it and to make it brighter and more visible.

propane [próupein] n. [화학] 프로판 (탄화수소의 일종)
A gas that is used for cooking and heating.

lantern [lǽntərn] n. 랜턴, 초롱
A lantern is a lamp in a metal frame with glass sides and with a handle on top so you can carry it.

recognition [rèkəgníʃən] n. 인지, 승인, 허가
The act of remembering who somebody is when you see them, or of identifying what something is.

bewildered [biwíldərd] a. 당황한, 어리둥절한
Very confused.

strike a chord idiom 뭔가 생각나게 하다; 상기시키다
Say or do something which speaks directly to somebody's emotions or memories.

appraise [əpréiz] vt. 살피다, 뜯어보다; (사람·능력을) 평가하다
To consider or examine somebody/something and form an opinion about them or it.

Vocabulary in New Moon

limp [limp] a. 기운이[활기가] 없는, 축 처진[늘어진]
If you describe something as limp, you mean that it is soft or weak when it should be firm or strong.

swift [swift] a. 빠른, 신속한 (swiftly ad. 빨리, 즉시)
A swift event or process happens very quickly or without delay.

babble [bǽbəl] n. 재잘거림, 왁자지껄; v. 실없이 지껄이다, 쓸데없는 말을 하다
The sound of many people speaking at the same time.

distort [distɔ́:rt] vt. 비틀다, 뒤틀다; 왜곡[곡해]하다; (얼굴 등을) 찡그리다, 찌푸리다
If something you can see or hear is distorted or distorts, its appearance or sound is changed so that it seems unclear.

sheriff [ʃérif] n. (미) 군(郡) 보안관; (영) 주(州) 장관
In the United States, a sheriff is a person who is elected to make sure that the law is obeyed in a particular county.

stagger [stǽgər] v. 비틀거리다; 흔들리게 하다; 주저하다; n. 비틀거림
If you stagger, you walk very unsteadily, for example because you are ill or drunk.

parade [pəréid] n. 행렬, 퍼레이드, 행진
A public celebration of a special day or event, usually with bands in the streets and decorated vehicles.

funeral [fjú:nərəl] n. 장례식
A ceremony for burying or burning the body of a dead person.

feeble [fí:bəl] a. 연약한, 약한, 힘없는 (feebly ad. 약하게; 힘없이; 희미하게)
Weak and without energy, strength or power.

gruff [grʌf] a. (목소리가) 거친, 쉰; 퉁명스러운
Deep and rough, and often sounding unfriendly.

significant [signífikənt] a. 중요한, 소중한; …을 의미하는, 나타내는
Large or important enough to have an effect or to be noticed.

3. THE END

grizzled [grízld] a. 회색이 도는, 회색의; 반백의
A grizzled person or a person with grizzled hair has hair that is grey or partly grey.

prod [prɑd] vt. 자극하다, 재촉하다; 찌르다, 쑤시다
If you prod someone into doing something, you remind or persuade them to do it.

Quileute n. 퀼렛 부족
현존하는 인디언계 퀴요 부족에서 따옴.

★ **reservation** [rèzərvéiʃən] n. (미) (인디언을 위한) 정부 지정 보류지
A reservation is an area of land that is kept separate for a particular group of people to live in.

★ **coastline** [kóustlàin] n. 해안선
A country's coastline is the outline of its coast.

surreptitious [sə̀:rəptíʃəs] a. 비밀의, 몰래 하는, 은밀한; 부정의
(surreptitiously ad. 몰래; 부정하게)
Done secretly or quickly, in the hope that other people will not notice.

★ **rumble** [rʌ́mbəl] vi. (천둥·지진 등이) 우르르 울리다; (배가) 꾸르륵거리다; n. 우르르 소리
To make a continuous low sound.

★ **probe** [proub] v. 탐구하다, 면밀히 조사하다
If you probe into something, you ask questions or try to discover facts about it.

★ **gland** [glænd] n. [생리·식물] 선(腺), 분비 기관
A gland is an organ in the body which produces chemical substances for the body to use or get rid of.

obedient [oubí:diənt] a. 말을 잘 듣는, 순종적인 (obediently ad. 고분고분하게, 정중하게)
Doing, or willing to do, what you have been told to do by someone in authority.

★ **exhaustion** [igzɔ́:stʃən] n. 극도의 피로, 기진맥진
Extreme tiredness.

Vocabulary in New Moon

* **creak** [kri:k] v. 삐걱삐걱 소리를 내며 움직이(게 하)다; n. 삐걱거리는 소리
  When a door or floorboard, etc. creaks, it makes a long low sound when it moves or is moved.

* **strain** [strein] v. 분투하다; 잡아당기다, 긴장시키다
  To try hard to do something, usually to see or hear something.

  alertness [ələ́:rtnis] n. 경계, 신경 씀, 기민함
  The quality of being alert or on the alert.

‡ **yawn** [jɔ:n] vi. 하품하다; n. 하품
  To open your mouth wide and breathe in deeply through it, usually because you are tired or bored.

  mystify [místəfài] vt. 혼란스럽게[얼떨떨하게] 만들다
  If you are mystified by something, you find it impossible to explain or understand.

‡ **cliff** [klif] n. 절벽, 낭떠러지
  A high area of rock with a very steep side, often on a coast.

* **irritation** [ìrətéiʃən] n. 짜증나게 함; 짜증, 화; 짜증나는 것, 자극하는 것
  Irritation is a feeling of annoyance, especially when something is happening that you cannot easily stop or control.

‡ **sarcastic** [sɑ:rkǽstik] a. 빈정대는, 비꼬는, 풍자적인 (sarcastically ad. 빈정대며, 비꼬아서)
  Saying things that are the opposite of what you mean, in order to make an unkind joke.

  grudging [grʌ́dʒiŋ] a. 인색한, 마지못해 하는 (grudgingly ad. 마지못해; 께쩨하게)
  Given or done unwillingly.

‡ **owe** [ou] vt. 빚지고 있다, 은혜를 입고 있다
  To have to pay somebody for something that you have already received or return money that you have borrowed.

‡ **sour** [sáuər] a. (사람이) 퉁한, 시큰둥한; 심술궂은
  Someone who is sour is bad-tempered and unfriendly.

3. THE END

incoherent [ìnko*u*híərənt] a. 조리가 서지 않는, 논리가 일관되지 않는, 모순된
If someone is incoherent, they are talking in a confused and unclear way.

★ **shuffle** [ʃʌ́fl] v. 질질 끌다, 발을 끌며 걷다; 카드를 뒤섞다; n. 발을 끌며 걷기; 뒤섞기
If you shuffle somewhere, you walk there without lifting your feet properly off the ground.

★ **bonfire** [bánfàiər] n. (축하의 큰) 햇불, (노천의) 화톳불, 모닥불
A bonfire is a fire that is made outdoors, usually to burn rubbish. Bonfires are also sometimes lit as part of a celebration.

rowdy [ráudi] a. 난폭한, 난장 치는, 싸움 좋아하는; 떠들썩한; 야비한
When people are rowdy, they are noisy, rough, and likely to cause trouble.

‡ **superstition** [sù:pərstíʃən] n. 미신, 맹신
Belief in an influence that certain (especially commonplace) objects, actions or occurrences have on events, people's lives, etc.

‡ **tribe** [traib] n. 종족, 부족
A group of people, often of related families, who live together, sharing the same language, culture and history.

‡ **ancestor** [ǽnsestər] n. (사람의) 조상, 선조
Your ancestors are the people from whom you are descended.

★ **folklore** [fóuklɔ̀:r] n. 민속, 민간전승
Folklore is the traditional stories, customs, and habits of a particular community or nation.

splutter [splʌ́tər] (= sputter) vi. 식식거리며[더듬거리며] 말하다; 캑캑거리다
To talk quickly in short confused phrases, especially because you are angry or surprised.

deflect [diflékt] v. 비키(게 하)다, 빗나가(게 하)다; (생각 등이[을]) 편향하다[시키다]
If you deflect something such as criticism or attention, you act in a way that prevents it from being directed towards you or affecting you.

shy away (from something) phrasal v. (불안하거나 무서워서) (…을) 피하다
To avoid doing something because you are nervous or frightened.

83

Vocabulary in New Moon

‡ **inevitable** [inévitəbəl] a. 피할 수 없는, 필연적인
Certain to happen and unable to be avoided or prevented.

‡ **abuse** [əbjúːz] v. 남용[오용]하다; n. 남용, 오용; 욕설, 학대
If someone is abused, they are treated cruelly and violently.

‡ **damp** [dæmp] a. 축축한
Slightly wet, especially in a way that is not pleasant or comfortable.

refold [rifóuld] vt. 다시 접다, 접은 상태로 되돌리다
To fold again.

messy [mési] a. 지저분한, 흐트러진, 산란한
Untidy.

‡ **remarkable** [rimáːrkəbəl] a. 비범한, 뛰어난; 주목할 만한
(remarkably ad. 두드러지게, 현저하게, 몹시)
Someone or something that is remarkable is unusual or special in a way that makes people notice them and be surprised or impressed.

★ **recoil** [rikɔ́il] vi. 움찔하다; 되돌아오다; 후퇴하다; n. 되튐, 반동
If something makes you recoil, you move your body quickly away from it because it frightens, offends, or hurts you.

unleash [ʌ̀nlíːʃ] vt. 속박을 풀다, 해방하다, 자유롭게 하다
If you say that someone or something unleashes a powerful force, feeling, activity, or group, you mean that they suddenly start it or send it somewhere.

‡ **claw** [klɔː] v. 발톱으로 할퀴다; n. (날카롭고 굽은) 갈고리발톱, 집게발
To scratch or tear somebody/something with claws or with your nails.

‡ **astonished** [əstɑ́niʃt] a. 깜짝 놀란, 크게 놀란
Very surprised about something.

★ **doubtful** [dáutfəl] a. 확신이 없는, 의심스러운
(doubtfully ad. 미심쩍게, 불확실하게, 애매하게)
(of a person) Not sure.

3. THE END

* **shimmer** [ʃímər] vi. 희미하게 반짝이다, 빛나다; n. 반짝임 (shimmering a. 반짝이는)
If something shimmers, it shines with a faint, unsteady light or has an unclear, unsteady appearance.

‡ **agony** [ǽgəni] n. 고뇌, 고통, 번민
Agony is great physical or mental pain.

* **frantic** [frǽntik] a. 광란의, 미친 듯 날뛰는
Behaving in a wild and uncontrolled way.

‡ **scramble** [skrǽmbəl] vt. 간신히 해내다; 기어오르다; 서로 (다투어) 빼앗다; n. 기어오르기
If you scramble to a different place or position, you move there in a hurried, awkward way.

lurch [ləːrtʃ] v. 비틀거리다; n. (배·차 등의) 갑자기 기울어짐; 비틀거림
To make a sudden, unsteady movement forward or sideways.

‡ **suspicion** [səspíʃən] n. 혐의, 용의, 의심
Suspicion is a belief or feeling that someone has committed a crime or done something wrong.

* **latch** [lætʃ] n. 걸쇠, 빗장; v. 걸쇠를 걸다
A latch is a fastening on a door or gate. It consists of a metal bar which you lift in order to open the door.

‡ **thorough** [θə́ːrou] a. 철저한, 완전한, 빈틈없는
A thorough action or activity is one that is done very carefully and in a detailed way so that nothing is forgotten.

‡ **consciousness** [kánʃəsnis] n. 의식, 자각
Your consciousness is your mind and your thoughts.

rear up phrasal v. 들이닥치다; 고개를 쳐들다
If something rears up, it appears in front of you and often seems to be leaning over you in a threatening way.

resurface [riːsə́ːrfis] vi. 다시 수면에 떠오르다; 표면화하다
To reappear.

Comprehension Quiz

 4. WAKING UP

1. What was Charlie's problem with Bella?

A. Bella wasn't nice to him.

B. Bella wanted to be with her mother rather than with him.

C. Bella spent too much time with her friends.

D. Bella wasn't doing anything with her life.

2. Charlie thought that _____ was the best thing for Bella.

A. writing a letter to Edward

B. staying inside until she feels better

C. moving to Florida with her mother

D. going on a trip

3. According to Bella, she heard Edward's voice because _____.

A. she spoke to an attractive man

B. she ignored her friend

C. she put herself in danger

D. she remembered a time when she was with Edward

4. WAKING UP

4. The night Bella heard Edward's voice, she felt that _____.

  A. the pain of Edward leaving her made her weaker over time
  B. she grew strong enough to bear the pain of Edward leaving her
  C. she would never be strong enough to endure the pain of Edward leaving her
  D. the pain she felt was going away

5. Bella had to believe that _____ to be able to live.

  A. Edward existed
  B. Edward loved her
  C. the Cullens were safe
  D. she would see Edward again

Vocabulary in New Moon

bruise [bru:z] n. 타박상, 멍; v. …에게 타박상을 주다, 멍들게 하다
A blue, brown or purple mark that appears on the skin after somebody has fallen, been hit, etc.

lull [lʌl] v. (활동 사이의) 잠잠한 시기, 소강상태
A short period of time when there is less activity or less noise than usual.

ponder [pándər] v. 숙고하다, 깊이 생각하다
To think carefully about something, especially for a noticeable length of time.

clarify [klǽrəfài] v. (의미 등을) 뚜렷하게[명백하게] 하다; 명백하게 설명하다
To make something clearer or easier to understand.

exasperation [igzæspəréiʃən] n. 격분, 격노
The state of being annoyed and frustrated.

crumple [krʌ́mpl] v. 구기다, 구겨지다, 쭈글쭈글하게 하다
To crush something into folds; To become crushed into folds.

curfew [kə́:rfju:] n. 외출 금지 시각
A time when children must be home in the evening.

leftover [léftòuvər] n. 나머지; (식사 후에) 남은 음식; a. 나머지의, 남은
Food that has not been eaten at the end of a meal.

scowl [skaul] vi. 얼굴을 찌푸리다, 싫은 기색을 하다; n. 찌푸린 얼굴
To look at someone or something with a very annoyed expression.

mystify [místəfài] vt. 혼란스럽게[얼떨떨하게] 만들다 (mystification n. 어리둥절하게 함)
If you are mystified by something, you find it impossible to explain or understand.

mope around phrasal v. 맥없이 돌아다니다; 침울하게 서성거리다
To walk about a place in an unhappy way, with no particular purpose.

moroseness [məróusnis] n. 성미 까다로움, 언짢음, 침울함
A gloomy ill-tempered feeling.

4. WAKING UP

* **concede** [kənsíːd] v. 인정[시인]하다; 부여하다; 허용하다
  To admit that something is true, logical, etc.

* **lifeless** [láiflis] a. 생명 없는, 활기 없는
  Dead or appearing to be dead.

* **accusation** [æ̀kjuzéiʃən] n. 비난, 규탄, 죄, 죄명
  The act of accusing someone of having done something wrong.

* **animate** [ǽnəmèit] vt. 살리다, 활기를 주다; a. 살아 있는, 활기 있는
  (animation n. 생기, 활기)
  To make someone seem more happy or active.

* **scrutinize** [skrúːtənàiz] v. 세밀히 조사하다, 철저히 검사하다, 파고 따지다
  To subject to scrutiny; To examine closely.

* **grimace** [gríməs] n. 얼굴을 찌푸림, 찌푸린 얼굴, 우거지상; vi. 얼굴을 찡그리다
  An ugly expression made by twisting your face, used to show pain, disgust, etc. or to make somebody laugh.

unimpressive [ʌ̀nimprésiv] a. 인상적이 못 되는, 특별하지 않은, 평범한
Ordinary; Not special in any way.

point out phrasal v. …을 지적하다
If you point out a fact or mistake, you tell someone about it or draw their attention to it.

‡ **shrink** [ʃriŋk] n. (속어) 정신과 의사; 심리학자; v. 움츠러들다, 뒷걸음치다; 오그라들다; 줄다
A shrink is a psychiatrist.

psychoanalysis [sàikouənǽləsis] n. 정신 분석(학); 정신 분석 요법
The treatment of someone who has mental problems by asking them about their feelings and their past in order to try to discover what may be causing their condition.

padded cell n. (정신 병원에서 환자의 자해를 막기 위해) 벽면에 패드를 댄 방
A padded cell is a small room with padded walls in a mental hospital or prison, where a person who may behave violently can be put so that they do not hurt themselves.

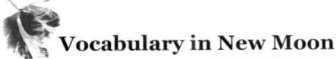

Vocabulary in New Moon

* **obstinate** [ábstənit] a. 완고한, 고집 센
  Unreasonably determined, especially to act in a particular way and not to change at all, despite argument or persuasion.

* **dense** [dens] a. (구어) 머리 나쁜, 우둔한; 빽빽한, 밀집한
  Stupid.

* **miserable** [mízərəbəl] a. 불쌍한, 비참한, 불행한, 딱한, 가엾은
  Unpleasant and causing unhappiness.

* **contemplate** [kántəmplèit] v. 깊이 생각하다, 응시하다, 찬찬히 보다
  To think carefully about and accept the possibility of something happening.

* **semester** [siméstər] n. 한 학기, 반 학년
  One of the two main periods into which the year is divided.

* **screw** [skru:] v. 나사로 죄다, 비틀다; 쥐어짜다; (종이 등을) 구겨서 말다; n. 나사
  (screw up phrasal v. 망치다, 엉망으로 만들다)
  To be brave enough to do something you are very nervous about.

* **glower** [gláuər] vi. 상을 찡그리다, 불쾌한 얼굴을 하다; 노려보다; n. 노려봄; 찌푸린 얼굴
  To look in an angry, aggressive way.

* **monotone** [mánətòun] n. 단조, 단조로움; a. 단조로운
  If someone speaks in a monotone, their voice does not vary at all in tone or loudness and so it is not interesting to listen to.

* **yank** [jæŋk] v. 홱 당기다; 홱 잡아당겨 …의 상태로 하다; n. 홱 잡아당김
  If you yank someone or something somewhere, you pull them there suddenly and with a lot of force.

* **dump** [dʌmp] vt. 내버리다; (구어) 차다; n. 쓰레기장; 쓰레기 더미
  To put something or unload it somewhere quickly and carelessly.

* **haste** [heist] n. 급함, 서두름, 신속함
  Speed, especially speed in an action.

* **end up** idiom 끝나다; (구어) 마침내는 (…으로) 되다
  To reach or come to a particular place or situation that you did not expect or intend to be in.

4. WAKING UP

calculus [kǽlkjələs] n. 미적분학
Calculus is a branch of advanced mathematics which deals with variable quantities.

★ **bubble** [bʌ́bəl] n. 환상, 망상; 거품; v. (말을) 신나게 하다; 차오르다; 거품이 일다
(burst somebody's bubble idiom 김 빼는 소리를 하다; 힘 빠지는 소식을 전하다)
A small amount of a feeling that somebody wants to express.

✤ **communism** [kάmjənìzəm] n. 공산주의
The political belief that all people are equal and that workers should control the means of producing things.

✤ **curriculum** [kəríkjələm] n. 교육 과정
A course of study, especially at school or university.

★ **distraction** [distrǽkʃən] n. 방심, 정신이 흐트러짐, 주의 산만
Something that turns your attention away from something you want to concentrate on.

★ **aisle** [ail] n. 통로, 측면의 복도
An aisle is a long narrow gap that people can walk along between rows of seats in a public building.

antisocial [æ̀ntisóuʃəl] a. 반사회적인, 비사교적인; 비우호적인
anti (pre. 반대하는) + social (a. 사회적인)

sulk [sʌlk] vi. 샐쭉해지다, 부루퉁해지다, 골내다; n. 샐쭉함, 부루퉁함
To be silent and childishly refuse to smile or be pleasant to people because you are angry about something that they have done.

✤ **loiter** [lɔ́itər] v. 빈둥거리다, 어슬렁어슬렁 걷다, 쉬엄쉬엄 가다
To move slowly around or stand especially in a public place without an obvious reason.

procrastinate [proukrǽstənèit] v. 지연하다, 꾸물거리다, 질질 끌다
If you procrastinate, you keep leaving things you should do until later, often because you do not want to do them.

interaction [ìntərǽkʃən] n. 상호 작용, 상호의 영향
A mutual or reciprocal action.

Vocabulary in New Moon

odometer [oudámitər] n. (자동차의) 주행 기록계
A device in a vehicle which shows how far the vehicle has travelled.

★ **mileage** [máilidʒ] n. (자동차의) 주행 거리[마일 수]
Mileage refers to the distance that you have travelled, measured in miles.

복습 **tempt** [tempt] vt. 유혹하다, 부추기다
Something that tempts you attracts you and makes you want it, even though it may be wrong or harmful.

goody-goody [gúdigùdi] n. (비격식 못마땅함) 착한 체하는 사람
If you call someone a goody-goody, you mean they behave extremely well in order to please people in authority.

stem from phrasal v. …에서 기인하다, 유래하다
To be caused by something; To be result of something.

‡ **dismiss** [dismís] v. 해산하다; 묵살하다; 떨쳐 버리다
If you dismiss something, you decide or say that it is not important enough for you to think about or consider.

복습 **wrinkle** [ríŋkəl] v. 주름살지게 하다, 구겨지다; n. 주름, 잔주름
When you wrinkle your nose or forehead, or when it wrinkles, you tighten the muscles in your face so that the skin folds.

★ **incredulous** [inkrédʒələs] a. 쉽사리 믿지 않는, 의심 많은, 회의적인
(incredulously ad. 의심스럽게, 회의적으로)
If someone is incredulous, they are unable to believe something because it is very surprising or shocking.

‡ **innocence** [ínəsns] n. 천진; 순결, 때 묻지 않음; 결백
Having no knowledge of the unpleasant and evil things in life.

tad [tæd] n. 조금
You can use a tad in expressions such as a tad big or a tad small when you mean that it is slightly too big or slightly too small.

‡ **suspicious** [səspíʃəs] a. 의심하는, 의심 많은, 수상쩍은
If you are suspicious of someone or something, you do not trust them, and are careful when dealing with them.

4. WAKING UP

genuine [dʒénjuin] a. 진짜의, 진품의; 진심의
Genuine refers to things such as emotions that are real and not pretended.

mollify [málifài] v. (사람을) 달래다[진정시키다]
If you mollify someone, you do or say something to make them less upset or angry.

hedge [hedʒ] v. 변명의 여지를 남겨두다; 얼버무리다; 울타리를 두르다; n. 울타리; 대비책
If you hedge against something unpleasant or unwanted that might affect you, especially losing money, you do something which will protect you from it.

clue [kluː] n. 단서, 실마리
A sign or some information which helps you to find the answer to a problem.

oddly [ádli] ad. 묘하게, 이상하게
In a strange or unusual way.

bubbliness [bʌbblinis] n. 명랑 쾌활함
bubbly (a. 항상 명랑 쾌활한) + -ness (suf. 성질, 상태, 성격을 나타냄)

leak [liːk] v. 새게 하다, 새어나오다; n. 새는 구멍[곳]
If a liquid or gas leaks, it comes out of a hole by accident.

grasp [græsp] v. 붙잡다, 움켜쥐다; n. 움켜잡기
To quickly take something in your hand(s) and hold it firmly.

tentative [téntətiv] a. 주저하는, 모호한; 잠정적인
If someone is tentative, they are cautious and not very confident because they are uncertain or afraid.

minimal [mínəməl] a. 극히 작은, 최소한도의
Very small in size or amount.

haze [heiz] n. 아지랑이, 엷은 연기
Smoke, dust, or mist in the air which is difficult to see through.

register [rédʒəstər] vt. 기재하다, 등록하다; (감정을) 나타내다, 표현하다
If you register your feelings or opinions about something, you do something that makes them clear to other people.

Vocabulary in New Moon

rubbish [rʌ́biʃ] n. 쓰레기, 폐물; 어리석은 짓
Waste material or unwanted or worthless things.

stray [strei] vi. 길을 잃다; (옳은 길에서) 빗나가다; a. 길 잃은, 벗어난
If your mind or your eyes stray, you do not concentrate on or look at one particular subject, but start thinking about or looking at other things.

claw [klɔː] v. 발톱으로 할퀴다; n. (날카롭고 굽은) 갈고리발톱, 집게발
To scratch or tear somebody/something with claws or with your nails.

honk [hɔːŋk] v. 경적을 울리다; (기러기가) 울다
If you honk the horn of a vehicle, you make the horn produce a short loud sound.

infuse [infjúːz] vt. 붓다, 주입하다, 불어넣다
To fill something or someone with a particular feeling or quality.

gratitude [grǽtətjùːd] n. 감사, 고마움
Gratitude is the state of feeling grateful.

fake [feik] vt. …인 체하다, 가장하다 (pretend); a. 가짜의, 위조의
To pretend to have a particular feeling, illness, etc.

scan through phrasal v. 대충 훑어 보다
To look quickly but not very carefully at a document, etc.

peek [piːk] vi. 살짝 들여다보다, 엿보다; n. 엿봄
If you peek at something or someone, you have a quick look at them.

squint [skwint] v. 곁눈질을 하다, 실눈으로 보다; a. 사시의; 곁눈질하는
If you squint at something, you look at it with your eyes partly closed.

tune [tjuːn] v. 조율하다, 조정하다; n. 곡조, 선율 (tune out phrasal v. …을 듣지 않다)
If you tune out something or someone, you stop listening to them.

eagerness [íːgərnis] n. 열의, 열심, 열망
A positive feeling of wanting to push ahead with something.

4. WAKING UP

- **launch** [lɔ:ntʃ] v. 시작하다; 맹렬히 덤비다; 발진시키다; 쏘다
  To launch a large and important activity, for example a military attack, means to start it.

- **sympathy** [símpəθi] n. 동정심, 공감, 연민
  Understanding and care for someone else's suffering.

- **comparison** [kəmpǽrisən] n. 비교, 대조; 비유
  The process of comparing two or more people or things.

- **prod** [prɑd] vt. 재촉하다, 자극하다; 찌르다, 쑤시다
  If you prod someone into doing something, you remind or persuade them to do it.

- **twilight** [twáilàit] n. (해뜨기 전·후의) 여명, 황혼, 어스름
  Twilight is the time just before night when the daylight has almost gone but when it is not completely dark.

- **preview** [prí:vjù:] n. (영화·텔레비전의) 예고편
  An occasion at which you can see a film/movie, a show, etc. before it is shown to the general public.

- **mutual** [mjú:tʃuəl] a. 서로의, 상호 관계있는, 공동의
  Felt by each of two or more people about the other or others.

- **gooey** [gú:i] a. 끈적끈적한, 들러붙는; n. 끈적거리는 것, 당밀
  Soft and sticky.

- **falseness** [fɔ́:lsnis] n. 거짓(말), 잘못; 허위; 불성실; 배반
  The quality of not being open or truthful.

- **urge** [ə:rdʒ] n. 강한 욕구[충동]; v. 몰아대다, 재촉하다; 충고하다, 설득하려 하다
  A strong wish to do or have something.

- **hum** [hʌm] v. 콧노래를 부르다, (벌·기계 등이) 윙윙거리다
  To sing without opening your mouth.

Vocabulary in New Moon

desperate [déspərit] a. 필사적인; 절망적인, 자포자기의
(desperately ad. 절망적으로; 자포자기하여; 필사적으로)
If you are desperate for something or desperate to do something, you want or need it very much indeed.

shush [ʃʌʃ] vt. 쉬잇 하여 입 다물게 하다; int. 쉿, 조용히
You say shush when you are telling someone to be quiet.

concession [kənséʃən] n. (미) (매장 등의) 토지 사용권; 구내매점
The right to sell something in a particular place; The place where you sell it, sometimes an area which is part of a larger building or store.

debate [dibéit] n. 논쟁, 토론; v. 토론하다, 논쟁하다
To discuss something, especially formally, before making a decision or finding a solution.

exposition [èkspəzíʃən] n. (상세한) 설명[해설]
An exposition of an idea or theory is a detailed explanation or account of it.

blare [blɛər] v. 울려 퍼지다, 크게 울리다
To make an unpleasantly loud noise.

comprise [kəmpráiz] v. …으로 구성되다[이뤄지다]
If you say that something comprises or is comprised of a number of things or people, you mean it has them as its parts or members.

gruesome [grú:səm] a. 소름 끼치는, 무시무시한; 힘든
Something that is gruesome is extremely unpleasant and shocking.

dwindle [dwíndl] vi. 줄다, 작아지다, 축소되다
To become gradually less or smaller.

haggard [hǽgərd] a. 여윈, 수척한, 초췌한
Someone who looks haggard has a tired expression and shadows under their eyes, especially because they are ill or have not had enough sleep.

shamble [ʃǽmbəl] vi. 비틀비틀[휘청휘청] 걷다
To walk in an awkward or lazy way, dragging your feet along the ground.

4. WAKING UP

* **shriek** [ʃriːk] v. 새된 소리를 지르다, 비명을 지르다; n. 비명
  When someone shrieks, they make a short, very loud cry.

* **survivor** [sərváivər] n. 살아남은 사람, 생존자
  A survivor of a disaster, accident, or illness is someone who continues to live afterwards in spite of coming close to death.

* **heroine** [hérouin] n. (소설·영화 등의) 여자 주인공
  The heroine of a book, play, film, or story is the main female character, who usually has good qualities.

  emotionless [imóuʃənlis] a. 무표정한, 무감동의; 감정이 담기지 않은
  Not showing any emotion.

* **pursuer** [pərsúːər] n. 뒤쫓는 사람, 추적[격]자
  Your pursuers are the people who are chasing or searching for you.

* **resemble** [rizémbəl] vt. …을 닮다, …와 공통점이 있다
  To be like or similar to someone or something else, especially in appearance.

* **ironic** [airánik] a. 반어의[적인]; 비꼬는; 풍자적인 (irony n. 아이러니, 풍자, 비꼬기)
  Showing that you really mean the opposite of what you are saying.

  wind up phrasal v. (어떤 장소·상황에) 처하게 되다; 끝을 맺다, 마무리하다
  To close a business, a company, etc.

  mythical [míθikəl] a. 신화의, 신화에 대한; 신화적인
  Existing only in ancient myths.

* **grotesque** [groutésk] a. 기괴한, 이상한, 괴상한
  You say that something is grotesque when it is so unnatural, unpleasant, and exaggerated that it upsets or shocks you.

* **corpse** [kɔːrps] n. 시체, 송장
  A dead body, especially the body of a human being.

* **coward** [káuərd] n. 겁쟁이, 비겁한 사람
  A person who is not brave or who does not have the courage to do things that other people do not think are especially difficult.

Vocabulary in New Moon

gush [gʌʃ] v. (구어) 지껄여대다; 분출하다, 내뿜다; n. 분출; 격발
If someone gushes, they express their admiration or pleasure in an exaggerated way.

apologetic [əpɑ̀lədʒétik] a. 미안해하는, 사과하는
(apologetically ad. 변명조로; 사과의 뜻으로)
Feeling or showing that you are sorry for doing something wrong or for causing a problem

unlit [ənlít] a. 점화되지 않은, 불이 켜져 있지 않은
An unlit street or building is dark because there are no lights switched on in it.

pirate [páiərət] n. 해적, 해적선; 약탈자; v. 약탈하다
Pirates are sailors who attack other ships and steal property from them.

dimly [dímli] ad. 어둑[흐릿·희미]하게
Not very brightly or clearly.

clink [kliŋk] v. (금속 따위가) 짤랑 울리다; 땡그랑 소리 나다
If objects clink or if you clink them, they touch each other and make a short, light sound.

brisk [brisk] a. 활발한, 팔팔한 (briskly ad. 활발하게, 힘차게)
Lively, active or quick.

déjà vu [dèiʒɑːvúː] n. 기시감(지금 자신에게 일어나는 일을 전에도 경험한 적이 있는 것 같이 느끼는 것)
The feeling that you have previously experienced something which is happening to you now.

coincidental [kouìnsədéntl] a. 우연의 일치인, 우연의
Something that is coincidental is the result of a coincidence and has not been deliberately arranged.

blur [bləːr] n. (기억이) 흐릿한 것; 흐릿한 형체; v. 흐릿해지다
Something that you cannot remember clearly.

tension [ténʃən] n. 긴장, 긴박, 팽팽함
A feeling of worry and anxiety which makes it difficult for you to relax.

4. WAKING UP

dryness [dráinis] n. 건조(한 상태); 무미건조; 냉담
The condition of not containing or being covered by a liquid.

* **decent** [díːsnt] a. (사회 기준에) 맞는, 점잖은, 의젓한
Decent is used to describe something which is considered to be of an acceptable standard or quality.

* **knuckle** [nʌ́kəl] n. 손가락 관절[마디]; v. 손가락 마디로 치다
One of the joints in the hand where your fingers bend, especially where your fingers join on to the main part of your hand.

* **indefinite** [indéfənit] a. 명확[분명]하지 않은, 애매한, 막연한
Something that is indefinite is not exact or clear.

* **imply** [implái] vt. 함축하다, 암시하다; 의미하다
To suggest or express something indirectly; To hint at it.

* **menace** [ménəs] n. 협박, 위협; (구어) 골칫거리; vt. 위협하다
Something that is likely to cause harm.

outnumber [àutnʌ́mbər] vt. …보다 수적으로 우세하다, …를 수로 압도하다
If one group of people or things outnumbers another, the first group has more people or things in it than the second group.

* **specific** [spisífik] a. 명확한, 구체적인, 특정의
In a detailed or exact way.

nebulous [nébjələs] a. 흐릿한, 모호한
Not clear.

* **impulse** [ímpʌls] n. 충동, 추진(력); a. 충동적인
A sudden strong desire to do something.

adrenaline [ədrénəlin] n. 아드레날린
A substance which your body produces when you are angry, scared, or excited. It makes your heart beat faster and gives you more energy.

absently [ǽbsəntli] a. 멍하니, 넋을 잃고
In a way that shows you are not looking at or thinking about what is happening around you.

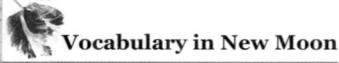

Vocabulary in New Moon

suicidal [sù:əsáidl] a. (사람이) 자포자기한; 자살의; 자살적인
Very dangerous and likely to lead to death; Likely to cause very serious problems or disaster.

★ **unquestionable** [ʌ̀nkwéstʃənəbəl] a. 의심할 나위 없는
(unquestionably ad. 의심할 여지없이, 확실히, 명백히)
Beyound question or doubt.

twinge [twindʒ] n. 쑤시는 듯한 아픔; (마음의) 고통, (양심의) 가책
A sudden short feeling of an unpleasant emotion.

‡ **blade** [bleid] n. (칼·도구 등의) 날
The flat part of a knife, tool or machine, which has a sharp edge or edges for cutting.

복습 **rhetorical** [ritɔ́(:)rikəl] a. 수사학의, 수사적인
(of a speech or piece of writing) Intended to influence people, but not completely honest or sincere.

‡ **amuse** [əmjú:z] vt. 즐겁게 하다, 재미나게 하다
To make somebody laugh or smile.

‡ **rebuke** [ribjú:k] vt. 힐책[질책]하다, 꾸짖다; n. 비난, 힐책
If you rebuke someone, you speak severely to them because they have said or done something that you do not approve of.

irate [áireit] a. 성난, 격분한
If someone is irate, they are very angry about something.

★ **exceptional** [iksépʃənəl] a. 이례적일 정도로 우수한, 특출한
(exceptionally ad. 예외적으로, 특별히, 유난히, 매우)
Unusually good.

‡ **pavement** [péivmənt] n. 포장 도로
A flat part at the side of a road for people to walk on.

slip away phrasal v. 사라지다, 없어지다
To leave quietly without attracting attention.

4. WAKING UP

turn down phrasal v. 줄이다; 소리를 줄이다[낮추다]
To adjust the controls on a piece of equipment in order to reduce the amount of heat, noise, light etc.

hallucination [həlù:sənéiʃən] n. 환각, 망상
A hallucination is the experience of seeing something that is not really there because you are ill or have taken a drug.

★ **trigger** [trígər] v. (장치를) 작동시키다; n. (총의) 방아쇠; 계기, 자극
If something triggers an event or situation, it causes it to begin to happen or exist.

layman [léimən] n. 평범한 사람들; 평신도; 아마추어
A person who does not have expert knowledge of a particular subject.

subconscious [sʌbkánʃəs] n., a. 잠재의식(의), 어렴풋이 의식(하는)
The mental processes that go on below the level of conscious awareness.

★ **fulfillment** [fulfílmənt] n. 이행, 수행, 완수; 실천; 실현
A feeling of satisfaction at having achieved your desires.

‡ **momentary** [móuməntèri] a. 순식간의, 찰나의
Something that is momentary lasts for a very short period of time.

★ **embrace** [embréis] vt. …을 껴안다, 포옹하다
If you embrace someone, you put your arms around them and hold them tightly, usually in order to show your love or affection for them.

‡ **incorrect** [ìnkərékt] a. 부정확한, 맞지 않는, 사실이 아닌
Something that is incorrect is wrong and untrue.

run amuck [rʌn əmʌ́k] idiom (특히 공공장소에서 갑자기) 미친 듯이 날뛰다
Behave in a wild or uncontrolled way.

hospitalize [háspitəlàiz] vt. 입원시키다
If someone is hospitalized, they are sent or admitted to hospital.

★ **sane** [sein] a. 제정신의, 온전한, 분별 있는
Having a normal healthy mind; Not mentally ill.

Vocabulary in New Moon

overwhelm [òuvərhwélm] vt. 압도하다, 제압하다; 질리게 하다
If you are overwhelmed by a feeling or event, it affects you very strongly, and you do not know how to deal with it.

trade-off [tréidɔ̀:f] n. (서로 대립되는 요소 사이의) 균형; 교환, 거래
A trade-off is a situation where you make a compromise between two things, or where you exchange all or part of one thing for another.

potential [pouténʃəl] a. 잠재적인, 가능성이 있는 (potentially ad. 가능성 있게, 잠재적으로)
If you say that someone or something has potential, you mean that they have the necessary abilities or qualities to become successful or useful in the future.

destructive [distrʌ́ktiv] a. 파괴적인, 해를 끼치는
Something that is destructive causes or is capable of causing great damage, harm, or injury.

unstable [ʌ̀nstéibəl] a. 안정되지 않은; 흔들리기 쉬운; 변하기 쉬운
Likely to change suddenly.

fabricate [fǽbrikèit] vt. (전설·거짓말 등을) 꾸며내다, 조작하다
To invent or produce something false in order to deceive.

dubious [djú:biəs] a. 의심스러운, 수상쩍은, 모호한
Feeling doubt or uncertainty.

dither [díðər] vi. (결정을 못 내리고) 머무적거리다[망설이다]
When someone dithers, they hesitate because they are unable to make a quick decision about something.

insanity [insǽnəti] n. 광기, 발광, 정신 이상
The state of being insane.

assurance [əʃúərəns] n. 확신; 보증, 보장
Guarantee or statement that something is true.

prejudiced [prédʒədist] a. 편견이 있는, 편파적인
Having an unreasonable dislike of someone or something.

4. WAKING UP

exquisite [ikskwízit] a. 정교한, 절묘한; 우아한, 섬세한
Extremely beautiful or carefully made.

snarl [snɑːrl] n. 으르렁거림; v. 으르렁거리다; 고함[호통]치다
A deep sound that an animal makes when it is angry and shows its teeth.

confident [kánfidənt] a. 확신하는, 자신 만만한
If you are confident about something, you are certain that it will happen in the way you want it to.

encouragement [enkə́ːridʒmənt] n. 격려, 고무
Encouragement is the activity of encouraging someone, or something that is said or done in order to encourage them.

gutter [gʌ́tər] n. 배수구, 도랑
The edge of a road where rain flows away.

analyze [ǽnəlàiz] vt. 분석적으로 검토하다, 분석하다
If you analyze something, you consider it carefully or use statistical methods in order to fully understand it.

flattered [flǽtərd] a. 우쭐한, 의기양양한
Plased because someone has shown you that they like or admire you.

baffle [bǽfəl] v. 당황하게 하다
To cause someone to be completely unable to understand or explain something.

compel [kəmpél] vt. 강제하다, 억지로 …시키다
To force someone to do something.

evaporate [ivǽpərèit] v. 증발하다, 사라지다
When a liquid evaporates, or is evaporated, it changes from a liquid state to a gas.

blonde [blɑnd] (= blond) n. 금발의 사람; 금색; a. 금발의
A woman with hair that is pale gold in color.

outrage [áutrèidʒ] n. 격분, 격노; v. (법률·도의 등을) 위반하다; 격분시키다
Outrage is an intense feeling of anger and shock.

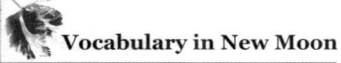

Vocabulary in New Moon

★ **betrayal** [bitréiəl] n. 배반, 배신
The act of betraying somebody/something or the fact of being betrayed.

rejoin [ri:dʒɔ́in] v. 다시 합류하다, 재결합하다
re (pre. 다시) + join (v. 합류하다)

★ **abstraction** [æbstrǽkʃən] n. 관념, 추상적 개념; 정신이 딴 데 팔려 있음
The act, or an example of, abstracting something.

★ **preoccupy** [pri:ɑ́kjəpài] vt. 먼저 점유하다, 선취하다; 마음을 빼앗다
pre (pre. 먼저) + occupy (v. 점유하다)

psychopath [sáikoupæ̀θ] n. 사이코패스(폭력성을 동반하는 이상 심리 소유자)
A psychopath is someone who has serious mental problems and who may act in a violent way without feeling sorry for what they have done.

★ **cooperative** [kouɑ́pərèitiv] a. 협력적인, 협동의, 협조적인
If you say that someone is cooperative, you mean that they do what you ask them to without complaining or arguing.

lyric [lírik] n. (보통 pl.) (유행가 따위의) 가사
The lyrics of a song are its words.

★ **reclaim** [rikléim] vt. 교정하다, 개선하다
To get something back or to ask to have it back after it has been lost, taken away, etc.

★ **core** [kɔ:r] n. 핵심, (사물의) 중심부
The most important or central part of something.

deprivation [dèprəvéiʃən] n. 박탈; 상실, 손실, 부족
The fact of not having something that you need, like enough food, money or a home; The process that causes this.

sleep away phrasal v. 잠자며 (시간을) 보내다; 잠자서 고치다[없애다]
To spend or waste a specific period of time sleeping.

4. WAKING UP

- **sieve** [siv] n. 체 (가루·물 등을 거르는 데 쓰는 부엌 도구)
  (have a memory/mind like a sieve : 기억력이 아주 나쁘다; 건망증이 심하다)
  A sieve is a tool used for separating solids from liquids or larger pieces of something from smaller pieces. It consists of a metal or plastic ring with a wire or plastic net underneath, which the liquid or smaller pieces pass through.

- **conviction** [kənvíkʃən] n. 신념, 확신; [법] 유죄 판결
  A strong belief or opinion.

- **absentminded** [ǽbsəntmaindid] a. 방심 상태의, 멍하고[얼빠져] 있는
  (absentmindedly ad. 건성으로, 방심하여)
  Someone who is absent-minded forgets things or does not pay attention to what they are doing, often because they are thinking about something else.

  humph [hʌmf] int. 흥!, 흠! (의심·경멸·불만을 나타냄)
  The way of writing the sound that people use to show they do not believe something or do not approve of it.

- **grunt** [grʌnt] vi. (돼지가) 꿀꿀거리다; (사람이) 툴툴거리다; n. 꿀꿀[툴툴]거리는 소리
  If you grunt, you make a low sound, especially because you are annoyed or not interested in something.

- **resign** [rizáin] v. 사직하다; 단념하다, 따르다
  To make yourself accept something that you do not like because you cannot change it.

- **cripple** [kripl] v. 심각한 손상을 주다, 제대로 기능을 못 하게 만들다
  (crippling a. 큰 손상[타격]을 주는)
  If something cripples a person, it causes them severe psychological or emotional problems.

  excise [éksaiz] vt. 삭제하다, 잘라내다, 절개하다
  If someone excises something, they remove it deliberately and completely.

- **vital** [váitl] a. 생명의, 생생한; 중요한; 치명적인
  Necessary for the success or continued existence of something; Extremely important.

Vocabulary in New Moon

- **organ** [ɔ́:rgən] n. (인체 내의) 장기[기관]
  An organ is a part of your body that has a particular purpose or function, for example your heart or lungs.

- **ragged** [rǽgid] a. 찢어진; 다 해진, 누더기가 된
  Torn and in bad condition.

- **gash** [gæʃ] n. 깊은 상처; (지면의) 갈라진 틈
  A gash is a long, deep cut in your skin or in the surface of something.

- **throb** [θrɑb] vi. (심장이) 고동치다, 맥이 뛰다; n. 고동, 맥박
  If part of your body throbs, you feel a series of strong and usually painful beats there.

- **bleed** [bli:d] vi. ① 출혈하다 ② 마음 아파하다
  When you bleed, you lose blood from your body as a result of injury or illness.

- **rationally** [rǽʃənləli] ad. 합리적으로; 이성적으로; 추리로
  (of behavior, ideas, etc.) Based on reason rather than emotions.

- **intact** [intǽkt] a. 완전한, 손상되지 않은
  Not broken, damaged, or spoiled.

- **pulse** [pʌls] n. 맥박, 고동; v. 맥이 뛰다, 고동치다
  Your pulse is the regular beating of blood through your body, which you can feel when you touch particular parts of your body, especially your wrist.

- **inward** [ínwərd] a. 안쪽으로[내부로] 향한; ad. 안으로, 속에서
  An inward movement is one towards the inside or center of something.

- **denial** [dináiəl] n. 부정, 부인, 거부
  A statement saying that something is not true.

- **evade** [ivéid] vt. 피하다, 면하다, 모면하다, 회피하다
  To escape or avoid something or someone by trickery or skill.

- **radiate** [réidièit] vi. (빛·열 등을) 발하다, 빛나다, 방출하다
  To send out rays (of light, heat, electromagnetic radiation, etc).

4. WAKING UP

wrack [ræk] v. 고문하다
To make somebody suffer great physical or mental pain.

☼ **limb** [lim] n. 사지(四肢), 팔다리
An arm or leg of a person or animal, or a large branch of a tree.

manageable [mǽnidʒəbəl] a. 다루기[제어하기] 쉬운; 순종하는
Something that is manageable is of a size, quantity, or level of difficulty that people are able to deal with.

☼ **weaken** [wíːkən] v. (능력·세력 등을) 약화시키다; 약화되다
If you weaken something or if it weakens, it becomes less strong or less powerful.

Comprehension Quiz

5. CHEATER

1. The men in Mike's store were talking about _____.

   A. the size of bear-safe canisters

   B. motorcycle crashes

   C. a large animal seen near the road

   D. the differences between hiking backpacks

2. What did Bella always do in her nightmare?

   A. She searched for something.

   B. She ran from something.

   C. She tried to find the exit to a maze.

   D. She drove through empty roads looking for her house.

3. Why did Bella want to get the motorcycles?

   A. Her father was interested in motorcycles.

   B. She wanted to do something reckless.

   C. She wanted an excuse to get closer to Jacob.

   D. She wanted to make new friends.

5. CHEATER

4. How did Bella feel when she saw Jacob?

　A. Pleased

　B. Upset

　C. Nervous

　D. Guilty

5. How would Jacob and Bella get the motorcycle parts?

　A. Jacob would use his savings.

　B. Bella would use her college savings.

　C. Jacob had the parts they needed in his garage.

　D. They would save money together and fix the bikes after a few months.

Vocabulary in New Moon

patron [péitrən] n. 고객, 단골손님; 보호자, 후원자
The patrons of a place such as a pub, bar, or hotel are its customers.

dedicate [dédikèit] vt. (시간·생애 등을) 바치다, 헌납하다
To give a lot of your time and effort to a particular activity or purpose because you think it is important.

pros and cons phrase 찬반양론[논쟁]
The arguments for and against something.

lightweight [láitwèit] a. (보통 것보다) 가벼운[경량의]
Something that is lightweight weighs less than most other things of the same type.

indulge [indʌ́ldʒ] v. 빠지다, 탐닉하다; (욕망·정열 따위를) 만족시키다, 충족시키다
To allow oneself or someone else pleasure or the pleasure of a specified thing.

numbness [nʌ́mnis] n. 무감각
Partial or total lack of sensation in a part of the body.

thickset [θíksét] a. 몸집이 떡 벌어진[튼튼한]
A man who is thickset is broad and heavy, with a solid-looking body.

beard [biərd] n. 턱수염
The hair that some men allow to grow on the lower part of their face.

grizzly [grízli] (= grizzly bear) n. (북미 서부산(産)의 큰) 회색곰
A grizzly or a grizzly bear is a large, fierce, greyish-brown bear.

Yellowstone n. 옐로스톤 강
미국 Wyoming 주 북서부에서 발원하여 Yellowstone 국립공원을 지나 Missouri 강으로 흘러듦.

brute [bru:t] n. 짐승, 야만인; a. 잔인한, 야만적인, 금수와 같은, 무정한
A rough and sometimes violent man.

cub [kʌb] n. (곰·사자·이리 등) 짐승 새끼, 어린 짐승
A young bear, lion, fox, etc.

5. CHEATER

- **tanned** [tænd] a. (피부가) 햇볕에 탄[그을은]
Having a darker skin color because you have been in the sun.

- **impressive** [imprésiv] a. 인상적인, 강한 인상을 주는, 감동적인
Producing admiration, wonder or approval.

- **crust** [krʌst] n. (물건의) 딱딱한 표면, 겉껍질, 딱딱한 껍질
A hard layer or surface, especially above or around something soft or liquid.

trailhead [tréilhèd] n. 자취[길]의 기점(起點)
The place where a trail begins.

turn away phrasal v. (얼굴을) 돌리다, 보려고 하지 않다, 외면하다
To move your body so that you are looking in a different direction.

canister [kǽnistər] n. (차·커피·담배 등을 넣는) 깡통, 보관용기
A canister is a strong metal container. It is used to hold gases or chemical substances.

- **hunch** [hʌntʃ] vt. (등을) 둥글게 구부리다
To bend down and forwards so that your back forms a curve.

- **brutal** [brú:tl] a. 잔인한, 야만적인; 모진, 혹독한
A brutal act or person is cruel and violent.

revisit [ri:vízit] v. 재방문하다; 다시 논의하다
If you revisit a place, you return there for a visit after you have been away for a long time, often after the place has changed a lot.

- **plural** [plúərəl] a. 복수형의
Relating to more than one.

immune [imjú:n] a. (전염병·독 등을) 면한, 면역성의, 영향을 받지 않는
Protected against a particular disease.

- **intruder** [intrú:dər] n. 침입자, 난입자; 훼방꾼, 방해자
A person who enters a building or an area illegally.

- **strangle** [strǽŋgəl] vt. 목 졸라 죽이다, 교살하다; 목을 조이다
To kill someone by squeezing their throat tightly so that they cannot breathe.

Vocabulary in New Moon

psychopath [sáikoupæ̀θ] n. 사이코패스 (폭력성을 동반하는 이상 심리 소유자)
A psychopath is someone who has serious mental problems and who may act in a violent way without feeling sorry for what they have done.

★ **maze** [meiz] n. 미로, 미궁
A complicated and confusing arrangement of streets, roads etc.

‡ **moss** [mɔ(:)s] n. 이끼
Moss is a very small soft green plant which grows on damp soil, or on wood or stone.

eardrum [íɾʌm] n. 중이(中耳); 귀청, 고막
The piece of thin tightly stretched skin inside the ear which is moved by sound waves, making you able to hear.

★ **dusk** [dʌsk] n. 땅거미, 황혼, 어스름
The time of day when the light has almost gone, but it is not yet dark.

‡ **gloom** [glu:m] n. 어둠침침함, 어둠, 그늘, 암흑
Almost total darkness.

★ **clumsy** [klʌ́mzi] a. 꼴사나운, 어색한, 서투른
Awkward in movement or manner.

‡ **dreary** [dríəri] a. 쓸쓸한, 황량한, 음산한, 울적한
Boring and making you feel unhappy.

nagging [nǽgiŋ] a. 끈질긴, 계속되는; (통증 등이) 사라지지 않는; 잔소리가 심한
Continuing for a long time and difficult to cure or remove.

steer [stiər] v. 키를 잡다, 조종하다; 향하다 (steering wheel n. 핸들)
To control the direction a vehicle is going, for example by turning a wheel.

torso [tɔ́:rsou] n. (인체의) 몸통; 토르소(머리·손발이 없는 나체 조각상); (비유) 미완성 작품
The main part of the body, not including the head, arms or legs.

★ **clarity** [klǽrəti] n. 명쾌함, 깨끗하고 맑음
The quality of being clear and easy to understand.

5. CHEATER

stomp [stɑmp] v. 짓밟다, 발을 구르며 걷다; n. 발구르기
To walk with heavy steps or to put your foot down very hard, especially.

incapacitate [ìnkəpǽsətèit] vt. 무능력하게 하다, 못하게 하다
To take away strength, power or ability; To make unfit.

lung [lʌŋ] n. [해부] 폐, 허파
Your lungs are the two organs inside your chest which fill with air when you breathe in.

irreversible [ìrivə́:rsəbəl] a. 거꾸로 할[뒤집을] 수 없는; 철회[취소·변경]할 수 없는
If a change is irreversible, things cannot be changed back to the way they were before.

reclaim [rikléim] vt. 교정하다, 개선하다
To get something back or to ask to have it back after it has been lost, taken away, etc.

insignificant [ìnsignífikənt] a. 무의미한, 하찮은, 사소한
Not big or valuable enough to be considered important.

equation [i(:)kwéiʒən] n. 방정식, 등식
A mathematical statement saying that two amounts or values are the same.

alter [ɔ́:ltər] v. 변하다, 바꾸다, 변경하다, 고치다
To change something, usually slightly, or to cause the characteristics of something to change.

sallow [sǽlou] a. (안색이 병적으로) 누르께한, 흙빛의, 혈색이 나쁜
(of a person's skin or face) Having a slightly yellow color that does not look healthy.

pallid [pǽlid] a. (안색이) 창백한, 해쓱한, 핏기가 가신
Pale, especially unhealthily so.

insanity [insǽnəti] n. 광기, 발광, 정신 이상
The state of being insane.

thump [θʌmp] v. 치다, 부딪치다; n. 때림, 세게 쥐어박음
If you thump something, you hit it hard, usually with your fist.

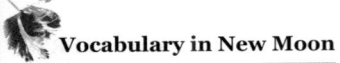

Vocabulary in New Moon

violate [váiəlèit] vt. 어기다, 위반하다, 방해하다
To disregard or break a law, agreement or oath.

humorless [hjúːmərlis] a. 유머가 없는, 멋없는
(humorlessly ad. 유머가 없이, 익살 부릴 줄 모르고)
Lacking humor or levity; Serious; Not funny, amusing, amused, or light-hearted.

proposition [pràpəzíʃən] n. 계획, 안(案)
A thing that you intend to do; A problem or task to be dealt with.

excruciating [ikskrúːʃièitiŋ] a. 고문을 당하는 듯한; 몹시 마음을 아프게 하는
Extremely painful or bad.

creativity [kriːeitívəti] n. 창조적임, 창조성; 독창[창조]력; (속어) 활기, 생기
The ability to create.

oath [ouθ] n. 맹세, 서약; 선서
A formal promise to do something or a formal statement that something is true.

sluggish [slʌ́giʃ] a. 둔한, 활발하지 못한; 느린, 굼뜬; 부진한 (sluggishily ad. 느리게)
Moving, reacting or working more slowly than normal and in a way that seems lazy.

pitiful [pítifəl] a. 가엾은, 비참한, 딱한
Deserving or causing you to feel pity.

drizzle [drizl] n. 이슬비, 가랑비; vi. 이슬비[가랑비]가 내리다
Drizzle is light rain falling in fine drops.

blink [bliŋk] v. 눈을 깜박거리다, (등불·별 등이) 깜박이다; n. 깜박거림
When you blink or when you blink your eyes, you shut your eyes and very quickly open them again.

blankly [blǽŋkli] ad. 멍하니, 우두커니
In a way that shows no emotion, understanding, or interest.

5. CHEATER

* **impair** [impéər] vt. (가치·힘·건강 등을) 감하다, 약하게 하다; 손상시키다, 해치다
  If something impairs something such as an ability or the way something works, it damages it or makes it worse.

복습 **menace** [ménəs] n. 위협, 협박; (구어) 골칫거리; vt. 위협하다
  Something that is likely to cause harm.

복습 **scrawl** [skrɔːl] vt. 휘갈겨 쓰다, 낙서하다
  To write something in a careless untidy way, making it difficult to read.

kismet [kízmet] n. 숙명, 운명
  The idea that everything that happens to you in your life is already decided and that you cannot do anything to change or control it.

fated [feitid] a. …할 운명인, 운명이 정해진; 운이 다 된
  Unable to escape a particular fate; Certain to happen because everything is controlled by fate.

dilapidated [dilǽpədèitid] a. 남루한, 초라한; 황폐한, 무너져가는
  Old and in very bad condition.

‡ **shortage** [ʃɔ́ːrtidʒ] n. 부족, 결핍
  A situation when there is not enough of the people or things that are needed.

hauler [hɔ́ːlər] n. 트럭 운송 회사; 화물 트럭
  A hauler is a company or a person that transports goods by road.

‡ **barrel** [bǽrəl] v. (통제가 안 되게) 쏜살같이 달리다[질주하다]
  If a vehicle or person is barreling in a particular direction, they are moving very quickly in that direction.

* **smear** [smiər] v. 바르다, 칠하다, 문질러 더럽히다
  If you smear a surface with an oily or sticky substance or smear the substance onto the surface, you spread a layer of the substance over the surface.

복습 **slosh** [slaʃ] v. 절벅절벅 휘젓다, 물을 튀기다; n. (액체가) 튀어 흩어짐, 튀어 오름
  To walk noisily in water or mud.

Vocabulary in New Moon

- **sandy** [sǽndi] a. (머리털이) 모래 빛깔의, 엷은 갈색의
  Sandy hair is light orangey-brown in color.

- **jerk** [dʒəːrk] v. 갑자기 움직이다; n. 갑자기 잡아당김; 바보
  If you jerk something or someone in a particular direction, or they jerk in a particular direction, they move a short distance very suddenly and quickly.

- **thumb** [θʌm] n. 엄지손가락
  Your thumb is the short thick part on the side of your hand next to your four fingers.

- **infer** [infə́ːr] v. 추측하다; 추론[추리]하다
  If you infer that something is the case, you decide that it is true on the basis of information that you already have.

- **clipping** [klípiŋ] n. 깎아[잘라·오려] 낸 조각
  Clippings are small pieces of something that have been cut from something larger.

- **scavenge** [skǽvəndʒ] v. (아직 쓸 만한 물건을) 쓰레기통에서 모으다; 찾아다니다
  To search through waste for things that can be used or eaten.

- **downpour** [dáunpɔ̀ːr] n. 억수 (같은 비), 호우
  A downpour is a sudden and unexpected heavy fall of rain.

- **spur-of-the-moment** [spə́ːrɑvðəmóumənt] a. 즉석의, 충동적인
  If you do something on the spur-of-the moment, you do it suddenly, without planning it beforehand.

- **whim** [hwim] n. 변덕, 잘 변하는 마음; v. 일시적인 기분으로 바라다
  A whim is a wish to do or have something which seems to have no serious reason or purpose behind it, and often occurs suddenly.

- **intact** [intǽkt] a. 완전한, 손상되지 않은
  Not broken, damaged, or spoiled.

- **snort** [snɔːrt] v. 콧김을 뿜다, (경멸·불찬성 등으로) 콧방귀 뀌다
  To breathe air in a noisy way out through your nose to show that you are annoyed.

5. CHEATER

- **reputation** [rèpjətéiʃən] n. 평판, 명성
  The opinion that people have about what somebody/something is like, based on what has happened in the past.

- **emergency** [imə́:rdʒənsi] n. 비상사태, 비상시, 위급, 급변
  An unexpected and serious happening which calls for immediate and determined action.

- **inspiration** [ìnspəréiʃən] n. 영감; 고취, 고무
  A sudden good idea.

- **bolt** [boult] n. 번개, 번갯불, 전광(電光)
  A bolt of lightning is a flash of lightning that is seen as a white line in the sky.

- **deputy** [dépjəti] n. 대리인; 대리역, 부관
  A person appointed to act on behalf of, or as an assistant to, someone else.

- **affable** [ǽfəbəl] a. 상냥한, 붙임성 있는, 사근사근한 (affably ad. 상냥하게)
  Someone who is affable is pleasant and friendly.

- **plead** [pli:d] v. 간청하다, 탄원하다; 변론하다; 변호하다
  If you plead with someone to do something, you ask them in an intense, emotional way to do it.

- **resemble** [rizémbəl] vt. …을 닮다, …와 공통점이 있다
  To be like or similar to someone or something else, especially in appearance.

- **barn** [ba:rn] n. (농가의) 헛간, 광
  A large building on a farm in which hay and grain are kept.

- **peer** [piər] vi. 응시하다, 자세히 보다; 희미하게 나타나다; 보이기 시작하다
  If you peer at something, you look at it very hard.

- **restriction** [ristríkʃən] n. 제한[제약]하는 것, 제약, 규정
  The act of limiting or controlling somebody/something.

- **shortcoming** [ʃɔ́:rtkʌ̀miŋ] n. 결점, 단점, 불충분한 점 (fault가 일반적); 부족
  Someone's or something's shortcomings are the faults or weaknesses which they have.

Vocabulary in New Moon

vivid [vívid] a. 선명한, 뚜렷한; 생생한, 발랄한
Produced very clear, powerful and detailed images in the mind.

russet [rʌ́sət] a. 적[황]갈색의, 팥빛의
Russet is used to describe things that are reddish-brown in color.

ponytail [póunitèil] n. 포니테일(뒤에서 묶어 아래로 드리운 머리)
A ponytail is a hairstyle in which someone's hair is tied up at the back of the head and hangs down like a tail.

lanky [lǽŋki] a. 마르고 키 큰, 호리호리한
(said of a person or animal) Thin and tall, especially in an awkward and ungainly way.

tendon [téndən] n. 힘줄, 건(腱)
A tendon is a strong cord in a person's or animal's body which joins a muscle to a bone.

prominent [prάmənənt] a. 현저한, 두드러진
Important or well known.

cheekbone [tʃíːkbòun] n. 광대뼈
The bone below the eye.

surge [səːrdʒ] n. 큰 물결, 쇄도; v. 파도처럼 밀려오다
A sudden increase of a strong feeling.

corresponding [kɔ̀ːrəspάndiŋ] a. 일치하는; 유사한; 상응하는
Having the same or nearly the same relationship.

accuse [əkjúːz] v. 비난하다, 고발하다
To say that someone has done something morally wrong, illegal or unkind.

satisfaction [sæ̀tisfǽkʃən] n. 만족, 만족감
(self-satisfaction n. 자기만족, 자부)
A pleasant feeling which you get when you do something or get something that you wanted to do.

5. CHEATER

beanpole [bíːnpòul] n. 몸이 마르고 키가 큰 사람, 키다리
If you call someone a beanpole, you are criticizing them because you think that they are extremely tall and thin.

bundle [bʌ́ndl] n. 묶음, 꾸러미
A number of things tied or wrapped together.

discomfort [diskʌ́mfərt] n. 불쾌, 불안; (약한) 고통; 귀찮은 일, 불편, 곤란
A feeling of slight pain or of being physically uncomfortable.

shrubbery [ʃrʌ́bəri] n. 관목을 심은 길, 관목 숲
A group of plants that have several woody stems.

conceal [kənsíːl] vt. 숨기다, 감추다; 비밀로 하다, 내색하지 않다
If you conceal something, you cover it or hide it carefully.

cinder block [síndər blàk] n. 콘크리트 블록 (concrete와 cinder(재)를 섞어서 만듦)
A cinder block is a large grey brick made from coal cinders and cement which is used for building.

grille [gril] n. 격자, 쇠창살; (매표구·교도소 따위의) 창살문
A screen made of metal bars or wire that is placed in front of a window, door or piece of machinery in order to protect it.

Volkswagen [vóukswæ̀gən] n. 폭스바겐 (독일의 대중용 소형 자동차; 상표명)

reluctance [rilʌ́ktəns] n. 싫음, 마음이 내키지 않음, 마지못해 함
A certain degree of unwillingness.

prom [prɑm] n. (대학·고교 따위의) 무도회, 댄스파티
A formal dance, especially one that is held at a high school.

bribe [braib] v. 뇌물을 주다, 매수하다; n. 뇌물
If one person bribes another, they give them a sum of money or something valuable that one person offers or gives to another in order to persuade him or her to do something.

purse [pəːrs] v. (불만 등의 표시로 입술을) 오므리다
If you purse your lips, you move them into a small, rounded shape, usually because you disapprove of something or when you are thinking.

Vocabulary in New Moon

- **offend** [əfénd] v. ···의 감정을 상하게 하다; 위반하다; 죄를 범하다
  To make someone upset or angry.

- **syllable** [síləbəl] n. 음절
  A syllable is a part of a word that contains a single vowel sound and that is pronounced as a unit.

- **tease** [ti:z] v. 놀리다, 희롱하다
  To laugh at or make fun of someone annoyingly.

- **mock** [mɑk] a. 가짜의, 모의의; vt. 조롱하다, 흉내 내며 놀리다; n. 조롱, 놀림감
  You use mock to describe something which is not real or genuine, but which is intended to be very similar to the real thing.

- **resentment** [rizéntmənt] n. 분함, 억울함, 분개
  A feeling of anger or unhappiness about something that you think is unfair.

- **sniff** [snif] v. 콧방귀를 뀌다; 코를 킁킁거리다, 냄새를 맡다; n. 냄새 맡음, 콧방귀
  To speak in an unpleasant way, showing that you have a low opinion of something.

- **reign** [rein] v. (특정 장소·순간을) 군림하다, 지배하다; 주권을 잡다
  If you say that a person reigns in a situation or area, you mean that they are very powerful or successful.

- **buoyant** [bɔ́iənt] a. 탄력이 있는; 경쾌한; 낙천적인
  If you are in a buoyant mood, you feel cheerful and behave in a lively way.

- **sneaky** [sní:ki] a. 교활한, 엉큼한
  If you describe someone as sneaky, you disapprove of them because they do things secretly rather than openly.

- **stroll** [stroul] vi. 한가롭게 거닐다, 산책하다; n. 산책
  If you stroll somewhere, you walk there in a slow, relaxed way.

- **appraise** [əpréiz] vt. 살피다, 뜯어보다; (사람·능력을) 평가하다
  To consider or examine somebody/something and form an opinion about them or it.

5. CHEATER

Harley Sprint n. 할리데이비드슨(미국제 대형 오토바이; 상표명)의 모터사이클 이름

★ **blacken** [blǽkən] v. 검게 하다, 어둡게 하다, 어두워지다
To make or become black or very dark in color.

schmollege 사전에 없는 저자가 합성한 단어
Schmo(n. 멍청이, 얼간이) + college(n. 대학)

☆ **skim** [skim] v. (돈을) 조금씩 훔치다[빼돌리다]; 걷어내다; 스치듯 지나가다; 훑어보다
To secretly use a piece of equipment that records someone's credit card details when they are paying for something, in order to use their credit card account illegally.

skulk [skʌlk] vi. 슬그머니 숨다; 살금살금…하다
To hide or move around as if trying not to be seen, usually with bad intentions.

★ **makeshift** [méikʃìft] a. 임시변통의, 일시적인; n. 임시변통 (수단), 미봉책
Makeshift things are temporary and usually of poor quality, but they are used because there is nothing better available.

복습 **contemplate** [kántəmplèit] v. 깊이 생각하다, 응시하다, 찬찬히 보다
To think carefully about and accept the possibility of something happening.

Comprehension Quiz

 6. FRIENDS

1. What was NOT true about the night Bella saw Jacob for the first time?

A. She was surprised that she laughed.

B. She didn't dream that night.

C. She felt guilty being around Jacob.

D. Charlie was shocked to see a change in Bella's mood.

2. How was spending time with Jacob different than Bella expected?

A. Bella forgot about why she wanted to fix the motorcycles.

B. Bella enjoyed herself more than she thought was possible.

C. Bella didn't care about building the motorcycles anymore.

D. Bella forgot about Edward.

3. How had Bella's nightmare changed?

A. She was no longer searching for something.

B. She didn't scream when the nightmare was over.

C. She was alone in her dream.

D. Sam Uley was in her dream.

6. FRIENDS

4. Why did Angela cancel her picnic?

A. It rained on Saturday.

B. The path in the woods was flooded with rainwater.

C. Her parents wouldn't allow her to go into the woods.

D. She and her friends saw a large animal.

5. Why did Angela thank Bella?

A. Bella made fun of Lauren.

B. Bella stood up for Angela.

C. Bella helped Angela with her homework.

D. Bella was kind to Mike at lunch.

Vocabulary in New Moon

* **shed** [ʃed] n. 헛간, 창고
A small simple building, usually built of wood or metal, used for keeping things in.

* **maneuver** [mənúːvər] v. 교묘히 이동하다; n. 책략, 술책
To move or turn skilfully.

‡ **chatter** [tʃǽtər] vi. 수다스레 재잘거리다; (춥거나 공포로) 이가 맞부딪치다
If you chatter, you talk quickly and continuously, usually about things which are not important.

nudge [nʌdʒ] n. (팔꿈치로) 슬쩍 찌르기; vt. 슬쩍 찌르다; 주의를 환기시키다
A slight push, usually with the elbow.

* **sophomore** [sάfəmɔ̀ːr] n. (대학·고교의) 2학년생
A student in the second year of college or high school.

복습 **chuckle** [tʃʌ́kl] vi. 낄낄 웃다; n. 낄낄 웃음
When you chuckle, you laugh quietly.

복습 **mumble** [mʌ́mbəl] v. 중얼거리다, 웅얼거리다; n. 중얼거림
If you mumble, you speak very quietly and not at all clearly with the result that the words are difficult to understand.

‡ **slender** [sléndər] a. 호리호리한, 가느다란; 빈약한
Thin and delicate.

복습 **swing** [swiŋ] v. (swang-swung) 흔들다; 매달리다, 빙 돌다
If something swings or if you swing it, it moves repeatedly backwards and forwards or from side to side from a fixed point.

burly [bə́ːrli] a. 억센, 건장한
A burly man has a broad body and strong muscles.

gleeful [glíːfəl] a. 매우 기뻐하는, 대단히 기분이 좋은 (gleefully ad. 매우 기뻐하여)
Someone who is gleeful is happy and excited, often because of someone else's bad luck.

‡ **buzz** [bʌz] n. (남성의) 스포츠 머리; 윙윙대는 소리; v. 윙윙거리다; 분주하게 돌아다니다
A hairstyle for men in which the hair is cut very short.

6. FRIENDS

brawny [brɔ́:ni] a. 근육의; 근육이 발달한; 억센, 건장한
Muscular; Strong.

halfhearted [hǽfhá:rtid] a. 마음이 내키지 않는 (halfheartedly ad. 어쩔 수 없이)
Showing a lack of enthusiasm and interest.

impish [ímpiʃ] a. 작은 요괴의[같은], 장난꾸러기의, 개구쟁이의
Showing a lack of respect for somebody/something in a way that is amusing rather than serious.

flex [fleks] v. 굽히다, 수축시키다; n. 굽힘
If you flex your muscles or parts of your body, you bend, move, or stretch them for a short time in order to exercise them.

bicep [báisep] n. (= biceps) 이두박근, 알통
The large muscle at the front of the upper arm.

release [rilí:s] vt. 석방하다, 풀어놓다, 방출하다
To give freedom or free movement to someone or something.

shove [ʃʌv] v. 밀(치)다, 밀어내다; n. 밀치기
If you shove something somewhere, you push it there quickly and carelessly.

inaccurate [inǽkjərit] a. 부정확한, 정밀하지 않은; 틀린
(inaccurately ad. 정확하지 않게)
If a statement or measurement is inaccurate, it is not accurate or correct.

chromosome [króuməsòum] n. [생물] 염색체
A chromosome is a part of a cell in an animal or plant. It contains genes which determine what characteristics the animal or plant will have.

immerse [imɔ́:rs] v. …에 몰두해[게 만들]다; 담그다, 가라앉히다, 적시다
To become completely involved in an activity.

bane [bein] n. 파멸(의 원인); 맹독; 죽음; 재난
A cause of continual trouble or unhappiness.

bankroll [bǽŋkròul] vt. 재정을 지원하다, 돈을 대다; n. 돈다발, 자금
To bankroll a person, organization, or project means to provide the financial resources that they need.

Vocabulary in New Moon

expertise [èkspərtíːz] n. 전문 기술[지식]
A high level of knowledge or skill.

★ **smack** [smæk] vt. 찰싹 치다, 쳐 날리다; n. 찰싹 하는 소리
To hit someone or something loudly and heavily, especially with your hand.

복습 **mutter** [mʌ́tər] v. 중얼거리다, 불평하다; n. 중얼거림, 불평
If you mutter, you speak very quietly so that you cannot easily be heard, often because you are complaining about something.

복습 **protest** [prətést] v. 항의하다, 이의를 제기하다; 주장하다; n. 항의
If you protest against something or about something, you say or show publicly that you object to it.

복습 **chorus** [kɔ́ːrəs] v. 합창을 하다, 이구동성으로 말하다; n. 합창; 일제히 내는 소리
When people chorus something, they say it or sing it together.

scuffle [skʌ́fəl] n. 실랑이, 옥신각신함
A scuffle is a short, disorganized fight or struggle.

intersperse [ìntərspə́ːrs] vt. 흩뿌리다, 산재시키다
If you intersperse one group of things with another or among another, you put or include the second things between or among the first things.

복습 **giggle** [gígəl] v. 낄낄 웃다; n. 낄낄 웃음
If someone giggles, they laugh in a childlike way, because they are amused, nervous, or embarrassed.

★ **flit** [flit] vi. 휙 지나가다, 오가다; 훌쩍 날다
To fly or move quickly and lightly.

복습 **cautious** [kɔ́ːʃəs] a. 조심성 있는, 신중한
Someone who is cautious acts very carefully in order to avoid possible danger.

※ **interrogation** [intèrəgéiʃən] n. 질문, 심문
Question; A sentence of inquiry that asks for a reply.

6. FRIENDS

- **dither** [díðər] vi. (결정을 못 내리고) 머무적거리다[망설이다]
  When someone dithers, they hesitate because they are unable to make a quick decision about something.

- **reluctantly** [rilʌ́ktəntli] ad. 마지못해, 싫어하면서
  Not very willing to do something and therefore slow to do it.

- **drain** [drein] v. 말라버리다, 고갈시키다, 쇠진하다; (액체가) 흘러나가다; n. 배수로, 하수구
  To make someone feel very tired and without any energy.

- **replace** [ripléis] v. 대신하다, 제자리에 놓다
  If one thing or person replaces another, the first is used or acts instead of the second.

- **dull** [dʌl] a. 흐릿한; 따분한, 재미없는; 둔한, 활기 없는
  Not very severe, but continuous.

- **numb** [nʌm] a. 감각을 잃은; 멍한, 망연자실한; vt. 감각을 잃게 하다; 망연자실케 하다
  If a part of your body is numb, you cannot feel anything there.

- **onslaught** [ánslɔ̀:t] n. 돌격, 맹공, 습격
  A very powerful attack.

- **squeeze** [skwi:z] vt. 꽉 쥐대[죄다], 압착하다; n. 압착, 짜냄
  If you squeeze something, you press it firmly, usually with your hands.

- **stun** [stʌn] vt. 어리벙벙하게 하다; 기절시키다; n. 놀라게 함
  If you are stunned by something, you are extremely shocked or surprised by it and are therefore unable to speak or do anything.

- **slippery** [slípəri] a. 미끄러운, 반들반들한
  Something that is slippery is smooth, wet, or oily and is therefore difficult to hold or to walk on.

- **precarious** [prikɛ́əriəs] a. 불확실한, 믿을 수 없는
  (of a situation) Not safe or certain.

- **appropriate** [əpróuprièit] a. 적절한, 알맞은
  Something that is appropriate is suitable or acceptable for a particular situation.

Vocabulary in New Moon

- **scrutiny** [skrú:təni] n. 응시, 찬찬히 쳐다보기; 정밀한 조사[검사]
  A penetrating or searching look.

- **cuff** [kʌf] n. 소매 끝동; (와이셔츠의) 커프스; 바지의 접힌 단
  The cuffs of a shirt or dress are the parts at the ends of the sleeves, which are thicker than the rest of the sleeve.

  don [dɑn] vt. (옷·모자 따위를) 걸치다, 입다, 쓰다
  To put on (clothing).

- **bucket** [bʌ́kit] n. 버킷, 양동이
  A round metal or plastic container for holding or carrying liquids.

- **muddy** [mʌ́di] a. 진창의, 진흙의, 질퍽한; 진흙투성이의
  Something that is muddy contains mud or is covered in mud.

  splatter [splǽtər] v. (물·흙탕물 등이) 튀다; 물보라 치며 떨어지다
  If a thick wet substance splatters on something or is splattered on it, it drops or is thrown over it.

- **slap** [slæp] v. 찰싹 때리다, 세게 치다; 아무렇게나 바르다; n. 찰싹 때리기[는 소리]
  To hit someone with the flat part of the hand or other flat object.

  unsupervised [ʌnsú:pərvàizd] a. 감독받지 않는
  Not supervised; Not being constantly observed.

  goodwrench n. (= GM Goodwrench) General Motors 회사의 수리서비스. 비유적으로 정비사를 의미

- **dump** [dʌmp] n. 쓰레기장, 쓰레기 더미; vt. 내버리다; (구어) 차다
  A place where waste or rubbish/garbage is taken and left.

- **fan** [fæn] vt. …에 불다, (바람을) 부치다[보내다]; n. 부채, 선풍기
  If something fans out, or if you fan it out, it spreads out or opens out into the shape of a circle or half circle.

- **ankle** [ǽŋkl] n. 발목
  Your ankle is the joint where your foot joins your leg.

6. FRIENDS

perpetual [pərpétʃuəl] a. 끊임없는, 그칠 새 없는; (구어) 계속 반복되는, 잦은
(perpetually ad. 끊임없이, 그칠 사이 없이)
Continual; Continually recurring.

aura [ɔ́ːrə] n. (어떤 사람이나 장소에 서려 있는 독특한) 기운[분위기]
An aura is a quality or feeling that seems to surround a person or place or to come from them.

earthbound [ɔ́ːrθbàund] a. (우주선 등이) 지구를 향한
Unable to leave the surface of the earth.

gravitational [grævətéiʃənl] a. 중력의, 인력(작용)의
Gravitational means relating to or resulting from the force of gravity.

dashboard [dǽʃbɔ̀ːrd] n. (자동차·비행기의) 계기판, 대시보드
The part of a car in front of the driver that has instruments and controls in it.

cavity [kǽvəti] n. (어떤 물체 속의) 구멍[빈 부분]
A hole or empty space inside something solid.

grease [griːs] n. (끈적끈적한) 기름, 그리스(기계의 윤활유)
Grease is a thick, oily substance which is put on the moving parts of cars and other machines in order to make them work smoothly.

Hoquiam n. 호퀴엄 (미국 워싱턴 주(州)에 있는 도시)

complain [kəmpléin] v. 불평하다, 투덜거리다
To say that something is wrong or not satisfactory.

maturity [mətjúərəti] n. 성숙, 숙성; 원숙, 완성; [의학] 화농
Maturity is the state of being fully developed or adult.

picky [piki] a. 까다로운, 별스러운
Someone who is picky is difficult to please and only likes a small range of things.

banter [bǽntər] v. (정감 어린) 농담을 주고받다; n. (가벼운) 농담, 놀림
If you banter with someone, you tease them or joke with them in an amusing, friendly way.

Vocabulary in New Moon

bookkeeping [búkkì:piŋ] n. 부기(덧붙여 적는 기록)
Bookkeeping is the job or activity of keeping an accurate record of the money that is spent and received by a business or other organization.

haul [hɔ:l] n. 소득, 벌이; 세게 잡아당김; 운반; v. 세게 잡아당기다; 운반하다
A haul is a quantity of things that are stolen, or a quantity of stolen or illegal goods found by police or customs.

perk [pə:rk] ① n. (급료 외의) 특전 ② v. 생기가 나다; (귀·꼬리 등을) 쫑긋 세우다
Something you receive as well as your wages for doing a particular job.

sneaky [sní:ki] a. 교활한, 엉큼한
If you describe someone as sneaky, you disapprove of them because they do things secretly rather than openly.

comb through phrasal v. 구석구석[철저히] 찾다
If you comb through information, you look at it very carefully in order to find something.

fascinating [fǽsənèitiŋ] a. 매력적인, 대단히 흥미로운
Extremely interesting.

precision [prisíʒən] n. 정확, 정말; 꼼꼼함; a. 정밀한
If you do something with precision, you do it exactly as it should be done.

waft [wɑ:ft] v. 둥둥 떠돌다, (냄새 따위가) 풍기다
To move gently through the air.

yell [jel] v. 소리치다, 고함치다; n. 고함, 부르짖음
If you yell, you shout loudly, usually because you are excited, angry, or in pain.

cloak-and-dagger [klóukəndǽgər] a. 비밀과 의문에 가득 찬, 첩보 영화 같은
A cloak-and-dagger activity is one which involves mystery and secrecy.

tow [tou] vt. 끌다, 밧줄[사슬]로 끌다, 견인하다; 끌고 가다
If one vehicle tows another, it pulls it along behind it.

superficial [sù:pərfíʃəl] a. 표면상의, 피상적인
Never thinking about things that are serious or important.

6. FRIENDS

hysteria [histíəriə] n. [병리] 히스테리; (개인이나 집단의) 병적 흥분, 광란
Extreme fear, excitement, anger, etc. which cannot be controlled.

absentminded [æbsəntmáindid] a. 방심 상태의, 멍하고[얼빠져] 있는
Someone who is absent-minded forgets things or does not pay attention to what they are doing, often because they are thinking about something else.

recipe [résəpìː] n. (요리의) 조리법; (약제 등의) 처방전
A list of ingredients and a set of instructions that tell you how to cook something.

generation [dʒènəréiʃən] n. 동시대의 사람들, 세대, 대(代)
All the people who were born at about the same time.

grave [greiv] a. 중대한, 근엄한, 엄숙한 n. 무덤, 묘; 묘석 (gravely ad. 중대하게; 근엄하게)
Giving cause for great concern; Very dangerous.

exotic [igzátik] a. 이국적인, 이국정서의; 색다른, 낭만적인
Something that is exotic is unusual and interesting, usually because it comes from or is related to a distant country.

copper [kápər] n. 구릿빛, 동색, 적갈색
Copper is sometimes used to describe things that are reddish-brown in color.

glisten [glisn] vi. 반짝이다, 빛나다
If something glistens, it shines, usually because it is wet or oily.

eyelash [áilæʃ] n. 속눈썹 (bat an eyelash : 눈을 깜박이다)
Your eyelashes are the hairs which grow on the edges of your eyelids.

duster [dʌ́stər] n. 먼지떨이, 총채; 먼지 터는 사람, 청소부
A duster is a cloth which you use for removing dust from furniture, ornaments, or other objects.

idolize [áidəlàiz] vt. 맹목적으로 숭배하다, 심취하다
If you idolize someone, you admire them very much.

Vocabulary in New Moon

dim [dim] a. 어둑한, 흐릿한, 희미한; v. 어둑하게 하다, 흐려지다
Dim light is not bright.

cholesterol [kəléstəròul] n. [생화학] 콜레스테롤
Cholesterol is a substance that exists in the fat, tissues, and blood of all animals. Too much cholesterol in a person's blood can cause heart disease.

unsuccessful [ʌ̀nsəksésfəl] a. 성공하지 못한, 실패한, 잘 안된
Something that is unsuccessful does not achieve what it was intended to achieve.

leafy [líːfi] a. 잎이 많은, 잎이 무성한
Leafy trees and plants have lots of leaves on them.

inconspicuous [ìnkənspíkjuːəs] a. 눈에 띄지 않는, 주의를 끌지 않는
Not attracting attention.

disguise [disgáiz] v. 위장하다, 숨기다; 변장하다; n. 변장(도구); 변장술
To disguise something means to hide it or make it appear different so that people will not know about it or will not recognize it.

meditation [mèdətéiʃən] n. 명상, 묵상, 심사숙고, 고찰
The act of giving your attention to only one thing, either as a religious activity or as a way of becoming calm and relaxed.

quit [kwit] v. 떠나다, 그만두다; (술·담배 등을) 끊다
To stop doing something or leave a job or a place.

sub [sʌb] v. (…의) 대리를 하다, 대행하다
To do somebody else's job for them for a short time.

kindergartener [kíndərgàːrtnər] n. 유치원생
Kindergarten student.

awe [ɔː] vt. 경외심을 갖게 하다 n. 경외, 경외심 (awed a. 경외심에 휩싸인)
If you are awed by someone or something, they make you feel respectful and amazed, though often rather frightened.

6. FRIENDS

* **envious** [énviəs] a. 시기심이 강한; 질투하는, 샘내는
  If you are envious of someone, you want something that they have.

* **reference** [réfərəns] n. 참조, 문의, 언급, 관련
  A thing you say or write that mentions somebody/something else; The act of mentioning it(them).

* **strictly** [stríktli] ad. 엄격히, 엄밀히, 정확히
  In all details; Exactly.

* **deprivation** [dèprəvéiʃən] n. 박탈, 상실, 손실; 부족
  The fact of not having something that you need, like enough food, money or a home; The process that causes this.

* **muffle** [mʌ́fəl] vt. (덮어서 소리를) 지우다, 억제하다; 덮다, 목도리로 감싸다
  If something muffles a sound, it makes it quieter and more difficult to hear.

* **alteration** [ɔ̀:ltəréiʃən] n. 변경, 개조; 수정
  An alteration is a change in or to something.

* **incline** [inkláin] v. 기울이다, (마음이) 기울다; n. 경사, 비탈
  To tend to think or behave in a particular way.

  peripheral [pərífərəl] a. 주위의, 주변에 있는
  Happening at the edge of something.

* **concrete** [kánkri:t] n. 콘크리트; a. 유형의, 구체적인
  Based on facts, not on ideas or guesses.

  chameleon [kəmí:liən] n. [동물] 카멜레온
  A chameleon is a kind of lizard whose skin changes color to match the color of its surroundings.

  disjointed [disdʒɔ́intid] a. 연결이 안 되는, 일관성이 없는; 흐트러진, 낱낱으로 된
  Not communicated or described in a clear or logical way.

  nonchalance [nànʃəlá:ns] n. 아랑곳하지 않음, 냉담, 태연
  Indifference; Carelessness; Coolness.

Vocabulary in New Moon

cold shoulder [kóuld ʃóuldər] n. (구어) 무시, 냉대
If one person gives another the cold shoulder, they behave towards them in an unfriendly way, to show them that they do not care about them or that they want them to go away.

literal [lítərəl] a. 글자 그대로의; 문자의
Being the basic or usual meaning of a word or phrase.

vent [vent] n. 통풍구, 배출구; 구멍; v. (감정 등을) 터뜨리다; (감정 등에) 배출구를 주다
A vent is a hole in something through which air can come in and smoke, gas, or smells can go out.

styrofoam peanut [staiərəfóum píːnʌt] n. 스티로폼으로 만들어진 땅콩
먹을 수 없는 땅콩이므로 가치가 없다는 의미로 무가치한, 무관심한 존재로 해석할 수 있다.

semester [siméstər] n. 한 학기, 반 학년
One of the two main periods into which the year is divided.

squeal [skwiːl] v. 끼익 소리 내다; 꽥꽥거리다, 비명을 지르다; n. 꽥꽥거리는 소리
If someone or something squeals, they make a long, high-pitched sound.

strident [stráidənt] a. 귀에 거슬리는, 소리가 불쾌한 (stridently ad. 귀에 거슬리게)
Having a loud, rough and unpleasant sound.

linoleum [linóuliəm] n. 리놀륨(마루의 깔개)
A stiff smooth material that is used for covering floors.

cut off phrasal v. 중단하다, 끊다
If you cut somebody off, you refuse to let the one have any of your money or property.

pixie [píksiː] n. 작은 요정; 장난꾸러기
An imaginary little creature like a fairy.

habitual [həbítʃuəl] a. 습관적인; 버릇이 된; 평소의 (habitually ad. 평소대로, 습관적으로)
Doing something from habit, and unable to stop doing it.

nasty [nǽsti] a. 더러운, 불쾌한, 몹시 싫은
Something that is nasty is very unpleasant to see, experience, or feel.

6. FRIENDS

* **scalp** [skælp] v. 머리가죽을 벗기다; n. 두피, 머리가죽
  To scalp someone means to remove the skin and hair from the top of their head.

  hesitant [hézətənt] a. 주저하는; 머뭇거리는
  If you are hesitant about doing something, you do not do it quickly or immediately, usually because you are uncertain, embarrassed, or worried.

  snicker [sníkər] vi. (미) 낄낄 웃다, 숨죽여 웃다; n. 낄낄 웃음
  To laugh at someone or something childishly and often unkindly.

* **explosion** [iksplóuʒən] n. 폭발
  A sudden, violent burst of energy, for example one caused by a bomb.

* **mortify** [mɔ́:rtəfài] vt. 굴욕을 느끼게 하다, 분하게 하다; 억제하다
  If you say that something mortifies you, you mean that it offends or embarrasses you a great deal.

  stutter [stʌ́tər] v. 말을 더듬다, 더듬거리며 말하다; n. 말더듬기
  If someone stutters, they have difficulty speaking because they find it hard to say the first sound of a word.

  trailhead [tréilhèd] n. 자취[길]의 기점(起點)
  The place where a trail begins.

  grizzly [grizli] (= grizzly bear) n. (북미 서부산(産)의 큰) 회색곰
  A grizzly or a grizzly bear is a large, fierce, greyish-brown bear.

* **confirm** [kənfə́:rm] vt. 굳게 하다, 확인하다
  If you confirm something that has been stated or suggested, you say that it is true because you know about it.

  hmph int. 짜증나거나 불쾌할 때, 성날 때 내는 소리
  A sound, usually made with a closed mouth, indicating annoyance.

  USC n. (= The University of South Carolina) 남가주 대학
  The University of South Carolina (also referred to as USC, SC, or Carolina).

Vocabulary in New Moon

tentative [téntətiv] a. 주저하는, 모호한; 잠정적인 (tentatively ad. 주저하며, 모호하게)
If someone is tentative, they are cautious and not very confident because they are uncertain or afraid.

irritated [írətèitid] a. 짜증이 나, 화 난
Feeling annoyed and impatient about something.

encouragement [enkə́:ridʒmənt] n. 격려[고무]
Encouragement is the activity of encouraging someone, or something that is said or done in order to encourage them.

reparable [répərəbəl] a. 수선할 수 있는; 보상[배상]할 수 있는
Able to be repaired.

eager [í:gər] a. 열망하는, 간절히 하고 싶어 하는
If you are eager to do or have something, you want to do or have it very much.

freak [fri:k] v. 괴상한 짓을 하다; n. 이상 현상, 기형, 변덕
If someone freaks out, they suddenly feel extremely surprised, upset, or confused.

insert [insə́:rt] vt. 끼워 넣다, 삽입하다, 넣다
To put something inside or into something.

sly [slai] a. 익살맞은; 은밀한, 음흉한
A sly look or expression shows that you know something that other people do not know.

gradual [grǽdʒuəl] a. 점진적인, 단계적인 (gradually ad. 서서히, 점차)
Happening or changing slowly over a long period of time or distance.

tray [trei] n. 쟁반, 음식 접시; 서류함
A tray is a flat piece of wood, plastic, or metal, which usually has raised edges and which is used for carrying things, especially food and drinks.

offensive [əfénsiv] n. 공격; 공격 태세; (적극적) 활동
A series of actions aimed at achieving something in a way that attracts a lot of attention.

6. FRIENDS

perceptive [pərséptiv] a. 통찰력[직관력]이 있는; 지각의
Having or showing the ability to see or understand things quickly, especially things that are not obvious.

Comprehension Quiz

7. REPETITION

1. Why did Bella visit the Cullen's house?
   A. She wanted to see if they were still in Forks.
   B. She wanted to hear Edward's voice again.
   C. She thought that the house would be gone.
   D. She wanted to see if Edward left anything there.

2. Why did Bella stop her truck on the side of the road before trying out the motorcycles?
   A. She thought she saw a large animal on the side of the road.
   B. She thought she heard Edward's voice.
   C. She saw someone jump off a cliff into the ocean.
   D. She was angry at Jacob and had to stop driving.

3. What bothered Jacob the most about Sam and his friends?
   A. Sam paid more attention to Jacob than anyone else.
   B. Sam and his friends acted like tough guys.
   C. Sam's friends followed Sam around all the time.
   D. Jacob was angry because Sam ignored him.

7. REPETITION

4. What was NOT true about the boys who were in Sam's group of friends?

    A. They missed school before becoming Sam's friend.
    B. They were all friends with Sam since childhood.
    C. They constantly followed Sam around.
    D. They called themselves protectors.

5. Why was Jacob's friendship strange to Bella?

    A. It was hard to relate to Jacob.
    B. It was strange to be close to someone emotionally.
    C. She was physically attracted to Jacob.
    D. She missed Edward more when she was around Jacob.

Vocabulary in New Moon

repetition [rèpətíʃən] n. 되풀이, 반복; 재주장
If there is a repetition of an event, usually an undesirable event, it happens again.

stupor [stjú:pər] n. 인사불성; 무감각; 마비, 혼수
Someone who is in a stupor is almost unconscious and is unable to act or think normally, especially as a result of drink or drugs.

masochistic [mǽsəkìstik] a. 자기학대 하는
If you describe someone's behavior as masochistic, you mean that they seem to be trying to get into a situation which causes them suffering or great difficulty.

torture [tɔ́:rtʃər] n. 고문, 고뇌; vt. 고문하다, 고통을 주다
If you say that something is torture or a torture, you mean that it causes you great mental or physical suffering.

overgrown [òuvərgróun] a. (풀 · 잡초 등이) 마구[제멋대로] 자란; 너무 커진
If a garden or other place is overgrown, it is covered with a lot of untidy plants because it has not been looked after.

lane [lein] n. 좁은 길, 골목, 작은 길
A narrow road in the country.

steer [stiər] v. 키를 잡다, 조종하다; 향하다 (steering wheel n. 핸들)
To control the direction a vehicle is going, for example by turning a wheel.

nothingness [nʌ́θiŋnis] n. 무(無), 공허; 존재하지 않음, 없음
Nothingness is the fact of not existing.

gnaw [nɔ:] v. 쏠다, 갉다, 물다
If people or animals gnaw something or gnaw at it, they bite it repeatedly.

nerve [nə:rv] n. 신경, 정신; 긴장, 불안; 용기
Nerves are long thin fibers that transmit messages between your brain and other parts of your body.

unattainable [ʌ̀nətéinəbəl] a. 얻기 어려운, 도달[성취]하기 어려운
Impossible to achieve or reach.

7. REPETITION

distract [distrǽkt] vt. (마음·주의를) 흐트러뜨리다, 딴 데로 돌리다
(distracted a. (주의가) 빗나간, 마음이 산란한)
Nervous, anxious or confused because you are worried about something.

toneless [tóunlis] a. 음[음조·색조·억양]이 없는; 단조로운 (tonelessly ad. 단조롭게)
A toneless voice is dull and does not express any feeling.

split [split] v. 쪼개다, 찢다, 째다
If something splits or if you split it, it is divided into two or more parts.

motivation [mòutəvéiʃən] n. 자극, 유도; 동기 부여
Enthusiasm for doing something.

delusion [dilúːʒən] n. 현혹, 기만; 망상, 착각
The act of believing or making yourself believe something that is not true.

errand [érənd] n. 심부름; 용건, 볼일
A short trip that you make in order to do a job for someone.

irresistible [ìrizístəbəl] a. 저항할 수 없는
Impossible to refuse or avoid because too pleasant, attractive or strong.

lure [luər] n. 매혹물, 미끼; vt. 유혹하다, 꾀어내다
A lure is an object which is used to attract animals so that they can be caught.

crawl [krɔːl] vi. 기어가다, 느릿느릿 가다; n. 기어감; 서행
When you crawl, you move forward on your hands and knees.

edgy [édʒi] a. (구어) 초조한; 신랄한
Nervous, especially about what might happen.

tangible [tǽndʒəbəl] a. 확실한, 명백한; 만져서 알 수 있는, 실체적인
Real or not imaginary; Able to be shown, touched or experienced.

pronounced [prənáunst] a. 뚜렷한; 명백한; 단호한
Very great or noticeable.

flora [flɔ́ːrə] n. (특정 장소·시대·환경의) 식물군(群)[상(相)]
The plants of a particular area, type of environment or period of time.

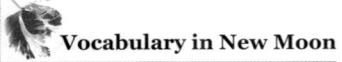
Vocabulary in New Moon

reclaim [rikléim] vt. 교정하다, 개선하다
To get something back or to ask to have it back after it has been lost, taken away, etc.

unguarded [ʌngáːrdid] a. 지키지 않는, 수비 없는
If something is unguarded, nobody is protecting it or looking after it.

fern [fəːrn] n. [식물] 양치류(의 식물)
A plant with large delicate leaves and no flowers that grows in wet areas or is grown in a pot.

infiltrate [infíltreit] v. 잠입[침투]하다[시키다]
If people infiltrate a place or organization, or infiltrate into it, they enter it secretly in order to spy on it or influence it.

meadow [médou] n. 목초지, 풀밭
A field with grass and often wild flowers in it.

trunk [trʌŋk] n. (나무의) 줄기, 몸뚱이; 여행 가방
The trunk of a tree is the large main stem from which the branches grow.

cedar [síːdər] n. [식물] 히말라야삼목; 삼나무 목재; a. 삼나무로 만들어진
A tall evergreen tree with wide spreading branches.

lawn [lɔːn] n. 잔디, 잔디밭
A lawn is an area of grass that is kept cut short and is usually part of someone's garden or backyard, or part of a park.

creepy [kríːpi] a. 소름이 끼치는; 꾸물꾸물 움직이는
If you say that something or someone is creepy, you mean they make you feel very nervous or frightened.

haunt [hɔːnt] n. 자주 가는[나타나는] 곳, 서식지; v. (유령이) 출몰하다; 늘 따라다니다; 자주 가다
A place that is the haunt of a particular person is one which they often visit because they enjoy going there.

barren [bǽrən] a. 불모의, 메마른
A barren landscape is dry and bare, and has very few plants and no trees.

7. REPETITION

vacant [véikənt] a. 빈, 비어 있는; 공허한
If something is vacant, it is not being used by anyone.

comforting [kʌ́mfərtiŋ] a. 기분을 돋우는, 격려하는; 위안이 되는
Making you feel less sad or anxious.

linger [líŋgər] vi. 오래 머무르다, 떠나지 못하다 (lingering a. 오래 끄는)
When something lingers, it continues to exist for a long time, often much longer than expected.

funeral [fjúːnərəl] n. 장례식
A ceremony for burying or burning the body of a dead person.

hideous [hídiəs] a. 끔찍한, 오싹한, 흉측한; 극악무도한 (hideously ad. 끔찍하게, 오싹하게)
Extremely ugly or bad.

addiction [ədíkʃən] n. 탐닉, 중독, 열중, 몰두
The condition of being addicted to something.

numbness [nʌ́mnis] n. 무감각
Partial or total lack of sensation in a part of the body.

barrel [bǽrəl] v. (통제가 안 되게) 쏜살같이 달리다[질주하다]
If a vehicle or person is barreling in a particular direction, they are moving very quickly in that direction.

throaty [θróuti] a. (목소리가) 목 안쪽에서 나오는, 묵직한, 목쉰
A throaty voice or laugh is low and rather rough.

jagged [dʒǽgid] a. 들쭉날쭉한; 톱니 같은; (목소리 등이) 귀에 거슬리는
Rough and uneven, with sharp points.

obsessive [əbsésiv] a. 강박적인, 사로잡혀 있는
Thinking or worrying about something all the time.

shrug [ʃrʌg] v. (양 손바닥을 내보이면서 어깨를) 으쓱하다; n. 으쓱하기
If you shrug, you raise your shoulders to show that you are not interested in something or that you do not know or care about something.

Vocabulary in New Moon

★ wrench [rentʃ] n. 렌치 (너트를 죄는 기구); vt. (갑자기·세게) 비틀다, 비틀어 돌리다
A wrench or a monkey wrench is an adjustable metal tool used for tightening or loosening metal nuts of different sizes.

underpriced [ʌ̀ndərpráist] a. 시세 이하의, 적정가보다 저가의
Something that is underpriced is sold at a price that is too low and less than its real value.

★ marvel [máːrvəl] v. …에 놀라다, 경탄하다
To be very surprised or impressed by something.

복습 tempt [tempt] vt. 유혹하다, 부추기다
Something that tempts you attracts you and makes you want it, even though it may be wrong or harmful.

복습 crack [kræk] v. 날카로운 소리를 내다; 갈라지다, 금이 가다; 깨지다
If something hard cracks, or if you crack it, it becomes slightly damaged, with lines appearing on its surface.

ceremonious [sèrəmóuniəs] a. 형식적인, 엄숙한; 의식적인
(ceremoniously ad. 형식적으로)
Behaving or performed in an extremely formal way.

★ toast [toust] v. 건배하다; n. 건배, 축배; 건배의 인사
To drink a glass of wine etc. to thank someone, wish someone luck, or celebrate something.

복습 reckless [réklis] a. 무모한, 분별없는 (recklessness n. 무모함, 분별없는 짓)
Showing a lack of care about danger and the possible results of your actions.

★ emphasize [émfəsàiz] vt. 강조하다; 역설하다
To emphasize something means to indicate that it is particularly important or true, or to draw special attention to it.

복습 relieve [rilíːv] vt. 안도케 하다, (긴장·걱정 등을) 덜다, 구제하다
To lessen or stop someone's pain, worry, boredom, etc.

★ exhaustive [igzɔ́ːstiv] a. (하나도 빠뜨리는 것 없이) 철저한[완전한]
If you describe a study, search, or list as exhaustive, you mean that it is very thorough and complete.

7. REPETITION

description [diskrípʃən] n. 기술, 서술; 설명서; 기재사항
An official list of the work and responsibilities that you have in your job.

aberrant [əbérənt] a. 정도를 벗어난, 비정상의
Aberrant means unusual and not socially acceptable.

resistant [rizístənt] a. 저항[반대]하는
Someone who is resistant to something is opposed to it and wants to prevent it.

animate [ǽnəmèit] vt. 살리다, 활기를 주다; a. 살아 있는, 활기 있는
To make someone seem more happy or active.

semester [siméstər] n. 한 학기, 반 학년
One of the two main periods into which the year is divided.

spill [spil] v. 쏟아져 나오다
If people or things spill out of a place, they come out of it in large numbers.

quit [kwit] v. 떠나다, 그만두다; (술·담배 등을) 끊다
To stop doing something or leave a job or a place.

wimp [wimp] n. (미·속어) 무기력한 사람, 겁쟁이
If you call someone a wimp, you disapprove of them because they lack confidence or determination, or because they are often afraid of things.

screw up phrasal v. 망치다, 결단내다
To make a mistake, or to spoil something.

exuberant [igzú:bərənt] a. 열광적인, 열의가 넘치는
Full of energy, excitement and happiness.

devoid [divɔ́id] a. 결여된, …이 없는; vt. 빼앗다
If you say that someone or something is devoid of a quality or thing, you are emphasizing that they have none of it.

sprawl [sprɔːl] v. 불규칙하게 퍼지게 하다; 팔다리를 펴다[뻗다]; n. 드러누움
To spread in an untidy way; To cover a large area.

Vocabulary in New Moon

lasagna [ləzá:njə] n. 라자냐 (치즈·토마토 소스·다진 고기 따위를 넣은 이탈리아의 요리)
Thin wide sheets of pasta, or savoury food consisting of layers of this combined with cheese and meat or vegetables.

occasionally [əkéiʒənəli] ad. 때때로, 가끔
Sometimes but not often.

waft [wɑ:ft] v. 둥둥 떠돌다, (냄새 따위가) 풍기다
To move gently through the air.

atone [ətóun] vi. 보상하다, 갚다, 속죄하다
If you atone for something that you have done, you do something to show that you are sorry you did it.

grudging [grʌ́dʒiŋ] a. 인색한, 마지못해 하는 (grudgingly ad. 마지못해; 쩨쩨하게)
Given or done unwillingly.

negotiable [nigóuʃiəbəl] a. 협상의 여지가 있는, 절충 가능한
Something that is negotiable can be changed or agreed when people discuss it.

sanity [sǽnəti] n. 제정신, 정신이 멀쩡함; 건전함, 온건함, (육체적인) 건강
The state of having a normal healthy mind.

mature [mətjúər] a. 성숙한, 익은; v. 성숙[발달]시키다; 익(히)다
Fully grown and developed.

unwilling [ʌ̀nwíliŋ] a. 마음 내키지 않는, 마지못해 하는
Not wanting to do something and refusing to do it.

scenery [sí:nəri] n. 배경, 무대 장치; 풍경
One's usual surroundings.

intersperse [ìntərspə́:rs] vt. 흩뿌리다, 산재시키다
If you intersperse one group of things with another or among another, you put or include the second things between or among the first things.

hemlock [hémlɑk] n. [식물] 북미 서부산 미송(美松)
A poisonous plant with a mass of small white flowers growing at the end of a stem that is covered in spots.

7. REPETITION

- **aimless** [éimlis] a. 목적이[목표가] 없는
  A person or activity that is aimless has no clear purpose or plan.

- **implication** [ìmpləkéiʃən] n. 함축, 암시
  A meaning that is not expressly stated but can be inferred.

- **splash** [splæʃ] n. 화사한 색[빛]; 첨벙 하는 소리; v. (물 등을) 끼얹다[튀기다]
  A splash of color is an area of a bright color which contrasts strongly with the colors around it.

- **shiny** [ʃáini] a. 빛나는, 해가 비치는, 해가 쬐는, 청명한, 광택이 있는
  Smooth and bright; Reflecting the light.

- **spruce** [spru:s] n. 가문비나무속(屬)의 식물 (갯솔·전나무 등)
  A kind of evergreen tree.

- **sparkle** [spá:rkəl] v. 불꽃을 튀기다, 생기가 넘치다; n. 불꽃, 광채 (sparkling a. 반짝거리는)
  If something sparkles, it is clear and bright and shines with a lot of very small points of light.

- **breathtaking** [bréθtèikiŋ] a. 깜짝 놀랄 만한, 아슬아슬한
  Very exciting or impressive (usually in a pleasant way).

- **horizon** [həráizən] n. 지평선, 수평선
  The line far away where the land or sea seems to meet the sky.

- **ledge** [ledʒ] n. 절벽에서 (선반처럼) 튀어나온 바위
  A ledge is a piece of rock on the side of a cliff or mountain, which is in the shape of a narrow shelf.

- **precipice** [présəpis] n. 절벽, 벼랑; 위기
  A very steep side of a cliff or a mountain.

- **chill** [tʃil] n. 냉기, 한기; 오싹한 느낌; v. 춥게 하다, 오싹하다; a. 냉랭한, 차가운
  To lower its temperature so that it becomes colder but does not freeze.

- **brink** [briŋk] n. (벼랑의 가장자리; 물가; (…하기) 직전
  The edge at the top of a steep place.

Vocabulary in New Moon

windshield [wíndʃìːld] n. (자동차 등의) 앞 유리
The windshield of a car or other vehicle is the glass window at the front through which the driver looks.

callous [kǽləs] a. 무감각한, 냉담한; 예사인; (피부가) 굳은, 못 박힌
Not caring about other people's feelings or suffering.

irritation [ìrətéiʃən] n. 짜증나게 함; 짜증, 화; 짜증나는 것, 자극하는 것
Irritation is a feeling of annoyance, especially when something is happening that you cannot easily stop or control.

★ **eternity** [itə́ːrnəti] n. 영원, 무궁; 불사, 불멸; 영원성
Eternity is time without an end or a state of existence outside time, especially the state which some people believe they will pass into after they have died.

insane [inséin] a. 미친, 광기의
Someone who is insane is permanently and seriously mentally ill so that they cannot live in normal society.

disgruntled [disgrʌ́ntld] a. 불만인, 심술 난
Annoyed or disappointed because something has happened to upset you.

★ **stunt** [stʌnt] n. 멍청한[위험한] 행동; 곡예; 스턴트[고난이도 연기]
A stunt is something interesting that is done in order to attract attention and get publicity for the person or company responsible for it.

grin [grin] v. 이를 드러내고 싱긋 웃다; n. 싱긋 웃음
When you grin, you smile broadly.

★ **disapprove** [dìsəprúːv] v. 찬성하지 않다, 안 된다고 하다
(disapproving a. 못마땅해 하는)
To think that somebody or something is not good or suitable.

grab [græb] v. 부여잡다, 움켜쥐다; n. 부여잡기
If you grab something, you take it or pick it up suddenly and roughly.

glacial [gléiʃəl] a. 얼음 같은, 몹시 추운; 얼음의; 빙하의
Made or left by a glacier.

7. REPETITION

breeze [briːz] n. 산들바람, 미풍; v. (주어 it) 산들산들 불다
A light and pleasant wind.

goose bumps [gúːsbʌ̀mps] n. (추위·공포로 인한) 소름
A condition in which there are raised spots on your skin because you feel cold, frightened or excited.

fascinate [fǽsənèit] v. 매혹하다, 황홀케 하다
To interest strongly.

fling [fliŋ] vt. (flung-flung) 던지다, 내던지다; (문 등을) 왈칵 열다
If you fling yourself into a particular activity, you do it with a lot of enthusiasm and energy.

cartwheel [káːrthwìːl] vi. 바퀴처럼 움직이다; 옆으로 재주넘다
To perform an acrobatic movement using both hands and feet.

utterly [ʌ́tərli] ad. 완전히, 순전히, 아주, 전혀
You use utterly to emphasize that something is very great in extent, degree, or amount.

irresponsible [ìrispánsəbəl] a. 무책임한, 신뢰할 수 없는
(of a person) Not thinking enough about the effects of what they do.

disgust [disgʌ́st] vt. 역겹게 하다, 넌더리나게 하다; n. 싫음, 혐오감
(disgusted a. 메스꺼운)
To disgust someone means to make them feel a strong sense of dislike and disapproval.

swear [swɛər] v. 맹세하다, 선서하다; n. 맹세, 선서
If you swear to do something, you promise in a serious way that you will do it.

Makah n. 마카 (인디언 거주지역 중 하나)
An indigenous North American people in the northwestern Olympic Peninsula of Washington state in North America.

rez [rɛz] n. (속어) 인디언 보호구역
Short form of Indian reservation.

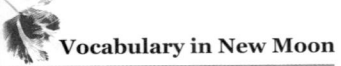

Vocabulary in New Moon

meth [méθ] n. (= METHEDRINE) (구어) 메탐페타민 (각성제)
A variety of amphetamine used for its stimulant action.

disciple [disáipəl] n. 제자[신봉자]
If you are someone's disciple, you are influenced by their teachings and try to follow their example.

ridiculous [ridíkjələs] a. 웃기는, 우스꽝스러운; 터무니없는
If you say that something or someone is ridiculous, you mean that they are very foolish.

resentment [rizéntmənt] n. 분함, 억울함, 분개
A feeling of anger or unhappiness about something that you think is unfair.

soothe [suːð] v. 달래다, 어르다; (통증 등을) 완화시키다, 누그러뜨리다
To make someone feel calmer and less anxious.

cheerful [tʃíərfəl] a. 쾌활한, 명랑한
Someone who is cheerful is happy and shows this in their behavior.

annoying [ənɔ́iiŋ] a. 성가신, 귀찮은, 약 오르는 (annoyingly ad. 짜증스럽게, 성가시게)
Someone or something that is annoying makes you feel fairly angry and impatient.

piss somebody off idiom …를 열 받게[지겹게] 하다
To make somebody annoyed or bored.

groan [groun] v. 신음하다, 끙끙거리다; n. 신음[끙끙거리는] 소리
If you groan, you make a long, low sound because you are in pain, or because you are upset or unhappy about something.

beefy [bíːfi] a. 살찐; 근육이 발달한; 견고한
Someone, especially a man, who is beefy has a big body and large muscles.

divert [divə́ːrt] vt. 전환하다, 딴 데로 돌리다
To divert means to follow a different route or go to a different destination than they originally intended.

7. REPETITION

bleak [bli:k] a. 황폐한, 쓸쓸한, 냉혹한
Without anything to make you feel happy or hopeful.

crap [kræp] n. 허튼소리, 헛소리
Nonsense.

scholarship [skálərʃìp] n. 장학금; 학문
If you get a scholarship to a school, your studies are paid for by the school or by some other organization.

peek [pi:k] vi. 살짝 들여다보다, 엿보다; n. 엿봄
If you peek at something or someone, you have a quick look at them.

offend [əfénd] v. …의 감정을 상하게 하다; 위반하다; 죄를 범하다
To make someone upset or angry.

execute [éksikjù:t] vt. 실행하다, 집행하다
To do or perform something, especially in a planned way.

head-up [hédʌp] n. 좀 모자라는[주의력이 없는] 녀석[선수]

intimidate [intímədèit] vt. 겁주다, 소심하게 만들다 (intimidating a. 위협적인)
To frighten or threaten someone, usually in order to persuade them to do something that you want them to do.

astride [əstráid] a. 걸터앉아; 올라타고; 두 다리를 크게 벌려
If you sit or stand astride something, you sit or stand with one leg on each side of it.

gingerly [dʒíndʒərli] ad. 지극히 조심스럽게, 주의 깊게
In a way that is careful or cautious.

fender [féndər] n. 펜더, 흙받기; 완충 장치
A fender is a low metal wall built around a fireplace, which stops any coals that fall out of the fire from rolling onto the carpet.

creep somebody out idiom …를 겁나게[불안하게] 만들다
To make somebody feel frightened and not safe.

Vocabulary in New Moon

upset [ʌpsét] v. 속상하게 하다; (계획·상황 등이) 잘못되게 만들다; a. 속상한, 마음이 상한
If something upsets you, it makes you feel worried or unhappy.

infuriate [infjúərièit] vt. 격노케 하다
To make someone extremely angry.

★ **monopolize** [mənápəlàiz] vt. 전매하다; 독점[전매]권을 얻다[가지다]
To have a monopoly or exclusive control of trade in a commodity or service.

복습 **terrify** [térəfài] vt. 무섭게[겁나게] 하다, 놀래다
If something terrifies you, it makes you feel extremely frightened.

tempo [témpou] n. 속도, 빠르기, 박자
The speed at which music is played or should be played.

복습 **tense** [tens] a. 팽팽한, 긴장한, 긴박한; v. 팽팽하게 하다, 긴장시키다[하다]
Nervous and anxious and unable to relax.

★ **bug** [bʌg] v. (구어) 귀찮게 굴다, 괴롭히다; n. 곤충; 결함
If someone or something bugs you, they worry or annoy you.

복습 **sarcastic** [sɑːrkǽstik] a. 반정대는, 비꼬는, 풍자적인
Saying things that are the opposite of what you mean, in order to make an unkind joke.

puberty [pjúːbərti] n. 사춘기
The period of a person's life during which their sexual organs develop and they become capable of having children.

복습 **instinctive** [instíŋktiv] a. 본능적인, 직관적인; 무의식적인 (instinctively ad. 본능적으로)
Instinctive behavior or reactions are not thought about, planned or developed by training.

복습 **embrace** [embréis] vt. …을 껴안다, 포옹하다
If you embrace someone, you put your arms around them and hold them tightly, usually in order to show your love or affection for them.

★ **emotional** [imóuʃənəl] a. 감정적인, 감동적인, 감정에 호소하는
(emotionally ad. 감정적으로)
Having and expressing strong feelings.

7. REPETITION

* **perspective** [pə:rspéktiv] n. 가망, 전망; 원근(화)법, 투시(화)법
A particular perspective is a particular way of thinking about something, especially one that is influenced by your beliefs or experiences.

* **dwarf** [dwɔ:rf] n. 난쟁이
An extremely small person, who will never grow to a normal size because of a physical problem; A person suffering from dwarfism.

* **crane** [krein] v. (목을) 쑥 내밀다; 달아 올리다
If you crane your neck, you stretch your neck in a particular direction in order to see something better.

* **pat** [pæt] v. 톡톡 가볍게 치다; 쓰다듬다; n. 톡톡[가볍게] 침[두드림]
If you pat something or someone, you tap them lightly, usually with your hand held flat.

* **porcelain** [pɔ́:rsəlin] a. 자기로 만든, 깨지기 쉬운; n. 자기(磁器), (pl.) 자기 제품
A hard but delicate shiny white substance made by heating a special type of clay to a high temperature, used to make cups, plates, decorations, etc.

albino [ælbáinou] n. 선천성 색소 결핍증[백피증]인 사람
A person or an animal that is born with no color (= pigment) in the hair or skin, which are white, or in the eyes, which are pink.

복습 **enthusiastic** [enθú:ziǽstik] a. 열렬한, 열광적인
If you are enthusiastic about something, you show how much you like or enjoy it by the way that you behave and talk.

Comprehension Quiz

8. ADRENALINE

1. Bella thought it was pointless to fear riding the motorcycle because _____.

   A. she knew how to ride motorcycles well

   B. she knew Jacob would give her excellent instructions

   C. she believed she already lived through the worst thing possible

   D. she didn't believe she could get hurt on the motorcycle with Jacob nearby

2. What was NOT a reason why Bella fell off the motorcycle?

   A. She pushed down on the breaks too hard.

   B. She was distracted by Edward's voice.

   C. The breaks on the motorcycle didn't work.

   D. Jacob didn't teach her how to turn.

8. ADRENALINE

3. Why did Bella want to go to the meadow?

A. She wanted to find a place with 'human' memories.

B. She wanted to share the meadow with Jacob.

C. She wanted to be attacked by the wild animal so she could hear Edward's voice.

D. She thought Edward's presence would be at the meadow.

4. According to Bella, how were Billy and Charlie different?

A. Charlie was a hard person to live with.

B. Billy was a stricter father than Charlie.

C. Billy was more relaxed than Charlie.

D. Billy didn't care about his child.

5. What made Bella's pain easier to bear?

A. Dreaming

B. Being with Jacob

C. Looking after Charlie

D. Remembering the meadow

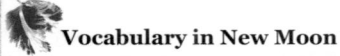

Vocabulary in New Moon

wobble [wábəl] v. 흔들흔들하다, 비틀대다; 동요하다; n. 흔들림
To shake or move from side to side in a way that shows a lack of balance.

throttle [θrátl] n. 조절판; v. 목을 조르다
The throttle of a motor vehicle or aircraft is the device, lever, or pedal that controls the quantity of fuel entering the engine and is used to control the vehicle's speed.

suspicious [səspíʃəs] a. 의심하는, 의심 많은, 수상쩍은 (suspiciously ad. 미심쩍다는 듯이)
If you are suspicious of someone or something, you do not trust them, and are careful when dealing with them.

gearshift [gíərʃìft] n. 변속 기어, (특히 자동차의) 기어 전환 장치
In a vehicle, the gearshift is the same as the gear lever.

nudge [nʌdʒ] vt. (팔꿈치로) 슬쩍 찌르다; 주의를 환기시키다; n. 슬쩍 찌르기
To push somebody gently, especially with your elbow, in order to get their attention.

calf [kæf] n. 장딴지, 종아리
The thick curved part at the back of the human leg between the knee and the foot.

pointless [pɔ́intlis] a. 효과가 없는; 요령부득의, 무의미한
Lacking purpose or meaning.

misty [místi] a. 희미한, 몽롱한; 안개가 짙은, 안개 자욱한
Not clear or bright.

damp [dæmp] a. 축축한
Slightly wet, especially in a way that is not pleasant or comfortable.

instruct [instrʌ́kt] vt. 가르치다, 지시[명령]하다
If you instruct someone to do something, you formally tell them to do it.

crucial [krúːʃəl] a. 결정적인, 중대한; 엄격한; 어려운
Extremely important, because it will affect other things.

grenade [grənéid] n. 수류탄
A small bomb that can be thrown by hand or fired from a gun.

8. ADRENALINE

grit [grit] v. 삐걱거리다, 쓸리다 (grit the teeth : 이를 갈다); n. 잔모래
If you grit your teeth, you press your top and bottom teeth together, often in anger.

slam [slæm] v. 털썩 내려놓다; (문 따위를) 탕 닫다, 세게 치다; n. 쾅 (하는 소리)
If you slam something down, you put it there quickly and with great force.

rip [rip] v. 벗겨내다, 찢다; 돌진하다; n. 잡아 찢음, 째진 틈 (ripping a. 찢는, 째는)
If you rip something away, you remove it quickly and forcefully.

thrust [θrʌst] v. 밀다, 떠밀다, 쑤셔 넣다; n. 밀침
To push something somewhere roughly.

encourage [enkə́:ridʒ] vt. 용기를 북돋우다, 장려하다
If you encourage someone, you give them confidence, hope, or support.

ignition [igníʃən] n. 점화, 발화, (내연 기관의) 점화; 점화 장치
The electrical system of a vehicle that makes the fuel begin to burn to start the engine; The place in a vehicle where you start this system.

snarl [snɑːrl] v. 으르렁거리다; 고함[호통]치다; n. 으르렁거림
If you snarl something, you say it in a fierce, angry way.

satisfaction [sæ̀tisfǽkʃən] n. 만족, 만족감
A pleasant feeling which you get when you do something or get something that you wanted to do.

gear [giər] n. 기어, 톱니바퀴; 장비, 도구
The gears on a machine or vehicle are a device for changing the rate at which energy is changed into motion.

notch [nɑtʃ] n. (구어) 단(段), 단계, 급(級)
A level on a scale, often marking quality or achievement.

idiotic [ìdiátik] a. 백치의, 천치의
Stupid.

fume [fjuːm] v. 몹시 화내다, 약이 오르다; 연기 나다, 그을리다; n. 연기, 김
If you fume over something, you express annoyance and anger about it.

157

Vocabulary in New Moon

- **buck** [bʌk] vi. (구어) (차가 덜커덕하고) 갑자기 움직이다
  To move up and down suddenly or in a way that is not controlled.

- **yank** [jæŋk] v. 홱 당기다; 홱 잡아당겨 …의 상태로 하다; n. 홱 잡아당김
  If you yank someone or something somewhere, you pull them there suddenly and with a lot of force.

- **collapse** [kəlǽps] v. 쓰러지다, 맥없이 주저앉다; 무너지다, 붕괴하다; n. 무너짐, 붕괴
  To fall down or fall in suddenly, often after breaking apart.

- **growl** [graul] v. 으르렁거리다, 고함치다; n. 으르렁거리는 소리 (growling a. 으르렁거리는)
  To make a low rough sound, usually in anger.

- **choke** [tʃouk] v. 숨 막히다[막히게 하다], 질식하다[시키다]
  To prevent or be prevented from breathing by an obstruction in the throat, fumes, emotion.

- **murmur** [mə́:rmər] v. 중얼거리다
  To speak or say very quietly.

- **daze** [deiz] vt. 멍하게 하다; 현혹시키다; n. 멍한 상태; 눈이 부심 (dazed a. 멍한, 아찔한)
  If someone is in a daze, they are feeling confused and unable to think clearly, often because they have had a shock or surprise.

- **swift** [swift] a. 빠른, 신속한 (swiftly ad. 빨리, 즉시)
  A swift event or process happens very quickly or without delay.

- **hallucination** [həlù:sənéiʃən] n. 환각, 망상
  A hallucination is the experience of seeing something that is not really there because you are ill or have taken a drug.

- **trigger** [trígər] v. (장치를) 작동시키다; n. (총의) 방아쇠; 계기, 자극
  If something triggers an event or situation, it causes it to begin to happen or exist.

- **vein** [vein] n. 혈관, 정맥, 광맥; 기질, 특질
  Any of the tubes that carry blood from all parts of the body towards the heart.

- **combination** [kɑ̀mbənéiʃən] n. 결합, 화합, 조합
  A combination of things is a mixture of them.

8. ADRENALINE

* **stupidity** [stju:pídəti] n. 어리석음, 어리석은 짓
  Behavior that shows a lack of thought or good judgement.

* **generate** [dʒénərèit] vt. (결과·행동·감정 등을) 일으키다, 초래하다, 가져오다
  To generate something means to cause it to begin and develop.

  stall [stɔ:l] v. (차량·엔진이) 멎다, 시동이 꺼지다; 시간을 벌다
  If a vehicle stalls or if you accidentally stall it, the engine stops suddenly.

‡ **speculation** [spèkjəléiʃən] n. 심사숙고, 사색, 고찰; 추측, 추론
  An act or instance, or the process or result, of speculating.

복습 **complicate** [kámpləkèit] vt. 복잡하게 하다, 뒤얽히게 만들다
  To complicate something means to make it more difficult to understand or deal with.

‡ **hover** [hʌ́vər] v. 공중을 맴돌다; 배회하다; n. 공중을 떠다님; 배회 (complicated a. 복잡한)
  To hover means to stay in the same position in the air without moving forwards or backwards.

  rev [rev] v. (엔진 등의) 회전 속도를 올리다; n. (구어) (엔진·레코드 등의) 회전
  When the engine of a vehicle revs, or when you rev it, the engine speed is increased as the accelerator is pressed.

* **experimental** [ikspèrəméntl] a. 실험적인; 실험의, 실험에 의한
  (experimentally ad. 실험적으로, 실험상)
  Something that is experimental is new or uses new ideas or methods, and might be modified later if it is unsuccessful.

‡ **sheer** [ʃiər] a. 순전한, 섞이지 않은; 얇은; ad. 완전히, 순전히
  You can use sheer to emphasize that a state or situation is complete and does not involve or is not mixed with anything else.

복습 **startle** [stá:rtl] v. 깜짝 놀라게 하다; 움찔하다; n. 깜짝 놀람
  If something sudden and unexpected startles you, it surprises and frightens you slightly.

복습 **wrench** [rentʃ] vt. (갑자기·세게) 비틀다, 비틀어 돌리다; n. 렌치 (너트를 죄는 기구)
  To make somebody feel great pain or unhappiness, especially so that they make a sound or cry.

159

Vocabulary in New Moon

- ★ **skull** [skʌl] n. 두개골
  The bone structure that forms the head and surrounds and protects the brain.

- **tug** [tʌg] v. 당기다, 끌다; 노력하다; n. 힘껏 당김
  If you tug something or tug at it, you give it a quick and usually strong pull.

- **tingle** [tíŋgəl] v. 설레다; 따끔따끔 아프다; n. 설렘, 흥분; 따끔거림
  If you tingle with a feeling such as excitement, you feel it very strongly.

- ★ **itch** [itʃ] vi. (몹시 …하고 싶어 몸이) 근질거리다[근지럽다]
  If you are itching to do something, you are very eager or impatient to do it.

- **unstable** [ʌnstéibəl] a. 안정되지 않은; 흔들리기 쉬운; 변하기 쉬운
  Likely to change suddenly.

- ★ **stationary** [stéiʃənèri] a. 움직이지 않는, 정지한
  Standing still instead of moving.

- ★ **mash** [mæʃ] vt. 짓찧다, 짓이기다, 찧어 섞다; n. 짓이긴 것, 갈아서 빻은 것
  If you mash food that is solid but soft, you crush it so that it forms a soft mass.

- **moss** [mɔ(:)s] n. 이끼
  Moss is a very small soft green plant which grows on damp soil, or on wood or stone.

- **dizzy** [dízi] a. 현기증 나는, 아찔한
  If you feel dizzy, you feel as if everything is spinning round and being unable to balance.

- **thrill** [θril] v. 감동[감격·흥분] 시키다; 오싹하다; n. 전율 (thrilled a. 흥분한, 감격한)
  If something thrills you, it gives you a feeling of great pleasure and excitement.

- **recipe** [résəpì:] n. (요리의) 조리법; (약제 등의) 처방전
  A list of ingredients and a set of instructions that tell you how to cook something.

8. ADRENALINE

crouch [krautʃ] v. 몸을 구부리다, 쭈그리다, 웅크리다
To bend your knees and lower yourself so that you are close to the ground and leaning forward slightly.

enthuse [inθúːz] v. 열광[열중]하다, 감격하다
To express excitement about something or great interest in it.

gush [gʌʃ] v. (액체 등이) 분출하다, 내뿜다; (구어) 지껄여대다; n. 분출; (감정의) 격발
If a liquid gushes, it flowes or pours out quickly and in large quantities.

clap [klæp] v. 가볍게 치다[두드리다]; 박수를[손뼉을] 치다
If you clap your hand or an object onto something, you put it there quickly and firmly.

sticky [stíki] a. 끈적[끈끈]한, 들러붙는, 점착성의
Made of or covered in a substance that sticks to things that touch it.

nausea [nɔ́ːziə] n. 메스꺼움, 욕지기; 뱃멀미
The feeling that you have when you want to vomit, for example because you are ill/sick or are disgusted by something.

bleed [bliːd] vi. ① 출혈하다 ② 마음 아파하다
When you bleed, you lose blood from your body as a result of injury or illness.

wad [wad] v. (단단한 덩이가 되게) 뭉치다, 뭉치로 만들다; 뭉쳐 넣다, 채우다
To fold or press something into a tight wad.

pebble [pébəl] n. 조약돌, 자갈
A smooth, round stone that is found in or near water.

athletic [æθlétik] a. (체격이) 스포츠맨다운, 강건한; 발랄한
An athletic person is fit, and able to perform energetic movements easily.

envious [énviəs] a. 시기심이 강한; 질투하는, 샘내는 (**enviously** ad. 시기하여, 부러워하여)
If you are envious of someone, you want something that they have.

barely [bɛ́ərli] ad. 간신히, 가까스로; 거의 …않다
Only with great difficulty or effort.

Vocabulary in New Moon

- **sprint** [sprint] v. 역주하다, 달려가다
  To run at full speed.

- **coax** [kouks] vt. 구슬려 ···시키다, 감언으로 설득하다, 어르다, 달래다
  To persuade someone gently to do something or go somewhere, by being kind and patient, or by appearing to be.

- **deafen** [défən] vt. 귀머거리를 만들다, 귀를 먹먹하게 하다
  If a noise deafens you, it is so loud that you cannot hear anything else at the same time.

- **sting** [stiŋ] vt. (stung-stung) 찌르다, 쏘다; n. 찌르기, 쏘기, (동물의) 침, 고통
  If something stings you, a sharp part of it is pushed into your skin so that you feel a sharp pain.

- **wound** [wu:nd] ① n. 상처, 부상, 상해; vt. 상처를 입히다 ② v. [waund] wind의 과거·과거분사
  A wound is damage to part of your body, especially a cut or a hole in your flesh, which is caused by a gun, knife, or other weapon.

- **ER** n. (= emergency room) 응급실
  The part of a hospital where people who need urgent treatment are taken.

- **cake** [keik] v. 들러붙다, 뭉쳐지다
  If something such as blood or mud cakes, it changes from a thick liquid to a dry layer or lump.

- **stitch** [stitʃ] n. [외과] (상처를 꿰매는) 한 바늘; v. 꿰매다; 바느질하다
  A stitch is a piece of thread that has been used to sew the skin of a wound together.

- **dire** [daiər] a. 대단히 심각한, 엄청난, 지독한
  Dire is used to emphasize how serious or terrible a situation or event is.

- **uncharacteristic** [ənkæriktərístik] a. 특징이 없는, 평소답지 않은
  Not typical of somebody; Not the way somebody usually behaves.

- **needless** [ní:dlis] a. 불필요한, 쓸데없는 (needlessly ad. 불필요하게)
  Something that is needless is completely unnecessary.

8. ADRENALINE

pathetic [pəθétik] a. 불쌍한, 애처로운; 가치 없는, (이익이) 매우 적은
Making you feel pity or sadness.

piggyback [pígibæk] n. (등에) 업기, 목말 타기
If you give someone a piggyback, you carry them high on your back, supporting them under their knees.

agony [ǽgəni] n. 고뇌, 고통, 번민
Agony is great physical or mental pain.

flinch [flintʃ] v. (고통·공포로) 주춤하다, 위축되다
To make a small sudden movement, especially when something surprises someone.

convincing [kənvínsiŋ] a. 설득력 있는, 납득이 가는
Making you believe that something is true or right.

disconnect [dìskənékt] vt. …의 전원을 끊다; …와의 연락을 끊다; (전화 등을) 끊다
To remove the supply of power, gas, water etc. from a machine or piece of equipment.

gruesome [grú:səm] a. 소름 끼치는, 무시무시한; 힘든
Something that is gruesome is extremely unpleasant and shocking.

muddy [mʌ́di] a. 진흙투성이의; 진창의, 진흙의, 질퍽한
Something that is muddy contains mud or is covered in mud.

clinical [klínikəl] a. (판단·묘사 등이) 극도로 객관적인, 분석적인, 냉정한
(clinically ad. 임상적으로, 냉담하게)
You use clinical to describe thought or behavior which is very logical and does not involve any emotion.

laundry [lɔ́:ndri] n. 세탁물, 세탁소
The dirty clothes and sheets which need to be, are being washed.

garment [gá:rmənt] n. 의복, 옷, 의류; 외피, 외관
A piece of clothing.

Vocabulary in New Moon

incriminate [inkrímənèit] vt. …이 잘못핸[유죄인] 것처럼 보이게 하다
If something incriminates you, it suggests that you are responsible for something bad, especially a crime.

frown [fraun] v. 눈살을 찌푸리다, 얼굴을 찡그리다; n. 찌푸린 얼굴
To make an angry, unhappy, bringing your eyebrows together.

shiver [ʃívər] v. (추위·공포로) 후들후들 떨다; 전율하다; n. 떨림, 전율
To shake slightly because you are cold, frightened, excited, etc.

huddle [hʌ́dl] v. (보통 춥거나 무서워서) 옹송그리다
If you huddle somewhere, you sit, stand, or lie there holding your arms and legs close to your body, usually because you are cold or frightened.

skeleton [skélətn] n. 해골; 골격, 뼈대
The frame of bones supporting a human or animal body.

wiry [wáiəri] a. 철사로 만든, 철사 같은, 빳빳한
Stiff and strong; Like wire.

scrutiny [skrúːtəni] n. 응시, 찬찬히 쳐다보기; 정밀한 조새[검사]
A penetrating or searching look.

impulsive [impʌ́lsiv] a. 충동적인, 감정에 끌린
If you describe someone as impulsive, you mean that they do things suddenly without thinking about them carefully first.

anesthetic [æ̀nəsθétik] n. 마취제; a. 마취의, 무감각한
A drug that causes temporary loss of bodily sensations.

sew [sou] v. 바느질하다, 꿰매다, 깁다
When you sew something such as clothes, you make them or repair them by joining pieces of cloth together by passing thread through them with a needle.

ironic [airánik] a. 반어의[적인]; 비꼬는; 풍자적인
Showing that you really mean the opposite of what you are saying.

throb [θrɑb] vi. (심장이) 고동치다, 맥이 뛰다; n. 고동, 맥박
If part of your body throbs, you feel a series of strong and usually painful beats there.

8. ADRENALINE

potency [póutənsi] n. 효능, 효과, 영향력
Potency is the power and influence that a person, action, or idea has to affect or change people's lives, feelings, or beliefs.

nothingness [nʌ́θiŋnis] n. 무(無), 공허; 존재하지 않음, 없음
Nothingness is the fact of not existing.

impatient [impéiʃənt] a. 성급한, 조급한, 몹시 …하고 싶어 하는
Easily annoyed by someone's mistakes or because you have to wait.

consciousness [kánʃəsnis] n. 의식, 자각
Your consciousness is your mind and your thoughts.

concussion [kənkʌ́ʃən] n. [병리] 뇌진탕
If you suffer concussion after a blow to your head, you lose consciousness or feel sick or confused.

edict [íːdikt] n. 명령
An edict is a command or instruction given by someone in authority.

prohibit [prouhíbit] vt. 금하다, 금지하다
To stop something from being done or used especially by law.

consequently [kánsikwəntli] ad. 그 결과(로서), 따라서; 논리적으로
As a result.

abrupt [əbrʌ́pt] a. 갑작스러운, 뜻밖의 (abruptly ad. 갑자기)
Sudden and unexpected.

launch [lɔːntʃ] v. 맹렬히 덤비다; 발진시키다, 쏘다, 내보내다
To jump forwards with a lot of force.

skeptical [sképtikəl] a. 의심 많은, 회의적인 (skeptically ad. 의심스럽게, 회의적으로)
Having doubts that a claim or statement is true or that something will happen.

rub off (on) idiom (습관·생각 따위가) …에 영향을 주다, 옮다
Of personal qualities, behaviour, opinions, etc. to become part of a person's character as a result of that person spending time with somebody who has those qualities, etc.

Vocabulary in New Moon

glare [glɛər] v. 노려보다; 번쩍번쩍 빛나다; n. 섬광; 노려봄
If you glare at someone, you look at them with an angry expression on your face.

unconvinced [ʌ̀nkənvínst] a. 설득되지 않은, 납득하지 않은
If you are unconvinced that something, you are not at all certain that it is true or right.

surreptitious [sə̀:rəptíʃəs] a. 비밀의, 몰래 하는, 은밀한; 부정의
(surreptitiously ad. 몰래; 부정하게)
Done secretly or quickly, in the hope that other people will not notice.

wildlife [wáildlàif] n. 야생 생물
Animals, birds, insects, etc. that are wild and live in a natural environment.

complaint [kəmpléint] n. 불평, 불만, 푸념
A statement in which you express your dissatisfaction with a particular situation.

mutate [mjú:teit] v. [생물] 돌연변이하다
If an animal or plant mutates, or something mutates it, it develops different characteristics as the result of a change in its genes.

grizzly [grízli] (= grizzly bear) n. (북미 서부산(産)의 큰) 회색곰
A grizzly or a grizzly bear is a large, fierce, greyish-brown bear.

crease [kri:s] v. 주름투성이로 만들다; 구기다; 주름이 생기다; n. 주름, 구김살
To make a crease or creases in (paper, fabric, etc); To develop creases.

nosy [nóuzi:] a. 참견하기 좋아하는, 꼬치꼬치 캐묻는
If you describe someone as nosy, you mean that they are interested in things which do not concern them.

closeness [klóusnis] n. 근사(近似); 접근
Nearness; The spatial property resulting from a relatively small distance.

creativity [krì:eitívəti] n. 창조적임, 창조성; 독창[창조]력; (속어) 활기, 생기
The ability to create.

8. ADRENALINE

stamp [stæmp] v. 짓밟다, (발을) 구르다
To put a foot down on the ground hard and quickly.

landmark [lǽndmɔ̀:rk] n. 주요 지형지물, 랜드마크(멀리서 보고 위치 파악에 도움이 되는 대형 건물 같은 것)
A landmark is a building or feature which is easily noticed and can be used to judge your position or the position of other buildings or features.

potential [pouténʃəl] n. 잠재력, 가능성; a. 잠재적인, 가능성이 있는
If you say that someone or something has potential, you mean that they have the necessary abilities or qualities to become successful or useful in the future.

backfire [bǽkfàiər] v. 역효과를 낳다
If a plan or project backfires, it has the opposite result to the one that was intended.

ache [eik] vi. 아프다, 쑤시다
To feel a continuous dull pain.

grid [grid] n. (지도의) 격자[바둑판] 눈금
A grid is something which is in a pattern of straight lines that cross over each other, forming squares. On maps the grid is used to help you find a particular thing or place.

confident [kάnfidənt] a. 확신하는, 자신 만만한
If you are confident about something, you are certain that it will happen in the way you want it to.

trailhead [tréilhèd] n. 자취[길]의 기점(起點)
The place where a trail begins.

topographical [tɑ̀pəgrǽfikəl] a. 지지(地誌)의, 지형상의, 지형학의
A topographical survey or map relates to or shows the physical features of an area of land, for example its hills, valleys, and rivers.

sprawl [sprɔ:l] v. 불규칙하게 퍼지게 하다; 팔다리를 펴다[뻗다]; n. 드러누움
To spread in an untidy way; To cover a large area.

Vocabulary in New Moon

perch [pəːrtʃ] v. 앉아 있다[쉬다]; 위치하다, 자리 잡다; (높은 곳에) 놓다, 앉히다
If you perch on something, you sit down lightly on the very edge or tip of it.

fuss [fʌs] n. 야단법석, 호들갑; 법석을 떨다; 안달하다
Attention and excitement given to small and unimportant matters.

sighting [sáitiŋ] n. 목격 (특히 특이한 것, 잠깐밖에 볼 수 없는 것에 대해 씀)
A sighting of something, especially something unusual or unexpected is an occasion on which it is seen.

refold [rifóud] vt. 다시 접다, 접은 상태로 되돌리다
To fold again.

dense [dens] a. 빽빽한, 밀집한; (구어) 머리 나쁜, 우둔한
Something that is dense contains a lot of things or people in a small area.

rebel [rébəl] n. 반항자, 반역자, 반도
Rebels are people who are fighting against their own country's army in order to change the political system there.

tune [tjuːn] n. 곡조, 선율; v. 조율하다, 조정하다
A tune is a series of musical notes that is pleasant and easy to remember.

radiate [réidièit] vi. (빛·열 등을) 발하다, 빛나다, 방출하다
To send out rays of light, heat, electromagnetic radiation, etc.

compliment [kámpləmənt] v. 경의를 표하다, 칭찬하다; n. 찬사, 칭찬의 말
If you compliment someone, you pay them a compliment.

inflated [infléitid] a. 부풀린, 과장된; 폭등한
Higher than is acceptable or reasonable.

hesitant [hézətənt] a. 주저하는; 머뭇거리는 (hesitantly ad. 주저하며, 머뭇대며)
If you are hesitant about doing something, you do not do it quickly or immediately, usually because you are uncertain, embarrassed, or worried.

playful [pléifəl] a. 놀기 좋아하는; 장난의 (playfully ad. 장난으로, 농담조로)
Full of fun.

8. ADRENALINE

- **sour** [sáuər] a. (사람이) 뚱한, 시큰둥한; 심술궂은
  Someone who is sour is bad-tempered and unfriendly.

- **gloom** [glu:m] n. 어둠침침함, 어둠, 그늘, 암흑
  A feeling of being sad and without hope.

- **kidnap** [kídnæp] vt. (어린이)를 유괴하다, 꾀어내다; (사람)을 납치하다
  To take somebody away illegally and keep them as a prisoner, especially in order to get money or something else for returning them.

- **doom** [du:m] vt. 운명 짓다, 선고하다; n. 운명, 파멸 (doomed a. 운이 다한, 불운한)
  If a fact or event dooms someone or something to a particular fate, it makes certain that they are going to suffer in some way.

- **fade** [feid] vi. 바래다, 시들다, 희미해지다
  To disappear gradually.

- **fern** [fə:rn] n. [식물] 양치류(의 식물)
  A plant with large delicate leaves and no flowers that grows in wet areas or is grown in a pot.

- **stomp** [stamp] v. 짓밟다, 발을 구르며 걷다; n. 발구르기
  To walk with heavy steps or to put your foot down very hard, especially.

- **gimpy** [gímpi] a. 절름발이의
  Limping, lame, with crippled legs.

- **moleskin** [móulskìn] n. (발에 붙이는) 반창고
  A type of strong cotton cloth with a soft surface, used for making clothes.

- **confess** [kənfés] vt. 자백하다, 인정하다
  If someone confesses to doing something wrong, they admit that they did it.

- **cab** [kæb] n. (버스·기차·트럭의) 운전석
  The cab of a truck or train is the front part in which the driver sits.

Comprehension Quiz

9. THIRD WHEEL

1. Jacob promised Bella _____.

   A. he would always make her happy

   B. he would always love her

   C. he would make her forget about Edward

   D. she could always count on him

2. What did Jacob notice about Bella's body?

   A. She was very pale.

   B. She had bags under her eyes.

   C. She had a scar on her hand.

   D. She was very thin.

3. Bella truly knew that _____.

   A. love was the most important thing in life

   B. she would always love Jacob more than anyone else in her life

   C. love gave someone the power to break her

   D. she would forget about Edward

9. THIRD WHEEL

4. Why did Bella feel guilty when she was in the car with Jacob and Mike?

A. Mike was sick and she wasn't.

B. She encouraged Jacob even though she didn't want a relationship with him.

C. She acted like she was dating Mike in front of Jacob.

D. She took both Jacob and Mike to the movie theater.

5. According to Jacob _____.

A. he didn't have the stomach flu

B. Mike was lying about having the stomach flu

C. he didn't want to be friends with Bella anymore

D. his father was being rude

Vocabulary in New Moon

third wheel idiom (속어) 쓸모없는 사람[존재]
The person who is the outsider when there is a group of three.

miserable [mízərəbəl] a. 불쌍한, 비참한, 불행한, 딱한, 가엾은
Unpleasant and causing unhappiness.

implication [ìmpləkéiʃən] n. 함축, 암시
A meaning that is not expressly stated but can be inferred.

cataclysmic [kætəklízmik] a. 격변하는; 대변동의 성질을 가진
A cataclysmic event is one that changes a situation or society very greatly, especially in an unpleasant way.

scenario [sinέəriòu] n. [영화] 시나리오, 영화 각본; [연극] 대본
If you talk about a likely or possible scenario, you are talking about the way in which a situation may develop.

desolation [dèsəléiʃən] n. 쓸쓸함, 외로움, 황량
The feeling of being very lonely and unhappy.

orbit [ɔ́ːrbit] n. [천문] 궤도
An orbit is the curved path in space that is followed by an object going round and round a planet, moon, or star.

gravity [grǽvəti] n. 중력
The force that makes objects fall to the ground.

bandage [bǽndidʒ] n. 붕대, 안대; vt. …에 붕대를 감다
A bandage is a long strip of cloth which is wrapped around a wounded part of someone's body to protect or support it.

frenzied [frénzid] a. 열광적인, 광포한
Frenzied activities or actions are wild, excited, and uncontrolled.

intensity [inténsəti] n. 강렬, 격렬; 집중, 전념
The state or quality of being intense.

impend [impénd] vi. (위험·사건 따위가) 절박[임박]하다, 바야흐로 일어나려 하다
Describes an event, usually something unpleasant or unwanted, that is going to happen soon.

9. THIRD WHEEL

palm [pɑːm] n. ① 손바닥 ② 종려나무, 야자나무
The palm of your hand is the inside part.

schmuck [ʃmʌk] n. 멍청이, 얼간이
A stupid person.

mock [mɑk] a. 가짜의, 모의의; vt. 조롱하다, 흉내 내며 놀리다; n. 조롱, 놀림감
You use mock to describe something which is not real or genuine, but which is intended to be very similar to the real thing.

entail [inteil] v. 수반하다; (논리적으로) 의미하다
If one thing entails another, it involves it or causes it.

hedge [hedʒ] v. 얼버무리다; 울타리를 두르다; n. 울타리; 대비책
If you hedge against something unpleasant or unwanted that might affect you, especially losing money, you do something which will protect you from it.

slave [sleiv] n. 노예; …에 빠진[사로잡힌] 사람; 헌신하는 사람
A slave is someone who is the property of another person and has to work for that person.

ER n. (= emergency room) 응급실
The part of a hospital where people who need urgent treatment are taken.

obsessive [əbsésiv] a. 강박적인, 사로잡혀 있는
Thinking or worrying about something all the time.

bunch [bʌntʃ] n. 떼, 한패; 다발, 송이
A group of people.

senior [síːniər] n. 연장자, 선배; a. 손위의; 상위의, 선배의, 최고 학년의
Someone who is high or higher in rank.

stab [stæb] n. 찌름, (찌르는 듯한) 고통; v. (칼 따위로) 찌르다
A sudden sharp feeling of pain or a strong emotion.

ordeal [ɔːrdíːəl] n. 호된 시련, 고된 체험
A difficult or unpleasant experience.

Vocabulary in New Moon

tempt [tempt] vt. 유혹하다, 부추기다 (tempting a. 솔깃한, 구미가 당기는)
Something that tempts you attracts you and makes you want it, even though it may be wrong or harmful.

gonna [góunə] etc. (미·구어) …할 예정인(going to)
Non-standard a way of saying or writing 'going to' in informal speech, when it refers to the future.

chortle [tʃɔ́ːrtl] vi. (좋아서) 깔깔 웃다; 아주 좋아하다
To laugh loudly with pleasure or because you are amused.

broach [broutʃ] vt. 끄집어 내다; 발의하다
To raise a subject, especially one likely to cause arguments or problems for discussion.

instantly [ínstəntli] ad. 즉각, 즉시
Immediately.

emphasize [émfəsàiz] vt. 강조하다; 역설하다
To emphasize something means to indicate that it is particularly important or true, or to draw special attention to it.

bloodbath [blʌ́dbæ̀θ] n. 피바다, 대학살
A situation in which many people are killed violently.

perk [pəːrk] ① v. 생기가 나다; (귀·꼬리 등을) 쫑긋 세우다; ② n. (급료 외의) 특전
(perk up phrasal v. 생기가 돌다, 활기를 띠다)
To become more cheerful and active in what is happening around you.

apparently [əpǽrəntli] ad. 보기에, 외관상으로; 분명히, 명백히
Used to say that something seems to be true, although it is not certain; Used when the real situation is different from what you thought it was.

★ **tack** [tæk] vt. 압정으로 고정시키다; n. 압정
(tack on phrasal v. …을 덧붙이다[보태다])
To attach something to a wall, board etc., using a short pin with a large round flat top.

grudging [grʌ́dʒiŋ] a. 인색한, 마지못해 하는 (grudgingly ad. 마지못해; 쩨쩨하게)
Given or done unwillingly.

9. THIRD WHEEL

foil [fɔil] v. 좌절시키다[저지하다]
If you foil someone's plan or attempt to do something, for example to commit a crime, you succeed in stopping them from doing what they want.

Suburban [səbə́:rbən] n. 서버밴 (7인승 승합차)

suspicion [səspíʃən] n. 혐의, 용의, 의심
Suspicion is a belief or feeling that someone has committed a crime or done something wrong.

sophomore [sáfəmɔ̀:r] n. (대학·고교의) 2학년생
A student in the second year of college or high school.

anniversary [æ̀nəvə́:rsəri] n. 기념일
A date on which some event took place in a previous year.

diminish [dəmíniʃ] v. 줄다, 감소[축소]되다 (diminished a. 감소된)
To become or to make something become smaller, weaker, etc.

dampen [dǽmpən] v. (기를) 꺾다, 풀이 죽게 하다; 축이다, 축축하게 하다
To make feelings, especially of excitement or enjoyment, less strong.

anticipation [æntìsəpéiʃən] n. 예상, 기대, 희망
A feeling of excitement about something that is going to happen.

Rotten Tomato n. 미국의 영화 사이트

maiden [meidn] a. 최초의, 처녀… (ex. 처녀비행, 처녀항해 등)
The maiden voyage or flight of a ship or aircraft is the first official journey that it makes.

incredible [inkrédəbəl] a. 놀라운, 훌륭한, 믿어지지 않는
Something is very unusual or surprising unbelievably.

unsurprised [ənsərpráizd] a. 놀라지 않는
Not surprised.

capitulation [kəpìtʃəléiʃən] n. 조건부 항복
The act of surrendering (usually under agreed conditions).

Vocabulary in New Moon

chug [tʃʌg] vi. (엔진이) 통통[칙칙]하는 소리를 내다; (음료를) 단숨에 들이켜다
When a vehicle chugs somewhere, it goes there slowly, noisily and with difficulty.

thoughtful [θɔ́:tfəl] a. 생각이 깊은, 생각에 잠긴 (thoughtfully ad. 생각에 깊게 잠겨)
Thinking deeply, or appearing to think deeply; Reflective.

persistence [pəːrsístəns] n. 끈덕짐, 고집, 완고, 버팀; 영속, 지속
If you have persistence, you continue to do something even though it is difficult or other people are against it.

annoying [ənɔ́iiŋ] a. 성가신, 귀찮은, 약 오르는
Someone or something that is annoying makes you feel fairly angry and impatient.

wary [wɛ́əri] a. 경계하는, 조심하는
Not completely trusting or certain about something or someone.

bail on idiom (속어) 억압하다, 괴롭게 하다; (데이트 약속을) 어기다, 바람맞히다

grim [grim] a. 엄한, 엄격한; 험상스러운
Looking or sounding very serious.

sarcasm [sáːrkæzəm] n. 빈정거림, 비꼼, 풍자
The use of remarks which clearly mean the opposite of what they say, and which are made in order to hurt someone's feelings or to criticize something in an amusing way.

sullen [sʌ́lən] a. 뚱한, 시무룩한; 음침한
Bad-tempered and not speaking, either on a particular occasion or because it is part of your character.

glum [glʌm] a. 음울한, 시무룩한, 풀죽은 (glumly ad. 시무룩하게, 침울하게)
Disappointed or unhappy, and quiet.

brag [bræg] v. 자랑하다, 자랑하며 말하다
If you brag, you say in a very proud way that you have something or have done something.

9. THIRD WHEEL

PTA [piːtiéi] n. 학부모회, 사친회
Parent-Teacher Association.

sulk [sʌlk] vi. 샐쭉해지다, 부루퉁해지다, 골나다; n. 샐쭉함, 부루퉁함
To be silent and childishly refuse to smile or be pleasant to people because you are angry about something that they have done.

strategy [strǽtədʒi] n. 전략, 작전
A plan that is intended to achieve a particular purpose.

petulance [pétʃələns] n. 토라짐, 심술사나움; 무례한 태도, 건방진 언동
An irritable petulant feeling.

serene [siríːn] a. 고요한, 화창한; 침착한, 평온한
Very charm or peaceful.

irritate [írətèit] vt. 짜증나게[초조하게] 하다, 화나게 하다
If something irritates you, it keeps annoying you.

hmph int. 짜증나거나 불쾌할 때, 성날 때 내는 소리. 감탄사
A sound, usually made with a closed mouth, indicating annoyance.

relative [rélətiv] a. 비교적인; 상대적인; n. 동족, 동류
Considered and judged by being compared with something else.

corrupt [kərʌ́pt] vt. 타락시키다, 매수하다
If someone is corrupted by something, it causes them to become dishonest and unjust and unable to be trusted.

innocence [ínəsns] n. 때 묻지 않음, 순결; 결백; 천진
Having no knowledge of the unpleasant and evil things in life.

snicker [sníkər] vi. (미) 킬킬 웃다, 숨죽여 웃다; n. 킬킬 웃음
To laugh at someone or something childishly and often unkindly.

quicken [kwíkən] v. 빨라지다, 빠르게 하다; 서두르게 하다
To become quicker or make something quicker.

Vocabulary in New Moon

behead [bihéd] vt. (사람을) 목 베다, 참수형에 처하다
If someone is beheaded, their head is cut off, usually because they have been found guilty of a crime.

wince [wins] vi. (아픔·무서움 때문에) 주춤하다, 움츠리다; n. 위축
If you wince, you suddenly look as if you are suffering because you feel pain.

fringe [frindʒ] n. (가장자리의) 술 (장식); 가장자리, 부차적인 것; v. 술을 달다, 테를 두르다
A fringe is a decoration attached to clothes, or other objects such as curtains, consisting of a row of hanging strips or threads.

endure [endjúər] v. 참다, 견디다, 인내하다
If you endure a painful or difficult situation, you experience it and do not avoid it or give up, usually because you cannot.

snigger [snígər] (= snicker) vi. 낄낄 웃다, 숨죽여 웃다
To laugh at someone or something childishly and often unkindly.

squirt [skwə́:rt] v. 분출하다, 뿜어 나오다; n. 건방진 벼락부자, 잘난 체하는 젊은이
To flow out through a narrow opening in a fast stream.

fake [feik] a. 가짜의, 위조의; vt. …인 체하다, 가장하다 (pretend)
Not real, but made to look or seem real.

flagpole [flǽgpòul] n. 깃대
A tall pole on which a flag is hung.

mayhem [méihem] n. 대혼란, 아수라장
Confusion and fear, usually caused by violent behavior or by some sudden shocking event.

relationship [riléiʃənʃìp] n. 관계, 관련
The way in which two people, groups or countries behave towards each other or deal with each other.

armrest [á:rmrèst] n. (의자 등의) 팔걸이
The part of a chair that supports the arm.

9. THIRD WHEEL

significance [signífikəns] n. 의의, 의미, 중요성
The significance of something is the importance that it has, usually because it will have an effect on a situation or shows something about a situation.

moan [moun] v. 신음하다, 끙끙대다; n. 신음
If you moan, you make a low sound, usually because you are unhappy or in pain.

bolt [boult] vi. 달아나다
To run away, especially in order to escape.

buck [bʌk] n. (미·속어) 달러
A dollar.

carnage [káːrnidʒ] n. 살육, 대학살
The violent killing of large numbers of people.

suck [sʌk] v. (속어) 엉망이다, 형편없다; 빨다, 흡수하다; n. 빨아들임
If someone says that something sucks, they are indicating that they think it is very bad.

duck [dʌk] ① vi. 몸을 홱 굽히다; (쑥) 들어가다 ② n. 오리
To move somewhere very quickly.

marshmallow [máːrʃmèlou] n. 마시멜로 (녹말·시럽·설탕·젤라틴 등으로 만드는 과자); (미·흑인 속어) 백인
Marshmallow is a soft, sweet food that is used in some cakes, puddings, and sweets.

vomit [vámit] v. 토하다, 게우다
To empty the contents of the stomach through the mouth.

velveteen [vèlvətíːn] n. 면 벨벳, 면 비로드
Velveteen is a soft fabric which looks and feels like velvet and is sometimes used as a cheaper alternative to velvet.

upholster [ʌphóulstər] vt. (의자 등에 속·스프링·커버 따위)를 대다; 커버를 씌우다
To cover a chair, etc. with soft material (= padding) and cloth.

Vocabulary in New Moon

- ★ **rejection** [ridʒékʃən] n. 거절, 배제, 기각, 부결
  The act of rejecting something.

- **grimace** [gríməs] vi. 얼굴을 찡그리다; n. 얼굴을 찡그림
  If you grimace, you twist your face in an ugly way because you are annoyed, disgusted, or in pain.

- **gut** [gʌt] n. 창자, 내장; 직감, 본능, 신경; (pl.) 용기, 결단; 실질, 핵심
  A person's or animal's guts are all the organs inside them.

- ★ **persistent** [pəːrsístənt] a. 고집하는, 집요한, 끈기 있는; 완고한
  Continuing with determination in spite of discouragement; Dogged; Tenacious.

- **cringe** [krindʒ] vi. (겁이 나서) 움츠리다[움찔하다]
  If you cringe at something, you feel embarrassed or disgusted, and making a slight movement.

- **obstinate** [ábstənit] a. 완고한, 고집 센 (obstinately ad. 완고하게)
  Unreasonably determined, especially to act in a particular way and not to change at all, despite argument or persuasion.

- **truthful** [trúːθfəl] a. 거짓말 안 하는, 성실한, 정직한; 정말의
  (truthfully ad. 거짓 없이, 진실하게)
  If a person or their comments are truthful, they are honest and do not tell any lies.

- **jerk** [dʒəːrk] v. 갑자기 움직이다; n. 갑자기 잡아당김; 바보
  If you jerk something or someone in a particular direction, or they jerk in a particular direction, they move a short distance very suddenly and quickly.

- **thumb** [θʌm] n. 엄지손가락
  Your thumb is the short thick part on the side of your hand next to your four fingers.

- **grumble** [grʌ́mbəl] v. 투덜거리다, 불평하다; n. 투덜댐, 불평
  To complain about someone or something in an annoyed way.

- **grenade** [grənéid] n. 수류탄
  A small bomb that can be thrown by hand or fired from a gun.

9. THIRD WHEEL

entitle [entáitl] vt. 권리[자격]를 주다; 제목을 붙이다, 칭하다
To give somebody the right to have or to do something.

pinky [píŋki] n. 새끼손가락
Your pinky is the smallest finger on your hand.

absently [ǽbsəntli] a. 멍하니, 넋을 잃고
In a way that shows you are not looking at or thinking about what is happening around you.

scar [skɑːr] n. 흉터, (화상·부스럼의) 자국
A mark that is left on the skin after a wound has healed.

silvery [sílvəri] a. 은과 같은; 은빛의; 은방울 같은
Silvery things look like silver or are the color of silver.

crescent [krésənt] n. 초승달, 초승달 모양(의 것); a. 초승달 모양의
A curved shape that is wide in the middle and pointed at each end.

scowl [skaul] vi. 얼굴을 찌푸리다, 싫은 기색을 하다; n. 찌푸린 얼굴
To look at someone or something with a very annoyed expression.

stumble [stʌ́mbəl] v. 비틀거리며 걷다, 발부리가 걸리다; n. 비틀거림
If you stumble, you put your foot down awkwardly while you are walking or running and nearly fall over.

ashen [ǽʃən] a. 회색의; (죽은 사람처럼) 매우 창백한, 핏기가 없는
Grey or very pale, usually from shock, illness, etc.

unsteady [ʌ̀nstédi] a. 굳세지 못한, 동요하는
Not completely in control of your movements so that you might fall.

heartless [hɑ́ːrtlis] a. 무정[박정]한, 무자비한, 냉혹한 (heartlessly ad. 무심[무정]하게)
Feeling no pity for other people.

malevolent [məlévələnt] a. 악의 있는; 남의 불행을 기뻐하는
Causing or wanting to cause harm or evil.

nauseate [nɔ́ːzièit] v. 구역질나(게 하)다, 메스껍게 하다; 싫어하다, 혐오감을 느까(게 하)다
To cause someone to feel as if they are going to vomit.

Vocabulary in New Moon

scold [skould] v. 꾸짖다, 잔소리하다
If you scold someone, you speak angrily to them because they have done something wrong.

stagger [stǽgər] v. 비틀거리다; 흔들리게 하다; 주저하다; n. 비틀거림
If you stagger, you walk very unsteadily, for example because you are ill or drunk.

concession [kənséʃən] n. 영업장소; (매점 등의) 토지 사용권
(concession stand : 구내 매점)
The place where you sell something, sometimes an area which is part of a larger building or store.

thrust [θrʌst] v. 밀다, 떠밀다, 쑤셔 넣다; n. 밀침
To push something somewhere roughly.

inhale [inhéil] v. 들이쉬다, 흡입하다
To take air, smoke, gas, etc. into your lungs as you breathe.

fit as a fiddle idiom 컨디션이 매우 좋아, 건강하여
Very healhy and active.

blaze [bleiz] vi. 타오르다; n. 불꽃, 화염, 섬광
To burn brightly and strongly.

defile [difail] vt. 더럽히다, 불결[부정(不淨)]하게 하다
To make something dirty or no longer pure, especially something that people consider important.

utterly [ʌ́tərli] ad. 완전히, 순전히, 아주, 전혀
You use utterly to emphasize that something is very great in extent, degree, or amount.

condemn [kəndém] vt. 비난하다, 힐난하다; 유죄 판결을 내리다
If you condemn something, you say that it is very bad and unacceptable.

uninhabitable [ʌ̀ninhǽbitəbəl] a. 사람이 살 수 없는, 주거하기에 부적합한
Not fit to live in; Impossible to live in.

9. THIRD WHEEL

investment [invéstmənt] n. 투자, 출자; 투자액; 투자의 대상
The act of investing money in something.

regardless [rigá:*r*dlis] ad. 개의치[상관하지] 않고
Paying no attention, even if the situation is bad or there are difficulties.

shudder [ʃʌ́dər] vi. 떨다, 몸서리치다; n. 몸이 떨림, 전율, 몸서리
If you shudder, you shake with fear, horror, or cold.

corny [kɔ́:rni] a. 감상적인, 멜로드라마적인; 곡류의; 케케묵은, 진부한; 촌스러운
If you describe something as corny, you mean that it is obvious or sentimental and not at all original.

legitimate [lidʒítəmit] a. 합법적인, 정당한; 합리적인
For which there is a fair and acceptable reason.

crutch [krʌtʃ] n. 목발, 버팀목; 지나치게 의지하게 되는 사람[것]
A person or thing that gives you help or support but often makes you depend on them too much.

doubtfully [dáutfəli] ad. 불확실하게, 애매하게, 미심쩍게
(of a person) Not sure.

tick by phrasal v. (시간이) 째깍째깍 흘러가다
To pass, especially when you feel it is passing too quickly or too slowly.

toneless [tounlis] a. 음[음조·색조·억양]이 없는; 단조로운 (tonelessly ad. 단조롭게)
A toneless voice is dull and does not express any feeling.

rude [ru:d] a. 무례한, 버릇없는
Having or showing a lack of respect for other people and their feelings.

disconnect [dìskənékt] vt. (전화 등을) 끊다; …와의 연락을 끊다; …의 전원을 끊다
To break the contact between two people who are talking on the telephone.

trudge [trʌdʒ] v. 터벅터벅 걷다; n. 터덕터덕 걸음
To walk slowly with a lot of effort, especially over a difficult surface or while carrying something heavy.

Vocabulary in New Moon

fret [fret] v. 애타다, 안달하다; 속타게 하다, 초조하게 하다; n. 애달음, 초조
If you fret about something, you worry about it.

Campbell n. 캠벨(통조림 상표명)

bathtub [bǽθtʌ̀b] n. (서양식) 욕조
A long container which is filled with water so that a person can sit or lie in it to wash their whole body.

instruct [instrʌ́kt] vt. 가르치다, 지시[명령]하다
If you instruct someone to do something, you formally tell them to do it.

hoarse [hɔːrs] a. 목쉰, 쉰 목소리의 (hoarsely ad. 목쉰 소리로)
If your voice is hoarse, your voice sounds rough and unclear.

crumple [krʌ́mpl] v. 구기다, 구겨지다, 쭈글쭈글하게 하다
To crush something into folds; To become crushed into folds.

hydrate [háidreit] v. 수화(水和)시키대[하다], 수산화시키대[하다]
To make something absorb water.

clump [klʌmp] v. (발로) 쿵쾅거리다
To put your feet down noisily and heavily as you walk.

parched [pɑːrtʃt] a. 몹시 목마른; 몹시 건조한, 바싹 말라버린
Deprived of natural moisture; Very thirsty.

stagnant [stǽgnənt] a. 흐르지 않는, 고여 있는, 정체된; 불경기의, 부진한
Not flowing or moving, and smelling unpleasant.

saltine [sɔːltíːn] n. (윗부분에 소금을 뿌린) 짭짤한 크래커
A saltine is a thin square biscuit with salt baked into its surface.

sympathetic [sìmpəθétik] a. 동정심 있는, 인정 있는; 마음에 드는
(sympathetically ad. 동정하여, 호의적으로)
If you are sympathetic to someone who is in a bad situation, you are kind to them and show that you understand their feelings.

tangible [tǽndʒəbəl] a. 만져서 알 수 있는, 실체적인, 확실한, 명백한, 현실의
Real or not imaginary; Able to be shown, touched or experienced.

9. THIRD WHEEL

복습 urgency [ə́ːrdʒənsi] n. 긴급, 화급; 절박, 위급, 위기
The state of being urgent.

Comprehension Quiz

10. THE MEADOW

1. Why did Harry Clearwater go to the hospital?

   A. He had a stomach flu.

   B. He broke his leg.

   C. He got some heart tests done.

   D. He had a heart attack.

2. What did Bella realize when she reached the meadow?

   A. She saw someone following her.

   B. The meadow wasn't special without Edward.

   C. She was too tired to go home.

   D. She wished Jacob was with her.

3. Bella told Laurent that _____.

   A. the Cullens were hunting

   B. she saw Victoria

   C. the Cullens went to Denali

   D. the Cullens visited Forks often

10. THE MEADOW

4. Laurent said Victoria wouldn't be happy because _____.

   A. he was going to kill Bella himself

   B. he told Bella to leave Forks

   C. edward was hunting her

   D. the wolves would kill Victoria

5. What happened when Laurent saw the wolves?

   A. He attacked Bella.

   B. He attacked the wolves.

   C. He didn't move at all.

   D. He ran away from the wolves.

Vocabulary in New Moon

‡ invitation [ìnvətéiʃən] n. 초대
A written or spoken request to come to an event such as a party, a meal, or a meeting.

‡ chat [tʃæt] vi. 잡담하다, 수다 떨다
To talk to someone in a friendly informal way.

‡ pinch [pintʃ] vt. 쥐어짜다, 죄다; 꼬집다; 수척[쇠잔]하게 하다; 위축시키다
If you pinch a part of someone's body, you take a piece of their skin between your thumb and first finger and give it a short squeeze.

mono [mánou] n. (구어) (= MONONUCLEOSIS) [병리] 단핵(세포)증, (특히) 전염성 단핵증
A disease which causes swollen glands, fever, and a sore throat.

‡ symptom [símptəm] n. [의학] 증후(症候), 증상
A sign that something exists, especially something bad.

복습 exhaustion [igzɔ́:stʃən] n. 극도의 피로, 기진맥진
Extreme tiredness.

복습 suspicious [səspíʃəs] a. 의심하는, 의심 많은, 수상쩍은
If you are suspicious of someone or something, you do not trust them, and are careful when dealing with them.

복습 skim [skim] v. 스치듯 지나가다; 훑어보다; (돈을) 조금씩 훔치다[빼돌리다]; 걷어내다
(skim through : 대강 훑어보다)
To read something very quickly in order to get a general impression or to find a particular point.

복습 enforce [enfɔ́:rs] v. 집행[시행·실시]하다
To enforce something means to force or cause it to be done or to happen.

‡ infectious [infékʃəs] a. 전염하는, (영향이) 옮기 쉬운
The act or process of causing or getting a disease.

pushy [púʃi] a. (구어) 억지가 센, 뻔뻔한, 나서기 잘하는
Trying hard to get what you want, especially in a way that seems rude.

10. THE MEADOW

generous [dʒénərəs] a. 관대한, 아끼지 않는, 후한
A generous person is friendly, helpful, and willing to see the good qualities in someone or something.

adrenaline [ədrénəlin] n. 아드레날린
A substance which your body produces when you are angry, scared, or excited. It makes your heart beat faster and gives you more energy.

distraction [distrǽkʃən] n. 방심, 정신이 흐트러짐, 주의 산만
Something that turns your attention away from something you want to concentrate on.

repress [riprés] v. …을 억제하다, 참다, 억누르다
To restrain (an impulse, desire, etc).

creep [kriːp] vi. (crept-crept) 기다, 살금살금 걷다; n. 포복
When people or animals creep somewhere, they move quietly and slowly.

nothingness [nʌ́θiŋnis] n. 무(無), 공허; 존재하지 않음, 없음
Nothingness is the fact of not existing.

fern [fəːrn] n. [식물] 양치류(의 식물)
A plant with large delicate leaves and no flowers that grows in wet areas or is grown in a pot.

hunch [hʌntʃ] vt. (등을) 둥글게 구부리다
To bend down and forwards so that your back forms a curve.

expectation [èkspektéiʃən] n. 예상, 기대
A belief that something will happen because it is likely.

phony [fóuni] a. (구어) 가짜의, 엉터리의
Not real or true.

babble [bǽbəl] v. 실없이 지껄이다, 쓸데없는 말을 하다; n. 재잘거림, 왁자지껄
If someone babbles, they talk in a confused or excited way.

perforate [pə́ːrfərèit] v. (…에) 구멍을 뚫다[내다] (perforated a. 구멍이 난, 관통된)
To perforate something means to make a hole or holes in it.

Vocabulary in New Moon

desolate [désəlit] a. 황폐한, 황량한, 쓸쓸한
Unattractive and empty, with no people or nothing pleasant in it.

absentminded [ǽbsəntmaindid] a. 방심 상태의, 멍하고[얼빠져] 있는
(absentmindedly ad. 건성으로, 방심하여)
Someone who is absent-minded forgets things or does not pay attention to what they are doing, often because they are thinking about something else.

stack [stæk] n. 더미; 많음, 다량; v. 쌓다, 쌓아올리다
A stack of things is a pile of them.

indecision [ìndisíʒən] n. 우유부단, 주저
The state of being unable to decide.

mopey [móupi] a. 생기 없는, 나른한; 시무룩한
mope (vi. 맥이 빠져 지내다) + -y (suf. …하는 경향이 있는)

fib [fib] vi. 악의 없는 거짓말을 하다; n. 악의 없는 거짓말, 사소한 거짓말
To tell a lie, usually about something that is not important.

calculus [kǽlkjələs] n. 미적분학
Calculus is a branch of advanced mathematics which deals with variable quantities.

ranger [réindʒər] n. 공원[삼림·자연] 관리원[경비 대원]
A person whose job is to take care of a park, a forest or an area of countryside.

vaguely [véigli] ad. 모호하게, 막연히
In a way that is not detailed or exact.

charade [ʃəréid] n. 빤히 들여다보이는 수작[속임수]
A situation in which people pretend that something is true when it clearly is not.

ferocious [fəróuʃəs] a. 지독한, 사나운, 잔인한 (ferociously ad. 사납게, 지독하게)
Fierce and violent.

emergency [imə́:rdʒənsi] n. 비상사태, 비상시, 위급, 급변
An unexpected and serious happening which calls for immediate and determined action.

10. THE MEADOW

- **eliminate** [ilímənèit] vt. 제거하다
  To remove or get rid of something/somebody.

- **twinge** [twindʒ] n. 쑤시는 듯한 아픔; (마음의) 고통, (양심의) 가책
  A sudden short feeling of an unpleasant emotion.

- **momentary** [móuməntèri] a. 순식간의, 찰나의
  Something that is momentary lasts for a very short period of time.

- **dryness** [dráinis] n. 건조(한 상태); 무미건조; 냉담
  The condition of not containing or being covered by a liquid.

- **chirp** [tʃəːrp] v. (즐거운 듯이) 말하다; 짹짹 울다; n. 짹짹 (새 등의 울음소리)
  You say that a person chirps when they say something in a cheerful, high-pitched voice.

- **buzz** [bʌz] v. 윙윙거리다; 분주하게 돌아다니다; n. 윙윙대는 소리; (남성의) 스포츠 머리
  If something buzzes or buzzes somewhere, it makes a long continuous sound, like the noise a bee makes when it is flying.

- **noisy** [nɔ́izi] a. 떠들썩한, 시끄러운; 화려한, 요란한
  (noisily ad. 요란하게, 소란스레, 시끄럽게)
  A noisy person or thing makes a lot of loud or unpleasant noise.

- **occasional** [əkéiʒənəl] a. 이따금씩, 때때로의
  Happening or done sometimes but not often.

- **scurry** [skə́ːri] vi. 종종걸음으로 달리다, 급히 가다
  To move quickly, with small short steps.

- **shrub** [ʃrʌb] n. 키 작은 나무, 관목
  A small bush with several woody stems.

- **squish** [skwiʃ] v. 찌부러뜨리다, 으깨다
  To crush something.

- **exertion** [igzə́ːrʃən] n. 노력, 분발
  Physical or mental effort.

Vocabulary in New Moon

torso [tɔ́:rsou] n. 토르소(머리·손발이 없는 나체 조각상); (인체의) 몸통; (비유) 미완성 작품
The main part of the body, not including the head, arms or legs.

banish [bǽniʃ] vt. 추방하다, 내쫓다
To order somebody to leave a place, especially a country, as a punishment.

numb [nʌ́m] vt. 감각을 잃게 하다; 망연자실케 하다; a. 감각을 잃은; 멍한, 망연자실한
If an event or experience numbs you, you can no longer think clearly or feel any emotion.

bushwhack [búʃhwæ̀k] vi. (삼림 속을) 길을 내며 가다
To cut your way through bushes, plants, etc. in wild country.

efficient [ifíʃənt] a. 능률적인, 효과적인, 유능한 (efficiently ad. 능률적으로, 유효하게)
Working or operating quickly and effectively in an organized way.

abruptness [əbrʌ́ptnis] n. 갑작스러움, 돌연함
The quality of happening with headlong haste or without warning.

disorient [disɔ́:riənt] vt. 길을 잃게 하다, 방향[감각]을 상실하게 하다
To cause to lose orientation or direction.

vine [vain] n. 포도나무, 덩굴식물
A vine is a plant that grows up or over things, especially one which produces grapes.

symmetrical [simétrikəl] a. 대칭적인; (몸·전체 등이) 균형이 잡힌, 조화된
If something is symmetrical, it has two halves which are exactly the same, except that one half is the mirror image of the other.

intentional [inténʃənəl] a. 계획적인, 고의의, 일부러 (intentionally ad. 고의적으로)
Done deliberately.

flawless [flɔ́:lis] a. 흠없는; (작품·사고·인격·용모 등이) 완전한, 완벽한
Without flaws and therefore perfect.

bubble [bʌ́bəl] v. 거품이 일다; (말을) 신나게 하다; 차오르다; n. 환상, 망상; 거품
To make a bubbling sound, especially when moving in the direction mentioned.

10. THE MEADOW

stun [stʌn] vt. 어리벙벙하게 하다; 기절시키다; n. 놀라게 함
(stunning a. 아연하게 하는; 놀랄 만큼 멋진)
If you are stunned by something, you are extremely shocked or surprised by it and are therefore unable to speak or do anything.

sway [swei] v. 흔들(리)다, 동요하다; 설득하다; n. 동요, 지배
To move slowly from side to side.

ripple [rípəl] n. 잔물결, 파문; v. 잔물결이 일다; 잔물결을 일으키다
Ripples are little waves on the surface of water caused by the wind or by something moving in or on the water.

instantaneous [ìnstəntéiniəs] a. 즉시의, 순간의; 동시에 일어나는, 동시적인
Happening immediately.

recognition [rèkəgníʃən] n. 인지, 승인, 허가
The act of remembering who somebody is when you see them, or of identifying what something is.

sink down idiom 맥없이 주저앉다; 지다; 안 보이게 하다
If you sink down, you fall down or sit down heavily, especially because you are very tired and weak.

kneel [ni:l] vi. (knelt-knelt) 무릎 꿇다
To lower oneself onto one's knees.

gasp [gæsp] v. (놀람 따위로) 숨이 막히다, 헐떡거리다; n. 헐떡거림
When you gasp, you take a short quick breath through your mouth, especially when you are surprised, shocked, or in pain.

correspond [kɔ̀:rəspánd] v. 일치하다, 부합하다, 조화하다
If one thing corresponds to another, there is a close similarity or connection between them. You can also say that two things correspond.

swirl [swə:rl] vi. 소용돌이치다, 빙빙 돌다
If liquid or flowing swirls, it moves round and round quickly.

disguise [disgáiz] v. 위장하다, 숨기다; 변장하다; n. 변장(도구); 변장술
To disguise something means to hide it or make it appear different so that people will not know about it or will not recognize it.

Vocabulary in New Moon

- **abyss** [əbís] n. 심연, 깊은 구렁
  A very deep wide space or hole that seems to have no bottom.

- **plunge** [plʌndʒ] v. 추락하다; 뛰어들다, 돌진하다; 던져 넣다; n. 돌진
  To fall suddenly and often a long way forward, down or into something.

- **fracture** [fræktʃər] vt. (뼈를) 부러뜨리다; 베다, 부수다, 깨다; n. 골절; 부러짐, 파손
  To break or crack; To make something break or crack.

- **satisfaction** [sæ̀tisfǽkʃən] n. 만족, 만족감
  A pleasant feeling which you get when you do something or get something that you wanted to do.

- **wrench** [rentʃ] vt. (갑자기·세게) 비틀다, 비틀어 돌리다; n. 렌치(너트를 죄는 기구)
  To make somebody feel great pain or unhappiness, especially so that they make a sound or cry.

- **precisely** [prisáisli] ad. 정밀하게, 정확히, 정확하게
  Exactly.

- **stillness** [stílnis] n. 고요; 평온, 침묵; 부동, 정지
  The quality of being quiet and not moving.

- **pallid** [pǽlid] a. (안색이) 창백한, 해쓱한, 핏기가 가신
  Pale, especially unhealthily so.

- **suppress** [səprés] vt. 억압하다, 참다, (사실을) 감추다
  To prevent something from being seen or expressed or from operating.

- **vicious** [víʃəs] a. 나쁜, 악덕의, 잔인한 (viciously ad. 잔인하게)
  A vicious person or a vicious blow is violent and cruel.

- **equally** [í:kwəli] ad. 똑같이, 균등하게, 동등하게
  To the same degree or level, or into amounts or parts that are the same.

- **lash** [læʃ] n. 채찍질; 채찍 끈; 속눈썹; v. 부딪히다; 후려치다
  A hit with a whip, given as a form of punishment.

- **grieve** [gri:v] v. 몹시 슬퍼하다, 슬프게 하다
  To feel or express great sadness.

10. THE MEADOW

stray [strei] a. 길 잃은, 벗어난; vi. 길을 잃다; (옳은 길에서) 빗나가다
Stray things have moved apart from similar things and are not in their expected or intended place.

irrational [irǽʃənəl] a. 이성을 잃은, 분별이 없는, 불합리한
Not based on, or not using, clear logical thought.

coven [kʌ́vən] n. 집회, 모임
A group or meeting of witches.

quarry [kwɔ́:ri] n. 사냥감(사냥·추적의 대상이 되는 동물·사람)
A person's or animal's quarry is the person or animal that they are hunting.

compunction [kəmpʌ́ŋkʃən] n. 양심의 가책, 죄책감, 거리낌
If you say that someone has no compunction about doing something, you mean that they do it without feeling ashamed or guilty.

overwhelm [òuvərhwélm] vt. 압도하다, 제압하다; 질리게 하다
If you are overwhelmed by a feeling or event, it affects you very strongly, and you do not know how to deal with it.

seek [si:k] v. (sought-sought) 찾다, 추구하다, 얻으려 하다
To try to find or get something, especially something which is not a physical object.

astonish [əstániʃ] vt. 깜짝 놀라게 하다
To surprise someone very much.

elate [iléit] vt. 기운을 돋우다, 의기양양하게 하다
Extremely happy and excited, often because something has happened or been achieved.

stroll [stroul] vi. 한가롭게 거닐다, 산책하다; n. 산책
If you stroll somewhere, you walk there in a slow, relaxed way.

bemuse [bimjú:z] vt. 멍하게 만들다, 어리벙벙하게 하다 (**bemused** a. 멍한, 어리벙벙한)
If something bemuses you, it puzzles or confuses you.

cock [kɑk] v. 위로 치올리다, (귀·꽁지)를 쫑긋 세우다
To move a part of your body upwards or in a particular direction.

Vocabulary in New Moon

eternity [itə́ːrnəti] n. 영원, 무궁; 불사, 불멸; 영원성
Eternity is time without an end or a state of existence outside time, especially the state which some people believe they will pass into after they have died.

greedy [gríːdi] a. 탐욕스러운; 열망하는
Wanting a lot more food, money, etc. than you need.

raw [rɔː] a. 생것의, 날것의, 가공하지 않은
Not cooked.

offense [əféns] n. 위반, 반칙, 죄; 법률 위반
An illegal act crime.

wry [rai] a. 찡그린, 뒤틀린; 삐딱한, 빈정대는 (wryly ad. 빈정대며, 뒤틀려)
Showing that you find a bad or difficult situation slightly amusing.

involuntary [inváləntèri] a. 무심결의, 무의식적인; 본의 아닌
Not done by choice; Done unwillingly, or without the decision or intention of the person involved.

kitten [kitn] n. 새끼 고양이; (작은 동물의) 새끼
A kitten is a very young cat.

deliberate [dilíbərèit] v. 숙고하다; 심의하다; a. 신중한; 계획적인
To think very carefully about something, usually before making a decision.

bluff [blʌf] n. 허세, 엄포, 속임수; v. 허세부리다
An attempt to trick somebody by making them believe that you will do something when you really have no intention of doing it.

temper [témpər] n. 기질, 성질; 화, 노여움
If you refer to someone's temper, you mean that they become angry very easily.

dismissive [dismísiv] a. 거부하는 듯한, 무시하는 (dismissively ad. 거부하듯이)
Showing that you do not believe a person or thing to be important or worth considering.

10. THE MEADOW

hysteria [histíəriə] n. [병리] 히스테리; (개인이나 집단의) 병적 흥분, 광란
Extreme fear, excitement, anger, etc. which cannot be controlled.

betray [bitréi] vt. 배반하다; (남편·아내·여자 등을) 속이다
To hurt somebody who trusts you, especially by not being loyal or faithful to them.

muse [mju:z] vi. 묵상하다, 곰곰이 생각하다
To think about something carefully and for a long time.

novelty [návəlti] n. 새로움, 신기함, 참신함, 진기함
The quality of being new, different and interesting.

restriction [ristríkʃən] n. 제한[제약]하는 것, 제약, 규정
The act of limiting or controlling somebody/something.

conspiratorial [kənspìrətɔ́:riəl] a. 공모의, 음모의
(conspiratorially ad. 음모가 있는 것처럼)
Relating to a secret plan to do something bad, illegal or against someone's wishes.

swallow [swálou] vt. 들이켜다, 삼키다, 꿀꺽 삼키다; 마른침을 삼키다
If you swallow something, you cause it to go from your mouth down into your stomach.

flicker [flíkər] v. (등불·희망·빛 등이) 깜박이다; n. 깜박임; (어떤 감정이 잠깐) 스침
If a light or flame flickers, it shines unsteadily.

instruct [instrʌ́kt] vt. 지시[명령]하다, 가르치다
If you instruct someone to do something, you formally tell them to do it.

instinct [ínstiŋkt] n. 본능, 직관, 천성
The way people or animals naturally react or behave, without having to think or learn about it.

uncontrollable [ʌ̀nkəntróuləbəl] a. 통제할 수 없는, 걷잡을 수 없는
Too strong or violent to be controlled.

Vocabulary in New Moon

desperate [déspərit] a. 필사적인; 절망적인, 자포자기의
If you are desperate for something or desperate to do something, you want or need it very much indeed.

diversion [divə́:rʒən] n. 전환, 딴 데로 돌림
The act of diverting; The state of being diverted.

furtive [fə́:rtiv] a. 몰래 하는, 내밀한, 은밀한
Behaving in a way that shows that you want to keep something secret and do not want to be noticed.

seductive [sidʌ́ktiv] a. 유혹하는, 매혹적인, 매력적인
Sexually attractive.

purr [pə:r] n. 목구멍을 울림[울리는 소리]; v. (차 엔진이) 낮은 소리를 내다; 낮고 부드럽게 말하다
To make a quiet, continuous, vibration sound.

frantic [fræntik] a. 광란의, 미친 듯 날뛰는
Behaving in a wild and uncontrolled way.

blithe [blaið] a. 즐거운, 유쾌한, 쾌활한; 경솔한, 부주의한 (blithely ad. 쾌활하게, 즐겁게)
Happy and without worry.

squeak [skwi:k] v. (그렇게 크지 않게) 끽[찍] 하는 소리를 내다
If something or someone squeaks, they make a short, high-pitched sound.

tear [tɛər] ① v. (tore-torn) 찢다, 찢어지다 ② n. 눈물
To damage something by pulling it hard or letting it touch something sharp.

serrate [sérət] a. 톱(니) 모양의, 톱니가 있는, 깔쭉깔쭉한
Notched like a saw with teeth pointing toward the apex.

oblivious [əblíviəs] a. (…이) 염두[안중]에 없는; 잘 잊어버리는, 건망증이 있는
Unaware or forgetful of it.

appropriate [əpróuprièit] a. 적절한, 알맞은
Something that is appropriate is suitable or acceptable for a particular situation.

10. THE MEADOW

flawed [flɔːd] a. 결함[결점·흠]이 있는
Something that is flawed has a mark, fault, or mistake in it.

revenge [rivéndʒ] n. 복수, 보복, 원한; vt. 복수하다, 원수를 갚다
Something that you do in order to make somebody suffer because they have made you suffer.

unprotected [ʌ̀nprətéktid] a. 보호받지 못하는, 무방비의
An unprotected person or place is not looked after or defended, and so they may be harmed or attacked.

mischievous [místʃivəs] a. 장난이 심한, 개구쟁이의; 유해한
Enjoying playing tricks and annoying people.

rearrange [rìːəréindʒ] vt. 재배열하다, 재정리하다
If you rearrange things, you change the way in which they are organized or ordered.

mouthwatering [máuθiwɔ́ːtəriŋ] a. 군침이 도는, 맛있어 보이는
입(mouth)에 침(water)이 나올 만큼(ing) 맛있어 보이는.

approval [əprúːvəl] n. 찬성, 동의, 승인
When someone likes something or someone and thinks that they are good.

compliment [kάmpləmənt] n. 찬사, 칭찬의 말; v. 경의를 표하다, 칭찬하다
A compliment is a polite remark that you say to someone to show that you like their appearance, appreciate their qualities, or approve of what they have done.

distort [distɔ́ːrt] vt. 비틀다, 뒤틀다; 왜곡[곡해]하다; (얼굴 등을) 찡그리다, 찌푸리다
If something you can see or hear is distorted or distorts, its appearance or sound is changed so that it seems unclear.

dread [dred] n. 두려움, 두려운 것, 공포; a. 대단히 무서운; v. 두려워하다
A feeling of great fear about something that might or will happen in the future; A thing that causes this feeling.

obediently [oubíːdiəntli] ad. 고분고분하게, 정중하게
Doing, or willing to do, what you have been told to do by someone in authority.

Vocabulary in New Moon

- **scent** [sent] n. 냄새, 향기; v. 냄새 맡다; 냄새를 풍기다
  The scent of something is the pleasant smell that it has.

- **investigate** [invéstəgèit] v. 조사하다, 연구하다, 심사하다
  To examine a crime, problem, statement, etc. carefully, especially to discover the truth.

- **falter** [fɔ́:ltər] vi. 비틀거리다, 말을 더듬다; 머뭇거리다, 움찔[멈칫]하다
  To become weaker or less effective.

- **lithe** [laið] a. 잘 휘는; 나긋나긋한, 유연한
  (of a person or their body) Moving or bending easily, in a way that is elegant.

- **placate** [pléikeit] vt. (화·감정을) 진정시키다, 달래다
  To make somebody feel less angry about something.

- **sniff** [snif] v. 코를 킁킁거리다, 냄새를 맡다; 콧방귀를 뀌다; n. 냄새 맡음; 콧방귀
  To smell something by taking air in through your nose.

- **squint** [skwint] v. 곁눈질을 하다, 실눈으로 보다; a. 사시의; 곁눈질하는
  If you squint at something, you look at it with your eyes partly closed.

- **furious** [fjúəriəs] a. 성난, 격노한; 맹렬한, 왕성한
  Someone who is furious is extremely angry.

- **overpower** [òuvərpáuər] vt. 압도하다, 억누르다, 제압하다
  To defeat or gain control over somebody completely by using greater strength.

- **scan** [skæn] v. 유심히 쳐다보다; 자세히 조사하다; 대충 훑어 보다; n. 정밀 검사; 스캔
  To look at something carefully, with the eyes, in order to obtain information.

- **retreat** [ri:trí:t] vi. 물러가다, 퇴각하다
  To move away from someone or something.

- **stalk** [stɔ:k] v. (화가 난 듯이) 성큼성큼 걷다; (적·먹이 등에) 몰래 접근하다
  If you stalk somewhere, you walk there in a stiff, proud, or angry way.

10. THE MEADOW

- **enormous** [inɔ́:rməs] a. 거대한, 막대한, 엄청난
  Something that is enormous is extremely large in size or amount.

- **muscular** [mʌ́skjələr] a. 근육의, 근육이 늠름한, 억센
  Connected with the muscles.

- **muzzle** [mʌ́zəl] n. (동물의) 주둥이, 부리(입·코 부분)
  The nose and mouth of an animal, especially a dog or a horse.

- **dagger** [dǽgər] n. 단도, 단검; vt. 단도로 찌르다, …에 칼표를 하다
  A dagger is a weapon like a knife with two sharp edges.

- **incisor** [insáizər] n. 앞니
  One of the eight sharp teeth at the front of the mouth that are used for biting.

- **grisly** [grizli] a. 섬뜩한, 소름끼치는
  Extremely unpleasant, especially because death or blood is involved.

- **gigantic** [dʒaigǽntik] a. 거대한, 막대한
  If you describe something as gigantic, you are emphasizing that it is extremely large in size, amount, or degree.

- **pad** [pæd] v. 조용히 걷다; 패드[보호대]를 대다; n. 패드; 편지지 등의 묶음
  When someone pads somewhere, they walk there with steps that are fairly quick, light, and quiet.

- **boggle** [bágəl] v. 상상할 수 없어 받아들이지 못하다, 믿어지지 않다
  If your mind boggles when you think of something, it is difficult for you to imagine or accept it.

- **distinct** [distíŋkt] a. 별개의, 다른; 뚜렷한, 명백한
  (distinctly ad. 뚜렷[명백]하게; 의심할 나위 없이; 정말로)
  Clearly separate and different from something else.

- **canine** [kéinain] a. 개의, 개 같은
  Canine means relating to dogs.

- **confusion** [kənfjú:ʒən] n. 혼동, 혼란, 뒤죽박죽
  A situation, often with a lot of activity and noise, in which people do not know what to do.

Vocabulary in New Moon

* **mammoth** [mǽməθ] a. 거대한(huge); n. [동물] 매머드
Extremely large.

* **flank** [flæŋk] v. …의 측면에 서다; 측면을 지키다[공격하다]; n. 옆구리; 측면
To be placed on one or both sides of something.

* **prowl** [praul] vi. 어슬렁거리다, 배회하다
To move quietly and carefully around an area, especially when hunting.

geese [giːs] n. gooes(거위)의 복수
Geese is the plural of goose.

* **rusty** [rʌ́sti] a. 녹슨
Covered with rust.

crush [krʌʃ] v. 부서지다; 짓밟다; 잔뜩 구겨지다[구기다]; n. 눌러 터뜨림
To crush something means to press it very hard so that its shape is destroyed or so that it breaks into pieces.

* **reddish** [rédiʃ] a. 불그스름한, 붉은색을 띤
Fairly red in color.

* **fraction** [frǽkʃən] n. 조금, 소량; 파편, 단편; [수학] 분수
(a fraction of a second : 아주 잠깐)
A fraction of something is a tiny amount or proportion of it.

gratitude [grǽtətjùːd] n. 감사, 고마움
Gratitude is the state of feeling grateful.

fairytale [féəritèil] a. 동화 같은; 믿을 수 없을 정도로 아름다운
Typical of something in a fairy tale.

russet [rʌ́sət] a. 적[황]갈색의, 팥빛의
Russet is used to describe things that are reddish-brown in color.

unconcealed [ənkənsíːld] a. (감정 등이) 숨김없는, 노골적인
An unconcealed emotion is one that someone has made no attempt to hide.

10. THE MEADOW

instinctive [instíŋktiv] a. 본능적인, 직관적인; 무의식적인 (instinctively ad. 본능적으로)
Instinctive behavior or reactions are not thought about, planned or developed by training.

swiftness [swíftnis] n. 신속, 빠름
The state of being swift.

buckle [bʌ́kəl] vi. 구부러지다, 휘어지다; 버클로 잠그다; n. 버클, 잠금장치
To become crushed or bent under a weight or force; To crush or bend something in this way.

chase [tʃeis] v. 쫓아내다, 뒤쫓다; 추구하다; n. 추적, 추격
If you chase someone, or chase after them, you run after them or follow them quickly in order to catch or reach them.

overgrown [òuvərgróun] a. 너무 커진; (풀·잡초 등이) 마구[제멋대로] 자란
That has grown too large.

granite [grǽnit] n. 화강암; 견고함
Granite is a very hard rock used in building.

extraordinary [ikstrɔ́:rdənèri] a. 보통이 아닌, 비범한, 대단한, 비상한
Unexpected, surprising or strange.

pursue [pərsú:] v. 쫓다, 추적하다; 추구하다
To follow or chase somebody or something, especially in order to catch them.

scramble [skrǽmbəl] vt. 간신히 해내다; 기어오르다; 서로(다투어) 빼앗다; n. 기어오르기
If you scramble to a place or position, you move there in a hurried, awkward way.

headlong [hédlɔ̀:ŋ] ad. 앞뒤 살피지 않고, 황급히; 허둥지둥
If you rush headlong into something, you do it quickly without thinking carefully about it.

menacing [ménəsiŋ] a. 위협적인, 으르는
If someone or something looks menacing, they give you a feeling that they are likely to cause you harm or put you in danger.

203

Vocabulary in New Moon

violent [váiələnt] a. 격렬한, 맹렬한 (violently ad. 격렬하게)
Involving or caused by physical force that is intended to hurt or kill someone.

muddy [mʌ́di] a. 진창의, 진흙의, 질퍽한; 진흙투성이의
Something that is muddy contains mud or is covered in mud.

squelch [skweltʃ] v. 찌부러뜨리다[지다]; n. 철벅철벅함[하는 소리]; 찌부러뜨림, 진압
To make a sucking sound like the one produced when you are walking on soft wet ground.

jaybird [dʒeibəːrd] n. (= jay) 어치(까마귓과의 새)
In Europe and Asia, a jay is a brownish-pink bird with blue and black wings.

spruce [spruːs] n. 가문비나무속(屬)의 식물(갯솔·전나무 등)
A kind of evergreen tree.

tangle [tǽŋgəl] v. 얽히게 하다; 엉키다; n. 엉킴; 혼란
If something is tangled or tangles, it becomes twisted together in an untidy way.

sap [sæp] n. 수액(樹液), (식물의) 액즙(液汁)
The liquid in a plant or tree that carries food to all its parts.

squirrel [skwə́ːrəl] n. 다람쥐
A small furry animal with a long furry tail which climbs trees and feeds on nuts and seeds.

hemlock [hémlɑk] n. [식물] 북미 서부산 미송(美松)
A poisonous plant with a mass of small white flowers growing at the end of a stem that is covered in spots.

exhaust [igzɔ́ːst] vt. 다 써버리다, 소진시키다 (exhausted a. 지칠 대로 지친)
If something exhausts you, it makes you so tired, either physically or mentally, that you have no energy left.

jog [dʒɑg] v. 천천히 달리다, 조깅하다; n. 조깅
To run slowly and steadily.

10. THE MEADOW

- **sob** [sɑb] vi. 흐느껴 울다
  To cry noisily, taking in deep breaths.

- **fiercely** [fíərsli] ad. 맹렬히, 지독히
  Extremely.

- **hasty** [héisti] a. 급한, 신속한 (hastily ad. 급히, 서둘러서)
  Hurried; Without enough thought or preparation.

- **ominous** [ámənəs] a. 불길한, 나쁜 징조의
  If you describe something as ominous, you mean that it worries you because it makes you think that something unpleasant is going to happen.

- **flora** [flɔ́:rə] n. (특정 장소·시대·환경의) 식물군(群)[상(相)]
  The plants of a particular area, type of environment or period of time.

  fauna [fɔ́:nə] n. 동물군(群)[상(相)], (분포상의) 동물 구계(區系); 동물지(誌)
  All the animals living in an area or in a particular period of history.

  bob [bɑb] v. 위아래로 움직이다[흔들리다]
  To move up and down repeatedly.

- **fervent** [fə́:rvənt] a. 열렬한, 강렬한, (감정 따위가) 격한; 뜨거운 (fervently ad. 열렬하게)
  Having or showing very strong and sincere feelings about something.

  fudge [fʌdʒ] vt. 날조하다, 지어내다; 조작하다; 속이다
  To avoid giving clear and accurate information, or a clear answer.

- **starve** [stɑ:rv] v. 굶주리다, 굶어죽다, 갈망하다
  To suffer or die because you do not have enough food to eat.

- **imply** [implái] vt. 함축하다, 암시하다; 의미하다
  To suggest or express something indirectly; To hint at it.

- **confront** [kənfrʌ́nt] vt. 직면하다, 마주 대하다; 대조하다
  To face, meet or deal with a difficult situation or person.

- **ditch** [ditʃ] vt. (사람을) 따돌리다; (관계를) 끊다; (물건을) 버리다; (일·책임 등에서) 도망치다
  If someone ditches someone, they end a relationship with that person.

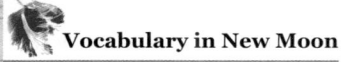

Vocabulary in New Moon

stymie [stáimi] vt. (계획 등을) 방해하다[좌절시키다]
If you are stymied by something, you find it very difficult to take action or to continue what you are doing.

opposable [əpóuzəbəl] a. 마주볼 수 있는; 적대할 수 있는
Apposable (of the thumb of primates, esp man) capable of being moved into a position facing the other digits so as to be able to touch the ends of each.

★ **cramp** [kræmp] vt. 속박하다, 제한하다, 가두다; n. 꺾쇠, 죔쇠
(cramped a. 비좁은, 갑갑한)
To limit someone, especially to prevent them from enjoying a full life.

복습 **quilt** [kwilt] n. (솜·털·깃털 따위를 둔) 누비이불; 누비 침대 커버
A thin cover filled with feathers or some other warm, soft material, which you put over your blankets when you are in bed.

복습 **horrify** [hɔ́:rəfài] vt. 소름끼치게 하다, 충격을 주다 (horrifying a. 몸서리치는, 소름끼치는)
If someone is horrified, they feel shocked or disgusted, because of something that they have seen or heard.

복습 **precaution** [prikɔ́:ʃən] n. 조심, 경계; 예방책
Something that is done in advance in order to prevent problems or to avoid danger.

nauseous [nɔ́:ʃəs] a. 욕지기나는, 메스꺼운
Feeling as if you want to vomit.

hairsbreadth [hɛ́ərzbrèdθ] n. 털끝만한 틈[폭·간격·거리]
A very small amount or distance.

tremor [trémər] n. 전율, 떨림; 겁; 떨리는 목소리; 진동
A slight shaking movement in a person's body, especially because of nervousness or excitement.

복습 **chatter** [tʃǽtər] v. (춥거나 공포로) 이가 맞부딪치다; 수다스레 재잘거리다
If your teeth chatter, they keep knocking together because you are very cold or very nervous.

10. THE MEADOW

fantasize [fǽntəsàiz] v. 꿈에 그리다, 공상하다
If you fantasize about an event or situation that you would like to happen, you give yourself pleasure by imagining that it is happening, although it is untrue or unlikely to happen.

massacre [mǽsəkər] vt. 학살하다, 짓밟다, (구어) 압승하다, 완패시키다
To kill a large number of people especially in a cruel way.

indestructible [ìndistrʌ́ktəbəl] a. 파괴할 수 없는, 불멸의
Not able to be destroyed.

immortal [imɔ́:rtl] a. 불사의, 불멸의, 영원한; n. 영생하는 존재; 불멸의 인물
Living or continuing for ever.

absurdity [əbsə́:rdəti] n. 부조리, 불합리, 모순; 어리석은 일[것]
The quality of being absurd or inconsistent with obvious truth, reason, or sound judgment.

unconsciousness [ʌnkʌ́nʃəsnis] n. 의식 불명[인사불성] (상태)
A state like sleep caused by injury or illness, when you are unable to use your senses.

lid [lid] n. 눈꺼풀(eyelid); 뚜껑
Your lids are the pieces of skin which cover your eyes when you close them.

thirst [θə:rst] n. 갈증, 갈망, 목마름
A strong desire for something.

anticipation [æntìsəpéiʃən] n. 예상, 기대, 희망
A feeling of excitement about something that is going to happen.

chaotically [keiátikəli] ad. 대혼란으로, 무질서하게
In a chaotic manner.

Comprehension Quiz

 11. CULT

1. At first, how did Charlie respond when Bella told him about Sam Uley?

   A. He promised he would tell Billy about the problem.

   B. He said Sam was a great person and was not a problem.

   C. He said he would go to La Push and find out more about Sam.

   D. He said he would talk to Jacob about Sam.

2. Why was Quil on the side of the road?

   A. He was looking for wolves.

   B. He was hiking in the woods.

   C. He was looking for Jacob and Embry.

   D. He was looking for Sam Uley.

3. What disturbed Bella the most when she saw Jacob?

   A. His short hair

   B. His large body

   C. The veins in his hands

   D. The expression on his face

11. CULT

4. Who did Jacob blame for his situation and they way he was acting?

A. Bella

B. The Cullens

C. Sam

D. His father

5. What did Jacob tell Bella?

A. Bella wasn't good enough to be his friend.

B. Sam ordered him not to be her friend.

C. He wasn't good enough to be her friend.

D. He didn't want to be around Bella if she wouldn't be his girlfriend.

Vocabulary in New Moon

- **ascertain** [æ̀sərtéin] vt. 알아내다, 확인하다
 If you ascertain the truth about something, you find out what it is, especially by making a deliberate effort to do so.

- **yearn** [jəːrn] vi. 그리워하다, 갈망하다
 To feel a great desire for it; To long for it.

- **infectious** [infékʃəs] a. 전염하는, (영향이) 옮기 쉬운
 If a feeling is infectious, it spreads to other people.

- **sanity** [sǽnəti] n. 제정신, 정신이 멀쩡함, 건전함, 온건함, (육체적인) 건강
 The state of having a normal healthy mind.

- **lethal** [líːθəl] a. 파괴적인, 치명적인
 Causing or able to cause death.

- **endanger** [endéindʒər] vt. 위험에 빠뜨리다, 위태롭게 하다
 To put somebody/something in a situation in which they could be harmed or damaged.

- **puncture** [pʌ́ŋktʃər] n. 구멍[상처]; 펑크 v. (바늘 따위로) 찌르다, 펑크 나다
 A puncture is a small hole in someone's skin that has been made by or with a sharp object.

- **nuisance** [njúːsəns] n. 방해물, 폐, 성가신 것
 Something or someone that annoys you or causes trouble for you.

- **subconscious** [sʌbkánʃəs] n., a. 잠재의식(의), 어렴풋이 의식(하는)
 The mental processes that go on below the level of conscious awareness.

- **verdict** [və́ːrdikt] n. 판단, 의견, 결정
 An opinion or decision made after judging the facts that are given, especially one made at the end of a trial.

- **revenge** [rivéndʒ] n. 복수, 보복, 원한; vt. 복수하다, 원수를 갚다
 Something that you do in order to make somebody suffer because they have made you suffer.

11. CULT

* **obsess** [əbsés] vt. (어떤 생각이 마음을) 사로잡다, …생각만 하게[집착하게] 하다
  If something obsesses you or if you obsess about something, you keep thinking about it and find it difficult to think about anything else.

  mutant [mjú:tənt] a. [생물] 변화한, 돌연변이의
  A mutant is an animal or plant that is physically different from others of the same species because of a change in its genes.

* **ragged** [rǽgid] a. 누더기가 된, 다 해진; 찢어진
  Someone who is ragged looks untidy and is wearing clothes that are old and torn.

  embarrassing [imbǽrəsiŋ] a. 쩔쩔매게[당황하게] 하는; 난처한, 곤란한
  (embarrassingly ad. 난처하게, 곤란하게)
  Making you feel shy, awkward or ashamed.

* **vague** [veig] a. 어렴풋한, 막연한
  Not clearly expressed, known, described or decided.

* **reservation** [rèzərvéiʃən] n. (미) (인디언을 위한) 정부 지정 보류지
  A reservation is an area of land that is kept separate for a particular group of people to live in.

  reach out phrasal v. …을 잡으려고 손을 내밀다[뻗다]
  To stretch your arm or your hand in order to touch or get something.

* **compulsory** [kəmpʌ́lsəri] a. 강제적인, 강제하는
  If something is compulsory, you must do it or accept it, because it is the law or because someone in a position of authority says you must.

* **priority** [praió(:)rəti] n. 우선, 보다 중요함, 우위, 상위
  Something that you think is more important than other things and should be dealt with first.

* **seclude** [siklú:d] v. (다른 사람들로부터) 은둔하다, 고립시키다 (secluded a. 한적한, 외딴)
  To keep yourself or somebody away from contact with other people.

* **rescue** [réskju:] n. 구출[구조] 작업, 구원; vt. 구조하다, 구출하다
  Rescue is help which gets someone out of a dangerous or unpleasant situation.

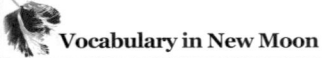
Vocabulary in New Moon

kidnap [kídnæp] vt. (어린이)를 유괴하다, 꾀어내다; (사람)을 납치하다
To take somebody away illegally and keep them as a prisoner, especially in order to get money or something else for returning them.

PBS n. 미국 공영 방송망(the Public Broadcasting Service)

deprogram [dì:próugræm] vt. 신념[신앙]을 버리게 하다
To free from the influence of a religious cult or political indoctrination.

brainwash [bréinwàʃ] v. 세뇌시키다
If you brainwash someone, you force them to believe something by continually telling them that it is true, and preventing them from thinking about it properly.

doomsday [dú:mzdèi] n. 최후의 심판일, 세상의 마지막 날
Doomsday is a day or time when you expect something terrible or unpleasant is going to happen.

★ **assumption** [əsʌ́mpʃən] n. (증거도 없이) 사실이라고 생각함; 가정, 가설
A belief or feeling that something is true or that something will happen, although there is no proof.

★ **weird** [wiərd] a. 기묘한, 이상한, 수상한
Very strange and unusual, unexpected or not natural.

bizarre [bizá:r] a. 기괴한, 이상야릇한
Something that is bizarre is very odd and strange.

reference [réfərəns] n. 참조, 문의, 언급, 관련
A thing you say or write that mentions somebody or something else; The act of mentioning it(them).

have a lot on one's plate idiom 해야 할 일이 산더미처럼 있다
To have something, usually a large amount of important work, to deal with.

crescent [krésənt] n. 초승달, 초승달 모양(의 것); a. 초승달 모양의
A curved shape that is wide in the middle and pointed at each end.

11. CULT

- **momentarily** [mòumənté́rəli] ad. 잠시, 잠깐
  Momentarily means for a short time.

- **stun** [stʌn] vt. 어리벙벙하게 하다; 기절시키다; n. 놀라게 함
  If you are stunned by something, you are extremely shocked or surprised by it and are therefore unable to speak or do anything.

- **confrontation** [kànfrəntéiʃən] n. 대면, 직면, 대립
  A conflict, fight, or battle between two groups of people.

- **outrun** [áutrʌ́n] vt. 달려서 이기다[앞서다]; …로부터 달아나다
  To move faster or further than someone or something.

- **curt** [kəːrt] a. 무뚝뚝한, 퉁명스런, 간략하게 (curtly ad. 퉁명스럽게)
  If speech is curt, it is rude as a result of being very brief.

- **frustrate** [frʌ́streit] vt. 좌절시키다, 실망시키다
  Feeling annoyed, upset, and impatient, because you cannot achieve something.

- **urgent** [ə́ːrdʒənt] a. 긴급한, 절박한
  If something is urgent, it needs to be dealt with as soon as possible.

- **mutter** [mʌ́tər] v. 중얼거리다, 불평하다; n. 중얼거림, 불평
  If you mutter, you speak very quietly so that you cannot easily be heard, often because you are complaining about something.

- **preoccupy** [priːɑ́kjəpài] vt. 먼저 점유하다; 선취하다; 마음을 빼앗다
  (preoccupied a. 어떤 생각이나 걱정에 사로잡힌[정신이 팔린])
  pre (pre. 먼저) + occupy (v. 점유하다)

- **Quileute** n. 퀼렛 부족
  현존하는 인디언게 퀴요 부족에서 따옴.

- **experimental** [ikspèrəméntl] a. 실험적인; 실험의, 실험에 의한
  Something that is experimental is new or uses new ideas or methods, and might be modified later if it is unsuccessful.

Vocabulary in New Moon

hormone [hɔ́ːrmoun] n. [생화학] 호르몬
A chemical substance produced in the body or in a plant that encourages growth or influences how the cells and tissues function.

※복습 **brooding** [brúːdiŋ] a. 음울한, 생각에 잠긴, 시무룩한
Sad and mysterious or threatening.

※복습 **dull** [dʌl] a. 활기 없는, 둔한; 흐릿한; 따분한, 재미없는 (dully ad. 활기 없이, 둔하게)
Not very lively or energetic.

morose [məróus] a. 까다로운, 기분이 언짢은; 침울한 (morosely ad. 언짢게, 까다롭게)
Unhappy, annoyed and unwilling to speak or smile.

※복습 **mumble** [mʌ́mbəl] v. 중얼거리다, 웅얼거리다; n. 중얼거림
If you mumble, you speak very quietly and not at all clearly with the result that the words are difficult to understand.

※복습 **shuffle** [ʃʌ́fl] v. 질질 끌다, 발을 끌며 걷다; 카드를 뒤섞다; n. 발을 끌며 걷기; 뒤섞기
If you shuffle somewhere, you walk there without lifting your feet properly off the ground.

※복습 **windshield** [wíndʃiːld] n. (자동차 등의) 앞 유리
The windshield of a car or other vehicle is the glass window at the front through which the driver looks.

✱ **crew** [kruː] n. 동료, 패거리; 승무원, 선원
A group of people who work together.

※복습 **yell** [jel] v. 소리치다, 고함치다; n. 고함, 부르짖음
If you yell, you shout loudly, usually because you are excited, angry, or in pain.

※복습 **distort** [distɔ́ːrt] vt. 비틀다, 뒤틀다; 왜곡[곡해]하다; (얼굴 등을) 찡그리다, 찌푸리다
If something you can see or hear is distorted or distorts, its appearance or sound is changed so that it seems unclear.

※복습 **grit** [grit] v. 삐걱거리다, 쓿리다 (grit the teeth : 이를 갈다); n. 잔모래
If you grit your teeth, you press your top and bottom teeth together, often in anger.

11. CULT

spit [spit] v. 뱉다, 토해내다, 뿜어내다
To force out the contents of the mouth, especially saliva.

prolonged [prəlɔ́:ŋd] a. 오래 계속되는, 장기적인
A prolonged event or situation continues for a long time, or for longer than expected.

crawl [krɔ:l] vi. 기어가다, 느릿느릿 가다; n. 기어감; 서행
When you crawl, you move forward on your hands and knees.

rectangle [réktæ̀ŋgəl] n. 직사각형
A rectangle is a four-sided shape whose corners are all ninety degree angles. Each side of a rectangle is the same length as the one opposite to it.

slump [slʌmp] v. 쿵 떨어지다; 털썩 앉다; n. (활동·원기의) 슬럼프; 쿵 떨어짐
To fall or lean against something because you are not strong enough to stand.

haunt [hɔ:nt] v. (유령이) 출몰하다; 늘 따라다니다; 자주 가다; n. 자주 가는[나타나는] 곳, 서식지
If something unpleasant haunts you, it keeps coming to your mind so that you cannot forget it.

stuffy [stʌ́fi] a. 통풍(通風)이 잘 안 되는, 숨 막히는; 무더운
If it is stuffy in a place, it is unpleasantly warm and there is not enough fresh air.

dashboard [dǽʃbɔ̀:rd] n. (자동차·비행기의) 계기판, 대시보드
The part of a car in front of the driver that has instruments and controls in it.

peripheral [pərífərəl] a. 주위의, 주변에 있는
Peripheral vision is your ability to see things to the side of you when you look straight ahead.

doodle [dú:dl] v. 낙서하다; 빈둥거리다; n. 낙서; (미·속어) 하찮은 것, 시시한 소리
To draw lines, shapes, etc., especially when you are bored or thinking about something else.

scrawl [skrɔ:l] vt. 휘갈겨 쓰다, 낙서하다
To write something in a careless untidy way, making it difficult to read.

Vocabulary in New Moon

growl [graul] v. 으르렁거리다, 고함치다; n. 으르렁거리는 소리
To make a low rough sound, usually in anger.

astonishment [əstániʃmənt] n. 놀람, 경악
A feeling of very great surprise.

radical [rǽdikəl] a. 근본적인, 기초적인 (radically ad. 원래는; 철저히; 근본적으로)
Radical changes and differences are very important and great in degree.

crop [krɑp] v. (머리를) 아주 짧게 깎다
To crop someone's hair means to cut it short.

tendon [téndən] n. 힘줄, 건(腱)
A tendon is a strong cord in a person's or animal's body which joins a muscle to a bone.

prominent [prámənənt] a. 현저한, 두드러진
Important or well known.

insignificant [ìnsignífikənt] a. 무의미한, 하찮은, 사소한
Not big or valuable enough to be considered important.

unrecognizable [ʌ̀nrékəgnàizəbəl] a. 식별할 수 없는, 인지[승인]할 수 없는
So changed or damaged that you do not recognize them or it.

alter [ɔ́:ltər] v. 변하다, 바꾸다, 변경하다, 고치다
To change something, usually slightly, or to cause the characteristics of something to change.

resentment [rizéntmənt] n. 노함, 분개; 적의, 원한
A feeling of anger or unhappiness about something that you think is unfair.

implode [implóud] v. 자체적으로 파열되다, 폭파하여 안쪽으로 붕괴하다
To burst or explode and collapse into the center.

resemblance [rizémbləns] n. 닮음, 비슷함, 유사함
The fact of being or looking similar to somebody or something.

11. CULT

- **intensify** [inténsəfài] v. 강렬하게 하다, 격렬하게 하다, 증강하다
  To become greater, more serious or more extreme, or to make something do this.

- **striking** [stráikiŋ] a. 현저한, 두드러진; 이목을[주의를] 끄는
  (strikingly ad. 두드러지게, 눈에 띄게)
  Something that is striking is very noticeable or unusual.

- **hostility** [hastíləti] n. 적의, 적개심; 교전
  Enmity, aggression or angry opposition.

- **malicious** [məlíʃəs] a. 악의 있는, 심술궂은; 고의의, 부당한
  Intended to harm or upset other people.

- **ache** [eik] vi. 아프다, 쑤시다
  To feel a continuous dull pain.

- **hollow** [hálou] a. 야윈, 오목한; 속이 빈; n. 구멍; 움푹 꺼진 곳 (hollowly ad. 속이 텅 비어)
  Something that is hollow has a space inside it, as opposed to being solid all the way through.

- **resentful** [rizéntfəl] a. 분개한, 화난
  Feeling angry and upset about something that you think is unfair.

- **reel** [ri:l] vi. 비틀거리다, 동요하기 시작하다, 어질어질하다
  If someone reels, they move about in an unsteady way as if they are going to fall.

- **taboo** [təbú:] n. 금기(禁忌), 터부, 금단, 꺼림
  If there is a taboo on a subject or activity, it is a social custom to avoid doing that activity or talking about that subject, because people find them embarrassing or offensive.

- **unperturbed** [ʌ̀npərtə́:rbd] a. 교란되지 않은, 평온[침착]한, 놀라지 않은
  Not worried or anxious.

- **permanent** [pə́:rmənənt] a. 영구적인, 영속하는, 변하지 않는
  (permanently ad. 영구히, 영구불변으로)
  Lasting for a long time or forever.

Vocabulary in New Moon

- **bitterly** [bítərli] ad. 쓸쓸하게, 따끔하게
  In a way that produces or shows feelings of great sadness or anger.

  unnerve [ʌnnə́ːrv] vt. 기운을 빼앗다[잃게 하다], 무기력하게 하다
  To make somebody feel nervous or frightened or lose confidence.

- **lump** [lʌmp] n. 덩어리, 한 조각; (구어) 땅딸보; 멍청이, 바보
  A piece of a solid substance, usually with no particular shape.

- **squish** [skwiʃ] v. 찌부러뜨리다, 으깨다
  To crush something.

  klutzy [klʌ́tsi] a. 서투른, 바보 같은
  Awkward, clumsy or socially inept.

- **spurt** [spəːrt] v. 쏟아져 나오다, 내뿜다; 갑자기 속도를 더 내다 n. 분출; 쏟아져 나옴
  To come out quickly and suddenly.

- **weary** [wíəri] a. 피로한, 지친
  If you are weary, you are very tired.

- **speculate** [spékjəlèit] vi. 숙고하다, 사색하다, 추측하다; 투기하다
  To consider the circumstances or possibilities regarding it, usually without any factual basis and without coming to a definite conclusion.

  Hallelujah [hæ̀ləlúːjə] n. '할렐루야'라고 외치는 소리

- **brittle** [britl] a. 부서지기 쉬운; 깨지기 쉬운; (소리 등이) 날카로운, 금속성의
  Hard but easily broken.

- **rage** [reidʒ] n. 격노, 분노; 열광; v. 격노하다[하게 하다]; 맹렬히 계속되다
  Rage is strong anger that is difficult to control.

- **dubious** [djúːbiəs] a. 의심스러운, 수상쩍은, 모호한
  (dubiously ad. 미심쩍어 하며, 의심스럽게)
  Feeling doubt or uncertainty.

- **defensive** [difénsiv] a. 방어적인, 방어의, 변호의 (defensively ad. 방어적으로, 변명으로)
  Behaving in a way that shows you protect yourself from being criticized.

11. CULT

wipe [waip] v. 훔치다, 씻다, 닦다, 비비다
To pass over, or rub on to.

reflex [rí:fleks] n. 반사 작용[운동]; 반사적인 반응[동작]
An action or a movement of your body that happens naturally in response to something and that you cannot control.

limp [limp] a. 기운이[활기가] 없는, 축 처진[늘어진] (limply ad. 힘없이, 축늘어져)
If you describe something as limp, you mean that it is soft or weak when it should be firm or strong.

retort [ritɔ́:rt] vt. 보복하다; 반론하여 말하다, 말대꾸하다
To reply quickly to a comment, in an angry, offended or humorous way.

glint [glint] v. 반짝이다, 빛나다; n. 반짝임, 섬광
If something glints, it produces or reflects a quick flash of light.

filthy [fílθi] a. 불결한, 더러운
Extremely or unpleasantly dirty.

reek [ri:k] v. 지독한 악취를 풍기다
To smell very strongly of something unpleasant.

bloodsucker [blʌ́dsʌ̀kər] n. 흡혈 동물, 흡혈귀; 고리대금업자
A bloodsucker is any creature that sucks blood from a wound that it has made in an animal or person.

whoosh [hwú(:)ʃ] v. 쉭 하고 움직이다; n. 휙[쉭] (하는 소리)
If something whooshes somewhere, it moves there quickly or suddenly.

correctly [kəréktli] ad. 바르게, 정확하게
Accurate or true, without any mistakes right.

indecision [ìndisíʒən] n. 우유부단, 주저
The state of being unable to decide.

fury [fjúəri] n. 격노, 격분; 격정, 열광; 맹렬함
Extreme anger.

Vocabulary in New Moon

scrutinize [skrú:tənàiz] v. 세밀히 조사하다, 철저히 검사하다, 파고 따지다
To subject to scrutiny; To examine closely.

denial [dináiəl] n. 부정, 부인, 거부
A statement saying that something is not true.

hater [héitər] n. (특정한 것을) 증오[싫어]하는 사람
hate (v. 증오하다, 싫어하다) + -er (suf. 사람, 도구, 기계)

superstitious [sù:pərstíʃəs] a. 미신의, 미신적인, 미신에 사로잡힌
Believing in superstitions.

feeble [fí:bəl] a. 연약한, 약한, 힘없는
Weak and without energy, strength or power.

mockery [mákəri] n. 비웃음, 냉소, 조롱, 조소
Comments or actions that are intended to make somebody or something seem ridiculous.

superstition [sù:pərstíʃən] n. 미신, 맹신
Belief in an influence that certain (especially commonplace) objects, actions or occurrences have on events, people's lives, etc.

accuse [əkjú:z] v. 비난하다, 고발하다
To say that someone has done something morally wrong, illegal or unkind.

hiss [his] v. 쉿 하는 소리를 내다; n. 쉿 (제지·힐책의 소리)
If people hiss at someone such as a performer or a person making a speech, they express their disapproval or dislike of that person.

caution [kɔ́:ʃən] v. 경고하다, 주의시키다; n. 조심, 신중
If someone cautions you, they warn you about problems or danger.

fume [fju:m] v. 약이 오르다, 몹시 화내다; 연기 나다, 그을리다; n. 연기, 김
If you fume over something, you express annoyance and anger about it.

quiver [kwívər] v. (떨리듯) 흔들리다, 떨다; n. 떨기
If something quivers, it shakes with very small movements.

11. CULT

delusion [dilú:ʒən] n. 현혹, 기만; 망상, 착각
The act of believing or making yourself believe something that is not true.

livid [livid] a. 납빛의, 흙빛의; 노발대발한, 격노한
Someone who is livid is extremely angry.

ridiculous [ridíkjələs] a. 웃기는, 우스꽝스러운; 터무니없는
If you say that something or someone is ridiculous, you mean that they are very foolish.

whirl [hwə:rl] v. 빙글 돌다, 선회하다
To move around or turn around very quickly.

freak out phrasal v. 흥분하다, 질겁하다
If somebody freaks out or if something freaks them out, they react very strongly to something that shocks, angers, excites or frightens them.

goad [goud] vt. 몰아세우다, 자극하다, 선동하다; n. 몰이 막대기
If you goad someone, you deliberately make them feel angry or irritated, often causing them to react by doing something.

slender [sléndər] a. 호리호리한, 가느다란; 빈약한
Thin and delicate.

trunk [trʌŋk] n. (나무의) 줄기, 몸뚱이; 여행 가방
The trunk of a tree is the large main stem from which the branches grow.

chase [tʃeis] v. 쫓아내다, 뒤쫓다; 추구하다; n. 추적, 추격
If you chase someone, or chase after them, you run after them or follow them quickly in order to catch or reach them.

inconsequential [inkànsikwénʃəl] a. 하찮은, 이치에 맞지 않는
Not important or worth considering trivial.

incredible [inkrédəbəl] a. 놀라운, 훌륭한, 믿어지지 않는
(incredibly ad. 믿을 수 없을 만큼)
Something is very unusual or surprising unbelievably.

potent [poutnt] a. 강력한, 유력한, 세력 있는
Having a strong effect on your body or mind.

Vocabulary in New Moon

bark out phrasal v. 갑자기 외치다, 고함지르다
To shout something loudly.

★ **semblance** [sémbləns] n. 외관, 외형, 모양, 모습
A situation in which something seems to exist although this may not, in fact, be the case.

★ **loneliness** [lóunlinis] n. 고독; 외로움
Loneliness is the unhappiness that is felt by someone because they do not have any friends or do not have anyone to talk to.

복습 **agony** [ǽgəni] n. 고뇌, 고통, 번민
Agony is great physical or mental pain.

복습 **swear** [swɛər] v. 맹세하다, 선서하다; n. 맹세, 선서
If you swear to do something, you promise in a serious way that you will do it.

★ **appall** [əpɔ́:l] vt. 오싹 소름이 끼치게 하다, 섬뜩하게 하다
To make someone have strong feelings of shock or of disapproval.

‡ **flutter** [flʌ́tər] v. (깃발 등이) 펄럭이다, (새 등이) 날갯짓하다; 심장이 두근거리다; n. 펄럭임
To make a series of quick delicate movements up and down or from side to side.

복습 **vacant** [véikənt] a. 빈, 비어 있는; 공허한 (vacantly ad. 멍하니, 멀거니)
Lacking expression; Blank.

복습 **drizzle** [drizl] vi. 이슬비[가랑비]가 내리다; n. 이슬비, 가랑비
If it is drizzling, it is raining very lightly.

‡ **slant** [slænt] v. 경사지게 하다, 기울이다; n. 경사, 비탈; 견해, 의견
To be at an angle as opposed to horizontal or vertical; To slope.

brine [brain] n. 소금물
Very salty water, used especially for preserving food.

‡ **whip** [hwip] v. 채찍질하다; 급히 움직이다; 홱 잡아채다; n. 채찍, 채찍질
If someone whips something out, they take it out very quickly and suddenly.

11. CULT

lash [læʃ] n. 속눈썹 (eyelash); 채찍질; v. 부딪히다, 후려치다
Your lashes are the hairs that grow on the edge of your upper and lower eyelids.

robotic [roubátik] a. (동작·표정 등이) 로봇 같은 (robotically ad. 로봇식으로, 뻣뻣하게)
Someone who is robotic acts like a robot by making stiff movements, not showing any human feelings etc.

slick [slik] a. 미끄러운, 매끈거리는
Smooth and difficult to hold or move on.

soak [souk] v. 적시다, 빨아들이다; 젖다, 스며들다; n. 적심
If a liquid soaks something or if you soak something with a liquid, the liquid makes the thing very wet.

plug up phrasal v. 막다, 막히게 하다
To fill or block a hole with a substance or piece of material that fits tightly into it.

carve [kɑːrv] vt. 새기다, 조각하다
To make something by cutting into especially wood or stone, or to cut into the surface of stone, wood, etc.

riddle [ridl] vt. 구멍을 숭숭 뚫다, 벌집같이 만들다
To make a lot of holes in somebody or something.

crumble [krʌ́mbl] v. 빻다, 부스러지다, 무너지다
To break, or cause something to break, into small pieces.

register [rédʒəstər] vt. (감정을) 나타내다, 표현하다; 기재하다, 등록하다
If you register your feelings or opinions about something, you do something that makes them clear to other people.

sodden [sɑ́dn] a. 흠뻑 젖은
Something that is sodden is extremely wet.

afghan [ǽfgæn] n. 모포[숄]의 일종
A blanket, wrap, or shawl of colored yarn.

Vocabulary in New Moon

splash [splæʃ] v. (물 등을) 끼얹다[튀기다]; n. 첨벙 하는 소리; 화사한 색[빛]
(of liquid) To fall noisily onto a surface.

linoleum [linóuliəm] n. 리놀륨(마루의 깔개)
A stiff smooth material that is used for covering floors.

cradle [kréidl] n. (전화기의) 수화기 거는 곳
The part of a telephone on which the receiver rests.

tiptoe [típtòu] vi. 발끝으로 걷다; 발돋움하다
If you tiptoe somewhere, you walk there very quietly without putting your heels on the floor when you walk.

unrequited [Ànrikwáitid] a. 상대방이 알아주지 않는, 짝사랑의
If you have unrequited love for someone, they do not love you.

crunch [krʌntʃ] v. 우두둑 부수다[깨물다]; n. 우두둑 부서지는 소리
If something crunches or if you crunch it, it makes a breaking or crushing noise.

gravel [grǽvəl] n. 자갈; vt. 자갈로 덮다, …에 자갈을 깔다
Small rounded stones, often mixed with sand.

leach [liːtʃ] vt. 걸러 내다; 거르다
To remove chemicals, minerals, etc. from soil.

crimson [krímzən] n. 진홍색; a. 진홍색의
A dark deep red color.

shear [ʃiər] v. (sheared-shorn) (머리를) 깎다; 털을 깎다
To cut off somebody's hair.

bronze [brɑnz] n. 청동, 구릿빛
A dark reddish-brown color, like bronze.

shatter [ʃǽtər] v. 충격을 주다; 산산조각이 나다, 파괴하다; n. 파편, 부서진 조각
If something shatters or is shattered, it breaks into a lot of small pieces.

11. CULT

vanish [vǽniʃ] v. 사라지다, 없어지다, 모습을 감추다
If you someone or something vanishes, they disappear suddenly or in a way that cannot be explained.

squeal [skwi:l] v. 꽥꽥거리다, 비명을 지르다; 끼익 소리 내다; n. 꽥꽥거리는 소리
If someone or something squeals, they make a long, high-pitched sound.

fingernail [fíŋgərnèil] n. 손톱
The thin hard layer that covers the outer tip of each finger.

Comprehension Quiz

 12. INTRUDER

1. Jacob wanted Bella to remember _____.

  A. why the Cullens left Forks

  B. the stories he told her on the beach

  C. a book that she read last year

  D. what Charlie said about the wild animals

2. Why wouldn't Jacob tell Bella about his situation?

  A. He wasn't allowed to share his secret.

  B. He didn't want Bella to know the truth about his situation.

  C. He didn't want Bella to worry about him.

  D. He didn't think Bella would believe him.

3. Why wouldn't Jacob run away with Bella?

  A. He didn't want to leave Billy alone.

  B. He didn't have enough money to run away.

  C. He couldn't run away from his situation.

  D. He didn't want to leave Sam and his friends.

12. INTRUDER

4. According to Jacob, why wasn't he supposed to see Bella?

    A. It was not safe to see Bella.

    B. Sam didn't like Bella.

    C. Someone dangerous was hunting Jacob.

    D. Charlie didn't want Jacob to go near Bella.

5. After Bella realized that Jacob and his friends were were-wolves, she thought _____.

    A. werewolves were safer to be around than vampires

    B. the werewolves were killing people around Forks

    C. Charlie was right to kill the werewolves

    D. she couldn't be friends with Jacob anymore

Vocabulary in New Moon

intruder [intrú:dər] n. 침입자, 난입자; 훼방꾼, 방해자
A person who enters a building or an area illegally.

muddled [mʌ́dld] a. 혼란스러워 하는, 갈피를 못 잡는
If someone is muddled, they are confused about something.

clumsy [klʌ́mzi] a. 꼴사나운, 어색한, 서투른
Awkward in movement or manner.

wobble [wábəl] v. 흔들흔들하다, 비틀대다; 동요하다; n. 흔들림
To shake or move from side to side in a way that shows a lack of balance.

erratic [irǽtik] a. 불규칙한, 산만한, 변덕스러운 (erratically ad. 산만하게, 불규칙적으로)
Not happening at regular times.

lurch [ləːrtʃ] v. 비틀거리다; n. (배·차 등의) 갑자기 기울어짐; 비틀거림
To make a sudden, unsteady movement forward or sideways.

stagger [stǽgər] v. 비틀거리다; 흔들리게 하다; 주저하다; n. 비틀거림
If you stagger, you walk very unsteadily, for example because you are ill or drunk.

terrify [térəfài] vt. 무섭게[겁나게] 하다, 놀래다
If something terrifies you, it makes you feel extremely frightened.

investigate [invéstəgèit] v. 조사하다, 연구하다, 심사하다
To examine a crime, problem, statement, etc. carefully, especially to discover the truth.

ouch [autʃ] int. 아얏, 아이쿠, 아야
'Ouch!' is used in writing to represent the noise that people make when they suddenly feel pain.

dimly [dímli] ad. 어둑[흐릿·희미]하게
Not very brightly or clearly.

cling [kliŋ] vi. 달라붙다, 매달리다
If you cling to someone or something, you hold onto them tightly.

12. INTRUDER

precarious [prikɛ́əriəs] a. 불확실한, 믿을 수 없는
(precariously ad. 불안정하게, 믿을 수 없게; 위태롭게)
(of a situation) Not safe or certain.

spruce [spru:s] n. 가문비나무속(屬)의 식물(갯솔·전나무 등)
A spruce is a kind of evergreen tree.

swing [swiŋ] v. (swang–swung) 흔들다; 매달리다, 빙 돌다
If something swings or if you swing it, it moves repeatedly backwards and forwards or from side to side from a fixed point.

dangle [dǽŋɡəl] v. 흔들흔들하다, 매달(리)다; n. 매달린 것
To hang loosely, or to hold something so that it hangs loosely.

huff [hʌf] v. 씩씩거리다, 씩씩거리며 말하다; 가쁘게 숨 쉬다; 헐떡이다; n. 분개, 골냄
If you huff, you indicate that you are annoyed or offended about something, usually by the way that you say something.

bounce [bauns] v. 펄쩍 뛰다, (공 등이) 튀(게 하)다; n. 튐, 바운드
To move up or away after hitting a surface.

blink [bliŋk] v. 눈을 깜박거리다; (등불·별 등이) 깜박이다; n. 깜박거림
When you blink or when you blink your eyes, you shut your eyes and very quickly open them again.

blurry [blə́:ri] a. 더러워진; 흐릿한
Without a clear outline.

snort [snɔ:rt] v. 콧김을 뿜다, (경멸·불찬성 등으로) 콧방귀 뀌다
To breathe air in a noisy way out through your nose to show that you are annoyed.

unamused [ənəmjú:zd] a. 재미가 없는, 즐기지 않는
un (pre. 부정) + amused (a. 즐거운, 재미있는)

momentum [mouméntəm] n. 여세, 힘, 타성; 운동량
A force that is gained by movement.

grunt [ɡrʌnt] n. 꿀꿀[툴툴]거리는 소리; vi. (돼지가) 꿀꿀거리다; (사람이) 툴툴거리다
A short low sound that a person or animal makes in their throat.

Vocabulary in New Moon

launch [lɔːntʃ] v. 맹렬히 덤비다; 쏘다, 내보내다; 발진시키다
To jump forwards with a lot of force.

agile [ǽdʒəl] a. (동작이) 기민[민첩]한, 날렵한 (agilely ad. 민첩하게, 날렵하게)
Someone who is agile can move quickly and easily.

thud [θʌd] n. 쿵[퍽·툭] (물건이 떨어지는 소리); v. 쿵[퍽·툭] 치다[떨어지다]; 쿵쿵거리다
A thud is a dull sound, such as that which a heavy object makes when it hits something soft.

muffle [mʌ́fəl] vt. (덮어서 소리를) 지우다, 억제하다; 덮다; 목도리로 감싸다
If something muffles a sound, it makes it quieter and more difficult to hear.

snore [snɔːr] v. 코를 골다
To breathe in a very noisy way while you are sleeping.

extremely [ikstríːmli] ad. 극단적으로, 극히, 매우
To a very high degree.

mockery [mάkəri] n. 비웃음, 냉소, 조롱, 조소
Comments or actions that are intended to make somebody or something seem ridiculous.

sincerity [sinsérəti] n. 성실, 성의
Honesty.

harsh [hɑːrʃ] a. 거친, 가혹한; 귀에 거슬리는, 불쾌한
Unpleasant, unkind, cruel or unnecessarily severe.

rejection [ridʒékʃən] n. 거절, 배제, 기각, 부결
The act of rejecting something.

infection [infékʃən] n. 전염, 감염
An infection is a disease caused by germs or bacteria.

sore [sɔːr] n. 상처; a. 아픈, 쓰린
A sore is a painful place on the body where the skin is infected.

insult [ínsʌlt] n. 모욕; vt. 모욕하다, 무례한 짓을 하다
A remark or an action that is said or done in order to offend somebody.

12. INTRUDER

injury [índʒəri] n. 부상, 상해; (물질적) 손해, 손상, 피해
Physical harm or damage.

smirk [smə:rk] vi. 능글맞게 웃다; n. 능글맞은 웃음
To smile in a self-satisfied, affected or foolish manner.

awkward [ɔ́:kwərd] a. 어색한, 불편한, 곤란한
An awkward situation is embarrassing and difficult to deal with.

vicious [víʃəs] a. 나쁜, 악덕의, 잔인한 (viciously ad. 잔인하게)
A vicious person or a vicious blow is violent and cruel.

wound [wu:nd] ① n. 상처, 부상, 상해; vt. 상처를 입히다 ② v. [waund] wind의 과거·과거분사
A wound is damage to part of your body, especially a cut or a hole in your flesh, which is caused by a gun, knife, or other weapon.

venom [vénəm] n. 악의, 원한; (독사 따위의) 독, 독액
Great anger or hated.

protest [prətést] v. 항의하다, 이의를 제기하다; 주장하다; n. 항의
If you protest against something or about something, you say or show publicly that you object to it.

shove [ʃʌv] v. 밀(치)다, 밀어내다; n. 밀치기
If you shove something somewhere, you push it there quickly and carelessly.

budge [bʌdʒ] v. (보통 부정문) 약간 움직이다[움직이게 하다]; 태도[견해]를 바꾸다
If something will not budge or you cannot budge it, it will not move.

crash down idiom (요란하게) 부서지다, 붕괴하다; 망하다, 파산하다; 폭락하다
To fall with a very lond noise.

en masse [enmæséi] ad. 일제히[집단으로]; 한 묶음으로, 통틀어서
All together, and usually in large numbers.

brutal [brú:tl] a. 모진, 혹독한; 잔인한, 야만적인 (brutally ad. 혹독하게, 잔인하게)
A brutal act or person is cruel and violent.

Vocabulary in New Moon

- **collapse** [kəlǽps] v. 무너지다, 붕괴하다; 쓰러지다, 맥없이 주저앉다; n. 무너짐, 붕괴
  If a building or other structure collapses, it falls down very suddenly.

- **sway** [swei] v. 흔들(리)다, 동요하다; 설득하다; n. 동요, 지배
  To move slowly from side to side.

- **unsteady** [ʌnstédi] a. 굳세지 못한; 동요하는 (unsteadily ad. 굳세지 못하게, 불안정하게)
  If you describe something as unsteady, you mean that it is not regular or stable, but unreliable or unpredictable.

- **elbow** [élbou] n. 팔꿈치
  The joint between the upper and lower parts of the arm where it bends in the middle.

- **steer** [stiər] v. 조종하다, 키를 잡다; 향하다
  To control the direction a vehicle is going, for example by turning a wheel.

- **plop** [plɑp] vt. 털썩 주저앉다[벌렁 드러눕다]
  To fall somewhere, making a sound like something dropping into water.

- ★ **anguish** [ǽŋgwiʃ] n. (심신의) 비통, 고뇌, 번민; v. 괴로워하다[괴롭히다]
  Anguish is great mental suffering or physical pain.

- **replace** [ripleis] v. 대신하다, 제자리에 놓다
  If one thing or person replaces another, the first is used or acts instead of the second.

- **bitterness** [bítərnis] n. 쓴맛, 쓰라림, 비통
  A rough and bitter manner.

- **crap** [kræp] n. 허튼소리, 헛소리
  Nonsense.

- **apology** [əpάlədʒi] n. 사죄, 사과
  An act of saying sorry.

- **cut off** phrasal v. 중단하다, 끊다
  If you cut somebody off, you refuse to let the one have any of your money or property.

12. INTRUDER

- **clench** [klentʃ] vt. (이를) 악물다, (손을) 꽉 쥐다
  To close one's teeth or one's fists tightly, especially in anger.

- **wrinkle** [ríŋkəl] v. 주름살지게 하다, 구겨지다; n. 주름, 잔주름
  When you wrinkle your nose or forehead, or when it wrinkles, you tighten the muscles in your face so that the skin folds.

- **exhale** [ekshéil] v. (숨 등을) 내쉬다; (증기·향기 등을) 발산[방출]하다
  To breathe out the air or smoke, etc. in your lungs.

- **confirmation** [kànfərméiʃən] n. 확정, 확립; 확인, 인가; 비준
  The act of confirming.

- **loyalty** [lɔ́iəlti] n. 충의, 충절
  A strong feeling that you want to be loyal to somebody or something.

- **riddle** [ridl] vt. 구멍을 숭숭 뚫다, 벌집같이 만들다
  A question or statement requiring thought to answer or understand.

- **abrupt** [əbrʌ́pt] a. 갑작스러운, 뜻밖의 (abruptly ad. 갑자기)
  Sudden and unexpected.

- **startle** [stá:rtl] v. 깜짝 놀라게 하다; 움찔하다; n. 깜짝 놀람
  If something sudden and unexpected startles you, it surprises and frightens you slightly.

- **hopelessness** [hóuplisnis] n. 가망 없음, 절망
  The lack of hope; Despair.

- **intensity** [inténsəti] n. 강렬, 격렬; 집중, 전념
  The state or quality of being intense.

- **eager** [í:gər] a. 열망하는, 간절히 하고 싶어하는
  If you are eager to do or have something, you want to do or have it very much.

- **tense** [tens] v. 팽팽하게 하다, 긴장시키다[하다]; a. 팽팽한, 긴장한, 긴박한
  If your muscles tense, if you tense, or if you tense your muscles, your muscles become tight and stiff, often because you are anxious or frightened.

Vocabulary in New Moon

lid [lid] n. 눈꺼풀(eyelid); 뚜껑
Your lids are the pieces of skin which cover your eyes when you close them.

clue [klu:] n. 단서, 실마리
A sign or some information which helps you to find the answer to a problem.

flirt [flə:rt] vi. 이성과 시시덕거리다, 장난삼아 연애하다
If you flirt with someone, you behave as if you are sexually attracted to them, although not seriously.

inept [inépt] a. 기량[능력]이 없는, 서투른 (ineptly ad. 서투르게)
Acting or done with no skill.

vital [váitl] a. 생명의, 생생한; 중요한, 치명적인
Necessary for the success or continued existence of something; Extremely important.

mute [mju:t] a. 무언의, 말없이; vt. …의 소리를 죽이다, …을 약하게 하다
(mutely ad. 말없이, 잠자코)
Someone who is mute is silent for a particular reason and does not speak.

churn [tʃə:rn] v. (분노·혼란스러움 등이) 들끓다; (흙탕물 등이[을]) 휘돌다[휘젓다]
To feel or to make somebody feel upset or emotionally confused.

inconsequential [inkànsikwénʃəl] a. 하찮은, 이치에 맞지 않는
Not important or worth considering trivial.

★ **prelude** [prélju:d] n. (다른 중요한 일의) 서곡[전주곡]
You can describe an event as a prelude to a more important event when it happens before it and acts as an introduction to it.

groan [groun] v. 신음하다, 끙끙거리다; n. 신음[끙끙거리는] 소리
If you groan, you make a long, low sound because you are in pain, or because you are upset or unhappy about something.

sarcastic [sɑ:rkǽstik] a. 빈정대는, 비꼬는, 풍자적인
Saying things that are the opposite of what you mean, in order to make an unkind joke.

12. INTRUDER

plunk [plʌŋk] (= plonk) v. (아무렇게나) 쿵 하고 놓다
To put something down heavily and without taking care.

wary [wéri] a. 경계하는, 조심하는 (warily ad. 조심하여, 방심 않고)
If you are wary of something or someone, you are cautious because you do not know much about them and you believe they may be dangerous or cause problems.

intention [inténʃən] n. 의향, 의지, 목적, 의도
What you intend or plan to do.

voluntary [váləntèri] a. 자발적인, 임의적인, 자진한
Voluntary actions or activities are done because someone chooses to do them and not because they have been forced to do them.

unrequited [ʌ̀nrikwáitid] a. 상대방이 알아주지 않는, 짝사랑의
If you have unrequited love for someone, they do not love you.

shear [ʃiər] v. (sheared-shorn) (머리를) 깎다; 털을 깎다
To cut off somebody's hair.

tremble [trémbəl] v. 떨다, 떨리다
To shake slightly, usually because you are cold or frightened.

pass out phrasal v. 의식을 잃다, 기절하다; 나가다, 퇴장하다
If you pass out, you faint or collapse.

frown [fraun] v. 눈살을 찌푸리다, 얼굴을 찡그리다; n. 찌푸린 얼굴
To make an angry, unhappy, bringing your eyebrows together.

incredible [inkrédəbəl] a. 놀라운, 훌륭한, 믿어지지 않는
(incredibly ad. 믿을 수 없을 만큼)
Something is very unusual or surprising unbelievably.

thrill [θril] n. 전율; v. 감동[감격·흥분]시키다; 오싹하다
A strong feeling of excitement or pleasure.

incomprehension [inkɑ̀mprihénʃən] n. 몰이해, 이해력이 없음
The state of not being able to understand somebody or something.

Vocabulary in New Moon

combination [kὰmbənéiʃən] n. 결합, 화합, 조합
A combination of things is a mixture of them.

★ **idiot** [ídiət] n. 얼간이, 바보
A stupid person or someone who has done something stupid.

stab [stæb] v. (칼 따위로) 찌르다; n. 찌름, (찌르는 듯한) 고통
To make a short forceful pushing movement with a finger or a long thin object.

plead [pli:d] v. 간청하다, 탄원하다; 변론하다; 변호하다
If you plead with someone to do something, you ask them in an intense, emotional way to do it.

squeaky [skwí:ki] a. 삐걱거리는, 찍찍 소리 내는
Making a short very high cry or sound.

yearn [jə:rn] vi. 그리워하다, 갈망하다
To feel a great desire for it; To long for it.

compulsion [kəmpʌ́lʃən] n. 강제, 강박(현상); 억제하기 어려운 욕망
A compulsion is a strong desire to do something, which you find difficult to control.

merely [míərli] ad. 단지, 다만 (…에 불과한)
Nothing more than; Just.

damp [dæmp] a. 축축한
Slightly wet, especially in a way that is not pleasant or comfortable.

brine [brain] n. 소금물
Very salty water, used especially for preserving food.

jade [dʒeid] n. 비취, 옥 (jade green : 비취색, 옥색)
Jade is a hard stone, usually green in color, that is used for making jewellery and ornaments.

grab [græb] v. 부여잡다, 움켜쥐다; n. 부여잡기
If you grab something, you take it or pick it up suddenly and roughly.

12. INTRUDER

ponytail [póunitèil] n. 포니테일(뒤에서 묶어 아래로 드리운 머리)
A ponytail is a hairstyle in which someone's hair is tied up at the back of the head and hangs down like a tail.

nape [neip] n. 목덜미
The back of the neck.

yank [jæŋk] v. 홱 당기다; 홱 잡아당겨 …의 상태로 하다; n. 홱 잡아당김
If you yank someone or something somewhere, you pull them there suddenly and with a lot of force.

déjà vu [dèiʒɑːvjúː] n. 기시감(지금 자신에게 일어나는 일을 전에도 경험한 적이 있는 것 같이 느끼는 것)
The feeling that you have previously experienced something which is happening to you now.

relive [riːliv] v. 다시 체험하다, 재현하다; 소생하다
If you relive something that has happened to you in the past, you remember it and imagine that you are experiencing it again.

dredge [dredʒ] vt. 상기하다, 들추어내다; (항만·강을) 준설하다, 물밑을 훑다
To remove mud, stones, etc. from the bottom of a river, canal, etc. using a boat or special machine, to make it deeper or to search for something.

detach [ditǽtʃ] v. 떼어놓다, 분리하다; 파견하다
If one thing detaches from another, it becomes separated from it.

★ **beckon** [békən] v. 손짓[고갯짓·몸짓]으로 부르다, 신호하다
To move your hand or head in a way that tells someone to come nearer.

★ **yelp** [jelp] v. 깽깽 울다, 큰소리로 말하다; (개가 성내어) 짖는 소리, 깽깽 우는 소리
If a person or dog yelps, they give a sudden short cry, often because of fear or pain.

★ **twitch** [twitʃ] vi. (손가락·근육 따위가) 씰룩거리다; 홱 잡아당기다, 잡아채다
Said of a muscle, limb, etc.; To move involuntarily with a spasm.

veer off phrasal v. 갑자기 방향을 바꾸다, 갑자기 변하다
To suddenly change direction.

Vocabulary in New Moon

meadow [médou] n. 목초지, 풀밭
A field with grass and often wild flowers in it.

gigantic [dʒaigǽntik] a. 거대한, 막대한
If you describe something as gigantic, you are emphasizing that it is extremely large in size, amount, or degree.

monstrous [mάnstrəs] a. 괴물 같은, 기괴한; 거대한
If you describe an unpleasant thing as monstrous, you mean that it is extremely large in size or extent.

intently [inténtli] ad. 골똘하게, 여념 없이, 오로지
Giving all your attention to something.

lung [lʌŋ] n. [해부] 폐, 허파
Your lungs are the two organs inside your chest which fill with air when you breathe in.

hysteric [histérik] n. 광란, 병적 흥분, 히스테리의 발작
If someone is in hysterics or is having hysterics, they are in a state of uncontrolled excitement, anger, or panic.

strangle [strǽŋgl] vt. 목을 조이다; 목 졸라 죽이다, 교살하다
To strangle something means to prevent it from succeeding or developing.

screech [skri:tʃ] vi. 날카로운[새된] 소리를 내다
To make a unpleasant loud high noise.

Noah and the ark n. 노아의 방주
In the Bible a large boat which Noah built to save his family and two of every type of animal from the flood.

descended [disendid] a. 전해진, 유래한 (from)
A person who is descended from someone who lived a long time ago is directly related to them.

treaty [trí:ti] n. 조약, 협정
A formal agreement between two or more countries.

12. INTRUDER

ancestor [ǽnsestər] n. (사람의) 조상, 선조
Your ancestors are the people from whom you are descended.

werewolf [wíərwùlf] n. 늑대 인간 (pl. werewolves)
In stories and films, a werewolf is a person who changes into a wolf.

lodge [lɑdʒ] v. 박아 넣다, 꽂다; 숙박하다 n. 조그만 집, 별장
If an object lodges somewhere, it becomes stuck there.

tilt [tilt] v. 기울이다; 기울다
If you tilt part of your body, usually your head, you move it slightly upwards or to one side.

axis [ǽksis] n. (사물의) (중심) 축, 축선
An axis is an imaginary line through the middle of something.

mythical [míθikəl] a. 신화의, 신화에 대한; 신화적인
Existing only in ancient myths.

fairy [fɛ́əri] n. 요정
(in stories) A creature like a small person, who has magic powers.

chunk [tʃʌŋk] n. 큰 덩어리, 상당한 양[액수]; v. 덩어리로 나누다
A chunk of something is a large amount or large part of it.

rearrange [rì:əréindʒ] vt. 재배열하다, 재정리하다
If you rearrange things, you change the way in which they are organized or ordered.

multihued [mʌ̀ltihú:d] (= multicolored) a. 다색의, 다채로운
Having multiple colors.

skid [skid] v. 미끄러지다; n. (무거운 물건을 굴릴 때 까는) 활제, 굴대; 미끄럼
To slide along a surface so that you have no control.

corkscrew [kɔ́:rkskrù:] n. 나사 모양, 나선형
Something to move in a particular direction while turning in circles.

ranger [réindʒər] n. 공원[삼림·자연] 관리원[경비 대원]
A person whose job is to take care of a park, a forest or an area of countryside.

Vocabulary in New Moon

- **armed** [ɑːrmd] a. 무장한, 무기를 가진
  Someone who is armed is carrying a weapon, usually a gun.

- **carcass** [kɑ́ːrkəs] n. (짐승의) 시체; (도살한 짐승의) 몸통
  The dead body of an animal, especially of a large one or of one that is ready for cutting up as meat.

- **firepower** [faiərpáuər] n. (군사) (부대·무기의) 화력, 사격 능력
  The number and size of guns that an army, a ship, etc. has available.

- **turn into** phrasal v. (외관·성질 따위가) …으로 변하다
  To change, or to make something change, into something different.

- **tree-hugger** [triːhʌ́gər] n. 급진적인 환경 보호 운동가
  Derogatory term for environmentalists who support restrictions on the logging industry and the preservation of forests.

- **paw** [pɔː] n. (동물·갈고리 발톱이 있는) 발; v. 앞발로 차다
  The paws of an animal such as a cat, dog, or bear are its feet, which have claws for gripping things and soft pads for walking on.

- **realization** [rìːələzéiʃən] n. 깨달음, 자각, 인식
  Coming to understand something clearly and distinctly.

- **hysterical** [histérikəl] a. 히스테리(성)의; 병적으로 흥분한, 이성을 잃은
  In a state of extreme excitement, and crying, laughing, etc. in an uncontrolled way.

- **pessimist** [pésəmist] n. 비관[염세]주의자
  A person who always expects bad things to happen.

- **loop** [luːp] n. 루프, 고리 (문맥상 '반복됨'의 의미가 있다.)
  The curved shape made when something long and thin, such as a piece of string, bends until one part of it nearly touches or crosses another part of it.

- **dizzy** [dízi] a. 현기증 나는, 아찔한
  If you feel dizzy, you feel as if everything is spinning round and being unable to balance.

12. INTRUDER

- **slaughter** [slɔ́:tər] vt. 도살하다, 학살하다
  To kill a large number of people or animals violently.

- **inevitable** [inévitəbəl] a. 피할 수 없는, 필연적인
  Certain to happen and unable to be avoided or prevented.

- **endure** [endjúər] v. 참다, 견디다, 인내하다
  If you endure a painful or difficult situation, you experience it and do not avoid it or give up, usually because you cannot.

- **ashamed** [əʃéimd] a. 부끄러운, 창피한, 수치스러운
  Feeling shame or embarrassment about somebody or something or because of something you have done.

- **bleed** [bli:d] vi. ① 출혈하다 ② 마음 아파하다
  When you bleed, you lose blood from your body as a result of injury or illness.

Comprehension Quiz

13. KILLER

1. Why did Quileute tribe werewolves exist?

    A. To protect humans from vampires

    B. To hunt down all of the vampires on Earth

    C. To protect the Cullens

    D. To hunt humans

2. What did Jacob and his friends to do Laurent?

    A. They chased him out of forks.

    B. They gave him a message for Victoria.

    C. They killed him.

    D. They chased him into the water.

3. In the last two weeks, who was killing people in the forest?

    A. Laurent

    B. Victoria

    C. Wolves

    D. The Volturi

13. KILLER

4. Jacob said _____ made the transformation easier for him.

A. his father

B. the voices in his head

C. bella

D. the stories his father told him

5. What happens when Jacob is a wolf?

A. He can hear the other wolf pack members.

B. He doesn't know who he is.

C. He cannot see as well as he can when he's human.

D. He will attack any human or vampire he sees.

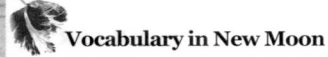
Vocabulary in New Moon

compromise [kámprəmàiz] n. 타협, 화해, 양보; v. 화해하다, 양보하다
Anything of an intermediate type which comes halfway between two opposing stages.

condone [kəndóun] vt. 용서하다, 묵과하다, 너그럽게 봐주다
To pardon or overlook (an offence or wrong).

cowardly [káuərdli] a. 겁이 많은; 비겁한, 비열한; ad. 겁을 내어
Lacking courage.

owe [ou] vt. 빚지고 있다, 은혜를 입고 있다
To have to pay somebody for something that you have already received or return money that you have borrowed.

thud [θʌd] v. 쿵[퍽·툭] 치다[떨어지다]; 쿵쿵거리다 ; n. 쿵[퍽·툭] (물건이 떨어지는 소리)
If something thuds somewhere, it makes a dull sound, usually when it falls onto or hits something else.

reverberate [rivə́:rbərèit] v. 반향하다(echo); 울려 퍼지다
To be repeated several times as it is reflected off different surfaces.

flick [flik] vt. (스위치 등을) 탁 누르다; 가볍게 치다, 튀기다; 휙 움직이다; n. 가볍게 치기
To press a button or switch quickly in order to turn a machine, etc. on or off.

knob [nab] n. 손잡이; 혹, 마디; (작은) 덩이
A round handle, or a small round device for controlling a machine or electrical equipment.

bathrobe [bǽθroub] n. 실내복, 가운 (주로 남성용)
A loose piece of clothing worn before and after taking a bath.

stoic [stóuik] (= stoical) a. 냉정한; 극기의, 금욕의
If you say that someone is a stoic, you approve of them because they do not complain or show they are upset in bad situations.

stall [stɔ:l] v. 시간을 벌다; (차량·엔진이) 멎다, 시동이 꺼지다
To delay.

13. KILLER

purse [pəːrs] v. (불만 등의 표시로 입술을) 오므리다
If you purse your lips, you move them into a small, rounded shape, usually because you disapprove of something or when you are thinking.

stalk [stɔːk] v. (화가 난 듯이) 성큼성큼 걷다; (적·먹이 등에) 몰래 접근하다
If you stalk somewhere, you walk there in a stiff, proud, or angry way.

bang [bæŋ] n. 쾅 하는 소리; v. 탕 치다, 쾅 닫(히)다; 부딪치다
A sudden loud noise.

sweat [swet] n. (pl.) 추리닝, 운동복 (= sweatsuit · sweatpants); 땀
A loose top and trousers, worn either by people who are training for a sport or exercising, or as informal clothing.

diagonal [daiǽgənəl] a. 대각선의; 비스듬한, 사선의
(diagonally ad. 대각선으로; 비스듬하게)
A diagonal line or movement goes in a sloping direction, for example, from one corner of a square across to the opposite corner.

slant [slænt] n. 경사, 비탈; 견해, 의견; v. 경사지게 하다, 기울이다
A sloping position.

gloomy [glúːmi] a. 어두운, 우울한
If a place is gloomy, it is almost dark so that you cannot see very well.

predawn [priːdɔ́ːn] n., a. 동트기 전(의)
Before the rising of the sun.

adjust [ədʒʌ́st] v. 적응하다; 조절[조정]하다; (옷매무새 등을) 바로 하다
To gradually become familiar with a new situation.

seawall [síːwɔ́ːl] n. 방파제
A large strong wall built to stop the sea from flowing onto the land.

driftwood [dríftwud] n. 유목(流木), 부목(浮木), 떠내려 온 나무
drift (v. 표류하다, 떠돌다) + wood (n. 나무)

materialize [mətíəriəlàiz] v. 나타나다, 가시화[사실화]되다
To become real, visible or tangible; To appear or take shape.

Vocabulary in New Moon

* **seaward** [síːwərd] a. 바다를 향한, 바다 쪽의
  Towards the sea; In the direction of the sea.

brittle [britl] a. 부서지기 쉬운, 깨지기 쉬운; (소리 등이) 날카로운, 금속성의
  Hard but easily broken.

tentacle [téntəkəl] n. (동물의) 촉수, 더듬이
  One of the long thin arm-like parts of some sea creatures.

vulnerable [vʌ́lnərəbəl] a. 상처를 입기 쉬운, 공격받기 쉬운, 취약성[약점]이 있는
  Weak and easily hurt physically or emotionally.

revulsion [rivʌ́lʃən] n. 극도의 불쾌감, 혐오감
  A strong feeling of disgust or horror.

dissolve [dizálv] v. 녹이다, 용해시키다
  To break up and merge with a liquid.

condemn [kəndém] vt. 비난하다, 힐난하다; 유죄 판결을 내리다
  If you condemn something, you say that it is very bad and unacceptable.

overpower [òuvərpáuər] vt. 압도하다, 억누르다, 제압하다
  To defeat or gain control over somebody completely by using greater strength.

illogical [ilɑ́dʒikəl] a. 비논리적인, 불합리한, 조리에 맞지 않는, 어리석은
  Not sensible or thought out in a logical way.

shelter [ʃéltər] v. 막아주다, 보호하다; 피하다; n. 피난처, 은신처
  If you shelter someone, usually someone who is being hunted by police or other people, you provide them with a place to stay or live.

forewarn [fɔːrwɔ́ːrn] vt. 미리 경계하다; 미리 주의[통고]하다
  To warn somebody about something bad or unpleasant before it happens.

* **silhouette** [sìluét] n. 윤곽, 실루엣; vt. …의 그림자를 비추다
  A silhouette is the solid dark shape that you see when someone or something has a bright light or pale background behind them.

13. KILLER

prickle [príkəl] v. 뜨끔뜨끔 쑤시다; 찌르다
To give somebody an unpleasant feeling on their skin, as if a lot of small sharp points are pushing into it.

acid [ǽsid] n. 매서움, 신랄함; [화학] 산(酸) (acidic a. 신랄한, 언짢은)
(of a person's remarks) Critical and unkind.

harsh [ha:rʃ] a. 거친, 가혹한; 귀에 거슬리는, 불쾌한 (harshly ad. 가혹하게, 냉혹히)
Unpleasant, unkind, cruel or unnecessarily severe.

clatter [klǽtər] v. 달가닥달가닥 울리다; n. (식기류 따위의) 덜걱덜걱 하는 소리
To move making a loud noise like hard objects knocking together.

castanet [kæstənét] n. 캐스터네츠
A musical instrument consisting of two small pieces of wood tied together by string and knocked against each other in the hand to make a noise.

halt [hɔ:lt] v. 멈춰서다, 정지하다; n. 정지, 휴식, 멈춤
To stop; To make somebody or something stop.

retort [ritɔ́:rt] vt. 보복하다; 반론하여 말하다, 말대꾸하다; n. 말대꾸; 반박
To reply quickly to a comment, in an angry, offended or humorous way.

snarl [sna:rl] n. 으르렁거림; v. 으르렁거리다; 고함[호통]치다
A deep sound that an animal makes when it is angry and shows its teeth.

spit [spit] v. 뱉다, 토해내다; 뿜어내다
To force out the contents of the mouth, especially saliva.

flinch [flintʃ] v. (고통·공포로) 주춤하다, 위축되다
To make a small sudden movement, especially when something surprises someone.

hostile [hástil] a. 적(군)의; 적의 있는, 적대하는, 반대하는, 냉담한
Angry and deliberately unfriendly towards someone and ready to argue with them.

hypocrite [hípəkrìt] n. 위선자, 겉으로 착한 체하는 사람
A person who pretends to have moral standards or opinions that they do not actually have.

Vocabulary in New Moon

ugh [ux] int. 위, 액, 왜, 캑 (혐오·경멸·공포 또는 기침 소리를 나타냄)
The way of writing the sound that people make when they think that something is disgusting or unpleasant.

temple [témpəl] n. 관자놀이; 신전, 사원
Your temples are the flat parts on each side of the front part of your head, near your forehead.

squeeze [skwi:z] vt. 꽉 쥐다[죄다], 압착하다; n. 압착, 짜냄
If you squeeze something, you press it firmly, usually with your hands.

rage [reidʒ] n. 격노, 분노, 열광; v. 격노하다[하게하다]; 맹렬히 계속되다
Rage is strong anger that is difficult to control.

caution [kɔ́:ʃən] v. 경고하다, 주의시키다; n. 조심, 신중
If someone cautions you, they warn you about problems or danger.

straighten [stréitn] v. (몸을) 똑바르게 하다; 정리[정돈]하다
To make your back straight.

disgust [disgʌ́st] n. 싫음, 혐오감; vt. 역겹게 하다, 넌더리나게 하다
Disgust is a feeling of very strong dislike or disapproval.

chortle [tʃɔ́:rtl] vi. (좋아서) 깔깔 웃다; 아주 좋아하다
To laugh loudly with pleasure or because you are amused.

vice [vais] n. 바이스 (기계공작에서, 공작물을 끼워 고정하는 기구)
A vice is a tool with a pair of parts that hold an object tightly while you do work on it.

morph [mɔ:rf] v. 변하다, 바뀌다; 바꾸다
To change, or make somebody or something change into something different.

solemn [sάləm] a. 엄숙한, 근엄한 (solemnly ad. 장엄하게, 진지하게)
Done, said, etc. in a very serious and sincere way.

stroke [strouk] vt. 쓰다듬다, 어루만지다; n. 쓰다듬기, 달램
If you stroke someone or something, you move your hand slowly and gently over them.

13. KILLER

- **furrow** [fə́:rou] v. 주름살지다, 이랑을 짓다; n. 밭고랑
  To make wrinkles on your face because you are thinking hard.

- **burden** [bə́:rdn] n. 무거운 짐, 부담
  Something difficult or unpleasant that you have to deal with.

- **blankly** [blǽŋkli] ad. 멍하니, 우두커니
  In a way that shows no emotion, understanding, or interest.

- **drain** [drein] v. (액체가) 흘러나가다; 말라버리다; 고갈시키다, 쇠진하다; n. 배수로, 하수구
  If you drain a liquid from a place or an object, you remove the liquid by causing it to flow somewhere else. If a liquid drains somewhere, it flows there.

- **wordless** [wə́:rdlis] a. 말없는
  Without saying any words.

- **cock** [kɑk] v. 위로 치올리다, (귀·꽁지를) 쫑긋 세우다
  To move a part of your body upwards or in a particular direction.

- **leech** [li:tʃ] n. 거머리 (본문에서는 컬린 일가의 사람들을 거머리에 비유)
  A leech is a small animal which looks like a worm and lives in water. Leeches feed by attaching themselves to other animals and sucking their blood.

- **fierce** [fiərs] a. 사나운; 격렬한, 지독한
  Physically violent and frightening.

  lone [loun] a. 고독한, 혼자의
  Without a companion.

- **qualify** [kwάləfài] v. (앞의 진술에) 단서를 달다; 자격을 주다, 권한을 주다
  To add to something that has already been said, in order to limit its effect or meaning.

- **stumble** [stʌ́mbəl] v. 비틀거리며 걷다, 발부리가 걸리다; n. 비틀거림
  If you stumble, you put your foot down awkwardly while you are walking or running and nearly fall over.

Vocabulary in New Moon

calf [kæf] n. 장딴지, 종아리 (pl. calves)
The thick curved part at the back of the human leg between the knee and the foot.

sink down idiom 지다; 맥없이 주저앉다; 안 보이게 하다
If you sink down, you fall down or sit down heavily, especially because you are very tired and weak.

babble [bǽbəl] v. 실없이 지껄이다, 쓸데없는 말을 하다; n. 재잘거림, 왁자지껄
(babbling n. 수다)
If someone babbles, they talk in a confused or excited way.

moist [mɔist] a. 축축한, 습한, 습기 있는
Slightly wet.

relieve [rilíːv] vt. 안도케 하다, (긴장·걱정 등을) 덜다, 구제하다
To lessen or stop someone's pain, worry, boredom, etc.

comforting [kʌ́mfərtiŋ] a. 기분을 돋우는, 격려하는; 위안이 되는
(comfortingly ad. 격려개[위안이] 되게)
Making you feel less sad or anxious.

ridden [ridn] a. 지배된, 시달린, 얽매인
Full of a particular unpleasant thing.

swear [swɛər] v. (swore-sworn) 맹세하다, 선서하다; n. 맹세, 선서
To make a serious promise to do something.

gasp [gæsp] v. (놀람 따위로) 숨이 막히다, 헐떡거리다; n. 헐떡거림
When you gasp, you take a short quick breath through your mouth, especially when you are surprised, shocked, or in pain.

ashen [ǽʃən] a. 회색의; (죽은 사람처럼) 매우 창백한, 핏기가 없는
Grey or very pale, usually from shock, illness, etc.

pissed off [pístɔːf] a. 열 받은, 화가 난
Annoyed, disappointed, or unhappy.

fade [feid] vi. 희미해지다, 바래다, 시들다
To disappear gradually.

13. KILLER

dew [dju:] v. 이슬로 적시다[젖다]; 축이다, 눅눅하게 하다; n. 이슬; 신선함, 상쾌함
To wet with or as with dew.

trunk [trʌŋk] n. (나무의) 줄기, 몸뚱이; 여행 가방
The trunk of a tree is the large main stem from which the branches grow.

convulse [kənvʌ́ls] vt. 경련시키다, 몸부림치게 하다; 진동시키다, 대소동을 일으키다
If someone convulses or if they are convulsed by or with something, their body moves suddenly in an uncontrolled way.

heave [hi:v] n. 메스꺼움, 구토; 들썩거리다; 들어 올리다
The act or an instance of gagging or vomiting.

horrify [hɔ́:rəfài] vt. 소름끼치게 하다, 충격을 주다 (horrified a. 겁에 질린, 충격 받은)
If someone is horrified, they feel shocked or disgusted, because of something that they have seen or heard.

nausea [nɔ́:ziə] n. 메스꺼움, 욕지기; 뱃멀미
The feeling that you have when you want to vomit, for example because you are ill/sick or are disgusted by something.

expel [ikspél] vt. 배출[방출]하다; 쫓아내다, 물리치다
To force air, water, or gas etc. out of your body or out of a container.

sickening [síkəniŋ] a. 병나게 하는, 욕지기나게 하는
(sickeningly ad. 구역질나게, 넌더리나게)
Making you feel disgusted or shocked.

nauseous [nɔ́:ʃəs] a. 욕지기나는, 메스꺼운
Feeling as if you want to vomit.

spasm [spǽzəm] n. 경련, 발작
A sudden and often painful contracting of a muscle, which you cannot control.

slump [slʌmp] n. (활동·원기의) 슬럼프; 쿵 떨어짐; v. 털썩 앉다; 쿵 떨어지다
A period when someone or something is in a bad state.

sag [sæg] v. 축 처지다[늘어지다]
When part of someone's body begins to sag, it starts to become less firm and hang down.

Vocabulary in New Moon

sweaty [swéti] a. (사람·몸·옷 등이) 땀이 나는, 땀투성이의
Covered or damp with sweat.

moan [moun] v. 신음하다, 끙끙대다; n. 신음
If you moan, you make a low sound, usually because you are unhappy or in pain.

pat [pæt] v. 톡톡 가볍게 치다; 쓰다듬다; n. 톡톡[가볍게] 침[두드림]
If you pat something or someone, you tap them lightly, usually with your hand held flat.

flex [fleks] v. 굽히다, 수축시키다; n. 굽힘
If you flex your muscles or parts of your body, you bend, move, or stretch them for a short time in order to exercise them.

scar [skɑːr] n. 흉터, (화상·부스럼의) 자국
A mark that is left on the skin after a wound has healed.

intently [inténtli] ad. 골똘하게, 여념 없이, 오로지
Giving all your attention to something.

flip [flip] v. 홱 뒤집(히)다, 휙 젖히다; (책장 등을) 넘기다; (너무 흥분하여) 확 돌아 버리다
To turn over into a different position with a sudden quick movement; To make something do this.

★ **slit** [slit] n. 갈라진 틈, 틈새; 길게 베어진 상처
A long narrow cut or opening.

shrug [ʃrʌg] v. (양 손바닥을 내보이면서 어깨를) 으쓱하다; n. 으쓱하기
If you shrug, you raise your shoulders to show that you are not interested in something or that you do not know or care about something.

★ **approximation** [əpràksəméiʃən] n. 접근, 근사; 비슷한 것
An estimate of a number or an amount that is almost correct, but not exact.

rumble [rʌ́mbəl] vi. (천둥·지진 등이) 우르르 울리다; (배가) 꾸르륵거리다; n. 우르르 소리
To make a continuous low sound.

13. KILLER

- **idiot** [ídiət] n. 얼간이, 바보
  A stupid person or someone who has done something stupid.

- **release** [rilíːs] vt. 풀어놓다, 석방하다, 방출하다
  To give freedom or free movement to someone or something.

- **sprint** [sprint] v. 역주하다, 달려가다
  To run at full speed.

- **parking lot** [páːrkiŋ làt] n. 주차장
  An open area for cars to park in.

- **flit** [flit] vi. 훌쩍 날다; 휙 지나가다, 오가다
  To fly or move quickly and lightly.

- **swift** [swift] a. 빠른, 신속한
  A swift event or process happens very quickly or without delay.

- ★ **sleek** [sliːk] a. 윤기 있는, 매끄러운
  Smooth, soft and glossy.

- **deer** [diər] n. 사슴
  A deer is a large wild animal that eats grass and leaves.

- **hyperventilate** [hàipərvéntəleit] v. (흥분·놀람으로) 숨을 크게 들이쉬다
  To breathe too quickly or too deeply, so that you get too much oxygen and feel dizzy.

- **mash** [mæʃ] vt. 짓찧다, 짓이기다, 찧어 섞다; n. 짓이긴 것, 갈아서 빻은 것
  If you mash food that is solid but soft, you crush it so that it forms a soft mass.

- **indestructible** [ìndistrʌ́ktəbəl] a. 파괴할 수 없는, 불멸의
  Not able to be destroyed.

- ★ **rap** [ræp] n. (재빨리 날카롭게) 톡[쾅] 때리기[두드리기]
  A quick sharp hit or knock.

- **yelp** [jelp] v. 깽깽 울다, 큰소리로 말하다; (개가 성내어) 짖는 소리, 깽깽 우는 소리
  If a person or dog yelps, they give a sudden short cry, often because of fear or pain.

Vocabulary in New Moon

복습 insult [insʌ́lt] vt. 모욕하다, 무례한 짓을 하다; n. 모욕
If someone insults you, they say or do something that is rude or offensive.

복습 weird [wiərd] a. 기묘한, 이상한, 수상한
Very strange and unusual, unexpected or not natural.

freaky [fríːki] a. 괴상한, 이상한
If someone or something is freaky, they are very unusual in some way.

복습 surreptitious [sə̀ːrəptíʃəs] a. 비밀의, 몰래 하는, 은밀한; 부정의
(surreptitiously ad. 몰래; 부정하게)
Done secretly or quickly, in the hope that other people will not notice.

복습 torso [tɔ́ːrsou] n. 토르소(머리·손발이 없는 나체 조각상); (인체의) 몸통; (비유) 미완성 작품
The main part of the body, not including the head, arms or legs.

복습 wry [rai] a. 찡그린, 뒤틀린; 삐딱한, 빈정대는 (wryly ad. 빈정대며, 뒤틀려)
Showing that you find a bad or difficult situation slightly amusing.

★ perception [pərsépʃən] n. 지각, 인식, 인지
Your perception of something is the way that you think about it or the impression you have of it.

복습 morose [məróus] a. 까다로운, 기분이 언짢은; 침울한
Unhappy, annoyed and unwilling to speak or smile.

복습 choke [tʃouk] v. 숨 막히다[막히게 하다], 질식하다[시키다]
To prevent or be prevented from breathing by an obstruction in the throat, fumes, emotion.

복습 chuckle [tʃʌ́kl] vi. 낄낄 웃다; n. 낄낄 웃음
When you chuckle, you laugh quietly.

★ compassion [kəmpǽʃən] n. 측은히 여김, 동정(심), 연민
Compassion is a feeling of pity, sympathy, and understanding for someone who is suffering.

♣ ignorant [ígnərənt] a. 무지한, 예의를 모르는, (어떤 일을) 모르는
Not polite or respectful.

13. KILLER

- **traitor** [tréitər] n. 반역자, 역적, 배신자
  Someone who is not loyal to their country, friends, or beliefs.

- **torture** [tɔ́ːrtʃər] vt. 고문하다, 고통을 주다; n. 고문, 고뇌
  To torture someone means to cause them to suffer mental pain or anxiety.

- **oblivious** [əblíviəs] a. (…이) 염두[안중]에 없는; 잘 잊어버리는, 건망증이 있는
  Unaware or forgetful of it.

- **reverie** [révəri] n. 공상, 환상, 몽상, 백일몽
  A day-dream or absent-minded idea or thought.

  midsection [mídsèkʃən] n. 중간부; 동체의 중간부
  The middle area of the human torso (usually in front).

- **throb** [θrɑb] vi. (심장이) 고동치다, 맥이 뛰다; n. 고동, 맥박
  If part of your body throbs, you feel a series of strong and usually painful beats there.

- **murmur** [mɔ́ːrmər] v. 중얼거리다
  To speak or say very quietly.

- **unseeing** [ʌ̀nsíːiŋ] a. 보고 있지 않는, 보려고 하지 않는
  (unseeingly ad. 보지 않고; 눈이 보이지 않게)
  Not noticing or really looking at anything although your eyes are open.

- **inhale** [inhéil] v. 들이쉬다, 흡입하다
  To take air, smoke, gas, etc. into your lungs as you breathe.

- **suck** [sʌk] v. 빨다, 흡수하다; (속어) 엉망이다, 형편없다; n. 빨아들임
  If you suck something, you hold it in your mouth and pull at it with the muscles in your cheeks and tongue, for example in order to get liquid out of it.

Comprehension Quiz

14. FAMILY

1. Why did Paul get angry and turn into a werewolf?

A. Jacob shared his secret and brought Bella to meet the wolf pack.

B. Jacob said he didn't care about the rules of the pack.

C. Sam told Paul to relax.

D. Jacob challenged Paul to fight him.

2. Why did Emery and Jared throw away Jacob's shoes?

A. The shoes were too small for Jacob.

B. The shoes broke when Jacob transformed into a wolf.

C. The shoes were wet from the rain.

D. Jacob forgot his shoes outside.

3. The Cullens could break the treaty with the Quileute Tribe by _____.

A. leaving Forks

B. killing animals near Forks

C. biting a human

D. attacking a vampire outside of La Push

14. FAMILY

4. What does Jacob describe as a wolf thing?

   A. Werewolves can quickly change from human to werewolf.

   B. Werewolves heal very quickly.

   C. Werewolves can see and hear very well.

   D. Werewolves can swim faster than vampires.

5. Emily had _____ and it made Sam uncomfortable when people stared at her.

   A. long, beautiful hair

   B. scars on the side of her face

   C. perfect skin

   D. different colored eyes

Vocabulary in New Moon

cower [káuər] vi. 움츠리다, 위축되다
To bend low and move back because you are frightened.

quadruplet [kwɑ́druplit] n. 네쌍둥이 중의 한 사람; (pl.) 네쌍둥이
Quadruplets are four children who are born to the same mother at the same time.

★ **synchronize** [síŋkrənaiz] v. 동시에 발생하다[움직이다] (synchronization n. 동기화)
If you synchronize two activities, processes, or movements, or if you synchronize one activity, process, or movement with another, you cause them to happen at the same time and speed as each other.

복습 **crop** [krɑp] v. (머리를) 아주 짧게 깎다
To crop someone's hair means to cut it short.

aging [éidʒiŋ] (= ageing) n. 나이 먹음, 노화
The process of growing old.

복습 **maturity** [mətjúərəti] n. 성숙, 숙성; 원숙, 완성; [의학] 화농
Maturity is the state of being fully developed or adult.

복습 **thrust** [θrʌst] v. 밀다, 떠밀다, 쑤셔 넣다; n. 밀침
To push something somewhere roughly.

복습 **tribe** [traib] n. 종족, 부족
A group of people, often of related families, who live together, sharing the same language, culture and history.

복습 **quiver** [kwívər] v. (떨리듯) 흔들리다, 떨다; n. 떨기
If something quivers, it shakes with very small movements.

복습 **sting** [stiŋ] vt. (stung-stung) 찌르다, 쏘다; n. 찌르기, 쏘기, (동물의) 침, 고통
If something stings you, a sharp part of it is pushed into your skin so that you feel a sharp pain.

‡ **criticism** [krítisìzəm] n. (좋지 못한 점을 지적하는) 비판, 비난
The act of expressing disapproval of somebody/something and opinions about their faults or bad qualities; A statement showing disapproval.

14. FAMILY

shudder [ʃʌ́dər] n. 몸이 떨림, 전율, 몸서리; vi. 떨다, 몸서리치다
A strong shaking movement.

ripple [rípəl] v. 잔물결이 일다; 잔물결을 일으키다
To move or to make something move in very small waves.

irritation [ìrətéiʃən] n. 짜증나게 함; 짜증, 화; 짜증나는 것, 자극하는 것
Irritation is a feeling of annoyance, especially when something is happening that you cannot easily stop or control.

outrage [áutrèidʒ] n. 격분, 격노; v. (법률·도의 등을) 위반하다; 격분시키다
Outrage is an intense feeling of anger and shock.

★ **convulsion** [kənvʌ́lʃən] n. 경련, 경기
A sudden shaking movement of the body that cannot be controlled.

heave [hiːv] v. 들썩거리다; 들어 올리다; n. 메스꺼움, 구토
To move up and down with very strong movements.

vibrate [vaibréit] v. 진동하다, (시계추처럼) 흔들리다
If something vibrates or if you vibrate it, it shakes with repeated small, quick movements.

rip [rip] v. 벗겨내다, 찢다; 돌진하다; n. 잡아 찢음, 째진 틈
If you rip something away, you remove it quickly and forcefully.

coalesce [kòuəlés] vi. 유착(癒着)하다; 합체(合體)하다
To come together to form one larger group, substance, etc.

massive [mǽsiv] a. 크고 무거운, 육중한, 굳센, 강력한
Something that is massive is very large in size, quantity, or extent.

crouch [krautʃ] v. 몸을 구부리다, 쭈그리다, 웅크리다
To bend your knees and lower yourself so that you are close to the ground and leaning forward slightly.

muzzle [mʌ́zəl] n. (동물의) 주둥이, 부리(입·코 부분)
The nose and mouth of an animal, especially a dog or a horse.

Vocabulary in New Moon

* **colossal** [kəlásəl] a. 거대한, (구어) 어마어마한, 굉장한
  If you describe something as colossal, you are emphasizing that it is very large.

* **enrage** [enréidʒ] vt. 노하게 하다
  To cause someone to become very angry.

* **tremor** [trémər] n. 전율, 떨림; 겁; 떨리는 목소리; 진동
  A slight shaking movement in a person's body, especially because of nervousness or excitement.

* **shiver** [ʃívər] v. (추위·공포로) 후들후들 떨다; 전율하다; n. 떨림, 전율
  To shake slightly because you are cold, frightened, excited, etc.

* **shred** [ʃred] n. 끄트러기, 조각, 파편; v. 조각조각으로 찢다, 갈가리 찢다
  A small thin piece that has been torn or cut from something.

* **blast** [blæst] v. 폭파하다, 큰 소리를 내다; n. 돌풍, 폭풍
  If something blasts water or air somewhere, it sends out a sudden, powerful stream of it.

* **russet** [rʌ́sət] a. 적[황]갈색의, 팥빛의
  Russet is used to describe things that are reddish-brown in color.

* **enormous** [inɔ́:rməs] a. 거대한, 막대한, 엄청난
  Something that is enormous is extremely large in size or amount.

* **flutter** [flʌ́tər] v. (깃발 등이) 펄럭이다, (새 등이) 날갯짓하다; 심장이 두근거리다; n. 펄럭임
  To make a series of quick delicate movements up and down or from side to side.

* **ram** [ræm] vt. (가끔은 일부러, 다른 차량·선박 등을) 들이받다
  To hit or push something with force.

* **conflict** [kánflikt] n. 투쟁, 전투; 충돌, 상충, 대립
  A situation in which people, groups or countries are involved in a serious disagreement or argument.

* **rapt** [ræpt] a. (넋·마음을) 빼앗긴, 정신이 팔린, 열중한, 몰두한
  If someone listens with rapt attention, they are extremely interested or fascinated.

14. FAMILY

snicker [sníkər] vi. (미) 낄낄 웃다, 숨죽여 웃다; n. 낄낄 웃음
To laugh at someone or something childishly and often unkindly.

grumble [grʌ́mbəl] v. 투덜거리다, 불평하다; n. 투덜댐, 불평
To complain about someone or something in an annoyed way.

grin [grin] v. 이를 드러내고 싱긋 웃다; n. 싱긋 웃음
When you grin, you smile broadly.

dangle [dǽŋgəl] v. 매달(리)다, 흔들흔들 하다; n. 매달린 것
To hang loosely, or to hold something so that it hangs loosely.

barefoot [bɛ́ərfùt] a. 맨발의
Not wearing anything on your feet.

sneaker [sníːkər] n. (주로 pl.) 고무창 운동화
Sneakers are casual shoes with rubber soles.

hop [hɑp] v. 깡충 뛰다, 뛰어 오르다; n. 깡충깡충 뜀
If you hop, you move along by jumping.

trash [træʃ] n. 폐물, 쓰레기(rubbish)
Something that you throw away because you no longer want or need them.

remnant [rémnənt] n. 나머지, 잔여
A small piece of cloth that is left when the rest has been sold.

wad [wad] v. 뭉쳐 넣다, 채우다; (단단한 덩이가 되게) 뭉치다, 뭉치로 만들다
To fill something with soft material for warmth or protection.

assess [əsés] vt. (사람·사물 등의) 성질을[가치를] 평가하다
To judge the quality or importance of something.

complain [kəmpléin] v. 불평하다, 투덜거리다
To say that something is wrong or not satisfactory.

glare [glɛər] v. 노려보다; 번쩍번쩍 빛나다; n. 섬광; 노려봄
If you glare at someone, you look at them with an angry expression on your face.

Vocabulary in New Moon

guffaw [gʌfɔ́ː] v. 시끄럽게[크게] 웃다
To laugh noisily.

blanch [blæntʃ] vt. (공포·질병 등이) (얼굴 등을) 창백하게 하다
To become pale because you are shocked or frightened.

phase [feiz] v. (단계적으로) 실행하다; n. 단계, 국면
To make something happen gradually in a planned way.

buck [bʌk] n. (미·속어) 달러
A dollar.

brutal [brúːtl] a. 모진, 혹독한; 잔인한, 야만적인
A brutal act or person is cruel and violent.

hurl [həːrl] v. 세게 내던지다, 집어던지다
If you hurl something, you throw it violently and with a lot of force.

ignition [igníʃən] n. 점화, 발화, (내연 기관의) 점화 장치
The electrical system of a vehicle that makes the fuel begin to burn to start the engine; The place in a vehicle where you start this system.

haul [hɔːl] vt. 세게 잡아당기다; 운반하다; n. 세게 잡아당김; 운송; 소득, 벌이
To pull something heavy slowly and with difficulty.

leapt [liːpt] v. leap(껑충 뛰다, 날뛰다, 뛰어오르다, 도약하다)의 과거·과거분사
To jump high into the air or to jump in order to land in a different place.

agile [ǽdʒəl] a. (동작이) 기민[민첩]한, 날렵한 (agilely ad. 민첩하게, 날렵하게)
Someone who is agile can move quickly and easily.

injunction [indʒʌ́ŋkʃən] n. 명령, 훈령, 지령
An official order given by a court which demands that something must or must not be done.

spill the beans idiom (비밀을) 무심코 말해 버리다
Tell somebody something that should be kept secret or private.

fiancee [fiːɑːnséi] n. 약혼녀
A man's fiancee is the woman to whom he is engaged to be married.

14. FAMILY

bug [bʌg] v. (구어) 귀찮게 굴다, 괴롭히다; n. 곤충; 결함
If someone or something bugs you, they worry or annoy you.

bloodsucker [blʌ́dsʌ̀kər] n. 흡혈 동물, 흡혈귀; 고리대금업자
A bloodsucker is any creature that sucks blood from a wound that it has made in an animal or person.

amuse [əmjúːz] vt. 즐겁게 하다, 재미나게 하다
To make somebody laugh or smile.

turf [təːrf] n. 세력권, 영역; (형사 등의) 담당 구역
The place where somebody lives and/or works, especially when they think of it as their own.

relative [rélətiv] n. 동족, 동류; a. 비교적인; 상대적인
If one animal, plant, language, or invention is a relative of another, they have both developed from the same type of animal, plant, language, or invention.

literal [lítərəl] a. 글자 그대로의; 문자의
Being the basic or usual meaning of a word or phrase.

easternmost [íːstərnmòust] a. 가장 동쪽의
The easternmost part of an area or the easternmost place is the one that is farthest towards the east.

lane [lein] n. 좁은 길, 골목, 작은 길
A narrow road in the country.

marigold [mǽrəgòuld] n. 금잔화, 금송화

meaningful [míːniŋfəl] a. 의미심장한, 뜻있는
(meaningfully ad. 의미 있게; 의의 있게, 유효하게)
If you describe something as meaningful, you mean that it is useful, serious or important.

timid [tímid] a. 소심한, 자신이 없는 (timidly ad. 소심하게)
If you describe someone's attitudes or actions as timid, you are criticizing them for being too cautious or slow to act.

Vocabulary in New Moon

satiny [sǽtəni] a. 공단[새틴] 같은; 윤기 있는; 매끈매끈한
Looking or feeling like satin.

copper [kάpər] n. 구릿빛, 동색, 적갈색
Copper is sometimes used to describe things that are reddish-brown in color.

grimace [gríməs] n. 얼굴을 찌푸림, 찌푸린 얼굴, 우거지상; vi. 얼굴을 찡그리다
An ugly expression made by twisting your face, used to show pain, disgust, etc. or to make somebody laugh.

stiffen [stífən] v. 딱딱[뻣뻣]해지다, 경직되다
If you stiffen, your body suddenly becomes firm, straight still because you feel angry or anxious.

nibble [níbəl] v. 조금씩 물어뜯다, 갉아먹다; n. 조금씩 물어뜯기, 한 입 분량
If you nibble food, you eat it by biting very small pieces of it.

chastise [tʃæstáiz] vt. 벌하다, 혼내주다; 꾸짖다
To criticize somebody for doing something wrong.

banter [bǽntər] v. (정감 어린) 농담을 주고받다; n. (가벼운) 농담, 놀림
If you banter with someone, you tease them or joke with them in an amusing, friendly way.

floorboard [flɔ́ːrbɔ̀ːrd] n. 바닥 널, 바닥; v. 전속력으로 운전하다
Floorboards are the long pieces of wood that a wooden floor is made up of.

crack [kræk] v. 갈라지다, 금이 가다; 날카로운 소리를 내다; 깨지다
If something hard cracks, or if you crack it, it becomes slightly damaged, with lines appearing on its surface.

pitcher [pítʃər] n. 물 주전자
A pitcher is a jug.

humongous [hjuːmʌ́ŋgəs] a. (미·속어) 거대한, 터무니없이[엄청나게] 큰
If you describe something or someone as humongous, you are emphasizing that they are very large or important.

14. FAMILY

batch [bætʃ] n. 한 솥, 한 차례 굽는 양; vt. 1회분으로 정리[처리]하다
A batch of things or people is a group of things or people of the same kind, dealt with at the same time.

★ **saturate** [sǽtʃərèit] vt. 흠뻑 적시다, 담그다
To make something completely wet.

intrusive [intrúːsiv] a. 침입의; 참견하는, 방해하는
Something that is intrusive disturbs your mood or your life in a way you do not like.

✱ **wretched** [retʃid] a. 비참한, 불쌍한; 초라한; 야비한, 비열한
Unhappy, unpleasant or of low quality.

★ **kidney** [kidni] n. 신장, 콩팥
Either of the two organs in the body that remove waste products from the blood and produce urine.

exultant [igzʌ́ltənt] a. 몹시 기뻐하는; 승리를 뽐내는, 의기양양한
Feeling or showing great pride or happiness especially because of something exciting that has happened.

복습 **barely** [bɛ́ərli] ad. 간신히, 가까스로; 거의 …않다
Only with great difficulty or effort.

sundown [sʌ́ndàun] n. 해넘이, 일몰
Sundown is the time when the sun sets.

복습 **smug** [smʌg] a. 잘난 체하는, 거만한
Too pleased or satisfied about something you have achieved or something you know.

skillet [skílit] n. (스튜용) 냄비 (긴 손잡이와 짧은 발이 달린)
A skillet is a shallow iron pan which is used for frying.

★ **avenge** [əvéndʒ] v. 복수를 하다, 앙갚음하다, 원수를 갚다
To punish or hurt somebody in return for something bad or wrong that they have done to you, your family or friends.

Vocabulary in New Moon

duck [dʌk] ① vi. 몸을 홱 굽히다; (쏙) 들어가다 ② n. 오리
If you duck, you move your head or the top half of your body quickly downwards to avoid something that might hit you, or to avoid being seen.

bait [beit] n. 미끼, 유혹물; v. 미끼로 꾀어 들이다
A small amount of food put on a hook or in a trap to attract fish or animals.

yank [jæŋk] v. 홱 당기다; 홱 잡아당겨 …의 상태로 하다; n. 홱 잡아당김
If you yank someone or something somewhere, you pull them there suddenly and with a lot of force.

flick [flik] vt. 휙 움직이다; 가볍게 치다, 튀기다; (스위치 등을) 탁 누르다; n. 가볍게 치기
If something flicks in a particular direction, or if someone flicks it, it moves with a short, sudden movement.

snag [snæg] v. (흔히 다른 사람보다 먼저) 잡아[낚아] 채다
To succeed in getting something quickly, often before other people.

unabashed [ˌʌnəbǽʃt] a. 부끄러운 줄 모르는, 뻔뻔한
If you describe someone as unabashed, you mean that they are not ashamed, embarrassed, or shy about something, especially when you think most people would be.

squabble [skwábəl] v. 승강이하다, 말다툼하다; n. 싸움, 말다툼
To argue noisily about something that is not very important.

split [split] v. 쪼개다, 찢다, 째다
If something splits or if you split it, it is divided into two or more parts.

fate [feit] n. 운명, 숙명; 죽음, 최후
The apparent power that determines the course of events, over which humans have no control.

perimeter [pərímitər] n. 둘레, 주변, 주위; 경계선
An area of land is the whole of its outer edge or boundary.

guarantee [ˌgærəntíː] n. 보증, 개런티; vt. 보증하다, 다짐하다
A firm promise that you will do something or that something will happen.

14. FAMILY

recoil [rikɔ́il] vi. 되돌아오다; 후퇴하다; 움찔하다; n. 되튐, 반동
If you recoil from doing something or recoil at the idea of something, you refuse to do it or accept it because you dislike it so much.

utterly [ʌ́tərli] ad. 완전히, 순전히, 아주, 전혀
Completely; Absolutely; Entirely.

unconcerned [ʌ̀nkənsə́:rnd] a. 개의치 않는, 무심한; 무관심한, 흥미 없는
If a person is unconcerned about something, usually something that most people would care about, they are not interested in it or worried about it.

audible [ɔ́:dəbl] a. 들리는, 들을 수 있는
Loud enough to be heard.

hoot [hu:t] n. 폭소; 비웃음, 콧방귀
A short loud laugh or shout.

amusement [əmjú:zmənt] n. 즐거움, 위안, 재미, 오락(물)
The feeling that you have when something is funny or amusing, or it entertains you.

symmetry [símətri] n. (좌우의) 대칭, 균형
The quality of being very similar or equal.

underlying [ʌ̀ndərláiiŋ] a. (겉으로 잘 드러나지는 않지만) 근본적인[근원적인]
The underlying features of an object, event, or situation are not obvious, and it may be difficult to discover or reveal them.

deformity [difɔ́:rməti] n. 신체적 기형[변형]
A condition in which a part of the body is not the normal shape because of injury, illness or because it has grown wrongly.

strategic [strətí:dʒik] a. 전략의, 전략상의, 전략적인
Done as part of a plan that is meant to achieve a particular purpose or to gain an advantage.

devour [diváuər] vt. 게걸스럽게 먹다, 먹어치우다
To eat something eagerly and in large amounts so that nothing is left.

Vocabulary in New Moon

buffet [bʌ́fit] n. 뷔페
A meal where people serve themselves from a variety of food.

midst [midst] n. 중앙, 한가운데, 한복판
The middle of a group of people or things.

bedlam [bédləm] n. 대소동, 소란한 장소
A very noisy confused place or situation.

affectionate [əfékʃənit] a. 애정 깊은, 사랑에 넘친, 다정한, 인정 많은
If you are affectionate, you show your love or fondness for another person in the way that you behave towards them.

suspicious [səspíʃəs] a. 의심하는, 의심 많은, 수상쩍은 (suspiciously ad. 미심쩍다는 듯이)
If you are suspicious of someone or something, you do not trust them, and are careful when dealing with them.

convenient [kənvíːnjənt] a. 편리한, 형편이 좋은
If a way of doing something is convenient, it is easy, or very useful or suitable for a particular purpose.

intermittent [ìntərmítənt] a. 간헐적인, 간간이 일어나는 (intermittently ad. 간헐적으로)
Something that is intermittent happens occasionally rather than continuously.

chase [tʃeis] v. 쫓아내다, 뒤쫓다; 추구하다; n. 추적, 추격
If you chase someone, or chase after them, you run after them or follow them quickly in order to catch or reach them.

foray [fɔ́ːrei] n. 전격적 침략; 급습
You can refer to a short journey that you make as a foray if it seems to involve excitement or risk, for example because it is to an unfamiliar place or because you are looking for a particular thing.

linger [líŋgər] vi. 오래 머무르다, 떠나지 못하다
When something lingers, it continues to exist for a long time, often much longer than expected.

honk [hɔːŋk] v. 경적을 울리다; (기러기가) 울다
If you honk the horn of a vehicle, you make the horn produce a short loud sound.

14. FAMILY

impatient [impéiʃənt] a. 성급한, 조급한, 몹시 …하고 싶어 하는
(impatiently ad. 성급하게, 조바심하며)
Easily annoyed by someone's mistakes or because you have to wait.

scant [skænt] a. 거의[별로] 없는, 부족한; vt. 아까워하다, 인색하게 굴다
You use scant to indicate that there is very little of something or not as much of something as there should be.

rearview mirror [ríərvju: mirər] n. (자동차의) 백미러
A mirror in which a driver can see the traffic behind.

misunderstanding [mìsʌndərstǽndiŋ] n. 오해, 잘못 생각함
A situation in which a comment, an instruction, etc. is not understood correctly.

maul [mɔ:l] vt. (짐승 등이) 할퀴어 상처 내다; 째다
To attack and injure somebody by tearing their flesh.

salmon [sǽmən] n. 연어
A large fish with silver skin and pink flesh that is used for food. Salmon live in the sea but swim up rivers to lay their eggs.

spawn [spɔ:n] v. (물고기·개구리 등이) 알을 낳다; n. 알; 산물, 결과
To lay eggs.

hypocrisy [hipákrəsi] n. 위선, 위선(적인) 행위
If you accuse someone of hypocrisy, you mean that they pretend to have qualities, beliefs, or feelings that they do not really have.

hypocrite [hípəkrìt] n. 위선자, 겉으로 착한 체하는 사람
A person who pretends to have moral standards or opinions that they do not actually have.

irrational [irǽʃənəl] a. 이성을 잃은, 분별이 없는, 불합리한
Not based on, or not using, clear logical thought.

Comprehension Quiz

15. PRESSURE

1. For Jacob, what was the hardest part of becoming a werewolf?

   A. Feeling out of control

   B. Not speaking to Bella

   C. Hiding his problems from his father

   D. Hearing voices in his head

2. How did Bella get the 'cold' scar on her arm?

   A. She got surgery on her arm the year before.

   B. Edward sucked venom out of her arm.

   C. James bit her arm.

   D. Bella fell into a glass table at her birthday party.

15. PRESSURE

3. How do the werewolves know how to kill vampires?

   A. They learned everything they needed to know about vampires by killing Laurent.

   B. Everything they needed to know was passed down from father to son for generations.

   C. The boys spent a lot of time researching werewolves at the library in La Push.

   D. When Sam turned into a werewolf, he was told what to do by voices in his head.

4. What reckless thing did Bella do to hear Edward's voice?

   A. She swam in the ocean during a storm.

   B. She tried to kill herself.

   C. She jumped off a cliff into the ocean.

   D. She went looking for Victoria.

5. Bella saw _____ when she was in the freezing water.

   A. Edward

   B. Alice

   C. Sharp rocks

   D. The shore

Vocabulary in New Moon

absorb [əbsɔ́:rb] vt. 받아들이다; 흡수하다; 열중시키다
If you absorb information, you learn and understand it.

ditch [ditʃ] vt. (사람을) 따돌리다; (관계를) 끊다; (물건을) 버리다; (일·책임 등에서) 도망치다
If someone ditches someone, they end a relationship with that person.

alert [əlɔ́:rt] n. 경보, 경계; v. 경고하다; a. 방심하지 않는
A warning to people to be prepared to deal with something dangerous.

assumption [əsʌ́mpʃən] n. 가정, 가설; (증거도 없이) 사실이라고 생각함
A belief or feeling that something is true or that something will happen, although there is no proof.

sophomore [sáfəmɔ̀:r] n. (대학·고교의) 2학년생
A student in the second year of college or high school.

disguise [disgáiz] v. 위장하다, 숨기다; 변장하다; n. 변장(도구); 변장술
To disguise something means to hide it or make it appear different so that people will not know about it or will not recognize it.

resentment [rizéntmənt] n. 노함, 분개; 적의, 원한
A feeling of anger or unhappiness about something that you think is unfair.

shrewd [ʃru:d] a. 예민한, 날카로운; 영리한, 빈틈없는 (shrewdly ad. 예민하게, 날카롭게)
Showing good judgement and likely to be right.

complicate [kámpləkèit] vt. 복잡하게 하다, 뒤얽히게 만들다 (complicated a. 복잡한)
To complicate something means to make it more difficult to understand or deal with.

cruel [krú:əl] a. 잔혹한, 무자비한
Extremely unkind and unpleasant and causing pain to people or animals intentionally.

harbor [háːrbər] vt. (계획·생각 등을) 품다; 숨겨주다; 잠복하다; n. 항구, 항만; 피난처
To keep feelings or thoughts, especially negative ones, in your mind for a long time.

15. PRESSURE

dissolve [dizálv] v. 녹이다, 용해시키다
To break up and merge with a liquid.

drawn [drɔːn] a. 찡그린, 일그러진
If someone or their face looks drawn, their face is thin and they look very tired, ill, worried, or unhappy.

exhaustion [igzɔ́ːstʃən] n. 극도의 피로, 기진맥진
Extreme tiredness.

blaze [bleiz] vi. 타오르다; n. 불꽃, 화염, 섬광 (blazing a. 타는 듯한)
To burn brightly and strongly.

flake [fleik] n. 얇은 조각, 박편
A flake is a small thin piece of something, especially one that has broken off a larger piece.

compartment [kəmpáːrtmənt] n. 구획, 칸막이
A smaller enclosed space inside something larger.

trigger [trígər] v. (장치를) 작동시키다; n. (총의) 방아쇠; 계기, 자극
If something triggers an event or situation, it causes it to begin to happen or exist.

temper [témpər] n. 기질, 성질; 화, 노여움
If you refer to someone's temper, you mean that they become angry very easily.

confusion [kənfjúːʒən] n. 혼동, 혼란, 뒤죽박죽
A situation, often with a lot of activity and noise, in which people do not know what to do.

enthusiastic [enθúːziǽstik] a. 열렬한, 열광적인
If you are enthusiastic about something, you show how much you like or enjoy it by the way that you behave and talk.

scar [skɑːr] n. 흉터, (화상·부스럼의) 자국
A mark that is left on the skin after a wound has healed.

Vocabulary in New Moon

★ **bulge** [bʌldʒ] v. 부풀다, 불룩해(게 하)다; n. 불룩한 것[부분]
If someone's eyes or veins are bulging, they seem to stick out a lot, often because the person is making a strong physical effort or is experiencing a strong emotion.

복습 **sallow** [sǽlou] a. (안색이 병적으로) 누르께한, 흙빛의, 혈색이 나쁜
(of a person's skin or face) Having a slightly yellow color that does not look healthy.

복습 **venom** [vénəm] n. (독사 따위의) 독, 독액; 악의, 원한
The venom of a creature such as a snake or spider is the poison that it puts into your body when it bites or stings you.

rattlesnake [rǽtlsnèik] n. [동물] 방울뱀
A rattlesnake is a poisonous American snake which can make a rattling noise with its tail.

복습 **twitch** [twitʃ] vi. 홱 잡아당기다, 잡아채다; (손가락·근육 따위가) 씰룩거리다
(said of a muscle, limb, etc.) To move involuntarily with a spasm.

복습 **lash** [læʃ] v. 부딪히다; 후려치다; n. 채찍 끈; 채찍질; 속눈썹
To hit with a lot of force.

복습 **tremble** [trémbəl] v. 떨다, 떨리다
To shake slightly, usually because you are cold or frightened.

복습 **tease** [tiːz] v. 놀리다, 희롱하다 (teasing a. 놀리는, 짓궂게 괴롭히는)
To laugh at or make fun of someone annoyingly.

복습 **weakly** [wíːkli] ad. 약하게, 가냘프게; 무기력하게; a. 몸이 약한, 허약한; 가냘픈
In a weak way.

복습 **tug** [tʌg] v. 당기다, 끌다; 노력하다; n. 힘껏 당김
If you tug something or tug at it, you give it a quick and usually strong pull.

복습 **pathetic** [pəθétik] a. 불쌍한, 애처로운; 가치 없는, (이익이) 매우 적은
Making you feel pity or sadness.

복습 **compel** [kəmpél] vt. 강제하다, 억지로 …시키다
To force someone to do something.

15. PRESSURE

- **calculus** [kǽlkjələs] n. 미적분학
  Calculus is a branch of advanced mathematics which deals with variable quantities.

- **awkwardness** [ɔ́:kwərdnis] n. 어색함, 다루기 어려움; 거북함
  The quality of an embarrassing situation.

- **scrub** [skrʌb] v. 북북 문지르다, 비벼서 씻다
  To rub something hard in order to clean it.

- **spotless** [spátlis] a. 더럽혀지지 않은, 오점이 없는
  spot (n. 얼룩, 반점) + -less (suf. …이 없는)

- **ascertain** [æ̀sərtéin] vt. 알아내다[확인하다]
  If you ascertain the truth about something, you find out what it is, especially by making a deliberate effort to do so.

- **aura** [ɔ́:rə] n. (어떤 사람이나 장소에 서려 있는 독특한) 기운[분위기]
  An aura is a quality or feeling that seems to surround a person or place or to come from them.

- **contentment** [kənténtmənt] n. 만족, 흡족함, 안도감
  A feeling of happiness or satisfaction.

- **dilute** [dilú:t] v. (효과 등을) 희석시키다[약화시키다]
  To make something weaker or less effective.

- **crescent** [krésənt] n. 초승달, 초승달 모양(의 것); a. 초승달 모양의
  A curved shape that is wide in the middle and pointed at each end.

- **distract** [distrǽkt] vt. (마음·주의를) 흐트러뜨리다, 딴 데로 돌리다
  Nervous, anxious or confused because you are worried about something.

- **terrify** [térəfài] vt. 무섭게[겁나게] 하다, 놀래다 (terrifying a. 놀라게 하는; 무서운)
  If something terrifies you, it makes you feel extremely frightened.

- **semidry** [sèmidrái] a. 반쯤 건조한
  Somewhat dry, but not severely arid.

Vocabulary in New Moon

comprehensible [kàmprihénsəbəl] a. 이해할 수 있는, 알기 쉬운
Something that is comprehensible can be understood.

deliberate [dilíbərèit] a. 신중한, 계획적인; v. 숙고하다; 심의하다
If you do something that is deliberate, you planned to do it beforehand, and so it happens on purpose.

horizon [həráizən] n. 지평선, 수평선
The line far away where the land or sea seems to meet the sky.

inspiration [ìnspəréiʃən] n. 영감; 고취, 고무
A sudden good idea.

uncomprehending [ənkàmprihéndiŋ] a. 잘 이해되지 않는, 이해력이 부족한
Not understanding a situation or what is happening.

addict [ədíkt] vt. 중독되게 하다, (악습에) 빠지게 하다; n. 중독자, 열광하는 사람
To cause (someone or oneself) to become dependent (on something, especially a narcotic drug).

etch [etʃ] vt. 선명하게 그리다, 뚜렷이 새기다[아로새기다]
To make a strong clear mark or pattern on something.

sneak [sni:k] v. (sneaked-sneaked 또는 snuck-snuck) 슬쩍하다, 몰래 움직이다, 살금살금 들어가다; n. 살금살금 몰래 함
To go somewhere secretly, trying to avoid being seen.

★ **downright** [dáunràit] ad. 철저하게, 완전히; a. 곧은, 철저한
Completely; Extremely.

★ **sultry** [sʌ́ltri] a. 무더운, 후텁지근한
Sultry weather is hot and damp.

hedge [hedʒ] v. 변명의 여지를 남겨두다; 얼버무리다; 울타리를 두르다; n. 울타리; 대비책
If you hedge against something unpleasant or unwanted that might affect you, especially losing money, you do something which will protect you from it.

complacent [kəmpléisənt] a. 마음에 흡족한, 자기만족의; 개의치 않는
Self-satisfied; Smug.

15. PRESSURE

tricky [tríki] a. 교묘한, 까다로운
If you describe a task or problem as tricky, you mean that it is difficult to do or deal with.

generation [dʒènəréiʃən] n. 동시대의 사람들, 세대, 대(代)
All the people who were born at about the same time.

lethal [líːθəl] a. 파괴적인, 치명적인
Causing or able to cause death.

flip [flip] v. (책장 등을) 넘기다; 홱 뒤집(히)다, 홱 젖히다; (너무 흥분하여) 확 돌아 버리다
If you flip through the pages of a book, for example, you quickly turn over the pages in order to find a particular one or to get an idea of the contents.

aimless [éimlis] a. 목적이[목표가] 없는 (aimlessly ad. 막연하게, 목적 없이)
A person or activity that is aimless has no clear purpose or plan.

claustrophobic [klɔ̀ːstrəfóubik] a. 밀실 공포증의
If you feel claustrophobic, you feel very uncomfortable or anxious when you are in a small, crowded, or enclosed place.

claustrophobia [klɔ̀ːstrəfóubiə] n. [의학] 밀실 공포, 폐소(閉所) 공포증
An extreme fear of being in a small confined place; The unpleasant feeling that a person gets in a situation which restricts them.

squirrel [skwə́ːrəl] n. 다람쥐
A small furry animal with a long furry tail which climbs trees and feeds on nuts and seeds.

eerie [íəri] a. 기분 나쁜, 무시무시한, 섬뜩한
Strange in a frightening and mysterious way.

perceptible [pərséptəbəl] a. 지각할 수 있는
Great enough for you to notice it.

sluggish [slʌ́giʃ] a. 둔한, 활발하지 못한; 느린, 굼뜬; 부진한
(sluggishly ad. 느리게, 둔하게)
Moving, reacting or working more slowly than normal and in a way that seems lazy.

277

Vocabulary in New Moon

gruesome [grú:səm] a. 소름 끼치는, 무시무시한; 힘든
Something that is gruesome is extremely unpleasant and shocking.

ferocious [fəróuʃəs] a. 사나운, 잔인한, 지독한
Fierce and violent.

bunker [bʌ́ŋkər] v. 벙커에 들어가다; n. 엄폐호; 은신처
To place or store in a bunker.

trudge [trʌdʒ] v. 터벅터벅 걷다; n. 터덕터덕 걸음
To walk slowly with a lot of effort, especially over a difficult surface or while carrying something heavy.

tangle [tǽŋgəl] v. 얽히게 하다; 엉키다; n. 엉킴; 혼란
If something is tangled or tangles, it becomes twisted together in an untidy way.

brooding [brú:diŋ] a. 생각에 잠긴, 음울한, 시무룩한 (broodingly ad. 음울하게)
Sad and mysterious or threatening.

unendurable [ʌnindjúərəbəl] a. 지탱할[참을] 수 없는
Too bad, unpleasant, etc. to bear.

shred [ʃred] n. 끄트러기, 조각, 파편; v. 조각조각으로 찢다, 갈가리 찢다
If there is not a shred of something, there is not even a small amount of it.

violate [váiəleit] vt. 어기다, 위반하다, 방해하다
To disregard or break (a law, agreement or oath).

condemn [kəndém] vt. 비난하다, 힐난하다; 유죄 판결을 내리다
If you condemn something, you say that it is very bad and unacceptable.

★ **bearable** [bɛ́ərəbəl] a. 견딜 수 있는, (추위·더위 등이) 견딜 만한
If an unpleasant situation is bearable, you can accept or deal with it.

fester [féstər] v. (상처가) 곪다, 곪게 하다; 괴롭히다, 괴로워하다
If a cut or other injury festers, it becomes infected and produces pus.

revenge [rivéndʒ] n. 복수, 보복, 원한; vt. 복수하다, 원수를 갚다
Something that you do in order to make somebody suffer because they have made you suffer.

15. PRESSURE

- **tame** [teim] vt. 길들이다; 재비하다; 억누르다; a. 길든, 길러서 길들인
  If someone tames a wild animal or bird, they train it not to be afraid of humans and to do what they say.

- **static** [stǽtik] n. 정전기
  Electricity that gathers on or in an object which is not a conductor of electricity.

  battering [bǽtəriŋ] n. 구타, 타격, 두들겨 패기, 통렬한 비난
  A violent attack that injures or damages somebody/something.

- **foam** [foum] n. 거품, 물거품, 포말(泡沫)(froth)
  Foam consists of a mass of small bubbles that are formed when air and a liquid are mixed together.

- **spiral** [spáiərəl] v. 소용돌이 꼴로 나아가다; n. 소용돌이, 나선
  To move in a spiral curve.

- **vivid** [vívid] a. 생생한; 발랄한; 선명한, 뚜렷한
  Producing very clear, powerful and detailed images in the mind.

- **flare** [flɛər] v. 불길이 너울거리다; n. 너울거리는 불길; 확 타오름
  If a fire flares, the flames suddenly become larger.

  agonizing [ǽgənàiziŋ] a. 고뇌하게 하는, 괴로워하는 (agonizingly ad. 괴로울 정도로)
  Something that is agonizing causes you to feel great physical or mental pain.

- **quench** [kwentʃ] v. (타는 불을) 끄다
  To stop a fire from burning.

- **intolerable** [intálərəbəl] a. 참을 수 없는, 견딜 수 없는
  So bad or difficult that you cannot tolerate it.

- **realization** [rìːələzéiʃən] n. 깨달음, 자각, 인식
  Coming to understand something clearly and distinctly.

- **jog** [dʒɑg] v. 천천히 달리다, 조깅하다; n. 조깅
  To run slowly and steadily.

  outcrop [áutkràp] n. (지층·광맥 따위의) 노출(부), 노두(露頭)
  A large mass of rock that stands above the surface of the ground.

Vocabulary in New Moon

- **splatter** [splǽtər] v. (물·흙탕 등이) 튀다; 물보라 치며 떨어지다
  If a thick wet substance splatters on something or is splattered on it, it drops or is thrown over it.

- **convince** [kənvíns] vt. 확신시키다; 설득하다
  To persuade someone or make them certain.

- **reckless** [réklis] a. 무모한, 분별없는
  Showing a lack of care about danger and the possible results of your actions.

- **eddy** [édi] n. (공기·먼지·물의) 회오리[소용돌이]
  A movement of air, dust or water in a circle.

- **blindly** [bláindli] ad. 맹목적으로, 무턱대고
  Without being able to see what you are doing.

- **caress** [kərés] vt. 애무하다, 껴안다, 어루만지다
  To touch or stroke gently and lovingly.

- **encounter** [enkáuntər] v. 만나다, 마주치다
  To experience something, especially something unpleasant or difficult, while you are trying to do something else.

- **exhale** [ekshéil] v. (숨 등을) 내쉬다; (증기·향기 등을) 발산[방출]하다
  To breathe out the air or smoke, etc. in your lungs.

- **shatter** [ʃǽtər] v. 산산조각이 나다; 파괴하다; 충격을 주다; n. 파편, 부서진 조각
  If something shatters or is shattered, it breaks into a lot of small pieces.

- **illusion** [ilúːʒən] n. 환영, 환각, 착각
  A false or misleading impression, idea, belief or understanding.

- **disapprove** [dìsəprúːv] v. 찬성하지 않다, 안 된다고 하다
  (disapproving a. 못마땅해 하는)
  To feel that something or someone is bad, wrong etc.

- **intonation** [ìntənéiʃən] n. (소리의) 억양, 어조
  The rise and fall of the voice in speaking, especially as this affects the meaning of what is being said.

15. PRESSURE

drench [drentʃ] vt. 흠뻑 젖게 하다
To drench something or someone means to make them completely wet.

ingrained [ingréind] a. (습관·태도 등이) 뿌리 깊은, 깊이 몸에 밴
Ingrained habits and beliefs are difficult to change or remove.

crouch [krautʃ] v. 몸을 구부리다, 쭈그리다, 웅크리다
To bend your knees and lower yourself so that you are close to the ground and leaning forward slightly.

fling [fliŋ] vt. (flung-flung) 던지다, 내던지다, (문 등을) 왈칵 열다
To open a door or window roughly, using a lot of force.

meteor [míːtiər] n. [천문] 유성(流星), 별똥별; 운석(隕石)
A piece of rock or metal that burns very brightly when it enters the earth's atmosphere from space.

exhilaration [igzìləréiʃən] n. 기분을 돋움; 유쾌한 기분, 들뜸; 흥분
Excitement and happiness.

vainly [véinli] ad. 헛사로, 헛되이
Without success.

unconquerable [ʌ̀nkɑ́ŋkərəbəl] a. 정복[극복]하기 어려운
Too strong to be defeated or changed.

gravity [grǽvəti] n. 중력
The force that makes objects fall to the ground.

twirl [twəːrl] v. 빠르게 돌다, 빙빙 돌리다; n. 회전, 비틀어 돌림
If you twirl something or if it twirls, it turns around and around with a smooth, fairly fast movement.

spiral [spáiərəl] n. 소용돌이, 나선
A shape or design, consisting of a continuous curved line that winds around a central point, with each curve further away from the center.

plunge [plʌndʒ] v. 던져 넣다; 추락하다; 뛰어들다, 돌진하다; n. 돌진
To fall suddenly and often a long way forward, down or into something.

Vocabulary in New Moon

adrenaline [ədrénəlin] n. 아드레날린
A substance which your body produces when you are angry, scared, or excited. It makes your heart beat faster and gives you more energy.

preoccupy [pri:ákjəpài] vt. 먼저 점유하다; 선취하다; 마음을 빼앗다
pre (pre. 먼저) + occupy (v. 점유하다)

sheer [ʃiər] a. 순전한, 섞이지 않은, 얇은; ad. 완전히, 순전히
You can use sheer to emphasize that a state or situation is complete and does not involve or is not mixed with anything else.

menace [ménəs] n. 협박, 위협; (구어) 골칫거리; vt. 위협하다
Something that is likely to cause harm.

lurk [lə:rk] vi. 숨다, 잠복하다; n. 잠복, 밀행
If someone lurks somewhere, they wait there secretly so that they cannot be seen, usually because they intend to do something bad.

halves [hævz] n. (pl.) 반으로 나눈 것 (half의 복수)
Either of the two equal or nearly equal parts that together make up a whole.

riptide [ríptàid] (= rip tide) n. 역조(逆潮: 둘 이상의 물결이 만나면서 물살이 거센 곳)
A riptide is an area of sea where two different currents meet or where the water is extremely deep. Riptides make the water very rough and dangerous.

parallel [pǽrəlèl] a. 평행의, 나란한; 유사한, 대응하는
Two or more lines that are parallel to each other are the same distance apart at every point.

downward [dáunwərd] a. 아래를 향한, 하향의; ad. 아래쪽으로
Towards a lower position.

rag [ræg] n. 넝마, 걸레 (rag doll n. 헝겊 인형, 봉제완구)
A piece of old, often torn, cloth used especially for cleaning things.

urgent [ə́:rdʒənt] a. 긴급한, 절박한 (urgently ad. 긴급하게)
If something is urgent, it needs to be dealt with as soon as possible.

numb [nʌm] a. 감각을 잃은; 멍한, 망연자실한; vt. 감각을 잃게 하다; 망연자실케 하다
If a part of your body is numb, you cannot feel anything there.

15. PRESSURE

buffeting [bʌ́fitiŋ] n. 난타
(of wind, rain, etc.) To hit something repeatedly and with great force.

dizzy [dízi] a. 현기증 나는, 아찔한 (dizziness n. 현기증)
If you feel dizzy, you feel as if everything is spinning round and being unable to balance.

yell [jel] v. 소리치다, 고함치다; n. 고함, 부르짖음
If you yell, you shout loudly, usually because you are excited, angry, or in pain.

lightheaded [láithedid] a. 머리가 어찔어찔한; 변덕스러운
(lightheadedness n. 생각 없음, 경솔함)
Not completely in control of your thoughts or movements.

cliché [kli(:)ʃéi] n. 진부한 표현, 상투적인 문구
A phrase or an idea that has been used so often that it no longer has much meaning and is not interesting.

subconscious [sʌbkánʃəs] n., a. 잠재의식(의), 어렴풋이 의식(하는)
The mental processes that go on below the level of conscious awareness.

flawless [flɔ́:lis] a. 흠 없는; (작품·사고·인격·용모 등이) 완전한, 완벽한
Without flaws and therefore perfect.

glint [glint] v. 반짝이다, 빛나다; n. 반짝임, 섬광
If something glints, it produces or reflects a quick flash of light.

nostril [nástril] n. 콧구멍
Your nostrils are the two openings at the end of your nose.

rage [reidʒ] n. 격노, 분노; 열광; v. 격노하다[하게 하다]; 맹렬히 계속되다
Rage is strong anger that is difficult to control.

cramp [kræmp] vt. 속박하다, 제한하다, 가두다; n. 꺾쇠, 침쇠
To limit someone, especially to prevent them from enjoying a full life.

gloom [glu:m] n. 어둠침침함, 어둠, 그늘, 암흑
A feeling of being sad and without hope.

whoosh [hwú(:)ʃ] v. 쉭 하고 움직이다; n. 휙[쉭] (하는 소리)
If something whooshes somewhere, it moves there quickly or suddenly.

Comprehension Quiz

 16. PARIS

1. Who saved Bella from the water?

  A. Sam

  B. Jacob

  C. Edward

  D. Charlie

2. What happened to Harry Clearwater?

  A. He died from a heart attack.

  B. He was killed by Victoria.

  C. He fell from a cliff and drowned.

  D. He hit his head and died.

3. Before Jacob smelled a vampire, Bella wanted to _____.

  A. tell Jacob everything and try to commit to him

  B. tell Jacob about her relationship with Edward

  C. kiss Jacob on the cheek

  D. tell Jacob that she couldn't be in a relationship with him

16. PARIS

4. Why did Bella think Carlisle was at house?

A. Jacob smelled a vampire.

B. She saw Carlisle's car outside of her house.

C. Edward's voice told her Carlisle was there.

D. She knew that Carlisle would help her if she was in danger.

5. After Bella stepped inside her house, she realized _____.

A. Victoria was inside her house

B. she was in love with Jacob

C. Edward was inside her house

D. she saw Victoria at the harbor

Vocabulary in New Moon

disorient [disɔ́:riənt] vt. 길을 잃게 하다, 방향[감각]을 상실하게 하다
To cause to lose orientation or direction.

slam [slæm] v. 털썩 내려놓다; (문 따위를) 탕 닫다, 세게 치다; n. 쾅 (하는 소리)
If you slam something down, you put it there quickly and with great force.

lung [lʌŋ] n. [해부] 폐, 허파
Your lungs are the two organs inside your chest which fill with air when you breathe in.

gush [gʌʃ] v. (액체 등이) 분출하다, 내뿜다; (구어) 지껄여대다; n. 분출; (감정의) 격발
If a liquid gushes, it flowes or pours out quickly and in large quantities.

torrent [tɔ́:rənt] n. 급류, 여울; (pl.) 억수, 연발
A large amount of water moving very quickly.

cruel [krú:əl] a. 잔혹한, 무자비한
Extremely unkind and unpleasant and causing pain to people or animals intentionally.

stab [stæb] n. 찌름, (찌르는 듯한) 고통; v. (칼 따위로) 찌르다
Sudden sharp pain or unpleasant feeling.

smack [smæk] vt. 찰싹 치다, 쳐 날리다; n. 찰싹 하는 소리
To hit someone or something loudly and heavily, especially with your hand.

shoulder blade [ʃóuldər bleid] n. 어깨뼈, 견갑골
One of the two flat bones on each side of your back.

volley [váli] n. 연발, 일제 사격
A volley of gunfire is a lot of bullets that travel through the air at the same time.

bloom [blu:m] vt. (빛나는 것을) 흐리게 하다; 꽃을 피우다; n. 꽃; 혈색
When a plant or tree blooms, it produces flowers. When a flower blooms, it opens.

whirl [hwə:rl] v. 빙글 돌다, 선회하다
To move around or turn around very quickly.

16. PARIS

tense [tens] a. 팽팽한, 긴장한, 긴박한; v. 팽팽하게 하다, 긴장시키다[하다]
Nervous and anxious and unable to relax.

swish [swiʃ] v. 휙 소리 내다, 휘두르다; 튀기다; n. 휙 소리
If something swishes or if you swish it, it moves quickly through the air, making a soft sound.

sickening [síkəniŋ] a. 병나게 하는, 욕지기나게 하는
(sickeningly ad. 구역질나게, 넌더리나게)
Making you feel disgusted or shocked.

jar [dʒɑːr] v. 깜짝 놀라게 하다; 충격을 주다[받다]; 삐걱거리다; 진동하다
If something jars on you, you find it unpleasant, disturbing, or shocking.

awareness [əwέərnis] n. 알아채고[깨닫고] 있음, 자각, 인식; 의식
Knowing that something exists and is important; Being interested in something.

grainy [gréini] a. (표면이) 오톨도톨한; 알갱이가 있는; 거친
Grainy means having a rough surface or texture, or containing small bits of something.

frantic [frǽntik] a. 광란의, 미친 듯 날뛰는
Behaving in a wild and uncontrolled way.

passageway [pǽsidʒwèi] n. 복도, 통로
A long narrow area with walls on either side which connects one place to another.

scrub [skrʌb] v. 북북 문지르다, 비벼서 씻다
To rub something hard in order to clean it.

fling [fliŋ] vt. 던지다, 내던지다; (문 등을) 왈칵 열다
To open a door or window roughly, using a lot of force.

croak [krouk] v. (낮고 거친 목소리로) 꺽꺽거리듯[목이 쉰 듯] 말하다
To speak or say something with a rough low voice.

Vocabulary in New Moon

gasp [gæsp] v. (놀람 따위로) 숨이 막히다, 헐떡거리다; n. 헐떡거림
When you gasp, you take a short quick breath through your mouth, especially when you are surprised, shocked, or in pain.

stutter [stʌ́tər] v. 말을 더듬다, 더듬거리며 말하다; n. 말더듬기
If someone stutters, they have difficulty speaking because they find it hard to say the first sound of a word.

hunch [hʌntʃ] vt. (등을) 둥글게 구부리다
To bend down and forwards so that your back forms a curve.

loll [lɑl] v. 축 늘어지다, 빈둥거리다
(of your head, tongue, etc.) To move or hang in a relaxed way.

vacant [véikənt] a. 빈, 비어 있는; 공허한 (vacantly ad. 멍하니, 멀거니)
If something is vacant, it is not being used by anyone.

furious [fjúəriəs] a. 맹렬한, 왕성한; 성난, 격노한
Furious is also used to describe something that is done with great energy, effort, speed, or violence.

lick [lik] vt. (불길이) 날름거리다; 넘실거리다; 핥다; n. 핥기
If flames or waves lick something, they touch it again and again with quick movements.

writhe [raið] v. 몸부림치다, 몸을 뒤틀다; n. 몸부림, 고뇌
To twist or move your body without stopping, often because you are in great pain.

weary [wíəri] a. 피로한, 지친 (wearily ad. 지쳐서, 지친 상태로)
If you are weary, you are very tired.

bay [bei] n. 만(灣), 후미, 내포 (보통 gulf보다 작음)
A bay is a part of a coast where the land curves inwards.

swirl [swəːrl] vi. 소용돌이치다, 빙빙 돌다
If liquid or flowing swirls, it moves round and round quickly.

churn [tʃəːrn] v. (흙탕물 등이[을]) 휘돌다[휘젓다]; (분노·혼란스러움 등이) 들끓다
If something churns water, mud, or dust, it moves about violently.

16. PARIS

rasp [ræsp] v. 귀에 거슬리는 소리로 말하다
To say something in a rough unpleasant voice.

turn into phrasal v. (외관·성질 따위가) …으로 변하다
To become something different.

chainsmoker [tʃéinsmòukər] n. 줄담배 피우는 사람, 골초
A chainsmoker is a person who smokes cigarettes or cigars continuously.

wince [wins] vi. (아픔·무서움 때문에) 주춤하다, 움츠리다; n. 위축
If you wince, you suddenly look as if you are suffering because you feel pain.

ridiculous [ridíkjələs] a. 웃기는, 우스꽝스러운; 터무니없는
If you say that something or someone is ridiculous, you mean that they are very foolish.

squint [skwint] v. 곁눈질을 하다, 실눈으로 보다; a. 사시의; 곁눈질하는
If you squint at something, you look at it with your eyes partly closed.

hammer [hǽmər] v. 망치로 두드리다; n. 해머, 망치
If you hammer an object such as a nail, you hit it with a hammer.

hoarse [hɔ́:rs] a. 목쉰, 쉰 목소리의 (hoarseness n. 목쉼)
If your voice is hoarse, your voice sounds rough and unclear.

absorb [əbsɔ́:rb] vt. 받아들이다, 흡수하다; 열중시키다
If you absorb information, you learn and understand it.

brainless [bréinlis] a. (머리가) 모자라는, 어리석은
Stupid; Not able to think or talk in an intelligent way.

dump [dʌmp] v. (아무렇게나) 내려놓다
If you dump something somewhere, you put it or unload it there quickly and carelessly.

bang [bæŋ] v. 탕 치다, 쾅 닫(히)다; 부딪치다; n. 쾅 하는 소리
To hit something hard, making a loud noise.

Vocabulary in New Moon

cramp [kræmp] vt. 속박하다, 제한하다, 가두다; n. 꺾쇠, 죔쇠
(cramped a. 비좁은, 갑갑한)
To limit someone, especially to prevent them from enjoying a full life.

desolate [désəlit] a. 황폐한, 황량한, 쓸쓸한
Unattractive and empty, with no people or nothing pleasant in it.

ominous [ámənəs] a. 불길한, 나쁜 징조의
If you describe something as ominous, you mean that it worries you because it makes you think that something unpleasant is going to happen.

exhaust [igzɔ́:st] vt. 다 써버리다, 소진시키다 (exhausted a. 지칠 대로 지친)
If something exhausts you, it makes you so tired, either physically or mentally, that you have no energy left.

yawn [jɔ:n] vi. 하품하다; n. 하품
To open your mouth wide and breathe in deeply through it, usually because you are tired or bored.

fervent [fə́:rvənt] a. 열렬한, 강렬한, (감정 따위가) 격한; 뜨거운
(fervently ad. 열렬하게, 격하게)
Having or showing very strong and sincere feelings about something.

★ **radiator** [réidièitər] n. (빛·열 등의) 방사[복사·방열]체; 방열기, 난방기
A hollow metal device for heating rooms. Radiators are usually connected by pipes through which hot water is sent.

soak [souk] v. 젖다, 스며들다; 적시다, 빨아들이다; n. 적심
If a liquid soaks something or if you soak something with a liquid, the liquid makes the thing very wet.

ache [eik] vi. 아프다, 쑤시다
To feel a continuous dull pain.

unconsciousness [ʌ̀nkánʃəsnis] n. 의식 불명[인사불성] (상태)
A state like sleep caused by injury or illness, when you are unable to use your senses.

vaguely [véigli] ad. 모호하게, 막연히
In a way that is not detailed or exact.

16. PARIS

snore [snɔːr] v. 코를 골다
To breathe in a very noisy way while you are sleeping.

soothe [suːð] v. 달래다, 어르다; (통증 등을) 완화시키다, 누그러뜨리다
To make someone feel calmer and less anxious.

lullaby [lʌ́ləbài] n. 자장가
A soft gentle song sung to make a child go to sleep.

ramshackle [rǽmʃæ̀kəl] a. 무너질 듯한, 덜커덩거리는; 건들건들하는, 약한
Badly or untidily made and likely to break or fall down easily.

quilt [kwilt] n. (솜·털·깃털 따위를 둔) 누비이불; 누비 침대 커버
A thin cover filled with feathers or some other warm, soft material, which you put over your blankets when you are in bed.

★ **meaningless** [míːniŋlis] a. 뜻[목적] 없는, 무의미한; 무익한
Without any purpose or reason and therefore not worth doing or having.

consciousness [kánʃəsnis] n. 의식, 자각
Your consciousness is your mind and your thoughts.

limp [limp] a. 기운이[활기가] 없는, 축 처진[늘어진]
If you describe something as limp, you mean that it is soft or weak when it should be firm or strong.

banish [bǽniʃ] vt. 추방하다, 내쫓다
To order somebody to leave a place, especially a country, as a punishment.

lid [lid] n. 눈꺼풀(eyelid); 뚜껑
Your lids are the pieces of skin which cover your eyes when you close them.

placeholder [pléishouldər] n. [언어] (문장에서) 필요하지만 의미가 없는 요소
An item which is necessary in a sentence, but does not have real meaning, for example the word 'it' in 'It's a pity she left'.

confide [kənfáid] v. 신임하다, 신뢰하다; 비밀을 털어놓다
To tell somebody secrets and personal information that you do not want other people to know.

Vocabulary in New Moon

devastate [dévəstèit] vt. (사람에게) 엄청난 충격을 주다; 비탄에 빠뜨리다
To make somebody feel very shocked and sad.

leftover [léftòuvər] a. 나머지의, 남은; n. 나머지; 남은 음식
You use leftover to describe an amount of something that remains after the rest of it has been used or eaten.

irresponsible [ìrispánsəbəl] a. 무책임한, 신뢰할 수 없는
(of a person) Not thinking enough about the effects of what they do.

Evel Knievel n. 이블 크니블 (오토바이로 14대 버스를 뛰어넘은 스턴트맨)

perspective [pəːrspéktiv] n. 가망, 전망; 원근(화)법, 투시(화)법
A particular perspective is a particular way of thinking about something, especially one that is influenced by your beliefs or experiences.

miserable [mízrəbl] a. 불쌍한, 비참한, 불행한, 딱한, 가엾은
Unpleasant and causing unhappiness.

hallucination [həlùːsənéiʃən] n. 환각, 망상
A hallucination is the experience of seeing something that is not really there because you are ill or have taken a drug.

thrash [θræʃ] v. 몸부림치다; 마구 때리다; n. 때림; 패배시킴
If someone thrashes their arms or legs about, they move in a wild or violent way.

sting [stiŋ] vt. 찌르다, 쏘다; n. 찌르기, 쏘기; (동물의) 침, 고통
If something stings you, a sharp part of it is pushed into your skin so that you feel a sharp pain.

squelch [skweltʃ] v. 찌부러뜨리다[지다]; n. 철벅철벅함[하는 소리]; 찌부러뜨림, 진압
To make a sucking sound like the one produced when you are walking on soft wet ground.

identifiable [aidéntəfàiəbəl] a. 인식 가능한, 알아볼 수 있는
Something or someone that is identifiable can be recognized.

uncharacteristic [ənkæ̀riktərístik] a. 특징이 없는, 특색을 나타내지 않는
(uncharacteristically ad. 평소답지 않게)
un (pre. 부정의 접두어) + characteristic (a. 특징적인, 특성이 있는)

16. PARIS

gravelly [grǽvəli] a. 목소리가 걸걸한; 자갈이 많은
Deep and with a rough sound.

momentarily [mòuməntérəli] ad. 잠시, 잠깐
Momentarily means for a short time.

startle [stá:rtl] v. 깜짝 놀라게 하다; 움찔하다; n. 깜짝 놀람
If something sudden and unexpected startles you, it surprises and frightens you slightly.

grunt [grʌnt] vi. (돼지가) 꿀꿀거리다; (사람이) 툴툴거리다; n. 꿀꿀[툴툴]거리는 소리
A short low sound that a person or animal makes in their throat.

grief [gri:f] n. 슬픔, 비탄
Grief is a feeling of extreme sadness.

composure [kəmpóuʒər] n. 침착, 냉정, 평정, 자제
Composure is the appearance or feeling of calm and the ability to control your feelings.

agonize [ǽgənàiz] v. 번민하다, 괴롭히다, 괴로워하다
If you agonize over something, you feel very anxious about it and spend a long time thinking about it.

gonna [góunə] etc. (미·구어) …할 예정인(going to)
Non-standard a way of saying or writing 'going to' in informal speech, when it refers to the future.

arrangement [əréindʒmənt] n. 정돈, 정리; 배열, 조정, 준비
A plan or preparation that you make so that something can happen.

swallow [swálou] vt. 들이켜다, 삼키다, 꿀꺽 삼키다; 마른침을 삼키다
If you swallow something, you cause it to go from your mouth down into your stomach.

hasty [héisti] a. 급한, 신속한 (hastily ad. 급히, 서둘러서)
Hurried; Without enough thought or preparation.

rim [rim] v. 둘러싸다, 테를 두르다; n. (둥근 물건의) 가장자리, 테두리
To form an edge around something.

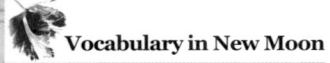

Vocabulary in New Moon

listlessly [lístlisli] ad. 마음 내키지 않아; 노곤하게; 무관심하게
Having no energy or enthusiasm.

peeping tom [pi:piŋ tám] n. 엿보기 좋아하는 사람, 관음증 환자
If you refer to someone as a Peeping Tom, you mean that they secretly watch other people, especially when those people are taking their clothes off.

peer [piər] vi. 자세히 보다, 응시하다; 희미하게 나타나다
If you peer at something, you look at it very hard.

grieve [gri:v] v. 몹시 슬퍼하다, 슬프게 하다
To feel or express great sadness.

fickle [fíkəl] a. 변하기 쉬운, 마음이 잘 변하는, 변덕스러운
Often changing their mind in an unreasonable way so that you cannot rely on them.

crush [krʌʃ] v. 부서지다; 짓밟다; 잔뜩 구겨지다[구기다]; n. 눌러 터뜨림
To crush something means to press it very hard so that its shape is destroyed or so that it breaks into pieces.

apologetic [əpàlədʒétik] a. 사죄의, 미안해하는
Showing that you are sorry that something has happened, especially because you feel guilty or embarrassed about it.

swear [swɛər] v. 맹세하다, 선서하다; n. 맹세, 선서
If you swear to do something, you promise in a serious way that you will do it.

throaty [θróuti] a. (목소리가) 목 안쪽에서 나오는, 묵직한, 목쉰
A throaty voice or laugh is low and rather rough.

circumstance [sə́:rkəmstæns] n. 상황, 환경, 사정
A fact, occurrence or condition, especially when relating to an act or event.

begrudge [bigrʌ́dʒ] vt. (…을) 주기를 꺼리다, 내놓기 아까워하다; (…하기를) 꺼리다
To feel unhappy about having to do, pay or give something.

assault [əsɔ́:lt] vt. 폭행하다; 급습하다; n. 습격; 폭행
To attack someone violently.

16. PARIS

ignition [igníʃən] n. 점화, 발화; (내연 기관의) 점화 장치
The electrical system of a vehicle that makes the fuel begin to burn to start the engine; The place in a vehicle where you start this system.

rev [rev] v. (엔진 등의) 회전 속도를 올리다; n. (구어) (엔진·레코드 등의) 회전
When the engine of a vehicle revs, or when you rev it, the engine speed is increased as the accelerator is pressed.

sputter [spʌ́tər] v. 푸푸 소리를 내다, 흥분하여 말하다
To make several quick explosive sounds.

falter [fɔ́:ltər] vi. 비틀거리다, 말을 더듬다; 머뭇거리다, 움찔[멈칫]하다
To become weaker or less effective.

dammit [dǽmit] (= damn it) int. (구어) 제기랄

rake [reik] vi. (무엇을 찾아 어디를) 샅샅이 뒤지다
To search a place carefully for something.

hiss [his] v. 쉿 하는 소리를 내다; n. 쉿 (제지·힐책의 소리)
If people hiss at someone such as a performer or a person making a speech, they express their disapproval or dislike of that person.

split [split] v. 쪼개다, 찢다, 째다 (split second n. 아주 짧은 순간)
If something splits or if you split it, it is divided into two or more parts.

scan [skæn] v. 자세히 조사하다; 유심히 쳐다보다; 대충 훑어 보다; n. 정밀 검사; 스캔
To look at something carefully, with the eyes, in order to obtain information.

squeal [skwi:l] v. 꽥꽥거리다, 비명을 지르다; 끼익 소리 내다 n. 꽥꽥거리는 소리
If someone or something squeals, they make a long, high-pitched sound.

pavement [péivmənt] n. 포장 도로
A flat part at the side of a road for people to walk on.

furthest [fə́:rðist] ad. 가장 멀리(에); 가장(most)
At or to the greatest distance in space or time.

autophile [ɔ́:toufàil] n. 자동차 애호가
auto (n. 자동차) + (-phile n. 사랑하는 사람)

Vocabulary in New Moon

Mercedes [mərséidi:z] n. 메르세데스 벤츠 (독일제 고급 승용차; 상표명)

horsepower [hɔ́:rspàuər] n. [기계] 마력
A unit for measuring the power of an engine.

purr [pə:r] vi. (차 엔진이) 낮은 소리를 내다, 낮고 부드럽게 말하다; n. 목구멍을 울림[울리는 소리]
To make a quiet continuous quiet, continuous, vibration sound.

dusk [dʌsk] n. 땅거미, 황혼, 어스름
The time of day when the light has almost gone, but it is not yet dark.

gun [gʌn] v. (차량을) 총알같이 몰기 시작하다; (엔진이) 고속으로 돌다; n. 총; 대포
To gun an engine or a vehicle means to make it start or go faster by pressing on the accelerator pedal.

stomp [stɑmp] v. 짓밟다, 발을 구르며 걷다; n. 발 구르기
To walk with heavy steps or to put your foot down very hard, especially.

dashboard [dǽʃbɔ̀:rd] n. (자동차·비행기의) 계기판, 대시보드
The part of a car in front of the driver that has instruments and controls in it.

aghast [əgǽst] a. 소스라치게 놀라서, 겁이 나서
Suddenly filled with strong feelings of shock and anxiety.

violent [váiələnt] a. 격렬한, 맹렬한
Involving or caused by physical force that is intended to hurt or kill someone.

pant [pænt] v. 헐떡거리다, 숨차다; 헐떡거리며 말하다
To breathe quickly and loudly through your mouth, usually because you have been doing something very energetic.

unwilling [ʌnwíliŋ] a. 마음 내키지 않는, 마지못해 하는
Not wanting to do something and refusing to do it.

congeal [kəndʒí:l] v. 얼리다, 얼다; 응결[응고]시키다[하다]; 고정화[경직]시키다
To become thick or solid.

spasm [spǽzəm] n. 경련, 발작
A sudden and often painful contracting of a muscle, which you cannot control.

16. PARIS

betrayal [bitréiəl] n. 배반, 배신
The act of betraying somebody/something or the fact of being betrayed.

emotionless [imóuʃənlis] a. 무표정한, 무감동의; 감정이 담기지 않은
Not showing any emotion.

slap [slæp] n. 찰싹 때리기[는 소리]; v. 찰싹 때리다, 세게 치다; 아무렇게나 바르다
The action of hitting somebody or something with the flat part of your hand.

unclench [ʌnkléntʃ] v. 펴다; 억지로 비틀어 열다
To open (something) that was clenched; To relax, especially one's muscles.

neutral [njúːtrəl] n. (기어 위치의) 중립
The position of the gears of a vehicle in which no power is carried from the engine to the wheels.

remorse [rimɔ́ːrs] n. 후회, 양심의 가책
A deep feeling of guilt, regret and bitterness for something wrong or bad which one has done.

concentration [kànsəntréiʃən] n. 집결, 집중(력)
The ability to think about something carefully or for a long time.

pang [pæŋ] n. 격통, 고통; 비통, 상심, 번민
A sudden strong feeling of physical or emotional pain.

doorknob [dɔ́ːrnàb] n. (문의) 손잡이
A type of round handle for a door, that you turn in order to open the door.

fumble [fʌ́mbəl] vi. 손으로 더듬어 찾다; 우물우물 말하다
If you fumble for something or fumble with something, you try and reach for it or hold it in a clumsy way.

harbor [háːrbər] n. 항구, 항만; 피난처; vt. (계획·생각 등을) 품다; 숨겨주다; 잠복하다
An area of water on the coast, protected from the open sea by strong walls, where ships can shelter.

Comprehension Quiz

 17. VISITOR

1. What did Alice notice about Bella?
A. Bella took the breakup with Edward well.

B. Bella smelled great.

C. Bella was lying to her about Jacob.

D. Bella looked and smelled bad.

2. Charlie said Bella threw a tantrum because _____ _____.
A. he wanted Bella to date Jacob

B. he told Bella she was silly for loving Edward

C. he stopped letting Bella see Jacob

D. he wanted Renee to take Bella to Florida

3. Where was Edward?
A. South America

B. Europe

C. South Africa

D. Alaska

17. VISITOR

4. What did Alice find out about her past?

A. A lot of information about her mother's life from old newspapers

B. Her sister was still alive in a small town.

C. The date she was put in the asylum and the date on her tombstone were the same.

D. Why her parents put her into an asylum.

5. Why was Alice annoyed when the doorbell rang?

A. She didn't want Bella being friends with werewolves.

B. She didn't want anyone interrupting her conversation with Bella.

C. She found out that werewolves interfered with her seeing the future.

D. She had to leave the house because Jacob was at the door.

Vocabulary in New Moon

headlong [hédlɔ̀:ŋ] ad. 앞뒤 살피지 않고, 황급히; 허둥지둥
If you rush headlong into something, you do it quickly without thinking carefully about it.

mingle [míŋɡəl] v. 섞다, 섞이다, 혼합하다
To mix or bring together in combination.

inhale [inhéil] v. 들이쉬다, 흡입하다
To take air, smoke, gas, etc. into your lungs as you breathe.

scent [sent] n. 냄새, 향기; v. 냄새 맡다; 냄새를 풍기다
The scent of something is the pleasant smell that it has.

floral [flɔ́:rəl] a. 꽃의, 꽃 같은; 꽃으로 덮인
You can use floral to describe something that contains flowers or is made of flowers.

citrus [sítrəs] n. [식물] 감귤류 식물의 총칭; 그 열매
A citrus fruit is a juicy fruit with a sharp taste such as an orange, lemon, or grapefruit.

musk [mʌsk] n. 사향(麝香)(의 향기), 인조 사향
Musk is a substance with a strong smell which is used in making perfume.

sob [sɑb] vi. 흐느껴 울다
To cry noisily, taking in deep breaths.

contour [kántuər] vi. …의 윤곽을 그리다; n. 윤곽(outline), 외형, 외곽
To shape the outer edges of something such as an area of land or someone's body.

blubber [blʌ́bər] ① v. 울면서 말하다; 엉엉 울다 ② n. 고래의 기름 ③ a. (입술이) 두툼한
To cry noisily.

bawl [bɔːl] v. 고함치다, 외치다, 울부짖다; (시끄럽게) 울어대다
To cry loudly, especially in an unpleasant and annoying way.

exuberant [iɡzúːbərənt] a. 열광적인, 열의가 넘치는
Full of energy, excitement and happiness.

17. VISITOR

strain [strein] v. 잡아당기다, 긴장시키다; 분투하다
If you strain to do something, you make a great effort to do it when it is difficult to do.

puff [pʌf] v. 숨을 헉헉[헐떡]거리다
If you are puffing, you are breathing loudly and quickly with your mouth open because you are out of breath after a lot of physical effort.

nut [nʌt] n. (구어) 괴짜, 바보, 미치광이; 머리(head); 견과(호두·밤 따위)
A strange or crazy person.

imitate [ímitèit] vt. 모방하다, 흉내 내다; 따르다, 본받다
To copy the way a person speaks or behaves, in order to amuse people.

quote [kwout] vt. 인용하다; n. 인용문, 따옴표
To repeat the exact words that another person has said or written

attune [ətjúːn] vt. (파장에) 맞추다, 동조(同調)하다; 조율하다, 맞추다
To bring into harmony.

misunderstanding [mìsʌndərstǽndiŋ] n. 오해, 잘못 생각함
A situation in which a comment, an instruction, etc. is not understood correctly.

suicide [súːəsàid] v. 자살하다; n. 자살, 자해
People who commit suicide deliberately kill themselves because they do not want to continue living.

dubious [djúːbiəs] a. 의심스러운, 수상쩍은, 모호한 (dubiously ad. 수상하게, 의심스럽게)
Feeling doubt or uncertainty.

recreational [rèkriéiʃənəl] a. 레크리에이션[오락]의
Recreational means relating to things people do in their spare time to relax.

redirect [rìːdirékt] vt. …을 다시(re) 향하다(direct), (다른 주소·방향으로) 다시 보내다
To send something to a different address or in a different direction.

cock [kɑk] v. 위로 치올리다, (귀·꽁지)를 쫑긋 세우다
To move a part of your body upwards or in a particular direction.

Vocabulary in New Moon

tow [tou] vt. 끌다, 밧줄[사슬]로 끌다, 견인하다; 끌고 가다
To pull a car or boat behind another vehicle, using a rope or chain.

frown [fraun] v. 눈살을 찌푸리다, 얼굴을 찡그리다; n. 찌푸린 얼굴
To make an angry, unhappy, bringing your eyebrows together.

perplexity [pərpléksəti] n. 당황, 곤혹; 분규, 혼란
Something that is difficult to understand.

enigmatic [ènigmǽtik] a. 수수께끼 같은, 불가사의한, 불가해한, 정체를 알 수 없는
Obscure, ambiguous or puzzling.

flit [flit] vi. 휙 지나가다, 오가다; 훌쩍 날다
To fly or move quickly and lightly.

imperfect [impə́ːrfikt] a. (지식·기능 등이) 불완전한, 불충분한; 결점[결함]이 있는
Something that is imperfect has faults and is not exactly as you would like it to be.

betray [bitréi] vt. 배반하다; (남편·아내·여자 등을) 속이다
To hurt somebody who trusts you, especially by not being loyal or faithful to them.

prone [proun] a. (좋지 않은 방향으로의) 경향이 있는, (…하기) 일쑤인, (…하기) 쉬운
To be prone to something, usually something bad, means to have a tendency to be affected by it or to do it.

idiocy [ídiəsi] n. 멍청한 행동; 백치
If you refer to something as idiocy, you mean that you think it is very stupid.

reluctance [rilʌ́ktəns] n. 싫음, 마음이 내키지 않음, 마지못해 함
A certain degree of unwillingness.

gnaw [nɔː] v. 물다, 쏠다, 갉다
If people or animals gnaw something or gnaw at it, they bite it repeatedly.

allegiance [əlíːdʒəns] n. 충성, 충절, 충직
A person's continued support for a political party, religion, ruler, etc.

17. VISITOR

Quileute n. 퀼렛 부족
현존하는 인디언계 퀴요 부족에서 따옴.

gawk [gɔːk] vi. 멍청히 바라보다; n. 둔한 사람, 얼간이
To gawk at someone or something means to stare at them in a rude, stupid, or unthinking way.

blink [bliŋk] v. 눈을 깜박거리다; (등불·별 등이) 깜박이다; n. 깜박거림
When you blink or when you blink your eyes, you shut your eyes and very quickly open them again.

porcelain [pɔ́ːrsəlin] a. 자기로 만든, 깨지기 쉬운; n. 자기(磁器), (pl.) 자기 제품
A hard but delicate shiny white substance made by heating a special type of clay to a high temperature, used to make cups, plates, decorations, etc.

crease [kriːs] v. 주름투성이로 만들다; 구기다; 주름이 생기다; n. 주름, 구김살
To make a crease or creases in (paper, fabric, etc.); To develop creases.

absently [ǽbsəntli] a. 멍하니, 넋을 잃고
In a way that shows you are not looking at or thinking about what is happening around you.

sheepish [ʃíːpiʃ] a. 양 같은, 수줍어하는 (sheepishly ad. 수줍어하면서)
Slightly uncomfortable or embarrassed because you know that you have done something silly.

glower [gláuər] vi. 노려보다; 상을 찡그리다, 불쾌한 얼굴을 하다; n. 노려봄; 찌푸린 얼굴
To look in an angry, aggressive way.

chime [tʃaim] n. 차임; v. (한 벌의 종·시계가) 울리다
A ringing sound, especially one that is made by a bell.

teensy [tíːnsi] a. (= tiny) (구어) 아주 작은[적은]
Something or someone that is tiny is extremely small.

gloss over something phrasal v. …을 얼버무리다
To treat something such as a problem, mistake, etc. as if it was not important and avoid discussing it in detail.

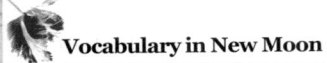
Vocabulary in New Moon

misadventure [mìsədvéntʃər] n. 불운, 불행; 불운한 사건, 재난
Bad luck or a small accident.

boredom [bɔ́:rdəm] n. 지루함, 권태
The state of being bored.

slit [slit] n. 갈라진 틈, 틈새; 길게 베어진 상처
A long narrow cut or opening.

occasionally [əkéiʒənəli] ad. 때때로, 가끔
Sometimes but not often.

carve [ka:rv] vt. 새기다, 조각하다
To make something by cutting into especially wood or stone, or to cut into the surface of stone, wood, etc.

permanent [pə́:rmənənt] a. 영구적인, 영속하는, 변하지 않는
(permanently ad. 영구적으로)
Lasting for a long time or forever.

grief [gri:f] n. 슬픔, 비탄
Grief is a feeling of extreme sadness.

murmur [mə́:rmər] v. 중얼거리다
To speak or say very quietly.

hysterical [histérikəl] a. 히스테리(성)의; 병적으로 흥분한, 이성을 잃은
In a state of extreme excitement, and crying, laughing, etc. in an uncontrolled way.

impulsive [impʌ́lsiv] a. 충동적인, 감정에 끌린 (impulsively ad. 충동적으로, 감정적으로)
If you describe someone as impulsive, you mean that they do things suddenly without thinking about them carefully first.

hyperventilate [hàipərvéntəleit] v. (흥분·놀람으로) 숨을 크게 들이쉬다
To breathe too quickly or too deeply, so that you get too much oxygen and feel dizzy.

enunciate [inʌ́nsièit] v. (또렷이) 말하다[발음하다]; 선언하다, 발표하다, 진술하다
To pronounce words clearly.

17. VISITOR

precision [prisíʒən] n. 정확, 정밀; 꼼꼼함; a. 정밀한
If you do something with precision, you do it exactly as it should be done.

stagger [stǽgər] v. 비틀거리다; 흔들리게 하다; 주저하다; n. 비틀거림
If you stagger, you walk very unsteadily, for example because you are ill or drunk.

scrutinize [skrú:tənàiz] v. 세밀히 조사하다, 철저히 검사하다, 파고 따지다
To subject to scrutiny; To examine closely.

sour [sáuər] a. (사람이) 뚱한, 시큰둥한; 심술궂은 (sourly ad. 까다롭게, 불쾌하게, 심술궂게)
Someone who is sour is bad-tempered and unfriendly.

squeeze [skwi:z] vt. 꽉 쥐다[죄다], 압착하다; n. 압착, 짜냄
If you squeeze something, you press it firmly, usually with your hands.

muse [mju:z] vi. 묵상하다, 곰곰이 생각하다
To think about something carefully and for a long time.

resign [rizáin] v. 단념하다, 따르다; 사직하다
To make yourself accept something that you do not like because you cannot change it.

skeptical [sképtikəl] a. 의심 많은, 회의적인 (skeptically ad. 의심스럽게, 회의적으로)
Having doubts that a claim or statement is true or that something will happen.

agenda [ədʒéndə] n. (단계적 수순을 담은) 계획, 행동 강령
A list of items to be discussed at a meeting.

brine [brain] n. 소금물
Very salty water, used especially for preserving food.

★ **seaweed** [síːwiːd] n. 해초, 해조(海藻)
Seaweed is a plant that grows in the sea. There are many kinds of seaweed.

hum [hʌm] v. 콧노래를 부르다, (벌·기계 등이) 윙윙거리다
To sing without opening your mouth.

Vocabulary in New Moon

tuneless [tjú:nlis] a. 음조가 맞지 않는; 비(非)선율적인
(tunelessly ad. 음이 맞지 않게; 듣기 싫게)
Not having a pleasant tune or sound.

casserole [kǽsəròul] n. 뚜껑 있는 찜냄비; 오지 냄비 요리; 고기·야채를 섞은 볶음
A casserole is a dish made of meat and vegetables that have been cooked slowly in a liquid.

★ **rotate** [róuteit] v. 돌다, 회전하다
To (cause to) turn in a circle, especially around a fixed point.

microwave [máikrouwèiv] n. 전자레인지
A microwave or a microwave oven is an oven which cooks food very quickly by electromagnetic radiation rather than by heat.

dehydrate [di:háidreit] v. 탈수하다[되다], 건조시키다, 마르다; 활력을 없애다
To lose too much water from your body; To make a person's body lose too much water.

★ **improvise** [ímprəvàiz] v. 즉석에서 하다; 즉흥 연주[작곡·노래]를 하다
To do something using whatever you have or without having planned it in advance.

butterscotch [bʌ́tərskàtʃ] n. 버터를 넣은 캔디, 버터 볼
A hard, light-brown colored, sweet food made by boiling butter and sugar together.

복습 **elate** [iléit] vt. 기운을 돋우다, 의기양양하게 하다
Extremely happy and excited, often because something has happened or been achieved.

복습 **distraction** [distrǽkʃən] n. 방심, 정신이 흐트러짐, 주의 산만
Something that turns your attention away from something you want to concentrate on.

복습 **Denali** n. 데날리
'The Great One'이란 뜻을 가진 알래스카 지역의 가장 높은 산.

복습 **cruiser** [krú:zər] n. 크라이슬러 PT 크루저(Chrysler PT Cruiser), 스테이션 웨건 콤팩트 카

17. VISITOR

embrace [embréis] vt. …을 껴안다, 포옹하다
If you embrace someone, you put your arms around them and hold them tightly, usually in order to show your love or affection for them.

fiercely [fíərsli] ad. 맹렬히, 지독히
Extremely.

blankly [blǽŋkli] ad. 멍하니, 우두커니
In a way that shows no emotion, understanding, or interest.

swivel [swívəl] v. 선회[회전]하다
To (cause to) turn round a central point in order to face in another direction.

glossy [glɔ́(:)si] a. 광택[윤]이 나는, 윤기 있는, 반질반질한
Smooth and shiny.

subdue [səbdjú:] vt. 정복하다, 진압하다; 억제하다 (subdued a. 억제된, 조용한)
To reduce the force of something, or to prevent something from existing or developing.

peer [piər] vi. 자세히 보다, 응시하다; 희미하게 나타나다
If you peer at something, you look at it very hard.

confirm [kənfə́:rm] vt. 굳게 하다, 확인하다
If you confirm something that has been stated or suggested, you say that it is true because you know about it.

plead [pli:d] v. 간청하다, 탄원하다; 변론하다; 변호하다
If you plead with someone to do something, you ask them in an intense, emotional way to do it.

shuffle [ʃʌ́fl] v. 질질 끌다, 발을 끌며 걷다; 카드를 뒤섞다; n. 발을 끌며 걷기; 뒤섞기
If you shuffle somewhere, you walk there without lifting your feet properly off the ground.

grim [grim] a. 엄한, 엄격한; 험상스러운 (grimly ad. 잔인하게, 험악하게)
Looking or sounding very serious.

Vocabulary in New Moon

- **oblivion** [əblíviən] n. 망각, 잊혀짐, 잊기 쉬움, 건망
  The state in which somebody/something has been forgotten and is no longer famous or important.

- **cringe** [krindʒ] vi. (겁이 나서) 움츠리다[움찔하다]
  If you cringe at something, you feel embarrassed or disgusted, and making a slight movement.

- **hospitalize** [háspitəlàiz] vt. 입원시키다
  If someone is hospitalized, they are sent or admitted to hospital.

- **catatonic** [kæ̀tətá:nik] a. (의학) 긴장증적인
  If you describe someone as being in a catatonic state, you mean that they are not moving or responding at all, usually as a result of illness, shock, or drugs.

- **vengeance** [véndʒəns] n. 복수, 앙갚음, 복수심
  The act of punishing or harming somebody in return for what they have done to you, your family or friends.

- **tantrum** [tǽntrəm] n. 언짢은 기분, 짜증, 불끈하기, 울화
  A sudden period of uncontrolled childish anger.

- **fury** [fjúəri] n. 격노, 격분; 격정, 열광, 광포, 격심함, 맹렬함
  Extreme anger.

- **bunch** [bʌntʃ] n. 다발, 송이; 떼, 한패
  A number of things of the same type which are growing or fastened together.

- **glum** [glʌm] a. 음울한, 시무룩한, 풀죽은
  Disappointed or unhappy, and quiet.

- **belligerent** [bəlídʒərənt] a. 적의가 있는, 도발적인; 호전적인
  Unfriendly and aggressive.

- **emotional** [imóuʃənəl] a. 감정적인, 감동적인, 감정에 호소하는
  (emotionally ad. 감정적으로)
  Having and expressing strong feel.

17. VISITOR

mature [mətjúər] v. 성숙[발달]시키다; 익(히)다; a. 성숙한, 익은
To develop emotionally and start to behave like a sensible adult.

gust [gʌst] n. 돌풍, 한바탕 부는 바람
A sudden strong movement of wind, air, rain etc.

overstate [òuvərstéit] vt. 과장하여 말하다, 허풍떨다
To say something in a way that makes it seem more important than it really is.

awkward [ɔ́:kwərd] a. 어색한, 불편한, 곤란한 (awkwardly ad. 어색하게, 거북하게)
An awkward situation is embarrassing and difficult to deal with.

suppress [səprés] vt. 억압하다, 참다, (사실을) 감추다
To prevent something from being seen or expressed or from operating.

reassure [rì:əʃúər] vt. 안심시키다, 재(re) 보증(assure)하다
To make someone feel less worried or frightened.

snort [snɔ:rt] v. (경멸·불찬성 등으로) 콧방귀 뀌다; 콧김을 뿜다
To breathe air in a noisy way out through your nose to show that you are annoyed.

assumption [əsʌ́mpʃən] n. (증거도 없이) 사실이라고 생각함; 가정, 가설
A belief or feeling that something is true or that something will happen, although there is no proof.

scoot [sku:t] v. 내닫다, 뛰어나가다
If you scoot somewhere, you go there very quickly.

faucet [fɔ́:sit] n. (수도)꼭지, 물 주둥이
A device that controls the flow of liquid, especially water, from a pipe.

splash [splæʃ] v. v. (물 등을) 끼얹다[튀기다]; n. 첨벙 하는 소리; 화사한 색[빛]
(of liquid) To fall noisily onto a surface.

bounce [bauns] v. 펄쩍 뛰다, (공 등이) 튀(게 하)다; n. 튐, 바운드
To move up or away after hitting a surface.

Vocabulary in New Moon

squeak [skwi:k] v. (쥐 따위가) 찍찍 울다, 끽끽거리며 말하다, 삐걱거리다
To make very high noises that are not loud.

yawn [jɔ:n] vi. 하품하다; n. 하품
To open your mouth wide and breathe in deeply through it, usually because you are tired or bored.

soreness [sɔ́:rnis] n. 아픔, 고통
sore (a. 아픈, 슬픔에 잠긴) + -ness (suf. 분사·형용사 등에 붙여서 성질·상태 등을 나타내는 추상 명사를 만듦)

rasp [ræsp] v. 귀에 거슬리는 소리로 말하다
To say something in a rough unpleasant voice.

charade [ʃəréid] n. 빤히 들여다보이는 수작[속임수]
A situation in which people pretend that something is true when it clearly is not.

eavesdrop [í:vzdrɑ̀p] v. 엿듣다, 도청하다
To listen secretly to a private conversation.

funeral [fjú:nərəl] n. 장례식
A ceremony for burying or burning the body of a dead person.

inevitable [inévitəbəl] a. 피할 수 없는, 필연적인
Certain to happen and unable to be avoided or prevented.

Ithaca [íθəkə] n. 이타카 (그리스 서쪽의 섬)

restore [ristɔ́:r] vt. 되돌리다, 복구하다, 회복시키다
To return to a former condition.

philosophy [filásəfi] n. 철학, 형이상학
Philosophy is the study or creation of theories about basic things such as the nature of existence, knowledge, and thought, or about how people should live.

accidental [æ̀ksidéntl] a. 우연한; 부수적인 (accidentally ad. 우연히)
An accidental event happens by chance or as the result of an accident, and is not deliberately intended.

17. VISITOR

uncover [ʌ̀nkʌ́vər] v. 폭로하다, 털어놓다, 적발하다
To discover something that was previously hidden or secret.

★ **asylum** [əsáiləm] n. (정신병자·고아·노인 등의) 보호소, 수용소
A place of safety or protection.

복습 **extreme** [ikstríːm] n. 극단; 극도; a. 극단의, 극도의
You can use extremes to refer to situations or types of behavior that have opposite qualities to each other, especially when each situation or type of behavior has such a quality to the greatest degree possible.

microfiche [máikrəfìːʃ] n. (서적 등의 여러 페이지 분을 수록하는) 마이크로필름 카드
A microfiche is a small sheet of film on which writing or other information is stored, greatly reduced in size.

‡ **engagement** [engéidʒmənt] n. 약혼; 약속, 계약
An engagement is an agreement that two people have made with each other to get married.

복습 **grave** [greiv] n. 무덤, 묘; 묘석; a. 중대한, 근엄한, 익숙한
A grave is a place where a dead person is buried.

filch [filtʃ] vt. 좀도둑질하다, 쓱싹하다, 훔치다
To steal something, especially something small or not very valuable.

archive [áːrkaiv] n. (pl.) 기록 보관소, 고(古)문서
A collection of historical records relating to a place, organization or family.

tombstone [túːmstòun] n. 묘석, 묘비
Large, flat stone that lies over a grave or stands at one end, that shows the name, age, etc. of the person buried there.

reassemble [rìːəsémbəl] v. 다시 모으다[모이다]; 새로 짜 맞추다
To come together again, or bring something together again, in a single place.

복습 **reservation** [rèzərvéiʃən] n. (미) (인디언을 위한) 정부 지정 보류지
A reservation is an area of land that is kept separate for a particular group of people to live in.

Vocabulary in New Moon

tiptoe [típtòu] vi. 발끝으로 걷다; 발돋움하다
To walk using the front parts of your feet only, so that other people cannot hear you.

recliner [rikláinər] n. 기대는 것, 안락의자
A soft comfortable chair with a back that can be pushed back at an angle so that you can lean back in it.

neglect [niglékt] vt. 무시[등한시]하다; 간과하다, 게을리[소홀히] 하다; n. 태만, 소홀
If you neglect someone or something, you fail to look after them properly.

chore [tʃɔːr] n. 지루한 일; 잡일, 허드렛일
A task that you do regularly.

doorjamb [dɔ́ːrdʒæ̀m] n. (문의) 양옆 기둥, 문설주
One of the two vertical posts on either side of an opening into which a door fits.

nonchalant [nɑ̀nʃəláːnt] a. 무관심[냉담]한; 태연한, 냉정한
Behaving in a calm and relaxed way.

emotionless [imóuʃənlis] a. 무표정한, 무감동의; 감정이 담기지 않은
Not showing any emotion.

literal [lítərəl] a. 글자 그대로의; 문자의 (literally ad. 글자 뜻대로, 말 그대로, 정말로)
Being the basic or usual meaning of a word or phrase.

Comet [kámit] n. 미국에서 판매되고 있는 청소액 제품의 이름

scrub [skrʌb] v. 북북 문지르다, 비벼서 씻다
To rub something hard in order to clean it.

bathtub [bǽθtʌ̀b] n. (서양식) 욕조
A long container which is filled with water so that a person can sit or lie in it to wash their whole body.

perplex [pərpléks] vt. 당황하게 하다, 당혹스럽게 하다, 난처하게 하다
To confuse and worry someone slightly by being difficult to understand or solve.

17. VISITOR

* **rinse** [rins] vt. 헹구어 내다, 씻어내다; n. 헹굼, 가심; 가셔냄
  To wash something with clean water only, not using soap.

* **frustration** [frʌstréiʃən] n. 좌절, 실패, 낙담; 장애물
  The feeling of being annoyed, or impatient, because you cannot achieve something.

  egregious [igríːdʒəs] a. 악명 높은; 지독한, 엄청난; 탁월한
  Extremely bad.

* **lapse** [læps] n. 착오, 실수; (시간의) 경과, 흐름; vi. … 상태가 되다; (정도에서) 벗어나다
  A small mistake, especially one that is caused by forgetting something or by being careless.

* **foresight** [fɔ́ːrsàit] n. 선견(지명), 예견
  The ability to predict what is likely to happen and to use this to prepare for the future.

* **silvery** [sílvəri] a. 은방울 같은; 은과 같은; 은빛의
  Silvery things look like silver or are the color of silver.

Comprehension Quiz

18. THE FUNERAL

1. Why couldn't Jacob protect Bella while Alice was in Forks?
   A. Jacob couldn't be near Alice.
   B. The other werewolves refused to help Bella because she was friends with a vampire.
   C. The werewolves could only watch their own land if a Cullen was in Forks.
   D. Alice was stronger than the werewolves and would be better at protecting Bella.

2. Who did Jacob talk to on the phone?
   A. Charlie
   B. Carlisle
   C. Rosalie
   D. Edward

3. What did Rosalie tell Edward?
   A. Alice visited Bella in Forks.
   B. Victoria killed Bella.
   C. Bella killed herself.
   D. Victoria was hunting Bella.

18. THE FUNERAL

4. What did Alice see in Edward's future?
- A. He would ask Victoria to kill him.
- B. He would leave South America and build a house in Italy.
- C. He would come back to Forks.
- D. He would ask the Volturi to kill him.

5. Why would Bella be in danger if she left with Alice?
- A. Bella smelled good and she knew too much about vampires.
- B. Bella was friends with werewolves.
- C. Victoria would follow her and the werewolves couldn't protect her.
- D. If Edward exposed himself as a vampire, then Bella would be considered his accomplice.

Vocabulary in New Moon

- **sprint** [sprint] v. 역주하다, 달려가다
  To run at full speed.

- **wrinkle** [ríŋkəl] v. 주름살지게 하다, 구겨지다; n. 주름, 잔주름
  When you wrinkle your nose or forehead, or when it wrinkles, you tighten the muscles in your face so that the skin folds.

- **hostility** [hɑstíləti] n. 적의, 적개심; 교전
  Enmity, aggression or angry opposition.

- **defensive** [difénsiv] a. 방어적인, 방어의, 변호의 (**defensively** ad. 방어적으로, 변명으로)
  Behaving in a way that shows you protect yourself from being criticized.

- **grind** [graind] vt. (ground-ground) 갈다, 타다; 가루로 만들다, 으깨다
  To break or crush something into very small pieces between two hard surfaces or using a special machine.

- **bug** [bʌg] v. (구어) 괴롭히다; 귀찮게 굴다; n. 곤충; 결함
  If someone or something bugs you, they worry or annoy you.

- **clench** [klentʃ] vt. (이를) 악물다, (손을) 꽉 쥐다
  To close one's teeth or one's fists tightly, especially in anger.

- **mumble** [mʌ́mbəl] v. 중얼거리다, 웅얼거리다; n. 중얼거림
  If you mumble, you speak very quietly and not at all clearly with the result that the words are difficult to understand.

- **slumber** [slʌ́mbər] n. (특히 가벼운) 잠, 선잠, 졸음, 얕은 잠
  (slumber party : 파자마파티, 밤샘파티)
  To sleep, especially lightly.

- **sarcastic** [sɑːrkǽstik] a. 빈정대는, 비꼬는, 풍자적인
  Saying things that are the opposite of what you mean, in order to make an unkind joke.

- **acid** [ǽsid] n. 매서움, 신랄함; [화학] 산(酸)
  (of a person's remarks) Critical and unkind.

18. THE FUNERAL

quotation [kwoutéiʃən] n. 인용(하기); 인용어[구 · 문]
A sentence or phrase taken from a book, poem, or play, which is repeated by someone else.

errand [érənd] n. 심부름; 용건, 볼일
A short trip that you make in order to do a job for someone.

edgy [édʒi] a. (구어) 초조한; 신랄한
Nervous, especially about what might happen.

quiver [kwívər] v. (떨리듯) 흔들리다, 떨다; n. 떨기
If something quivers, it shakes with very small movements.

restless [réstlis] a. 침착하지 못한; 불안한
If someone is restless, they keep moving around because they find it difficult to keep still.

mutter [mʌ́tər] v. 중얼거리다, 불평하다; n. 중얼거림, 불평
If you mutter, you speak very quietly so that you cannot easily be heard, often because you are complaining about something.

antagonism [æntǽgənìzəm] n. 반대, 적대, 대립; 반항심, 반발
Antagonism between people is hatred or dislike between them. Antagonisms are instances of this.

bloodsucker [blʌ́dsʌ̀kər] n. 흡혈 동물, 흡혈귀; 고리대금업자
A bloodsucker is any creature that sucks blood from a wound that it has made in an animal or person.

serene [sirí:n] a. 고요한, 화창한; 침착한, 평온한
Very calm and peaceful.

thoughtful [θɔ́:tfəl] a. 생각이 깊은, 생각에 잠긴 (thoughtfully ad. 생각에 깊게 잠겨)
Thinking deeply, or appearing to think deeply; Reflective.

belligerence [bəlídʒərəns] n. 호전성, 투쟁성
A natural disposition to be hostile.

Vocabulary in New Moon

invitation [ìnvətéiʃən] n. 초대
A written or spoken request to come to an event such as a party, a meal, or a meeting.

probe [proub] v. 탐구하다, 면밀히 조사하다 (probing a. 진실을 캐기 위한; 면밀히 살피는)
If you probe into something, you ask questions or try to discover facts about it.

conceal [kənsíːl] vt. 숨기다, 감추다; 비밀로 하다, 내색하지 않다
If you conceal something, you cover it or hide it carefully.

tension [ténʃən] n. 긴장, 긴박, 팽팽함
A feeling of worry and anxiety which makes it difficult for you to relax.

grudging [grʌ́dʒiŋ] a. 인색한, 마지못해 하는 (grudgingly ad. 마지못해; 쩨쩨하게)
Given or done unwillingly.

annoyance [ənɔ́iəns] n. 성가심, 불쾌감; 괴로움, 곤혹
The feeling of being slightly angry.

rekindle [riːkíndl] vt. (감정·생각 등을) 다시 불러일으키다[불붙이다]
To make something become active again.

swift [swift] a. 빠른, 신속한 (swiftly ad. 빨리, 즉시)
A swift event or process happens very quickly or without delay.

marvel [máːrvəl] v. …에 놀라다, 경탄하다
To be very surprised or impressed by something.

alienate [éiljənèit] vt. 멀리하다, 소원케하다; 양도하다, 매각하다
If you alienate someone, you make them become unfriendly or unsympathetic towards you.

slump [slʌmp] vi. 쿵 떨어지다; 털썩 앉다 n. (활동·원기의) 슬럼프; 쿵 떨어짐
To sit or fall heavily and suddenly.

hindsight [háindsàit] n. (일이 다 벌어진 뒤에) 사정을 다 알게 됨, 뒤늦은 깨달음
The understanding that you have of a situation only after it has happened and that means you would have done things in a different way.

18. THE FUNERAL

sparkle [spáːrkəl] v. 불꽃을 튀기다, 생기가 넘치다; n. 불꽃, 광채
(sparkling a. 반짝거리는)
If something sparkles, it is clear and bright and shines with a lot of very small points of light.

revulsion [rivʌ́lʃən] n. 극도의 불쾌감, 혐오감
A strong feeling of disgust or horror.

sniff [snif] v. 코를 킁킁거리다, 냄새를 맡다; 콧방귀를 뀌다; n. 냄새 맡음; 콧방귀
To smell something by taking air in through your nose.

gruff [grʌf] a. (목소리가) 거친, 쉰; 퉁명스러운 (gruffly ad. 거칠게, 퉁명스럽게)
Deep and rough, and often sounding unfriendly.

sniffle [snifl] vi. 코를 훌쩍이다, 코를 훌쩍거리며 말하다; n. 코를 훌쩍거림
If you sniffle, you keep sniffing, usually because you are crying or have a cold.

wipe [waip] v. 훔치다, 씻다, 닦다, 비비다
To pass over, or rub on to.

nasty [nǽsti] a. 더러운, 불쾌한, 몹시 싫은
Something that is nasty is very unpleasant to see, experience, or feel.

catch-22 n. (모순된 규칙[상황]에) 꼭 묶인 상태; 곤경; a. 궁지에 빠진, 옴짝달싹할 수 없는
If you describe a situation as a Catch-22, you mean it is an impossible situation because you cannot do one thing until you do another thing, but you cannot do the second thing until you do the first thing.

on the one hand idiom 한편으로는
From one point of view.

metaphorical [mètəfɔ́(ː)rikəl] a. 은유[비유]의, 은유적인
(metaphorically ad. 은유[비유]적으로)
Connected with or containing metaphors.

treaty [tríːti] n. 조약, 협정
A formal agreement between two or more countries.

Vocabulary in New Moon

recoil [rikɔ́il] vi. 되돌아오다; 후퇴하다; 움찔하다; n. 되튐, 반동
If you recoil from doing something or recoil at the idea of something, you refuse to do it or accept it because you dislike it so much.

smolder [smóuldər] v. 그을(리)다, 연기피우다; (감정이) 사무치다; 울적하다; n. 연기 (남)
To burn slowly without a flame.

wistful [wístfəl] a. 탐내는, 그리워하는; 곰곰이 생각하는
Someone who is wistful is rather sad because they want something and know that they cannot have it.

release [rilí:s] vt. 석방하다, 풀어놓다, 방출하다
To give freedom or free movement to someone or something.

palm [pɑ:m] n. ① 손바닥 ② 종려나무, 야자나무
The palm of your hand is the inside part.

consequence [kánsikwèns] n. 결과, 결말; 중요성, 중대함
The consequences of something are the results or effects of it.

harbor [há:rbər] n. 항구, 항만; 피난처; vt. (계획·생각 등을) 품다; 숨겨주다; 잠복하다
An area of water on the coast, protected from the open sea by strong walls, where ships can shelter.

enchant [entʃǽnt] vt. 매혹하다, 황홀케 하다 (enchanted a. 마법에 걸린; 황홀해하는)
To charm or please someone greatly.

fairy [fɛ́əri] n. 요정
(in stories) A creature like a small person, who has magic powers.

protocol [próutəkɑ̀l] n. 절차, 순서; 의례, 의식
The system of rules and acceptable behavior used at official ceremonies and occasions.

mundane [mʌ́ndein] a. 재미없는, 일상적인; 현세의, 세속적인; 보통의, 우주의
Not interesting or exciting.

undecided [ʌ̀ndisáidid] a. 아직 결정되지 않은; 확실치 않은, 모호한
Not having made a decision about somebody/something.

18. THE FUNERAL

- **shrill** [ʃril] a. (소리가) 날카로운, 새된; 신랄한; v. 새된 소리로 말하다, 새된 소리를 내다
  Having a loud and high sound that is unpleasant or painful to listen to.

- **muddled** [mʌdld] a. 혼란스러워 하는, 갈피를 못 잡는
  If someone is muddled, they are confused about something.

- **residence** [rézidəns] n. 주거, 거주
  Living in a particular place, especially officially.

- **alter** [ɔ́:ltər] v. 변하다, 바꾸다, 변경하다, 고치다
  To change something, usually slightly, or to cause the characteristics of something to change.

- **straighten** [stréitn] v. (몸을) 똑바르게 하다; 정리[정돈]하다
  To make your back straight.

- **measly** [mí:zli] a. 빈약한; 쥐꼬리만한
  Very small in size or quantity; Not enough.

- **menacing** [ménəsiŋ] a. 위협적인, 으르는
  If someone or something looks menacing, they give you a feeling that they are likely to cause you harm or put you in danger.

- **filthy** [fílθi] a. 불결한, 더러운
  Extremely or unpleasantly dirty.

- **infuriate** [infjúərièit] vt. 격노케 하다
  To make someone extremely angry.

- **sneer** [sniər] v. 비웃다, 냉소하다; n. 비웃음, 냉소
  If you sneer at someone or something, you express your contempt for them by the expression on your face or by what you say.

- **etiquette** [étikit] n. 에티켓, 예의, 예법; 법도
  The formal rules of correct or polite behavior in society or among members of a particular profession.

- **cuss** [kʌs] v. 욕하다
  If someone cusses, they swear at someone or use bad language.

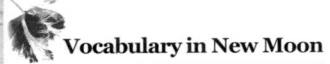
Vocabulary in New Moon

bobble [bábəl] vi. (깐닥깐닥) 위아래로 움직이다; (구어) 잘못[실수]하다; (공을) 놓치다
To move with an irregular bouncing motion.

choke [tʃouk] v. 숨 막히다[막히게 하다], 질식하다[시키다]
To prevent or be prevented from breathing by an obstruction in the throat, fumes, emotion.

scramble [skræmbəl] v. 기어오르다; 서로 (다투어) 빼앗다; 간신히 해내다; n. 기어오르기
If you scramble over rocks or up a hill, you move quickly over them or up it using your hands to help you.

lurch [ləːrtʃ] v. 비틀거리다; n. (배·차 등의) 갑자기 기울어짐; 비틀거림
To make a sudden, unsteady movement forward or sideways.

daze [deiz] vt. 멍하게 하다; 현혹시키다; n. 멍한 상태; 눈이 부심 (dazed a. 멍한, 아찔한)
If someone is in a daze, they are feeling confused and unable to think clearly, often because they have had a shock or surprise.

turmoil [tə́ːrmɔil] n. 소란, 소동, 혼란
A state of confusion, disorder or great anxiety.

abrupt [əbrʌ́pt] a. 갑작스러운, 뜻밖의 (abruptly ad. 갑자기)
Sudden and unexpected.

implication [ìmpləkéiʃən] n. 함축, 암시
A meaning that is not expressly stated but can be inferred.

hollow [hálou] a. 야윈, 오목한; 속이 빈; n. 구멍; 움푹 꺼진 곳
Something that is hollow has a space inside it, as opposed to being solid all the way through.

sway [swei] v. 흔들(리)다, 동요하다; 설득하다; n. 동요, 지배
To move slowly from side to side.

stairway [stέərwèi] n. 계단
A set of stairs inside or outside a building.

tilt [tilt] v. 기울이다; 기울다; n. 경사; 기울기
To move, or make something move, into a position with one side or end higher than the other.

18. THE FUNERAL

profanity [prəfǽnəti] n. 신성 모독, 불경
Behavior that shows a lack of respect for God or holy things.

vague [veig] a. 어렴풋한, 막연한
Not clearly expressed, known, described or decided.

earthquake [ə́:rθkwèik] n. 지진
A sudden shaking of the earth's surface that often causes a lot of damage.

retort [ritɔ́:rt] vt. 보복하다; 반론하여 말하다, 말대꾸하다
To reply quickly to a comment, in an angry, offended or humorous way.

dizzy [dízi] a. 현기증 나는, 아찔한 (dizziness n. 어지럼증, 현기증)
If you feel dizzy, you feel as if everything is spinning round and being unable to balance.

relocate [ri:lóukeit] vt. 다시 배치하다
To move or to move somebody/something to a new place to work or operate.

appall [əpɔ́:l] vt. 오싹 소름이 끼치게 하다, 섬뜩하게 하다
To make someone have strong feelings of shock or of disapproval.

remorse [rimɔ́:rs] n. 후회, 양심의 가책
A deep feeling of guilt, regret and bitterness for something wrong or bad which one has done.

torture [tɔ́:rtʃər] vt. 고문하다, 고통을 주다; n. 고문, 고뇌
To torture someone means to cause them to suffer mental pain or anxiety.

blurt [blə:rt] vt. 불쑥 말하다, 무심결에 말하다; n. 엉겁결에 말함
If someone blurts something, they say it suddenly, after trying hard to keep quiet or to keep it secret.

penetrate [pénətrèit] v. 꿰뚫다, 통과하다; 간파하다
If something or someone penetrates a physical object or an area, they succeed in getting into it or passing through it.

flinch [flintʃ] v. (고통·공포로) 주춤하다, 위축되다
To make a small sudden movement, especially when something surprises someone.

Vocabulary in New Moon

resentful [rizéntfəl] a. 분개한, 화난 (resentfully ad. 분개하여, 억울하게)
Feeling angry and upset about something that you think is unfair.

spit [spit] v. 뱉다, 토해내다, 뿜어내다
To force out the contents of the mouth, especially saliva.

tremor [trémər] n. 전율, 떨림; 겁; 떨리는 목소리; 진동
A slight shaking movement in a person's body, especially because of nervousness or excitement.

spine [spain] n. 등뼈, 척추
Your spine is the row of bones down your back.

moan [moun] v. 신음하다, 끙끙대다; n. 신음
If you moan, you make a low sound, usually because you are unhappy or in pain.

sink [siŋk] v. (sank-sunk 혹은 sunken) 가라앉다, 침몰하다, 빠지다
If something sharp sinks or is sunk into something solid, it goes deeply into it.

snarl [snɑːrl] v. 으르렁거리다; 고함[호통]치다; n. 으르렁거림
If you snarl something, you say it in a fierce, angry way.

bewilder [biwíldər] vt. 당황하게 하다, 어리둥절하게 하다
If something bewilders you, it is so confusing that you cannot understand it.

rely on phrasal v. …에 의지[의존]하다, …을 필요로 하다
To trust or depend on someone or something to do what you need or expect them to do.

fade [feid] vi. 바래다, 시들다, 희미해지다
To disappear gradually.

rot [rɑt] v. 썩이다, 못쓰게 만들다; n. 썩음, 부패 (rotten a. 끔찍한)
When food, wood, or another substance rots, or when something rots it, it becomes softer and is gradually destroyed.

comprehend [kàmprihénd] vt. 이해하다, 파악[인식]하다; 포함[함축]하다
To understand something fully.

18. THE FUNERAL

imitation [ìmitéiʃən] n. 모방, 흉내; 모조, 모사
An imitation of something is a copy of it.

delusion [dilúːʒən] n. 현혹, 기만; 망상, 착각
The act of believing or making yourself believe something that is not true.

shred [ʃred] v. 조각조각으로 찢다, 갈가리 찢다; n. 끄트러기, 조각, 파편
If you shred something such as food or paper, you cut it or tear it into very small, narrow pieces.

gape [geip] v. 틈이 벌어지다[생기다]; 갈라지다; n. 갈라진 틈, 큰 차이
If you gape, you look at something in surprise, usually with an open mouth.

provoke [prəvóuk] vt. 화나게 하다, 도발하다; 일으키다, 유발시키다
To annoy or infuriate someone, especially deliberately.

shriek [ʃriːk] v. 새된 소리를 지르다, 비명을 지르다; n. 비명
When someone shrieks, they make a short, very loud cry.

irritate [írətèit] vt. 짜증나게[초조하게] 하다, 화나게 하다
If something irritates you, it keeps annoying you.

denial [dináiəl] n. 부정, 부인, 거부
A statement saying that something is not true.

impatience [impéiʃəns] n. 성급함, 초조, 조급함, 안달
Annoyance at having to accept delays, other people's weakness etc.

trash [træʃ] n. 폐물, 쓰레기(rubbish) (trash can : 쓰레기통)
Something that you throw away because you no longer want or need them.

indecision [ìndisíʒən] n. 주저, 우유부단
The state of being unable to decide.

flex [fleks] v. 굽히다, 수축시키다; n. 굽힘
If you flex your muscles or parts of your body, you bend, move, or stretch them for a short time in order to exercise them.

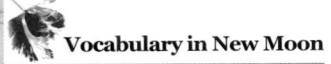
Vocabulary in New Moon

sporadical [spərǽdikəl] a. 때때로 일어나는, 우발적인, 단발성의
(sporadically ad. 우발적으로, 돌발적으로)
Happening only occasionally or at intervals that are not regular.

emphasize [émfəsàiz] vt. 강조하다; 역설하다
To emphasize something means to indicate that it is particularly important or true, or to draw special attention to it.

feverish [fíːvəriʃ] a. 열이 있는, 열띤; 열광적인 (feverishly ad. 열광적으로, 병적으로)
Showing strong feelings of excitement or worry, often with a lot of activity or quick movements.

protective [prətéktiv] a. 보호하는, (위험에서) 지키는, 방어하는
Protective means designed or intended to protect something or someone from harm.

frustration [frʌstréiʃən] n. 좌절, 실패, 낙담; 장애물
The feeling of being annoyed, or impatient, because you cannot achieve something.

theatrical [θiǽtrikəl] a. 연극조의, 과장된; 연극의
Theatrical can be used to describe something that is grand and dramatic, as if it is part of a performance in a theatre.

tendency [téndənsi] n. 성향, 기질; 경향; 동향; 추세
A tendency is a part of your character that makes you behave in an unpleasant or worrying way.

accomplice [əkámplis] n. 공범자, 연루자; 동료, 협력자
A person who helps another to commit a crime or to do something wrong.

eliminate [ilímənèit] vt. 제거하다
To remove or get rid of something/somebody.

tabulate [tǽbjəlèit] vt. 표로 만들다, 일람표로 만들다; 평면으로 하다
To arrange facts or figures in columns or lists so that they can be read easily.

disgust [disgʌ́st] n. 싫음, 혐오감; vt. 역겹게 하다, 넌더리나게 하다
A strong feeling of dislike or disapproval for somebody/something that you feel is unacceptable, or for something that looks, smells, etc. unpleasant.

18. THE FUNERAL

screw [skru:] v. (종이 등을) 구겨서 말다; 비틀다; 나사로 죄다; 쥐어짜다; n. 나사
If you screw something such as a piece of paper into a ball, you squeeze it or twist it tightly so that it is in the shape of a ball.

scowl [skaul] vi. 얼굴을 찌푸리다, 싫은 기색을 하다; n. 찌푸린 얼굴
To look at someone or something with a very annoyed expression.

urgent [ə́:rdʒənt] a. 긴급한, 절박한 (urgently ad. 긴급하게)
If something is urgent, it needs to be dealt with as soon as possible.

drawer [drɔ́:ər] n. 서랍
A box-shaped container without a top which is part of a piece of furniture. It slides in and out to open and close and is used for keeping things in.

tear [tɛər] ① v. (tore-torn) 찢다, 찢어지다 ② n. 눈물
To damage something by pulling it hard or letting it touch something sharp.

tear off phrasal v. 잡아떼다, 떼어내다
If you tear off something, you remove it quickly by pulling violently.

ground [graund] vt. (자녀에 대한 벌로) 나가 놀지[외출하지] 못하게 하다
When parents ground a child, they forbid them to go out and enjoy themselves for a period of time, as a punishment.

forge [fɔ:rdʒ] vt. 위조[모조]하다; (거짓말 등을) 꾸며 내다, 날조하다
To make an illegal copy of something in order to cheat people.

gratitude [grǽtətjù:d] n. 감사, 고마움
Gratitude is the state of feeling grateful.

sweatpants [swétpænts] n. 스웨트 팬츠 (운동선수가 입는 느슨한 바지)
Loose warm trousers/pants, usually made of thick cotton and worn for relaxing or playing sports in.

hurl [hə:rl] v. 세게 내던지다, 집어던지다
If you hurl something, you throw it violently and with a lot of force.

Vocabulary in New Moon

- **déjà vu** [dèiʒɑ:vjú:] n. 기시감(지금 자신에게 일어나는 일을 전에도 경험한 적이 있는 것 같이 느끼는 것)
  The feeling that you have previously experienced something which is happening to you now.

- **stifle** [stáifəl] v. 숨을 막다; 억누르다
  To stop a feeling from being expressed.

- **confrontation** [kànfrəntéiʃən] n. 대면, 직면, 대립
  A conflict, fight, or battle between two groups of people.

- **reappearance** [rì:əpíərəns] n. 재등장, 다시 나타남
  The reappearance of someone or something is their return after they have been away or out of sight for some time.

- **leech** [li:tʃ] n. 거머리(본문에서는 컬린 일가의 사람들을 거머리에 비유)
  A leech is a small animal which looks like a worm and lives in water. Leeches feed by attaching themselves to other animals and sucking their blood.

- **accuse** [əkjú:z] v. 비난하다, 고발하다
  To say that someone has done something morally wrong, illegal or unkind.

- **instinct** [ínstiŋkt] n. 본능, 직관, 천성
  The way people or animals naturally react or behave, without having to think or learn about it.

- **unaware** [ʌnəwɛ́ər] a. 알지 못하는
  un (pre. 부정) + aware (a. 알고 있는)

- **growl** [graul] v. 으르렁거리다, 고함치다; n. 으르렁거리는 소리
  To make a low rough sound, usually in anger.

- **haste** [heist] n. 급함, 서두름, 신속함
  Speed, especially speed in an action.

- **glisten** [glisn] vi. 반짝이다, 빛나다
  If something glistens, it shines, usually because it is wet or oily.

18. THE FUNERAL

lump [lʌmp] n. 덩어리, 한 조각; (구어) 땅딸보; 멍청이, 바보
A piece of a solid substance, usually with no particular shape.

thrum [θrʌm] v. 똑똑 두드리다; (현악기를) 퉁겨 소리 내다; n. 퉁기는 소리; (악기를) 손가락으로 뜯음)
When something such as a machine or engine thrums, it makes a low beating sound.

rev [rev] v. (엔진 등의) 회전 속도를 올리다; n. (구어) (엔진·레코드 등의) 회전
When the engine of a vehicle revs, or when you rev it, the engine speed is increased as the accelerator is pressed.

spatter [spǽtər] v. 튀(기)다, 흩어지다; n. 튀김, 튀기는 소리, 후두두 하는 소리
If a liquid spatters a surface or you spatter a liquid over a surface, drops of the liquid fall on an area of the surface.

screech [skri:tʃ] vi. 날카로운[새된] 소리를 내다
To make a unpleasant loud high noise.

Comprehension Quiz

 19. RACE

1. Why couldn't Jasper and Emmett stop Edward?
   A. If Edward knew they were coming, he would try to be taken down by the Volturi faster.
   B. They promised Edward that they wouldn't interfere with his decision.
   C. They couldn't get a flight to Italy in time to stop Edward.
   D. Edward wanted to die even if Bella was alive.

2. What is the most important rule for vampires?
   A. They cannot hunt humans in Volterra.
   B. They must join the Volturi if they have a special power.
   C. They cannot live in large groups.
   D. They must keep their existence a secret.

3. Why did the Volturi refuse to destroy Edward?
   A. They thought Edward was lying about Bella.
   B. They thought destroying his talent was wasteful.
   C. They didn't want Jasper and Emmett to attack Volterra.
   D. Carlisle begged the Volturi not to destroy Edward.

4. How would Edward expose himself as a Vampire?

　　A. He would kill someone inside Volterra's walls.

　　B. He would try to kill Aro.

　　C. He would let humans see him standing in the sun.

　　D. He would throw a car into the clock tower.

5. If Alice and Bella lived through their time in Volterra, Alice would _____ in the future.

　　A. change Bella into a vampire

　　B. introduce Bella to the Volturi

　　C. stop Edward from seeing Bella again

　　D. kill Victoria herself

Vocabulary in New Moon

tarmac [tá:rmæk] n. 타맥 포장도로[활주로]
The tarmac is an area with a surface made of tarmac, especially the area from which planes take off at an airport.

attendant [əténdənt] n. 시중드는 사람, 안내원
Someone whose job is to be in a place and help visitors or customers.

stroll [stroul] vi. 한가롭게 거닐다, 산책하다; n. 산책
If you stroll somewhere, you walk there in a slow, relaxed way.

aisle [ail] n. 통로, 측면의 복도
An aisle is a long narrow gap that people can walk along between rows of seats in a public building.

pat [pæt] v. 톡톡 가볍게 치다; 쓰다듬다; n. 톡톡[가볍게] 침[두드림]
If you pat something or someone, you tap them lightly, usually with your hand held flat.

cockpit [kákpìt] n. (항공) 조종실
The small enclosed space where the pilot sits in an aircraft.

bounce [bauns] v. 펄쩍 뛰다, (공 등이) 튀(게 하)다; n. 튐, 바운드
To move up or away after hitting a surface.

gradual [grǽdʒuəl] a. 점진적인, 단계적인
Happening or changing slowly over a long period of time or distance.

achieve [ətʃíːv] v. 이루다, 성취[완수]하다, 달성하다; (명성을) 얻다; 쟁취하다
To succeed in reaching a particular goal, status or standard, especially by making an effort for a long time.

liftoff [líftɔ̀(ː)f] n. 수직 이륙, 발진, 발사 (순간)
Lift-off is the beginning of a rocket's flight into space, when it leaves the ground.

frenzied [frénzid] a. 열광적인, 광포한
Frenzied activities or actions are wild, excited, and uncontrolled.

19. RACE

- **stewardess** [stjúːərdis] n. (여객기의) 스튜어디스, (기선·열차 등의) 여승무원
A stewardess is a woman who works on a ship, plane, or train, looking after passengers and serving meals to them.

disapproval [dìsəprúːvəl] n. 안 된다고 함, 불승인, 불찬성, 불만
A feeling of disliking something or what someone is doing.

protest [prətést] v. 항의하다, 이의를 제기하다; 주장하다; n. 항의
If you protest against something or about something, you say or show publicly that you object to it.

spree [spriː] n. 흥청거림; 연회, 주연; 탐닉; vi. 흥겹게 마시고 떠들다
If you spend a period of time doing something in an excessive way, you can say that you are going on a particular kind of spree.

inaudible [inɔ́ːdəbəl] a. 알아들을 수 없는, 들리지 않는
Too quiet to be heard.

plead [pliːd] v. 간청하다, 탄원하다; 변론하다; 변호하다
If you plead with someone to do something, you ask them in an intense, emotional way to do it.

sneak up phrasal v. 살금살금[몰래] 다가가다
To approach somebody very quietly, so that they do not see or hear you until you reach them.

Buick [bjuːik] n. 뷰익 (미국 GM사의 승용차; 상표명)

beseech [bisíːtʃ] vt. 간청[탄원]하다, 애원하다
To ask somebody for something in an anxious way because you want or need it very much.

clarity [klǽrəti] n. 명쾌함, 깨끗하고 맑음
The quality of being clear and easy to understand.

mute [mjuːt] a. 무언의, 말없는; vt. ···의 소리를 죽이다, ···을 약하게 하다
Someone who is mute is silent for a particular reason and does not speak.

Vocabulary in New Moon

endanger [endéindʒər] vt. 위험에 빠뜨리다, 위태롭게 하다
To put somebody/something in a situation in which they could be harmed or damaged.

guarantee [gæ̀rəntíː] vt. 보증하다, 다짐하다; n. 보증, 개런티
If you guarantee something, you promise that it will definitely happen, or that you will do or provide it for someone.

irritation [ìrətéiʃən] n. 짜증나게 함; 짜증, 화; 짜증나는 것, 자극하는 것
Irritation is a feeling of annoyance, especially when something is happening that you cannot easily stop or control.

conspicuous [kənspíkjuəs] a. 눈에 띄는, 현저한
(conspicuously ad. 눈에 띄게, 두드러지게)
Easy to see or notice.

antagonize [æntǽgənàiz] vt. 대항하다, 적대하다
If you antagonize someone, you make them feel angry or hostile towards you.

speculate [spékjəlèit] vi. 숙고하다, 사색하다, 추측하다; 투기하다
To consider the circumstances or possibilities regarding it, usually without any factual basis and without coming to a definite conclusion.

abstain [əbstéin] vi. 삼가다, 절제하다
To choose not to take, have, do or undertake it.

tolerance [tálərəns] n. 관용, 아량, 용인; 내성, 저항력
Allowing other people to say and do as they like, even if you do not agree with it.

apt [æpt] a. 적절한, 적당한; …하기 쉬운
An apt remark, description, or choice is especially suitable.

description [diskrípʃən] n. 기술, 서술, 설명서, 기재사항
An official list of the work and responsibilities that you have in your job.

permanent [pə́ːrmənənt] a. 영구적인, 영속하는, 변하지 않는
Lasting for a long time or forever.

19. RACE

transitory [trǽnsətɔ́:ri] a. 일시적인, 잠시 동안의; 덧없는
Continuing for only a short time.

★ **formidable** [fɔ́:rmidəbəl] a. 무서운, 무시무시한; 만만찮은, 얕잡을 수 없는; 굉장히 많은
Causing you to have fear or respect for something or someone because they are impressive, powerful or difficult.

‡ **parlor** [pá:rlər] a. 객실(용)의; n. 거실, 응접실; 영업실
A parlor is a room in a house for sitting in.

복습 **confrontation** [kɑ̀nfrəntéiʃən] n. 대면, 직면, 대립
A conflict, fight, or battle between two groups of people.

★ **wintry** [wíntri] a. 겨울의, 겨울 같은; 추운
Typical of winter; Cold.

millennium [miléniəm] n. 천년간 (pl. millennia)
A millennium is a period of one thousand years, especially one which begins and ends with a year ending in '000', for example the period from the year 1000 to the year 2000.

복습 **enforce** [enfɔ́:rs] v. 집행[시행·실시]하다
To enforce something means to force or cause it to be done or to happen.

‡ **translate** [trænsléit] v. (다른 상태·성질로) 바꾸다, 변형하다; 번역하다
To change or move from one state, condition, person, place, etc to another.

★ **transgress** [trænsgrés] vt. 어기다, 위반하다, 범하다 (transgressor n. 범법자, 범죄자)
To go beyond the limit of what is morally or legally acceptable.

★ **decisive** [disáisiv] a. 결정적인, 의심할 여지가 없는, 단호한 (decisively ad. 단호하게)
Determining or having the power to determine an outcome.

복습 **chuckle** [tʃʌ́kl] n. 낄낄 웃음; vi. 낄낄 웃다
When you chuckle, you laugh quietly.

복습 **core** [kɔ:r] n. 핵심, (사물의) 중심부
The most important or central part of something.

Vocabulary in New Moon

restriction [ristrík∫ən] n. 제한[제약]하는 것, 제약, 규정
The act of limiting or controlling somebody/something.

compromise [kámprəmàiz] n. 타협, 화해, 양보; v. 화해하다, 양보하다
Anything of an intermediate type which comes halfway between two opposing stages.

flout [flaut] vt. (법 등을 공공연히) 어기다[무시하다]
If you flout something such as a law, an order, or an accepted way of behaving, you deliberately do not obey it or follow it.

Etruscan [itrÁskən] n. 에트루리아 사람

annihilate [ənáiəlèit] vt. 전멸[절멸·멸망]시키다
To destroy somebody or something completely.

maverick [mǽvərik] n. 개성이 강한[독립적인] 사람; 독립독행하는 사람
A person who does not behave or think like everyone else, but who has independent, unusual opinions.

suicidal [sù:əsáidl] a. 자살의; 자살적인; (사람이) 자포자기한
Very dangerous and likely to lead to death; Likely to cause very serious problems or disaster.

stiffen [stífən] v. 딱딱[뻣뻣]해지다, 경직되다
If you stiffen, your body suddenly becomes firm, straight still because you feel angry or anxious.

scout [skaut] n. 보이 스카우트의 한 사람 (미국에서는 종종 걸 스카우트의 일원에도 말함)
A boy or girl who is a member of the Scouts.

temple [témpəl] n. 관자놀이; 신전, 사원
Your temples are the flat parts on each side of the front part of your head, near your forehead.

fascination [fæsənéi∫ən] n. 매혹, 매료, 황홀케 함, 홀린 상태
The state of being greatly interested in or delighted by something.

sculpture [skÁlpt∫ər] n. 조각, 조각상; v. 조각하다
An object made out of stone, wood, clay etc by an artist.

19. RACE

anticipate [æntísəpèit] vt. 예기하다, 예상[예지·예견]하다
To see what might happen in the future and take action to prepare for it.

dither [díðər] vi. (결정을 못 내리고) 머무적거리다[망설이다]
When someone dithers, they hesitate because they are unable to make a quick decision about something.

eternity [itə́:rnəti] n. 영원, 무궁; 불사, 불멸; 영원성
Eternity is time without an end or a state of existence outside time, especially the state which some people believe they will pass into after they have died.

jar [dʒɑ:r] v. 삐걱거리다; 진동하다; 깜짝 놀라게 하다; 충격을 주다[받다]
(jarring a. 삐걱거리는, 귀에 거슬리는)
To have an unpleasant or annoying effect.

stupor [stjú:pər] n. 무감각; 마비; 혼수; 인사불성
Someone who is in a stupor is almost unconscious and is unable to act or think normally, especially as a result of drink or drugs.

gleam [gli:m] vi. 어슴푸레 빛나다; 환하다, 반짝이다; n. 번득임; 어스레한 빛
To shine with a pale clear light.

dim [dim] a. 어둑한, 흐릿한, 희미한; v. 어둡게 하다, 흐려지다
Dim light is not bright.

groggy [grάgi] a. 비틀거리는, 그로기가 된
Weak and unable to think clearly or walk correctly.

tiptoe [típtòu] vi. 발끝으로 걷다; 발돋움하다
If you tiptoe somewhere, you walk there very quietly without putting your heels on the floor when you walk.

hush [hʌʃ] vt. 조용하게 하다, 침묵시키다; n. 침묵 (hushed a. 조용한; 소리를 낮춘)
If you hush someone or if they hush, they stop speaking or making a noise.

rebuke [ribjú:k] n. 비난, 힐책; vt. 힐책[질책]하다, 꾸짖다
An expression of strong disapproval.

Vocabulary in New Moon

* **comparative** [kəmpǽrətiv] a. 다른 것과 비교한 경우의, 상대적인, 상당한
(comparatively ad. 비교적, 상당히, 꽤)
Connected with studying things to find out how similar or different they are.

stumble [stʌ́mbəl] v. 비틀거리며 걷다, 발부리가 걸리다; n. 비틀거림
If you stumble, you put your foot down awkwardly while you are walking or running and nearly fall over.

* **intrigue** [intríːg] v. 호기심을 돋우다; 음모를 꾸미다; n. 음모
If something intrigues you, it interests you and you want to know more about it.

* **wasteful** [wéistfəl] a. 낭비적인; 비경제적인, 허비의; 소모성의
Using more of something than is necessary; Not saving or keeping something that could be used.

attune [ətjúːn] vt. (가락에) 맞추다, 동조(同調)하다; 조율하다, 맞추다
(attuned a. 익숙한, 적절히 대응하는)
To bring into harmony.

debate [dibéit] v. 토론하다, 논쟁하다; n. 논쟁, 토론
If you debate whether to do something or what to do, you think or talk about possible courses of action before deciding exactly what you are going to do.

bizarre [bizɑ́ːr] a. 기괴한, 이상야릇한
Something that is bizarre is very odd and strange.

hypothetical [hàipəθétikəl] a. 가설의, 가상의, 가정의; n. 가정에 근거한 상황[사물]
Based on situations or ideas which are possible and imagined rather than real and true.

encourage [enkə́ːridʒ] vt. 용기를 북돋우다, 장려하다
If you encourage someone, you give them confidence, hope, or support.

grumble [grʌ́mbəl] v. 투덜거리다, 불평하다; n. 투덜댐, 불평
To complain about someone or something in an annoyed way.

* **chaotic** [keiátik] a. 대혼란의, 무질서한; 혼돈된
Something that is chaotic is in a state of complete confusion and lack of order.

19. RACE

incomprehension [inkàmprihénʃən] n. 몰이해, 이해력이 없음
The state of not being able to understand somebody/something.

meadow [médou] n. 목초지, 풀밭
A field with grass and often wild flowers in it.

shimmer [ʃímər] vi. 희미하게 반짝이다, 빛나다; n. 반짝임 (shimmering a. 반짝이는)
If something shimmers, it shines with a faint, unsteady light or has an unclear, unsteady appearance.

inconspicuous [ìnkənspíkjuːəs] a. 눈에 띄지 않는, 주의를 끌지 않는
Not attracting attention.

speculative [spékjəlèitiv] a. 추측에 근거한; 사색적인, 명상적인
(speculatively ad. 추측하여, 사색적으로)
Based on guessing or on opinions that have been formed without knowing all the facts.

theft [θeft] n. 훔침, 도둑질, 절도
The crime of stealing something from a person or place.

Porsche [pɔ́ːrʃ] n. 포르셰 (독일제 스포츠카)

scrawl [skrɔːl] vt. 휘갈겨 쓰다, 낙서하다
To write something in a careless untidy way, making it difficult to read.

cursive [kə́ːrsiv] a. 초서체의, 흘림글씨의; 필기체의
(of handwriting) With the letters joined together.

sheesh [ʃiːʃ] int. 체, 치, 제기 (분노·불쾌감·놀람의 소리; Jesus 또는 shit의 완곡적 표현)
An exclamation of surprise or annoyance.

complain [kəmpléin] v. 불평하다, 투덜거리다
To say that something is wrong or not satisfactory.

tint [tint] v. 색깔을 넣다; (머리를) 염색하다; n. 엷은 빛깔
To slightly change the color of something.

Vocabulary in New Moon

fumble [fʌ́mbəl] vi. 손으로 더듬어 찾다; 우물우물 말하다
If you fumble for something or fumble with something, you try and reach for it or hold it in a clumsy way.

roadblock [róudblàk] n. (도로상의) 바리케이드, 방책(防柵); 노상 장애물; 장애(물)
A barrier put across the road by the police or army so that they can stop and search vehicles.

trill [tril] v. 명랑하게 말하다, 떨리는 소리로 노래[연주]하다; n. 떨리는 목소리; 지저귐
To say something in a high cheerful voice.

Tuscan [tʌ́skən] n. 토스카나 사람, 토스카나의

ironic [airánik] a. 반어의[적인]; 비꼬는; 풍자적인
Showing that you really mean the opposite of what you are saying.

sardonic [sɑːrdánik] a. 냉소적인, 조소하는; 가소롭다는 듯한
Showing that you think that you are better than other people and do not take them seriously.

bleed [bliːd] vi. ① 출혈하다 ② 마음 아파하다
When you bleed, you lose blood from your body as a result of injury or illness.

speedometer [spiːdámitər] n. (자동차 등의) 속도계; 주행 기록계
A device in a vehicle which shows how fast the vehicle is moving.

concussion [kənkʌ́ʃən] n. [병리] 뇌진탕
If you suffer concussion after a blow to your head, you lose consciousness or feel sick or confused.

groan [groun] v. 신음하다, 끙끙거리다; n. 신음[끙끙거리는] 소리
If you groan, you make a long, low sound because you are in pain, or because you are upset or unhappy about something.

klutzy [klʌ́tsi] a. 서투른, 바보 같은 (klutziness n. 바보스러움, 어리석음)
Awkward, clumsy or socially inept.

sienna [siénə] n. 시에나색, 황갈색
A type of dark yellow or red clay used for giving color to paints, etc.

19. RACE

- **dread** [dred] a. 대단히 무서운; v. 두려워하다; n. 두려움; 두려운 것, 공포
  Terrible and greatly feared.

- **thrill** [θril] n. 전율; v. 감동[감격·흥분]시키다; 오싹하다
  A sudden strong feeling that produces a physical effect.

Comprehension Quiz

20. VOLTERRA

1. **Why did Bella's clothing get wet when she ran through the crowd?**
   A. It was raining outside.
   B. She ran through a fountain.
   C. She ran into some tourists holding drinks.
   D. Her legs were bleeding from scraping them on some stones.

2. **How did Bella and Alice get into Volterra?**
   A. They drove over a police fence.
   B. Bella begged a guard to let them inside.
   C. They got onboard a tour bus.
   D. Alice bribed a guard.

3. **When Bella reached Edward at the clock tower, he thought _____.**
   A. he was dead.
   B. he was dreaming.
   C. Alice played a trick on him.
   D. Bella was crazy for saving him.

20. VOLTERRA

4. Why did Alice and Edward agree to meet with the Volturi?

A. Demetri threatened to kill them.

B. Alice knew that the Volturi wouldn't hurt Bella.

C. Jane told them to follow her.

D. Edward wanted to tell the Volturi he didn't want to die.

5. What stopped Bella from being scared of the tunnels and the vampires?

A. Knowing Alice could see the future

B. Receiving affection from Edward

C. Believing none of the vampires killed humans

D. Knowing that Jacob would take care of Charlie if she died

Vocabulary in New Moon

Peugeot [pə́:ʒou] n. 푸조 (프랑스 Peugeot사의 자동차)

soothe [su:ð] v. 달래다, 어르다; (통증 등을) 완화시키다, 누그러뜨리다
To make someone feel calmer and less anxious.

chisel [tʃízl] v. 조각하다; 끌로 파다, 새기다; n. 끌, 조각칼
To cut or shape wood or stone with a chisel.

tug [tʌg] v. 당기다, 끌다; 노력하다; n. 힘껏 당김
If you tug something or tug at it, you give it a quick and usually strong pull.

billow [bílou] vi. 크게 굽이치다; (돛 등이) 부풀다; n. 큰 물결
When something made of cloth billows, it swells out and moves slowly in the wind.

crimson [krímzən] a. 진홍색의; n. 진홍색
Having a dark deep red color.

scarf [skɑ:rf] n. 스카프, 목도리(muffler)
A piece of cloth that is worn around the neck, for example for warmth or decoration. Women also wear scarves over their shoulders or hair.

flutter [flʌ́tər] v. (깃발 등이) 펄럭이다, (새 등이) 날갯짓하다; 심장이 두근거리다; n. 펄럭임
To make a series of quick delicate movements up and down or from side to side.

dull [dʌl] a. 흐릿한; 따분한, 재미없는; 둔한, 활기 없는
Not interesting or exciting.

alleyway [ǽliwèi] n. 골목, 좁은 길[통로]
A narrow passage behind or between buildings.

accelerate [æksélərèit] vt. 속력을 빠르게 하다, 가속하다; 촉진하다
To happen or to make something happen faster or earlier than expected.

frantic [frǽntik] a. 광란의, 미친 듯 날뛰는
(frantically ad. 미친 듯이, 광포하게, 광란하여)
Behaving in a wild and uncontrolled way.

20. VOLTERRA

grab [græb] v. 부여잡다, 움켜쥐다; n. 부여잡기
If you grab something, you take it or pick it up suddenly and roughly.

striking [stráikiŋ] a. 현저한, 두드러진; 이목을[주의를] 끄는
(strikingly ad. 두드러지게, 눈에 띄게)
Something that is striking is very noticeable or unusual.

★ **allure** [əlúər] vt. 유혹하다, 부추기다 (alluring a. 매혹적인)
To entice by charm or attraction.

★ **retrieve** [ritríːv] vt. 되찾다, 회수하다
To find and bring back something.

wee [wiː] a. 작은, 조그마한; n. 아주 조금, 잠깐
Small; Little.

cobble [kábəl] vt. (도로에) 자갈을 깔다
To pave with cobblestones.

★ **cinnamon** [sínəmən] n. 계피
Cinnamon is a sweet spice used for flavoring food.

spurt [spəːrt] n. 분출; 쏟아져 나옴; v. 쏟아져 나오다, 내뿜다; 갑자기 속도를 더 내다
A sudden gush.

pavement [péivmənt] n. 포장 도로
A flat part at the side of a road for people to walk on.

thrash [θræʃ] v. 요동치다, 몸부림치다; 마구 때리다; n. 때림; 패배시킴
If someone thrashes their arms or legs about, they move in a wild or violent way.

shove [ʃʌv] v. 밀(치)다, 밀어내다; n. 밀치기
If you shove something somewhere, you push it there quickly and carelessly.

lane [lein] n. 좁은 길, 골목, 작은 길
A narrow road in the country.

whoosh [hwú(ː)ʃ] v. 쉭 하고 움직이다; n. 휙[쉭] (하는 소리)
If something whooshes somewhere, it moves there quickly or suddenly.

345

Vocabulary in New Moon

fling [fliŋ] vt. 던지다, 내던지다; (문 등을) 왈칵 열다
To open a door or window roughly, using a lot of force.

exclamation [èkskləméiʃən] n. 외침, 절규; 외치는 소리
A word or expression uttered suddenly and loudly.

coil [kɔil] vt. 똘똘 감다, 사리다; n. 고리, 사리, [전기] 코일
To wind into a series of circles.

gruesome [grú:səm] a. 소름 끼치는, 무시무시한; 힘든
Something that is gruesome is extremely unpleasant and shocking.

wound [wu:nd] ① n. 상처, 부상, 상해; vt. 상처를 입히다 ② v. [waund] wind의 과거·과거분사
A wound is damage to part of your body, especially a cut or a hole in your flesh, which is caused by a gun, knife, or other weapon.

fang [fæŋ] n. (육식 동물의) 송곳니, 엄니
A long sharp tooth.

throng [θrɔ(:)ŋ] n. 군중; vi. 떼 지어 모이다
A large group of people in one place.

jostle [dʒásl] v. (난폭하게) 떠밀다, 헤치고 나아가다
To push roughly against somebody in a crowd.

pitiless [pítilis] a. 무자비한, 매정한, 가차 없는; 냉혹한
Showing no pity; Cruel.

vicious [víʃəs] a. 나쁜, 악덕의, 잔인한 (viciously ad. 잔인하게; 부정하게)
A vicious person or a vicious blow is violent and cruel.

springboard [spríŋbɔ:rd] n. 도약대, 출발점, (…에의) 계기를 주는 것
A strong board that you jump on and use to help you jump high in diving and gymnastics.

splatter [splǽtər] v. (물·흙탕물 등이) 튀다; 물보라 치며 떨어지다
If a thick wet substance splatters on something or is splattered on it, it drops or is thrown over it.

20. VOLTERRA

- **boom** [buːm] vi. (소리가) 쿵 하고 울리다; 활기를 띠우다, 붐이 일다
  (booming a. 꽝 하고 울리는)
  When something such as someone's voice booms, it makes a loud, deep resounding sound.

- **chime** [tʃaim] n. 차임; v. (한 벌의 종·시계가) 울리다
  A chime is a ringing sound made by a bell, especially when it is part of a clock.

- **throb** [θrɑb] vi. 떨리다; (악기 등이) 진동하다
  To beat or sound with a strong, regular rhythm.

- **exertion** [igzə́ːrʃən] n. 노력, 분발
  Physical or mental effort.

- **toll** [toul] v. 울리다, 치다
  When a bell tolls or when someone tolls it, it rings slowly and repeatedly, often as a sign that someone has died.

- **dazzle** [dǽzəl] vt. 현혹시키다, 감탄시키다; n. 현혹, 눈부신 빛
  (dazzling a. 눈부신; 현혹적인)
  If someone or something dazzles you, you are extremely impressed by their skill, qualities, or beauty.

- **blazer** [bléizər] n. 블레이저(코트) (화려한 빛깔의 운동선수용 상의)
  A jacket, not worn with matching trousers/pants, often showing the colors or badge of a club, school, team, etc.

- **barrel** [bǽrəl] v. (통제가 안 되게) 쏜살같이 달리다[질주하다]
  If a vehicle or person is barreling in a particular direction, they are moving very quickly in that direction.

- **mill around** phrasal v. 특히 많은 사람들이 무리지어 서성거리다
  If a large group of people mill around, or mill around a place, they move around without going anywhere in particular, often while waiting for something to happen.

- **aimless** [eimlis] a. 목적이[목표가] 없는 (aimlessly ad. 막연하게, 목적 없이)
  A person or activity that is aimless has no clear purpose or plan.

Vocabulary in New Moon

★ **edifice** [édəfis] n. 건물; 대건축물
A large impressive building.

hurtle [hə́:rtl] vi. 돌진하다, 고속으로 움직이다; 충돌하다
To move very fast, especially in what seems a dangerous way.

★ **clamp** [klæmp] vt. (죔쇠 등으로) 죄다; 덮어서 가리다
To clamp something in a particular place means to put it or hold it there firmly and tightly.

복습 **giggle** [gígəl] v. 낄낄 웃다; n. 낄낄 웃음
If someone giggles, they laugh in a childlike way, because they are amused, nervous, or embarrassed.

★ **swerve** [swə:rv] v. 벗어나다, 빗나가다; n. 벗어남, 빗나감
To change direction, especially suddenly.

‡ **gloomy** [glú:mi] a. 어두운, 우울한
If a place is gloomy, it is almost dark so that you cannot see very well.

복습 **hallucination** [həlù:sənéiʃən] n. 환각, 망상
A hallucination is the experience of seeing something that is not really there because you are ill or have taken a drug.

flawed [flɔ:d] a. 결함[결점·흠]이 있는
Something that is flawed has a mark, fault, or mistake in it.

복습 **appreciate** [əprí:ʃièit] vt. 진가를 인정하다; 평가하다, 감상하다; 고맙게 생각하다
To recognize the good qualities of something.

복습 **amuse** [əmjú:z] vt. 즐겁게 하다, 재미나게 하다
To make somebody laugh or smile.

복습 **bemuse** [bimjú:z] vt. 멍하게 만들다, 어리벙벙하게 하다 (**bemused** a. 멍한, 어리벙벙한)
If something bemuses you, it puzzles or confuses you.

복습 **vein** [vein] n. 혈관, 정맥, 광맥; 기질, 특질
Any of the tubes that carry blood from all parts of the body towards the heart.

20. VOLTERRA

tomb [tu:m] n. 무덤, 묘(墓); (지하) 납골당
A large grave, especially one built of stone above or below the ground.

furrow [fə́:rou] v. 주름살지다, 이랑을 짓다; n. 밭고랑
To make wrinkles on your face because you are thinking hard.

yank [jæŋk] v. 홱 당기다; 홱 잡아당겨 …의 상태로 하다; n. 홱 잡아당김
If you yank someone or something somewhere, you pull them there suddenly and with a lot of force.

protective [prətéktiv] a. 보호하는, (위험에서) 지키는, 방어하는
(protectively ad. 보호하여)
Protective means designed or intended to protect something or someone from harm.

peek [pi:k] vi. 살짝 들여다보다, 엿보다; n. 엿봄
If you peek at something or someone, you have a quick look at them.

appropriate [əpróuprièit] a. 적절한, 알맞은
Something that is appropriate is suitable or acceptable for a particular situation.

venue [vénju:] n. 행위[사건]의 현장, 발생지, 회합 장소; 개최 예정지
A place where people meet for an organized event, for example a concert, sporting event or conference.

menacing [ménəsiŋ] a. 위협적인, 으르는 (menacingly ad. 위협적으로)
If someone or something looks menacing, they give you a feeling that they are likely to cause you harm or put you in danger.

instruction [instrʌ́kʃən] n. 가르침, 교훈; (pl.) 지령, 지시
The written information that tells you how to do or use something.

merely [míərli] ad. 단지, 다만 (…에 불과한)
Nothing more than; Just.

proximity [prɑksíməti] n. 근접, 가까움
The state of being near in space or time.

Vocabulary in New Moon

undulate [ʌ́ndʒəlèit] v. 물결치다, 파도처럼 움직이다, 파동치다
To move or to make something move in or like waves.

★ **inject** [indʒékt] vt. 주사하다, 주입하다, 삽입하다
If you inject a new, exciting, or interesting quality into a situation, you add it.

leer [liər] n. 음흉한 시선[미소]; vi. 곁눈질하다, (짓궂게) 노려보다
An unpleasant look or smile that shows somebody is interested in a person in an evil or sexual way.

★ **pretense** [priténs] n. 겉치레, 가식(假飾), 가면, 위장, 허위
The act of behaving in a particular way, in order to make other people believe something that is not true.

★ **civility** [sivíləti] n. 정중, 공손, 예의바름
Polite behavior.

infinitesimal [infinitésəməl] a. 미소한, 극미한; 극미량의
(infinitesimally ad. 무한소로, 극미량으로)
Extremely small.

regretful [rigrétfəl] a. 유감스러워[애석해] 하는 (듯한); 후회하는
(regretfully ad. 유감스럽게도, 유감스러운 듯, 애석한 듯)
Feeling or showing sadness or disappointment because of something that has happened or something that you have done or not done.

^{복습} **invitation** [ìnvətéiʃən] n. 초대
A written or spoken request to come to an event such as a party, a meal, or a meeting.

★ **alley** [ǽli] n. 좁은 길; 골목, 샛길
An alley is a narrow passage or street with buildings or walls on both sides.

^{복습} **purr** [pəːr] v. 낮고 부드럽게 말하다; (차 엔진이) 낮은 소리를 내다; n. 목구멍을 울렘[울리는 소리]
To make or utter a soft vibrant sound.

^{복습} **doom** [duːm] vt. 운명 짓다, 선고하다; n. 운명, 파멸
If a fact or event dooms someone or something to a particular fate, it makes certain that they are going to suffer in some way.

20. VOLTERRA

lilt [lilt] n. 쾌활한 곡조[리듬·동작]; vi. 즐겁게 노래하다 (lilting a. 경쾌한, 즐겁고 신나는)
The pleasant way in which a person's voice rises and falls.

stance [stæns] n. [야구·골프] (공을 칠 때의) 발의 위치, 스탠스
A position in which you stand, especially when playing a sport.

underlying [ʌ̀ndərláiiŋ] a. (겉으로 잘 드러나지는 않지만) 근본적인[근원적인]
The underlying features of an object, event, or situation are not obvious, and it may be difficult to discover or reveal them.

tension [ténʃən] n. 긴장, 긴박, 팽팽함
A feeling of worry and anxiety which makes it difficult for you to relax.

fragile [frǽdʒəl] a. 부서지기[깨지기] 쉬운
Easily damaged, broken or harmed.

swing [swiŋ] v. (swang-swung) 흔들다; 매달리다, 빙 돌다
If something swings or if you swing it, it moves repeatedly backwards and forwards or from side to side from a fixed point.

gust [gʌst] n. 돌풍, 한바탕 부는 바람
A sudden strong movement of wind, air, rain etc.

★ **funnel** [fʌ́nl] v. (깔때기처럼 좁은 통로)를 통과하다, 한 곳에 모이다; 깔때기 모양이 되다
To move or make something move through a narrow space, or as if through a funnel.

apparently [əpǽrəntli] ad. 보기에, 외관상으로; 분명히, 명백히
Used to say that something seems to be true, although it is not certain; Used when the real situation is different from what you thought it was.

audible [ɔ́:dəbl] a. 들리는, 들을 수 있는 (audibly ad. 들리도록, 들을 수 있게)
Loud enough to be heard.

reedy [rí:di] a. 갈대피리 소리 같은; (목소리가) 새된
(of a voice or sound) High and not very pleasant.

lank [læŋk] a. 여윈, 호리호리한, 나긋나긋한
Long and thin and often limp.

Vocabulary in New Moon

trim [trim] v. 다듬다, 정돈하다; n. 건물의 외면 장식, 외장; 정돈(된 상태)
To make something neater, smaller, better, etc., by cutting parts from it.

androgynous [ændrádʒənəs] a. 양성(兩性)의 특징을 가진; 중성 같은
Having both male and female characteristics; Looking neither strongly male nor strongly female.

gargoyle [gáːrgɔil] n. [건축] (고딕 건축에서) 괴물 꼴 홈통 주둥이; 추한 용모의 사람
A gargoyle is a decorative stone carving on old buildings. It is usually shaped like the head of a strange and ugly creature, and water drains through it from the roof of the building.

iris [áiris] n. [해부] (안구의) 홍채
The round colored part that surrounds the pupil of your eye.

insignificant [ìnsignífikənt] a. 무의미한, 하찮은, 사소한
Not big or valuable enough to be considered important.

resignation [rèzignéiʃən] n. 포기, 단념, 체념
The acceptance of an unpleasant situation because you realize that you cannot change it.

monotone [mánətòun] n. 단조, 단조로움; a. 단조로운
If someone speaks in a monotone, their voice does not vary at all in tone or loudness and so it is not interesting to listen to.

smirk [sməːrk] vi. 능글맞게 웃다; n. 능글맞은 웃음
To smile in a self-satisfied, affected or foolish manner.

conversational [kɑ̀nvərséiʃənəl] a. 회화(체)의, 좌담식의, 말을 잘하는
(conversationally ad. 회화적으로, 스스럼없이)
Not formal; As used in conversation.

extreme [ikstríːm] a. 극단의, 극도의; n. 극단; 극도
Very great in degree.

stalk [stɔːk] v. (적·먹이 등에) 몰래 접근하다; (화가 난 듯이) 성큼성큼 걷다
If you stalk a person or a wild animal, you follow them quietly in order to kill them, catch them, or observe them carefully.

20. VOLTERRA

werewolf [wíərwùlf] n. 늑대 인간 (pl. werewolves)
In stories and films, a werewolf is a person who changes into a wolf.

drain [drein] n. 배수로, 하수구; v. (액체가) 흘러나가다; 말라버리다; 고갈시키다, 쇠진하다
A pipe that carries away dirty water or other liquid waste.

paving [péiviŋ] n. (땅에 널돌 등을 깔아 만든) 포장된 표면, 포석(鋪石); a. 포장(용)의
Paving is flat blocks of stone or concrete covering an area.

balk [bɔːk] vi. 망설이다, 난색을 보이다; 뒷걸음질 치다; (사람이) 멈춰 서다
To stop suddenly and refuse to jump a fence, etc.

doubtful [dáutfəl] a. 확신이 없는, 의심스러운
(doubtfully ad. 미심쩍게, 불확실하게, 애매하게)
(of a person) Not sure.

smug [smʌg] a. 잘난 체하는, 거만한
Too pleased or satisfied about something you have achieved or something you know.

crouch [krautʃ] v. 몸을 구부리다, 쭈그리다, 웅크리다
To bend your knees and lower yourself so that you are close to the ground and leaning forward slightly.

tremble [trémbəl] v. 떨다, 떨리다
To shake slightly, usually because you are cold or frightened.

reassure [rìːəʃúər] vt. 안심시키다, 재(re) 보증(assure)하다
To make someone feel less worried or frightened.

scrunch [skrʌntʃ] vt. 구기다[뭉치다]; (자갈·눈 위를 밟을 때와 같은) 저벅저벅[뽀득뽀득] 소리를 내다
To crush material such as paper or cloth into a rough ball in the hand.

huff [hʌf] n. 분개, 골냄; v. 씩씩거리다, 씩씩거리며 말하다; 가쁘게 숨쉬다, 헐떡이다
Feeling angry or bad-tempered, especially because someone has offended you.

exhale [ekshéil] v. (숨 등을) 내쉬다; (증기·향기 등을) 발산[방출]하다
To breathe out the air or smoke, etc. in your lungs.

Vocabulary in New Moon

vanish [vǽniʃ] v. 사라지다, 없어지다, 모습을 감추다
If someone or something vanishes, they disappear suddenly or in a way that cannot be explained.

radiance [réidiəns] n. 광휘, 찬연히 빛남
Radiance is a glowing light shining from something.

thumb [θʌm] n. 엄지손가락; v. (책을) 엄지손가락으로 넘기다
The short thick finger at the side of the hand, slightly apart from the other four.

reunion [ri:jú:niən] n. 재결합, 재회; 화해, 융화
The act of reuniting or state of being reunited.

offset [ɔ́(:)fsét] v. 차감 계산하다, 상쇄하다; (장점이) (단점을) 벌충하다
To use one cost, payment or situation in order to cancel or reduce the effect of another.

subterranean [sʌ̀btəréiniən] a. 지하의
Under the ground.

prowl [praul] vi. 어슬렁거리다, 배회하다
To move quietly and carefully around an area, especially when hunting.

compel [kəmpél] vt. 강제하다, 억지로 …시키다
To force someone to do something.

motivation [mòutəvéiʃən] n. 자극, 유도, 동기 부여
Enthusiasm for doing something.

desperate [déspərit] a. 필사적인; 절망적인, 자포자기의
(**desperately** ad. 절망적으로; 자포자기하여; 필사적으로)
If you are desperate for something or desperate to do something, you want or need it very much indeed.

slant [slænt] v. 경사지게 하다, 기울이다; n. 경사, 비탈; 견해, 의견
To be at an angle as opposed to horizontal or vertical; To slope.

claustrophobic [klɔ̀:strəfóubik] a. 밀실공포증의
If you feel claustrophobic, you feel very uncomfortable or anxious when you are in a small, crowded, or enclosed place.

20. VOLTERRA

- **ebony** [ébəni] a. 흑단으로 만든; (흑단처럼) 새까만
  Something that is ebony is a very deep black color.

- **moisture** [mɔ́istʃər] n. 습기, 수분, 물기, (공기 중의) 수증기
  Very small drops of water that are present in the air, on a surface or in a substance.

- **chatter** [tʃǽtər] vi. 수다스레 재잘거리다; (춥거나 공포로) 이가 맞부딪치다
  If you chatter, you talk quickly and continuously, usually about things which are not important.

- **wintry** [wíntri] a. 겨울의, 겨울 같은; 추운
  Typical of winter; Cold.

- **chafe** [tʃeif] vt. (손 등을) 비벼서 따뜻하게 하다
  If skin chafes, or if something chafes it, it becomes sore because the thing is rubbing against it.

- **friction** [fríkʃən] n. [역학·물리] 마찰
  The action of one object or surface rubbing against another.

- **interlace** [ìntərléis] vt. 서로 엇갈리게 짜다, 섞어 짜다; 얽히게 하다
  To twist things together over and under each other; To be twisted together in this way.

- **duck** [dʌk] ① vi. 몸을 홱 굽히다; (쑥) 들어가다 ② n. 오리
  If you duck, you move your head or the top half of your body quickly downwards to avoid something that might hit you, or to avoid being seen.

- **grille** [gril] n. 격자, 쇠창살; (매표구·교도소 따위의) 창살문
  A screen made of metal bars or wire that is placed in front of a window, door or piece of machinery in order to protect it.

- **clang** [klæŋ] v. 뗑[철커덩] 울리다; n. 철커덩[뗑그렁] 하는 소리
  To make a loud deep ringing sound.

Comprehension Quiz

21. VERDICT

1. What is Aro's talent?

　A. He can read the minds of people around him from a distance.

　B. He can control the minds of the people around him.

　C. He can hurt people without touching them.

　D. He can read the minds of the people he touches.

2. Marcus was surprised by _____.

　A. Edward being physically close to Bella

　B. the intensity of Bella and Edward's relationship

　C. what Alice saw in the future

　D. Edward refusing to join the Volturi

3. Why did Aro want Bella to join the Volturi?

　A. He wanted to taste Bella's blood.

　B. Bella was immune to everyone's powers.

　C. He thought if Bella joined the Volturi then Edward would join, too.

　D. He wanted Bella to replace Jane in the group.

21. VERDICT

4. What is Jane's talent?

A. She can control people's minds and change their decisions.

B. She can read people's minds.

C. She can cause people pain using her mind.

D. She can control people's bodies.

5. Why did the Volturi allow Bella to leave?

A. Edward promised Aro that he would turn Bella into a vampire.

B. Aro didn't want to kill Bella because she meant a lot to Edward.

C. Alice said that she would turn Bella into a vampire.

D. Alice shows Aro a vision of Bella as a vampire in the future.

Vocabulary in New Moon

verdict [vɚ́ːrdikt] n. 판단, 의견, 결정
An opinion or decision made after judging the facts that are given, especially one made at the end of a trial.

unremarkable [ənrimáːrkəbəl] a. 남의 주의[흥미]를 끌지 않는, 평범한
Ordinary; Not special or remarkable in any way.

rectangular [rektǽŋgjələr] a. 직사각형[장방형]의
Something that is rectangular is shaped like a rectangle.

fluorescent [fluərésnt] a. 형광을 발하는, 형광성의; 산뜻한, 빛나는
Producing bright light by using some forms of radiation.

benign [bináin] a. 자비로운, 인자한, 친절한
Kind and gentle; Not hurting anybody.

gloom [gluːm] n. 어둠침침함, 어둠, 그늘, 암흑
A feeling of being sad and without hope.

ghoulish [gúːliʃ] a. 송장 먹는 귀신 같은; 잔인한, 엽기적인; 병적인
Something that is ghoulish looks or behaves like a ghoul.

★ **sewer** [sjúːər] n. 하수구, 하수도
A large pipe, usually underground, which is used for carrying waste water and human waste, such as urine and excrement, away from buildings to a place where they can be safely got rid of.

★ **assessment** [əsésmənt] n. (과세를 위한) 사정, 평가
The act of judging the quality of something, especially pupils' or students' work.

creak [kriːk] v. 삐걱삐걱 소리를 내며 움직이(게 하)다; n. 삐걱거리는 소리
When a door or floorboard, etc. creaks, it makes a long low sound when it moves or is moved.

apathetic [æ̀pəθétik] a. 무감각한; 냉담한
Showing no interest or enthusiasm.

chalky [tʃɔ́ːki] a. 분필처럼 흰, 백악질의
Like or consisting of chalk.

21. VERDICT

pallor [pǽlər] n. (안색의) 해쓱함, 창백
Paleness, especially of complexion.

crop [krɑp] v. (머리를) 아주 짧게 깎다
To crop someone's hair means to cut it short.

pupil [pjúːpəl] n. 눈동자, 동공
The circular black area in the center of your eye, through which light enters.

nondescript [nàndiskrípt] a., n. 정체를 알 수 없는 (사람[것]); 막연한 (사람[것])
Having no interesting or unusual features or qualities.

cower [káuər] vi. 움츠리다, 위축되다
To bend low and move back because you are frightened.

Tuscan [tʌ́skən] n. 토스카나의, 토스카나 사람

glossy [glɔ́(ː)si] a. 광택[윤]이 나는, 윤기 있는, 반질반질한
Smooth and shiny.

vibrant [váibrənt] a. (색·빛이) 선명한, 번쩍거리는 (vibrantly ad. 선명하게)
(of colors) Very bright and strong.

bouquet [boukéi] n. 부케, 꽃다발
An arrangement of flowers, especially one that you give to someone.

gawk [gɔːk] vi. 멍청히 바라보다; n. 둔한 사람, 얼간이
To gawk at someone or something means to stare at them in a rude, stupid, or unthinking way.

astonishment [əstɑ́niʃmənt] n. 놀람, 경악
A feeling of very great surprise.

comprehend [kàmprihénd] vt. 이해하다, 파악[인식]하다; 포함[함축]하다
To understand something fully.

glint [glint] v. 반짝이다, 빛나다; n. 반짝임, 섬광
If something glints, it produces or reflects a quick flash of light.

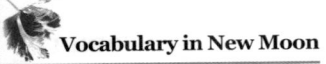
Vocabulary in New Moon

dimly [dímli] ad. 어둑[흐릿·희미]하게
Not very brightly or clearly.

disheveled [diʃévəld] a. 흩어진, 헝클어진; 단정하지 못한
If someone's appearance or their clothes, hair etc. is disheveled, they look very untidy.

comparative [kəmpǽrətiv] a. 다른 것과 비교한 경우의, 상대적인, 상당한
(comparatively ad. 비교적, 상당히, 꽤)
Connected with studying things to find out how similar or different they are.

hideous [hídiəs] a. 끔찍한, 오싹한, 흉측한, 극악무도한
Extremely ugly or bad.

giggle [gígəl] v. 낄낄 웃다; n. 낄낄 웃음
If someone giggles, they laugh in a childlike way, because they are amused, nervous, or embarrassed.

coo [ku:] v. 정답게 소곤거리다; 구구 울다; n. 구구 (비둘기 우는 소리)
When someone coos, they speak in a very soft, quiet voice which is intended to sound attractive.

marginally [má:rdʒənəli] ad. 아주 조금, 미미하게
Very slightly; Not very much.

cling [kliŋ] vi. (clung-clung) 달라붙다, 매달리다
If you cling to someone or something, you hold onto them tightly.

contemptuous [kəntémptʃuəs] a. 경멸적인, 남을 얕잡아보는
If you are contemptuous of someone or something, you do not like or respect them at all.

dibs [dibz] int. 내 몫이야[차례야] (주로 어린이 말)
A claim of rights.

ornate [ɔ:rnéit] a. 잘 꾸민; (문체가) 화려한
Covered with a lot of decoration, especially when this involves very small or complicated designs.

21. VERDICT

* **sheathe** [ʃi:ð] vt. 씌우다, 싸다, 외장하다 (with, in)
  Something to cover something in a material, especially in order to protect it.

* **alley** [ǽli] n. 좁은 길; 골목, 샛길
  An alley is a narrow passage or street with buildings or walls on both sides.

  antechamber [ǽntitʃèimbər] n. (큰 방으로 통하는) 곁방, 대기실
  An antechamber is a small room leading into a larger room.

  cavernous [kǽvərnəs] a. 동굴 같은, 동굴이 많은; 움푹한, 깊은
  A cavernous room or building is very large inside, and so it reminds you of a cave.

* **turret** [tə́:rit] n. (주건물에 부속된) 작은 탑
  A turret is a small narrow tower on top of a building or a larger tower.

* **artificial** [à:rtəfíʃəl] a. 인공적인
  Made by people, often as a copy of something natural.

* **massive** [mǽsiv] a. 크고 무거운, 육중한, 굳센, 강력한
  Something that is massive is very large in size, quantity, or extent.

  convene [kənvíːn] v. 모으다, 소집하다
  To arrange for people to come together for a formal meeting.

* **seemingly** [síːmiŋli] ad. 보기엔, 외관상; 겉으로는, 표면적으로는
  If something is seemingly the case, you mean that it appears to be the case, even though it may not really be so.

* **prism** [prizm] n. 프리즘, 분광기
  A prism is a block of clear glass or plastic which separates the light passing through it into different colors.

* **sienna** [siénə] n. 시에나색, 황갈색
  A type of dark yellow or red clay used for giving color to paints, etc.

* **exquisite** [ikskwízit] a. 우아한, 섬세한; 정교한, 절묘한
  Extremely beautiful or carefully made.

Vocabulary in New Moon

immortal [imɔ́ːrtl] n. 영생하는 존재; 불멸의 인물; a. 불사의, 불멸의, 영원한
A god or other being who is believed to live for ever.

evident [évidənt] a. 분명한, 명백한, 뚜렷한
Easily seen or understood; Obvious.

surreal [səríːəl] a. 환각적인, 환상적인, 비현실의
Being in the style of Surrealism.

astonish [əstániʃ] vt. 깜짝 놀라게 하다
To surprise someone very much.

attractive [ətrǽktiv] a. 사람의 마음을 끄는, 매력적인, 눈에 뜨이는, 흥미를 돋우는
Very pleasing in appearance or sound, or causing interest or pleasure.

converge [kənvə́ːrdʒ] vi. 모이다, 집중하다
To move towards or meet at one point.

alert [əlɔ́ːrt] n. 경보, 경계; v. 경고하다; a. 방심하지 않는
A warning to people to be prepared to deal with something dangerous.

translucent [trænsljúːsənt] a. 반투명의 (translucently ad. 반투명하게)
Allowing light to pass through but not transparent.

onionskin [ʌ́njənskìn] n. 양파 껍질; 얇은 반투명지
onion (n. 양파) + skin (n. 껍질, 피부)

horrify [hɔ́ːrəfài] vt. 소름끼치게 하다, 충격을 주다
(horrifying a. 몸서리처지는, 소름끼치는)
If someone is horrified, they feel shocked or disgusted, because of something that they have seen or heard.

powdery [páudəri] a. 가루 (모양)의; 가루투성이의
Something that is powdery looks or feels like powder.

haze [heiz] n. 아지랑이, 엷은 연기
Smoke, dust, or mist in the air which is difficult to see through.

glide [glaid] v. 미끄러지듯 움직이다; n. 활주, 활공
If you glide somewhere, you move silently and in a smooth and effortless way.

21. VERDICT

- **angelic** [ændʒélik] a. 천사의, 천사 같은; 청아한, 고결한
  Angelic means like angels or relating to angels.

- **misty** [místi] a. 희미한, 몽롱한; 안개가 짙은, 안개 자욱한
  Not clear or bright.

  ecstatic [ekstǽtik] a. 완전히 마음이 팔린, 열중한; 무아경의, 황홀한
  Very happy, excited and enthusiastic.

- **rejoice** [ridʒɔ́is] v. 기뻐하다, 즐겁게 하다
  To feel, show or express great happiness or joy.

- **clap** [klæp] v. 박수를[손뼉을] 치다; 가볍게 치다[두드리다]
  When you clap, you hit your hands together to show appreciation or attract attention.

  hulk [hʌlk] n. 덩치 큰 사람; 부피가 큰 물건 (hulking a. 몸집이 큰; 보기 흉한)
  A very large person, especially one who moves in an awkward way.

- **escort** [ésko:rt] n. 호위대[원]; vt. 호위하다, 동행하다
  An escort is a person who travels with someone in order to protect or guard them.

- **scold** [skould] v. 꾸짖다, 잔소리하다
  If you scold someone, you speak angrily to them because they have done something wrong.

- **infallible** [infǽləbəl] a. 절대 오류가 없는
  Never wrong, failing or making a mistake.

- **dazzle** [dǽzəl] vt. 현혹시키다, 감탄시키다; n. 현혹, 눈부신 빛 (dazzling a. 눈부신)
  If someone or something dazzles you, you are extremely impressed by their skill, qualities, or beauty.

- **modest** [mɑ́dist] a. 겸손한; (질·양·정도 등이) 별로 많지[크지] 않은
  If you say that someone is modest, you approve of them because they do not talk much about their abilities or achievements.

- **chide** [tʃaid] v. 꾸짖다, 책망하다
  To criticize or blame somebody because they have done something wrong.

Vocabulary in New Moon

* **exploit** [éksplɔit] n. 위업, 공적; vt. 개척[개발]하다; (부당하게) 이용하다; (노동력을) 착취하다
  If you refer to someone's exploits, you mean the brave, interesting, or amusing things that they have done.

* **peculiar** [pikjú:ljər] a. 기묘한, 이상한, 특이한; 특유한, 고유의
  Unusual and strange, sometimes in an unpleasant way.

* **envious** [énviəs] a. 시기심이 강한; 질투하는, 샘내는
  If you are envious of someone, you want something that they have.

  exponential [èkspounénʃəl] a. 기하급수적인, 급격한
  (exponentially ad. 전형적으로; 기하급수적으로)
  Growing or increasing very rapidly.

* **incline** [inkláin] v. 기울이다, (마음이) 기울다; n. 경사, 비탈
  To bend the head or body forward.

* **convenient** [kənví:njənt] a. 편리한, 형편이 좋은
  If a way of doing something is convenient, it is easy, or very useful or suitable for a particular purpose.

* **utterly** [ʌ́tərli] ad. 완전히, 순전히, 아주, 전혀
  You use utterly to emphasize that something is very great in extent, degree, or amount.

* **millennium** [miléniəm] n. 천년간 (pl. millennia)
  A millennium is a period of one thousand years, especially one which begins and ends with a year ending in '000', for example the period from the year 1000 to the year 2000.

  papery [péipəri] a. 종이 같은; 얇고 건조한
  Like paper; Thin and dry.

* **crumple** [krʌ́mpl] v. 구기다, 구겨지다, 쭈글쭈글하게 하다
  To crush something into folds; To become crushed into folds.

* **ridiculous** [ridíkjələs] a. 웃기는, 우스꽝스러운; 터무니없는
  If you say that something or someone is ridiculous, you mean that they are very foolish.

21. VERDICT

* **frail** [freil] a. 약한, 부서지기 쉬운, 무른
  Weak or unhealthy, or easily damaged, broken or harmed.

* **frustrate** [frʌ́streit] vt. 좌절시키다, 실망시키다 (frustrated a. 실망한, 좌절한)
  Feeling annoyed, upset, and impatient, because you cannot achieve something.

* **relationship** [riléiʃənʃip] n. 관계, 관련
  The way in which two people, groups or countries behave towards each other or deal with each other.

* **chaotic** [keiátik] a. 대혼란의, 무질서한; 혼돈된
  In a state of complete confusion and lack of order.

* **intensity** [inténsəti] n. 강렬, 격렬; 집중; 전념
  The state or quality of being intense.

* **outshine** [àutʃáin] vt. …보다 더 낫다[뛰어나다]
  If you outshine someone at a particular activity, you are much better at it than they are.

* **impatient** [impéiʃənt] a. 성급한, 조급한, 몹시 …하고 싶어 하는
  Easily annoyed by someone's mistakes or because you have to wait.

* **eager** [íːgər] a. 열망하는, 간절히 하고 싶어 하는
  If you are eager to do or have something, you want to do or have it very much.

* **preliminary** [prilímənèri] n. 사전 준비; 서두, 서론; a. 예비[준비]의; 임시의; 서문의
  A preliminary is something that you do at the beginning of an activity, often as a form of preparation.

* **gratify** [grǽtəfài] vt. 기쁘게 하다, 만족시키다
  To please someone, or to satisfy a wish or need.

* **exceedingly** [iksíːdiŋli] ad. 대단히, 매우, 몹시
  To a very great degree; Extremely.

* **unorthodox** [ʌnɔ́ːrθədàks] a. 정통적이 아닌, 특이한
  Different from what is usual or accepted.

Vocabulary in New Moon

- **scoff** [skɔːf] v. 비웃다, 조소하다, 조롱하다
  To laugh and speak about a person in a way which shows that you think they are stupid.

- **restraint** [riːstréint] n. 제지, 금지, 억제
  The act of controlling or limiting something because it is necessary or sensible to do so.

- **admiration** [ӕdməréiʃən] n. 감탄, 칭찬
  A feeling of respect and liking for somebody of something.

  seething [síːðiŋ] a. (화·흥분 등으로) 속이 끓어 오르는; 격렬한, 펄펄 끓는; 소용돌이치는
  When you are seething, you are very angry about something but do not express your feelings about it.

- **rude** [ruːd] a. 무례한, 버릇없는
  Having or showing a lack of respect for other people and their feelings.

- **fascinate** [fӕsəneit] v. 매혹하다, 황홀케 하다 (fascinated a. 마음을 다 빼앗긴, 매료된)
  To interest strongly.

  overt [óuvəːrt] a. 명시적인, 공공연한
  An overt action or attitude is done or shown in an open and obvious way.

- **politeness** [pəláitnis] n. 공손[정중]함; 우애[고상]함
  The act of showing regard for others.

- **perverse** [pərvə́ːrs] a. 괴팍한, 심술궂은, 별난; 외고집의 (perversely ad. 괴팍하게, 별나게)
  Showing deliberate determination to behave in a way that most people think is wrong, unacceptable or unreasonable.

- **intrigue** [intríːg] v. 호기심을 돋우다; 음모를 꾸미다; n. 음모
  If something intrigues you, it interests you and you want to know more about it.

- **encouragement** [enkə́ːridʒmənt] n. 격려, 고무
  Encouragement is the activity of encouraging someone, or something that is said or done in order to encourage them.

21. VERDICT

alien [éiljən] a. 생경한; 외국의, 성질이 다른; 우주의
Strange and frightening; Different from what you are used to.

insubstantial [ìnsəbstǽnʃəl] a. 실체가 없는, 비현실적인
Not real or solid.

brittle [britl] a. 부서지기 쉬운, 깨지기 쉬운; (소리 등이) 날카로운, 금속성의
Hard but easily broken.

shale [ʃeil] n. [암석] 혈암(頁岩), 이판암
A type of soft stone that splits easily into thin flat layers.

granite [grǽnit] n. 화강암; 견고함
Granite is a very hard rock used in building.

mesmerize [mésməràiz] vt. …에게 최면술을 걸다; 매혹시키다, 감화시키다
If you are mesmerized by something, you are so interested in it or so attracted to it that you cannot think about anything else.

waver [wéivər] v. 흔들리다, 펄럭이다; 동요하다, 머뭇거리다
To lose strength, determination or purpose, especially temporarily.

incredulity [ìnkridʒúːləti] n. 쉽사리 믿지 않음, 의심 많음, 불신
If someone reacts with incredulity to something, they are unable to believe it because it is very surprising or shocking.

immune [imjúːn] a. 영향을 받지 않는; (전염병·독 등을) 면한, 면역성의
Not affected by something.

restrain [ristréin] vt. 억제하다, 구속하다
To stop someone doing something by using force.

rip [rip] v. 벗겨내다, 찢다; 돌진하다; n. 잡아 찢음, 째진 틈
If you rip something away, you remove it quickly and forcefully.

baleful [béilfəl] a. 재앙의, 해로운, 불길한
Evil; Harmful.

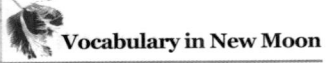
Vocabulary in New Moon

faux pas [fóu-páː] n. 잘못, 과실, 실책, 무례
An action or a remark that causes embarrassment because it is not socially correct.

★ **sulky** [sʌ́lki] a. 샐쭉한, 뚱한, 골난, 부루퉁한
Bad-tempered or not speaking because you are angry about something.

복습 **barely** [bɛ́ərli] ad. 간신히, 가까스로; 거의 …않다
Only with great difficulty or effort.

‡ **ghost** [goust] v. (유령처럼) …에 붙어 다니다, 나타나다, 소리 없이 움직이다; n. 유령
Move like a ghost.

entourage [àːnturáːʒ] n. 측근자, 주위 사람들
A group of people who travel with an important person.

beatific [bìːətífik] a. 기쁨이 넘치는, 더없이 행복해 하는
Showing great joy and peace.

복습 **launch** [lɔːntʃ] v. 맹렬히 덤비다; 발진시키다, 쏘다, 내보내다
To jump forwards with a lot of force.

복습 **formidable** [fɔ́ːrmidəbəl] a. 무서운, 무시무시한; 만만찮은, 얕잡을 수 없는; 굉장히 많은
Causing you to have fear or respect for something or someone because they are impressive, powerful or difficult.

복습 **shriek** [ʃriːk] v. 새된 소리를 지르다, 비명을 지르다; n. 비명
When someone shrieks, they make a short, very loud cry.

복습 **grasp** [græsp] v. 붙잡다, 움켜쥐다; n. 움켜잡기
To quickly take something in your hand(s) and hold it firmly.

복습 **tranquil** [trǽŋkwil] a. 조용한, 평온한, 평화로운
Quiet and peaceful.

복습 **pointless** [pɔ́intlis] a. 효과가 없는; 요령부득의, 무의미한
(pointlessly ad. 무의미하게, 효과 없이)
Lacking purpose or meaning.

21. VERDICT

- **glare** [glɛər] v. 노려보다; 번쩍번쩍 빛나다; n. 섬광; 노려봄
  If you glare at someone, you look at them with an angry expression on your face.

- **shrink** [ʃriŋk] v. (shrank-shrunk) 움츠러들다, 뒷걸음치다; 오그라들다; 줄다; n. (속어) 정신과 의사; 심리학자
  To become smaller, or to make something smaller.

- **surrender** [səréndər] v. 항복하다, 내어주다, 넘겨주다; n. 항복, 굴복
  To stop fighting and admit defeat.

- **confound** [kənfáund] v. 어리둥절[당혹]하게 만들다
  If someone or something confounds you, they make you feel surprised or confused, often by showing you that your opinions or expectations of them were wrong.

- **chortle** [tʃɔ́:rtl] vi. (좋아서) 깔깔 웃다; 아주 좋아하다
  To laugh loudly with pleasure or because you are amused.

- **grimace** [gríməs] vi. 얼굴을 찡그리다; n. 얼굴을 찌푸림, 찌푸린 얼굴, 우거지상
  If you grimace, you twist your face in an ugly way because you are annoyed, disgusted, or in pain.

- **hiss** [his] v. 쉿 하는 소리를 내다; n. 쉿 (제지·힐책의 소리)
  If people hiss at someone such as a performer or a person making a speech, they express their disapproval or dislike of that person.

- **potential** [pouténʃəl] n. 잠재력, 가능성; a. 잠재적인, 가능성이 있는
  If you say that someone or something has potential, you mean that they have the necessary abilities or qualities to become successful or useful in the future.

- **affectionate** [əfékʃənit] a. 애정 깊은, 사랑에 넘친, 다정한, 인정 많은
  (affectionately ad. 애정을 담고, 애정 어리게, 자애롭게)
  If you are affectionate, you show your love or fondness for another person in the way that you behave towards them.

- **prospective** [prəspéktiv] a. 예기되는, 가망이 있는, 장래의
  You use prospective to describe something that is likely to happen soon.

Vocabulary in New Moon

caustic [kɔ́:stik] a. 신랄한, 통렬한, 빈정대는; [화학] 부식성의, 가성(苛性)의
A caustic remark is extremely critical, cruel, or bitter.

fume [fju:m] v. 몹시 화내다; 약이 오르다, 연기 나다, 그을리다; n. 연기, 김
If you fume over something, you express annoyance and anger about it.

rumble [rʌ́mbəl] n. 우르르 소리; vi. (천둥·지진 등이) 우르르 울리다; (배) 꾸르륵거리다
A rumble is a low continuous noise.

temper [témpər] n. 기질, 성질; 화, 노여움
If you refer to someone's temper, you mean that they become angry very easily.

irate [áireit] a. 성난, 격분한
If someone is irate, they are very angry about something.

astonished [əstániʃt] a. 깜짝 놀란, 크게 놀란
Very surprised about something.

charade [ʃəréid] n. 빤히 들여다보이는 수작[속임수]
A situation in which people pretend that something is true when it clearly is not.

sustain [səstéin] vt. (생명을) 유지하다, 떠받치다
To keep going.

scoff [skɔ:f] v. 비웃다, 조소하다, 조롱하다
To laugh and speak about a person in a way which shows that you think they are stupid.

vulnerability [vʌ̀lnərəbíləti] n. 약점이 있음, 취약성, 상처 받기 쉬움
The state of being vulnerable or exposed.

forfeit [fɔ́:rfit] vt. 상실하다, 몰수되다; n. 벌금; 상실, 박탈
To lose something or have something taken away from you because you have done something wrong.

immortality [ìmɔ:rtǽləti] n. 불사, 영원(성); 영원한 생명[존재]
The state of being immortal.

21. VERDICT

loathsome [lóuðsəm] a. 싫은, 지긋지긋한; 불쾌한; 역겨운
Extremely unpleasant.

acquisitive [əkwízətiv] a. 소유욕[물욕]이 많은
Wanting very much to buy or get new possessions.

bent [bent] a. 굽은, 구부러진; 열중한, 결심한; n. 경향
Not straight; Curved or having a bend.

agonize [ǽgənàiz] v. 번민하다, 괴롭히다, 괴로워하다 (agonizing a. 고통스러운)
If you agonize over something, you feel very anxious about it and spend a long time thinking about it.

fret [fret] v. 애타다, 안달하다; 속 타게 하다, 초조하게 하다; n. 애달음, 초조
If you fret about something, you worry about it.

alternative [ɔːltə́ːrnətiv] a. 하나를 택해야 할, 양자택일의; n. 대안, 선택 가능한 것
An alternative plan or method is one that you can use if you do not want to use another one.

annoyance [ənɔ́iəns] n. 성가심, 불쾌감; 괴로움, 곤혹
The feeling of being slightly angry.

terrify [térəfài] vt. 무섭게[겁나게] 하다, 놀래다
If something terrifies you, it makes you feel extremely frightened.

enthrall [enθrɔ́ːl] vt. 매혹하다, 마음을 빼앗다, 사로잡다, 노예(상태)로 하다
To keep someone completely interested.

lidded [lídid] a. 눈(꺼풀)이 반쯤 감긴; 뚜껑이 있는
Lidded is used to describe a container that has a lid.

lizard [lízərd] n. 도마뱀
A reptile with short legs and a long tail.

amuse [əmjúːz] vt. 즐겁게 하다, 재미나게 하다 (amused a. 재밌어[즐거워] 하는)
To make somebody laugh or smile.

urgent [ə́ːrdʒənt] a. 긴급한, 절박한
If something is urgent, it needs to be dealt with as soon as possible.

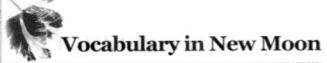

Vocabulary in New Moon

chagrin [ʃəgrín] n. 원통함, 억울함, 분함
A feeling of being disappointed or annoyed.

babble [bǽbəl] v. 실없이 지껄이다, 쓸데없는 말을 하다; n. 재잘거림, 왁자지껄
If someone babbles, they talk in a confused or excited way.

coarse [kɔːrs] a. 조잡한, 조악한, 열등한; 거친, 올이 성긴; 야비한, 상스러운
Rough and not smooth or soft, or not in very small pieces.

medieval [mìːdiíːvəl] a. 중세의, 중세풍의
Something that is medieval relates to or was made in the period of European history between the end of the Roman Empire in 476 AD and about 1500 AD.

shrill [ʃril] a. (소리가) 날카로운, 새된; 신랄한; v. 새된 소리로 말하다, 새된 소리를 내다
Having a loud and high sound that is unpleasant or painful to listen to.

gush [gʌʃ] v. (액체 등이) 분출하다, 내뿜다; (구어) 지껄여대다; n. 분출; (감정의) 격발
To express a positive feeling, especially praise, in such a strong way that it does not sound sincere.

rosary [róuzəri] n. (로마 가톨릭교의) 묵주
A rosary is a string of beads that members of certain religions, especially Catholics, use for counting prayers.

gorgeous [gɔ́ːrdʒəs] a. 호화로운, 찬란한, 화려한
Extremely beautiful or attractive.

statuesque [stætʃuésk] a. 조각상 같은; 조각상을 연상시키는, (조각상 같이) 완벽한, 균형이 잡힌; 당당한, 위엄이 있는
Large and beautiful in an impressive way, like a statue.

exceptional [iksépʃənəl] a. 이례적일 정도로 우수한, 특출한
Unusually good.

unforgettable [ʌ̀nfərgétəbəl] a. 잊을 수 없는, 언제까지나 기억에 남는
If something is unforgettable, you cannot forget it, usually because it is so beautiful, interesting, enjoyable, etc.

21. VERDICT

emphasize [émfəsàiz] vt. 강조하다; 역설하다
To emphasize something means to indicate that it is particularly important or true, or to draw special attention to it.

extremely [ikstrí:mli] ad. 극단적으로, 극히, 매우
To a very high degree.

lustrous [lʎstrəs] a. 광택 있는, 번쩍번쩍하는, 빛나는
Soft and shining.

tint [tint] n. 엷은 빛깔
A shade or small amount of a particular color.

compliment [kámpləmənt] v. 경의를 표하다, 칭찬하다; n. 찬사, 칭찬의 말
If you compliment someone, you pay them a compliment.

fisherman [fíʃərmən] n. 어부; 낚시꾼
A fisherman is a person who catches fish as a job or for sport.

bait [beit] n. 미끼, 유혹물; v. 미끼로 꾀어 들이다
A small amount of food put on a hook or in a trap to attract fish or animals.

stun [stʌn] vt. 어리벙벙하게 하다; 기절시키다; n. 놀라게 함
(stunning a. 아연하게 하는; 놀랄 만큼 멋진)
If you are stunned by something, you are extremely shocked or surprised by it and are therefore unable to speak or do anything.

Comprehension Quiz

22. FLIGHT

1. Why did Gianna work for the Volturi?

   A. She was a relative of one of the vampires.

   B. She wanted to become a vampire.

   C. She was a vampire but wanted to become part of the Volturi.

   D. The Volturi promised to turn her into a vampire after a year of work.

2. Bella was Edward's 'singer' because _____.

   A. her blood sang to him

   B. she could manipulate the people around her

   C. she reminded Aro of his favorite opera singer

   D. she had a beautiful voice

3. Bella told Edward she didn't want to sleep because _____.

   A. she wanted to talk to him

   B. she wanted to see his face

   C. she was afraid he would leave

   D. she would have nightmares

22. FLIGHT

4. Why did Esme say thank you to Bella?

A. Bella didn't kill herself.

B. Bella brought Esme a present from Florence.

C. Bella apologized to Esme.

D. Bella saved Edward.

5. Why was Bella surprised when Rosalie spoke to her?

A. Rosalie asked her for an apology.

B. It was the first time Rosalie spoke directly to her.

C. Rosalie apologized to her.

D. Rosalie woke her up from a deep sleep.

Vocabulary in New Moon

opulent [ápjələnt] a. 화려한; 무성한; 부유한, 풍부한
Made or decorated using expensive materials.

reception [risépʃən] n. (호텔의) 프론트; 수령, 받아들임; [통신] 청취(상태), 수신(율)
The place in a hotel or office building where people go when they first arrive.

tinkle [tíŋkəl] v. 딸랑딸랑 울리다
To make light ringing sounds, or to make something do this.

shrewd [ʃruːd] a. 예민한, 날카로운; 영리한, 빈틈없는
Showing good judgement and likely to be right.

speculation [spèkjəléiʃən] n. 심사 숙고, 사색, 고찰; 추측, 추론
An act or instance, or the process or result, of speculating.

vibrate [váibreit] v. 진동하다, (시계추처럼) 흔들리다
If something vibrates or if you vibrate it, it shakes with repeated small, quick movements.

chatter [tʃǽtər] v. (춥거나 공포로) 이가 맞부딪치다; 수다스레 재잘거리다
To knock together continuously because you are cold or frightened.

counterpart [káuntərpàːrt] n. [음악] 대응부
Someone's or something's counterpart is another person or thing that has a similar function or position in a different place.

cheery [tʃíəri] a. 기분 좋은; 명랑한; 원기 있는
If you describe a person or their behavior as cheery, you mean that they are cheerful and happy.

hysteric [histérik] n. 광란, 병적 흥분, 히스테리의 발작
If someone is in hysterics or is having hysterics, they are in a state of uncontrolled excitement, anger, or panic.

slap [slæp] v. 찰싹 때리다, 세게 치다; 아무렇게나 바르다
To hit someone with the flat part of the hand or other flat object.

frantic [frǽntik] a. 광란의, 미친 듯 날뛰는
Behaving in a wild and uncontrolled way.

22. FLIGHT

- ★ **chant** [tʃænt] v. 단조로운 어조로[되풀이하여] 말하다
  To sing or say a religious song or prayer using only a few notes that are repeated many times.

- **wasteful** [wéistfəl] a. 낭비적인; 비경제적인, 허비의; 소모성의
  something using more of something than is necessary; Not saving or keeping something that could be used.

- **insanity** [insǽnəti] n. 광기, 발광, 정신 이상
  The state of being insane.

- **rosary** [róuzəri] n. (로마 가톨릭교의) 묵주
  A rosary is a string of beads that members of certain religions, especially Catholics, use for counting prayers.

- **detach** [ditǽtʃ] v. 떼어놓다, 분리하다; 파견하다
  If one thing detaches from another, it becomes separated from it.

- **hostile** [hástil] a. 적(군)의; 적의 있는, 적대하는, 반대하는; 냉담한
  Angry and deliberately unfriendly towards someone and ready to argue with them.

- **oblivious** [əblíviəs] a. (…이) 염두[안중]에 없는; 잘 잊어버리는, 건망증이 있는
  Unaware or forgetful of it.

- **hoarse** [hɔːrs] a. 목쉰, 쉰 목소리의
  If your voice is hoarse, your voice sounds rough and unclear.

- **shudder** [ʃʌdər] vi. 떨다, 몸서리치다; n. 몸이 떨림, 전율, 몸서리
  If you shudder, you shake with fear, horror, or cold.

- **hideous** [hídiəs] a. 끔찍한, 오싹한, 흉측한, 극악무도한
  Extremely ugly or bad.

- ★ **fleeting** [flíːtiŋ] a. 어느덧 지나가는, 덧없는, 무상한 (fleetingly ad. 빨리, 덧없이)
  Something which lasts only for a very short time.

  inexcusable [ìnikskjúːzəbəl] a. 변명할 도리가 없는; 용서할 수 없는
  Too bad to accept or forgive.

Vocabulary in New Moon

- **iris** [áiris] n. [해부] (안구의) 홍채
  The round colored part that surrounds the pupil of your eye.

- **unwilling** [ʌ̀nwíliŋ] a. 마음 내키지 않는, 마지못해 하는
  Not wanting to do something and refusing to do it.

- **bubble** [bʌ́bəl] v. 차오르다; 거품이 일다; (말을) 신나게 하다; n. 환상, 망상, 거품
  If a feeling or activity bubbles, it continues to exist.

- **imperfect** [impə́:rfikt] a. (지식·기능 등이) 불완전한, 불충분한; 결점[결함]이 있는
  Something that is imperfect has faults and is not exactly as you would like it to be.

- **fantasize** [fǽntəsàiz] v. 꿈에 그리다, 공상하다
  If you fantasize about an event or situation that you would like to happen, you give yourself pleasure by imagining that it is happening, although it is untrue or unlikely to happen.

- **motivation** [mòutəvéiʃən] n. 자극, 유도, 동기 부여
  Enthusiasm for doing something.

- **idly** [áidli] ad. 하는 일 없이, 빈둥거려; 게으르게
  Without any particular reason, purpose or effort; Doing nothing.

- **Porsche** [pɔ́:rʃ] n. 포르셰 (독일제 스포츠카)

- **weary** [wíəri] a. 피로한, 지친 (weariness n. 피로, 기진맥진)
  If you are weary, you are very tired.

- ★ **dormant** [dɔ́:rmənt] a. 잠자는, 휴지 상태에 있는
  Not active or not growing at the present time but able to be active later.

- **smack** [smæk] n. 찰싹 하는 소리; vt. 찰싹 치다, 쳐 날리다
  A short loud sound.

- **spotless** [spátlis] a. 더럽혀지지 않은, 오점이 없는
  spot (n. 얼룩, 반점) + -less (suf. …이 없는)

- **lifelong** [láiflɔ̀(:)ŋ] a. 일생의, 필생의
  Lifelong means existing or happening for the whole of a person's life.

22. FLIGHT

linger [líŋgər] vi. 오래 머무르다, 떠나지 못하다
When something lingers, it continues to exist for a long time, often much longer than expected.

competence [kámpətəns] n. 능력; 적성
The ability to do something well.

relieve [rilíːv] vt. 안도케 하다, (긴장·걱정 등을) 덜다, 구제하다
To lessen or stop someone's pain, worry, boredom, etc.

tasteful [téistfəl] a. 고상한, 우아한, 세련된 (tastefully ad. 우아하게, 세련되게)
Attractive and of good quality and showing that the person who chose them can recognize good things.

luxurious [lʌgʒúəriəs] a. 사치스러운, 호화로운
Very expensive, beautiful, and comfortable.

medieval [mìːdiíːvəl] a. 중세의, 중세풍의
Something that is medieval relates to or was made in the period of European history between the end of the Roman Empire in 476 AD and about 1500 AD.

elaborate [ilǽbərèit] a. 공들인, 고심하여 만들어 낸
Very complicated and detailed.

façade [fəsáːd] n. 정면, (비유적) (사물의) 표면, 외관, 겉보기, 허울
A false appearance that hides the reality.

turret [tə́ːrit] n. (주건물에 부속된) 작은 탑
A turret is a small narrow tower on top of a building or a larger tower.

swift [swift] a. 빠른, 신속한 (swiftly ad. 빨리, 즉시)
A swift event or process happens very quickly or without delay.

cobble [kábəl] vt. (도로에) 자갈을 깔다 (cobbled a. 자갈을 깐)
To pave with cobblestones.

fang [fæŋ] n. (육식 동물의) 송곳니, 엄니
A long sharp tooth.

Vocabulary in New Moon

retrieve [ritríːv] vt. 되찾다, 회수하다
To find and bring back something.

stash [stæʃ] vt. (물건을) 살며시 치우다, 감추다
To store something in a safe or secret place.

considerably [kənsídərəbli] ad. 상당히, 꽤, 적지 않게
Much; A lot.

archway [áːrtʃwèi] n. [건축] 아치 길; 통로 위의 아치
A passage or an entrance with an arch over it.

portcullis [pɔːrtkʌ́lis] n. (옛날 성문 등의) 내리닫이 격자문(格子門)
A portcullis is a strong gate above an entrance to a castle and used to be lowered to the ground in order to keep out enemies.

vaguely [véigli] ad. 모호하게, 막연히
In a way that is not detailed or exact.

dashboard [dǽʃbɔ̀ːrd] n. (자동차·비행기의) 계기판, 대시보드
The part of a car in front of the driver that has instruments and controls in it.

fabulous [fǽbjələs] a. 굉장한, 멋진, 믿어지지 않는
If you describe something as fabulous, you are emphasizing that you like it a lot or think that it is very good.

curvy [kə́ːrvi] a. (길 등이) 구불구불한, 굽은 (데가 많은)
Containing a lot of curves.

hollow [hálou] n. 구멍; 움푹 깨진 곳; a. 오목한, 야원; 속이 빈
Something that is hollow has a space inside it, as opposed to being solid all the way through.

stubborn [stʌ́bərn] a. 완고한, 고집 센
Determined not to change your opinion or attitude.

lid [lid] n. 눈꺼풀(eyelid); 뚜껑
A cover on a container, which can be removed.

22. FLIGHT

trash [træʃ] n. 폐물, 쓰레기(rubbish)
Something that you throw away because you no longer want or need them.

alley [ǽli] n. 좁은 길; 골목, 샛길
An alley is a narrow passage or street with buildings or walls on both sides.

fatigue [fətí:g] n. 피로, 피곤
A feeling of being extremely tired, usually because of hard work or exercise.

attendant [əténdənt] n. 시중드는 사람, 안내원
Someone whose job is to be in a place and help visitors or customers.

disapproving [dìsəprú:viŋ] a. 못마땅해 하는, 불찬성의
(disapprovingly ad. 못마땅하여; 불찬성의 뜻을 나타내어)
Showing that you do not approve of somebody or something.

tolerance [tálərəns] n. 내성, 저항력; 관용, 아량, 용인
The degree to which someone can suffer pain, difficulty etc. without being harmed or damaged.

despair [dispέər] vi. 절망하다, 체념하다; n. 절망, 자포자기
If you despair, you feel that everything is wrong and that nothing will improve.

uninterrupted [ʌ̀nintərʌ́ptid] a. 중단되지 않은, 연속된
Not stopped or blocked by anything.

mute [mju:t] vt. …의 소리를 죽이다, …을 약하게 하다; a. 무언의, 말없는
To make the sound of something, especially a musical instrument, quieter or softer.

exhaustion [igzɔ́:stʃən] n. 극도의 피로, 기진맥진
Extreme tiredness.

perverse [pərvə́:rs] a. 괴팍한, 심술궂은, 별난; 외고집의 (perversely ad. 괴팍하게, 별나게)
Showing deliberate determination to behave in a way that most people think is wrong, unacceptable or unreasonable.

Vocabulary in New Moon

flawed [flɔ:d] a. 결함[결점·흠]이 있는
Something that is flawed has a mark, fault, or mistake in it.

postpone [poustpóun] vt. 연기하다, 미루다
To arrange for an event, etc. to take place at a later time or date.

Scheherazade [ʃəhérəzá:də] n. 셰헤라자드
「아라비안 나이트」에 등장하는 페르시아 왕의 아내. 천일(千一) 밤마다 왕에게 재미있는 얘기를 들려주고 죽음을 면했다고 함.

mangle [mǽŋgəl] vt. 난도질하다, 엉망으로 만들다
To destroy something by twisting or tearing it so that its original form is changed.

fragile [frǽdʒəl] a. 부서지기[깨지기] 쉬운
Easily damaged, broken or harmed.

shatter [ʃǽtər] v. 파괴하다; 충격을 주다; 산산조각이 나다; n. 파편, 부서진 조각
If something shatters or is shattered, it breaks into a lot of small pieces.

detector [ditéktər] n. 탐지기
A device used to find particular substances or things.

pillar [pílər] n. 기둥, 주석; (국가·사회 등의) 중심 세력[인물]
A pillar is a tall solid structure, which is usually used to support part of a building.

fiercely [fíərsli] ad. 맹렬히, 지독히
Extremely.

awkward [ɔ́:kwərd] a. 어색한, 불편한, 곤란한 (awkwardly ad. 어색하게, 거북하게)
An awkward situation is embarrassing and difficult to deal with.

repentant [ripéntənt] a. 후회하는, 뉘우치는, 후회를 나타내는
Feeling or showing that you are sorry for something wrong that you have done.

overpower [òuvərpáuər] vt. 압도하다, 억누르다, 제압하다
To defeat or gain control over somebody completely by using greater strength.

22. FLIGHT

disconnect [dìskənékt] vt. (전화 등을) 끊다; …와의 연락을 끊다; …의 전원을 끊다
To break the contact between two people who are talking on the telephone.

scold [skould] v. 꾸짖다, 잔소리하다
If you scold someone, you speak angrily to them because they have done something wrong.

dim [dim] a. 어둑한, 흐릿한, 희미한; v. 어둑하게 하다, 흐려지다
Dim light is not bright.

revive [riváiv] v. 되살리다, 소생하게 하다
To come or bring something back to life, health, existence, or use.

stiffen [stífən] v. 딱딱[뻣뻣]해지다, 경직되다
If you stiffen, your body suddenly becomes firm, straight still because you feel angry or anxious.

garbled [gá:rbəld] a. (메시지나 이야기가) 잘 알아들을 수 없는
A garbled statement or report is very unclear and confusing.

amend [əménd] vt. 고치다, 수정하다 (make amends : …에게[을] 보상[변충]하다)
To correct, improve or make minor changes.

plead [pli:d] v. 간청하다, 탄원하다; 변론하다; 변호하다
If you plead with someone to do something, you ask them in an intense, emotional way to do it.

glower [gláuər] vi. 상을 찡그리다, 불쾌한 얼굴을 하다; 노려보다; n. 노려봄; 찌푸린 얼굴
To look in an angry, aggressive way.

absurd [əbsə́:rd] a. 불합리한, 부조리한, 터무니없는 (absurdly ad. 터무니없이, 부조리하게)
If you say that something is absurd, you are criticizing it because you think that it is ridiculous or that it does not make sense.

eyelid [áilìd] n. (보통 pl.) 눈꺼풀(lid)
Either of the two pieces of skin which can close over each eye.

brusque [brʌsk] a. 무뚝뚝한, 퉁명스러운
Using very few words and sounding rude.

Vocabulary in New Moon

generous [dʒénərəs] a. 관대한, 아끼지 않는, 후한
A generous person is friendly, helpful, and willing to see the good qualities in someone or something.

wretched [rétʃid] a. 비참한, 불쌍한; 초라한; 야비한, 비열한
Unhappy, unpleasant or of low quality.

stilted [stíltid] a. 부자연스러운, 지나치게 격식적인
If someone speaks in a stilted way, they speak in a formal or unnatural way, for example because they are not relaxed.

★ **embarrassment** [imbǽrəsmənt] n. 당황, 곤혹, 난처
Embarrassment is the feeling you have when you are ashamed.

grasp [græsp] v. 붙잡다, 움켜쥐다; n. 움켜잡기
To quickly take something in your hand(s) and hold it firmly.

damn [dæm] a. 빌어먹을, 우라질; v. 저주[매도·욕설]하다
Damn is used to express anger with someone or something.

thrum [θrʌm] n. 튕기는 소리; (악기를) 손가락으로 뜯음; v. 똑똑 두드리다; (현악기를) 튕겨 소리 내다
A low beating sound.

stupor [stjúːpər] n. 인사불성; 무감각; 마비, 혼수
Someone who is in a stupor is almost unconscious and is unable to act or think normally, especially as a result of drink or drugs.

nerve [nəːrv] n. 용기, 정신력; (pl.) 신경질, 스트레스
The courage to do something difficult or dangerous.

★ **bellow** [bélou] vi. 큰 소리로 울다; 고함지르다
To shout in a loud voice, or (of a cow or large animal) to make a loud, deep sound.

yell [jel] v. 소리치다, 고함치다; n. 고함, 부르짖음
If you yell, you shout loudly, usually because you are excited, angry, or in pain.

22. FLIGHT

cling [kliŋ] vi. (clung-clung) 달라붙다, 매달리다
If you cling to someone or something, you hold onto them tightly.

tenacious [tinéiʃəs] a. 꼭 쥐고 놓지 않는, 들러붙어 떨어지지 않는; 끈기 있는
If you are tenacious, you are very determined and do not give up easily.

bleary [blíəri] a. (특히 피곤해서) 흐릿한[게슴츠레한]
Not able to see clearly, especially because you are tired.

kay [kei] ad. 좋아, 알았어 (okay의 의미)
Yes, alright.

trudge [trʌdʒ] v. 터벅터벅 걷다; n. 터덕터덕 걸음
To walk slowly with a lot of effort, especially over a difficult surface or while carrying something heavy.

swirl [swə:rl] vi. 소용돌이치다, 빙빙 돌다
If liquid or flowing swirls, it moves round and round quickly.

concrete [kánkri:t] n. 콘크리트; a. 유형의, 구체적인
Concrete is a substance used for building which is made by mixing together cement, sand, small stones, and water.

pry [prai] vt. 떼어놓다 (from); (돈·비밀 등을) 알아내다
If you pry something open or pry it away from a surface, you force it open or away from a surface.

Comprehension Quiz

23. THE TRUTH

1. Why was Bella confused when she woke up?

   A. It was dark outside.

   B. She couldn't see Edward.

   C. She thought she was dreaming.

   D. She thought she was still in Italy.

2. What did Edward do while he was away?

   A. He tried tracking Victoria.

   B. He looked for vampires who didn't kill humans.

   C. He refused to tell Bella what he did while he was away.

   D. He tried to start a new life in South America.

3. Edward said he went to the Volturi because _____ _____.

   A. he felt guilty

   B. he wanted to join them if he couldn't be with Bella

   C. he didn't want to live without Bella

   D. he thought Bella started a relationship with Jacob

23. THE TRUTH

4. What was Bella's second greatest problem?
   A. Victoria trying to kill her
   B. The Volturi looking for her
   C. Being grounded by Charlie
   D. Staying friends with Jacob

5. Why did Bella want to see the Cullens?
   A. She wanted them to vote on her relationship with Edward.
   B. She wanted to ask Alice what was in the future.
   C. She wanted to move in with them because Charlie was angry.
   D. She wanted them to vote on her mortality.

Vocabulary in New Moon

- **fiend** [fi:nd] n. 마귀, 악마(the Devil), 악령
  An evil and cruel person.

- **ghastly** [gǽstli] a. 무시무시한, 소름끼치는; ad. 무섭게
  If you describe someone or something as ghastly, you mean that you find them very unpleasant.

- **genteel** [dʒentíːl] a. 품위 있는, 우아한; (반어적) 거드름 피우는, 고상한 체하는
  Quiet and polite, often in an exaggerated way; From, or pretending to be from, a high social class.

- **civility** [sivíləti] n. 정중, 공손, 예의바름
  Polite behavior.

- **alert** [əláːrt] n. 경보, 경계; v. 경고하다; a. 방심하지 않는
  A warning to people to be prepared to deal with something dangerous.

- **inhale** [inhéil] v. 들이쉬다, 흡입하다
  To take air, smoke, gas, etc. into your lungs as you breathe.

- **substantial** [səbstǽnʃəl] a. 상당한, 많은; 실체의, 실재하는; 튼튼한; 실속 있는
  Large in amount, value or importance.

- **wrench** [rentʃ] vt. (갑자기·세게) 비틀다, 비틀어 돌리다; n. 렌치(너트를 죄는 기구)
  To make somebody feel great pain or unhappiness, especially so that they make a sound or cry.

- **dispel** [dispél] vt. 쫓아 버리다; (공포·불안)을 떨쳐 버리다
  To make something, especially a feeling or belief, go away or disappear.

- **illusion** [ilúːʒən] n. 환영, 환각, 착각
  A false or misleading impression, idea, belief or understanding.

- **hallucination** [həlùːsənéiʃən] n. 환각, 망상
  A hallucination is the experience of seeing something that is not really there because you are ill or have taken a drug.

- **delusion** [dilúːʒən] n. 현혹, 기만; 망상, 착각
  The act of believing or making yourself believe something that is not true.

23. THE TRUTH

scent [sent] n. 냄새, 향기; v. 냄새 맡다; 냄새를 풍기다
The scent of something is the pleasant smell that it has.

figment [fígmənt] n. 꾸며낸 것, 허구, 가공의 일
If you say that something is a figment of someone's imagination, you mean that it does not really exist and that they are just imagining it.

iris [áiris] n. [해부] (안구의) 홍채
The round colored part that surrounds the pupil of your eye.

hallucinatory [həlú:sənətɔ̀:ri] a. 환각의, 환각을 초래하는
Connected with or causing hallucinations.

preamble [prí:æmbəl] n. ('앞서 걸어가는'이라는 의미에서) 서문, 머리말, 서론
An introduction to a book or a written document; An introduction to something you say.

crap [kræp] n. 허튼소리, 헛소리
Nonsense.

croak [krouk] v. (낮고 거친 목소리로) 꺽꺽거리듯[목이 쉰 듯] 말하다
To speak or say something with a rough low voice.

gonna [góunə] etc. (미·구어) …할 예정인(going to)
Non-standard a way of saying or writing 'going to' in informal speech, when it refers to the future.

cheekbone [tʃí:kbòun] n. 광대뼈
The bone below the eye.

idiot [ídiət] n. 얼간이, 바보
A stupid person or someone who has done something stupid.

reassign [rì:əsáin] v. 다시 맡기다, 새로 발령 내다
To give somebody a duty, position, or responsibility again.

refer [rifə́:r] vi. 언급하다; 참조하다
To talk or write about someone or something, especially briefly.

Vocabulary in New Moon

massacre [mǽsəkər] vt. 학살하다, 짓밟다, (구어) 압승하다, 완패시키다
To kill of a large number of people especially in a cruel way.

muse [mju:z] vi. 곰곰이 생각하다; 묵상하다
To think about something carefully and for a long time.

Albuquerque n. 엘버커키, 미국 뉴멕시코 주(州)에 있는 도시

coherent [kouhíərənt] a. 시종일관한; 분명히 말할 수 있는
(of ideas, thoughts, arguments, etc.) Logical and well organized.

ban [bæn] vt. 금지하다; n. 금지, 금제, 금지령
To decide or say officially that something is not allowed.

fury [fjúəri] n. 격노, 격분; 격정, 열광, 광포, 격심함, 맹렬함
Extreme anger.

adulthood [ədʌ́lthùd] n. 성인[어른]임; 성년
Adulthood is the state of being an adult.

prohibition [pròuhəbíʃən] n. 금지, 금제
The act of stopping something being done or used, especially by law.

genuine [dʒénjuin] a. 진짜의, 진품의; 진심의 (genuinely ad. 진정으로)
Genuine refers to things such as emotions that are real and not pretended.

fabulous [fǽbjələs] a. 굉장한, 멋진, 믿어지지 않는
If you describe something as fabulous, you are emphasizing that you like it a lot or think that it is very good.

flawless [flɔ́:lis] a. (작품·사고·인격·용모 등이) 완전한, 완벽한; 흠 없는
Without flaws and therefore perfect.

vitally [váitəli] ad. 치명적으로, 사활에 관계될 만큼; 극히 중요하게
Extremely.

scornful [skɔ́:rnfəl] a. 경멸하는, 비웃는 (scornfully ad. 경멸적으로, 깔보면서)
If you are scornful of someone or something, you show contempt for them.

23. THE TRUTH

- **criticize** [krítisàiz] n. 비판[비난]하다
  If you criticize someone or something, you express your disapproval of them by saying what you think is wrong with them.

- **intrigue** [intríːg] v. 호기심을 돋우다; 음모를 꾸미다; n. 음모
  (intrigued a. 흥미 있는, 호기심을 가진)
  If something intrigues you, it interests you and you want to know more about it.

- **consequence** [kánsikwèns] n. 중요성, 중대함; 결과, 결말
  Importance.

- **agitate** [ǽdʒətèit] v. 흔들다, 선동하다, 교란하다 (agitated a. 흥분한; 동요한)
  If something agitates you, it worries you and makes you unable to think clearly or calmly.

- **overconfidence** [òuvərkánfədəns] n. 지나친 자신[자부], 과신
  An excessive degree of confidence.

- **bond** [band] n. (인간관계의) 유대, 연분, 연고, 결속
  Something that unites or joins people together.

- **immature** [ìmətjúər] a. 미숙한, 생경한; 미완성의
  Behaving in a way that is not sensible and is typical of people who are much younger.

- **core** [kɔːr] n. 핵심, (사물의) 중심부
  The most important or central part of something.

- **miserable** [mízərəbəl] a. 불쌍한, 비참한, 불행한, 딱한, 가엾은
  Unpleasant and causing unhappiness.

- **agonize** [ǽgənàiz] v. 번민하다, 괴롭히다, 괴로워하다
  If you agonize over something, you feel very anxious about it and spend a long time thinking about it.

- **obligation** [àbləgéiʃən] n. 의무, 책무; 은혜, 의리
  The state of being forced to do something because it is your duty, or because of a law.

Vocabulary in New Moon

anguish [ǽŋgwiʃ] n. (심신의) 비통, 고뇌, 번민; v. 괴로워하다[괴롭히다]
Anguish is great mental suffering or physical pain.

irresponsible [ìrispánsəbəl] a. 무책임한, 신뢰할 수 없는
(of a person) Not thinking enough about the effects of what they do.

incomprehension [inkàmprihénʃən] n. 몰이해, 이해력이 없음
The state of not being able to understand somebody/something.

funeral [fjúːnərəl] n. 장례식
A ceremony for burying or burning the body of a dead person.

stack [stæk] v. 쌓다, 쌓아올리다; n. 더미; 많음, 다량
To arrange things in an ordered pile.

dubious [djúːbiəs] a. 의심스러운, 수상쩍은, 모호한 (dubiously ad. 수상하게, 의심스럽게)
Feeling doubt or uncertainty.

negate [nigéit] vt. 부정[부인]하다; 취소하다, 무효로 하다
To stop something from having any effect.

misapprehension [mìsæprihénʃən] n. 오해
A wrong idea about something, or something you believe to be true that is not true.

ripple [rípəl] v. 잔물결이 일다; 잔물결을 일으키다
To move or to make something move in very small waves.

rigid [rídʒid] a. 굳은, 단단한; 엄격한, 완고한
Stiff or fixed; Not able to be bent, moved, changed or persuaded.

wince [wins] vi. (아픔·무서움 때문에) 주춤하다, 움츠리다; n. 위축
If you wince, you suddenly look as if you are suffering because you feel pain.

excruciating [ikskrúːʃièitiŋ] a. 고문을 당하는 듯한; 몹시 마음을 아프게 하는
Extremely painful or bad.

absurd [əbsə́ːrd] a. 불합리한, 부조리한, 터무니없는
If you say that something is absurd, you are criticizing it because you think that it is ridiculous or that it does not make sense.

23. THE TRUTH

- **incomprehensible** [ìnkɑmprihénsəbəl] a. 이해할 수 없는
  Something that is incomprehensible is impossible to understand.

- **rattle** [rǽtl] v. 달가닥 소리나다[움직이다]; n. 덜거덕거리는 소리
  When something rattles or when you rattle it, it makes short sharp knocking sounds because it is being shaken or it keeps hitting against something hard.

- **blasphemy** [blǽsfəmi] n. 신성 모독, 불경스러운[모독적인] 언동
  Behavior or language that insults or shows a lack of respect for God or religion.

- **ooze** [uːz] v. 스며 나오다, 새어나오다; n. 보드라운 진흙, 습지
  To flow slowly out of something through a small opening, or to slowly produce a thick sticky liquid.

- **revise** [riváiz] vt. 개정하다, 정정하다
  To look at or consider again an idea, piece of writing, etc. in order to correct or improve it.

- **idiotic** [ìdiátik] a. 백치의, 천치의
  Stupid.

- **crumble** [krʌ́mbl] v. 빻다, 부스러지다, 무너지다
  To break, or cause something to break, into small pieces.

- **jagged** [dʒǽgid] a. 들쭉날쭉한; 톱니 같은; (목소리 등이) 귀에 거슬리는
  Rough and uneven, with sharp points.

- **disjointed** [disdʒɔ́intid] a. 흐트러진, 낱낱으로 된; 연결이 안 되는, 일관성이 없는
  Not communicated or described in a clear or logical way.

- **greedy** [gríːdi] a. 탐욕스러운; 열망하는 (greedily ad. 욕심내어, 탐욕스럽게)
  Wanting a lot more food, money, etc. than you need.

- **skepticism** [sképtəsìzəm] n. 의심, 회의; [철학] 회의론[주의]; 회의적 태도
  The disbelief in any claims of ultimate knowledge.

- **constantly** [kɑ́nstəntli] ad. 변함없이; 끊임없이, 빈번하게
  All the time.

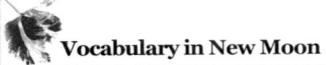

Vocabulary in New Moon

- ★ **merciless** [mə́:rsilis] a. 무자비한, 무정한, 잔인한
  If you describe someone as merciless, you mean that they are very cruel or determined and do not show any concern for the effect their actions have on other people.

- ★ **hypothesis** [haipάθəsis] n. 가설, 가정
  An idea or explanation of something that is based on a few known facts but that has not yet been proved to be true or correct.

- **clinical** [klínikəl] a. (판단·묘사 등이) 극도로 객관적인, 분석적인, 냉정한
  You use clinical to describe thought or behavior which is very logical and does not involve any emotion.

- **flinch** [flintʃ] v. (고통·공포로) 주춤하다, 위축되다
  To make a small sudden movement, especially when something surprises someone.

- **perspective** [pə:rspéktiv] n. 가망, 전망; 원근(화)법, 투시(화)법
  A particular perspective is a particular way of thinking about something, especially one that is influenced by your beliefs or experiences.

- **brooding** [brú:diŋ] a. 음울한, 생각에 잠긴, 시무룩한
  Sad and mysterious or threatening.

- **meteor** [mí:tiər] n. [천문] 유성(流星), 별똥별; 운석(隕石)
  A piece of rock or metal that burns very brightly when it enters the earth's atmosphere from space.

- ★ **brilliancy** [bríljənsi] n. 광휘, 찬란함
  A shining quality; Brilliance; An act of being brilliant.

- **mumble** [mʌ́mbəl] v. 중얼거리다, 웅얼거리다; n. 중얼거림
  If you mumble, you speak very quietly and not at all clearly with the result that the words are difficult to understand.

- **luxuriate** [lʌgʒúərièit] vi. 무성하다, 우거지다; (세포 등이) 증식하다; 현저하게 확대되다
  Thrive profusely or flourish extensively.

23. THE TRUTH

- **stutter** [stʌ́tər] v. 말을 더듬다, 더듬거리며 말하다; n. 말더듬기
  If someone stutters, they have difficulty speaking because they find it hard to say the first sound of a word.

- **outrage** [áutrèidʒ] v. (법률·도의 등을) 위반하다; 격분시키다; n. 격분, 격노
  If you are outraged by something, it makes you extremely shocked and angry.

- **taint** [teint] v. 더럽히다, 오염시키다; 더러워지다, 오염되다; 감염되다
  If something bad taints a situation or person, it makes the person or situation seem bad.

- **choke** [tʃouk] v. 숨 막히다[막히게 하다], 질식하다[시키다]
  To prevent or be prevented from breathing by an obstruction in the throat, fumes, emotion.

- **durable** [djúərəbəl] a. 영속성 있는, 항구적인; 오래 견디는, 튼튼한
  Likely to last for a long time without breaking or getting weaker.

- **compatible** [kəmpǽtəbəl] a. 양립하는, 조화되는, 모순되지 않는
  If things are compatible, they work well together or can exist together successfully.

- **expedition** [èkspədíʃən] n. 원정, (탐험 등의) 여행
  An organized journey for a particular purpose.

- **snarl** [snɑːrl] n. 으르렁거림; v. 으르렁거리다; 고함[호통]치다
  A deep sound that an animal makes when it is angry and shows its teeth.

- **pronounce** [prənáuns] v. 발음하다; 선언하다 (pronounced a. 확연한; 단호한)
  To make the sound of a word or letter in a particular way.

- **hasty** [héisti] a. 급한, 신속한
  Hurried; Without enough thought or preparation.

- **snort** [snɔːrt] v. (경멸·불찬성 등으로) 콧방귀 뀌다; 콧김을 뿜다
  To breathe air in a noisy way out through your nose to show that you are annoyed.

Vocabulary in New Moon

adolescent [ædəlésənt] a. 청춘[청년]기의, 청춘의, 한창 젊은
Adolesecent is used to describe young people who are no longer children but who have not yet become adults.

inconsequential [inkànsikwénʃəl] a. 하찮은, 이치에 맞지 않는
Not important or worth considering trivial.

suspicious [səspíʃəs] a. 의심하는, 의심 많은, 수상쩍은
If you are suspicious of someone or something, you do not trust them, and are careful when dealing with them.

subdue [səbdjúː] vt. 정복하다, 진압하다; 억제하다 (subdued a. 정복된, 억제된, 조용한)
To reduce the force of something, or to prevent something from existing or developing.

dew [djuː] v. 이슬로 적시다[젖다]; 축이다, 눅눅하게 하다; n. 이슬; (시어) 신선함, 상쾌함
To wet with or as with dew.

rim [rim] n. (둥근 물건의) 가장자리, 테두리, 테; v. 둘러싸다, 테를 두르다
The outer, often curved or circular, edge of something.

gravitational [græ̀vətéiʃənl] a. 중력의, 인력(작용)의
Gravitational means relating to or resulting from the force of gravity.

leak [liːk] v. 새어나오다, 새게 하다; n. 새는 구멍[곳]
If a liquid or gas leaks, it comes out of a hole by accident.

fixation [fikséiʃən] n. 고집, 집착
A very strong interest in somebody/something, that is not normal or natural.

revulsion [rivʌ́lʃən] n. 극도의 불쾌감, 혐오감
A strong feeling of disgust or horror.

onyx [ániks] n. [광물] (줄무늬가 있는 보석) 마노
Onyx is a stone which can be various colors. It is used for making ornaments, jewelry, or furniture.

asinine [ǽsənàin] a. 나귀(ass)의, 나귀 같은; 우둔한, 고집이 센, 완고한
Extremely stupid.

23. THE TRUTH

decisive [disáisiv] a. 결정적인, 의심할 여지가 없는, 단호한
Determining or having the power to determine an outcome.

grin [grin] v. 이를 드러내고 싱긋 웃다; n. 싱긋 웃음
When you grin, you smile broadly.

acid [ǽsid] n. 매서움, 신랄함; [화학] 산(酸) (acidic a. 신랄한, 언짢은)
(of a person's remarks) Critical and unkind.

brusque [brʌsk] a. 무뚝뚝한, 퉁명스러운
Using very few words and sounding rude.

fumble [fʌ́mbəl] vi. 손으로 더듬어 찾다; 우물우물 말하다
If you fumble for something or fumble with something, you try and reach for it or hold it in a clumsy way.

ground [graund] vt. (자녀에 대한 벌로) 나가 놀지[외출하지] 못하게 하다
When parents ground a child, they forbid them to go out and enjoy themselves for a period of time, as a punishment.

no dice idiom 안 돼, 싫어 (강하게 거절할 때); 소용없다, 헛수고다
Used to show that you refuse to do something or that something cannot be done.

encourage [enkə́:ridʒ] vt. 용기를 북돋우다, 장려하다
If you encourage someone, you give them confidence, hope, or support.

tease [ti:z] v. 놀리다, 희롱하다 (teasing a. 놀리는, 짓궂게 괴롭히는)
To laugh at or make fun of someone annoyingly.

extraordinary [ikstrɔ́:rdənèri] a. 보통이 아닌, 비범한, 대단한, 비상한
(extraordinarily ad. 엄청나게, 유별나게, 비상하게,)
Unexpected, surprising or strange.

opinionated [əpínjənétid] a. 자기 의견을 고집하는, 독선적인
Having very strong opinions that you are not willing to change.

mortality [mɔ:rtǽləti] n. 죽음을 면할 수 없음, 사망
State of being human and not living for ever.

Comprehension Quiz

 24. VOTE

1. What was Bella's greatest problem?

   A. The Volturi trying to kill her

   B. Charlie never forgiving her

   C. Victoria trying to kill her

   D. Edward

2. What is Demetri's talent?

   A. He can read people's minds from far away.

   B. He can move faster than any other vampire.

   C. He can track people over immense distances.

   D. He is stronger than any other vampire.

3. Why did Rosalie vote no?

   A. She wouldn't have chosen to be a vampire.

   B. She didn't want Bella as a sister.

   C. She didn't like Bella's relationship with Edward.

   D. She thought Bella would get the family killed.

24. VOTE

4. Carlisle promised he would change Bella into a vampire _____.

A. next Christmas

B. when the Volturi checked on her

C. when Edward agreed to her becoming a vampire

D. after her high school graduation

5. Edward agreed to change Bella if _____.

A. she finished college

B. she married him

C. she moved out of Charlie's house

D. charlie agreed to Bella becoming a vampire

Vocabulary in New Moon

lithe [laið] a. 유연한, 나긋나긋한; 잘 휘는 (lithely ad. 유연하게, 나긋나긋하게)
(of a person or their body) Moving or bending easily, in a way that is elegant.

seething [síːðiŋ] a. (화·흥분 등으로) 속이 끓어 오르는; 격렬한; 펄펄 끓는; 소용돌이치는
When you are seething, you are very angry about something but do not express your feelings about it.

disapproval [dìsəprúːvəl] n. 안 된다고 함, 불승인, 불찬성, 불만
A feeling of disliking something or what someone is doing.

routine [ruːtíːn] n. 판에 박힌 일; 틀에 박힌 연기
The normal order and way in which you regularly do things.

evident [évidənt] a. 분명한, 명백한, 뚜렷한 (evidently ad. 분명히, 명백히)
Easily seen or understood; Obvious.

damp [dæmp] a. 축축한
Slightly wet, especially in a way that is not pleasant or comfortable.

exhilarate [igzílərèit] vt. 원기를 돋우다, 기분을 들뜨게 하다, 유쾌하게 하다
(exhilarating a. 아주 신나는[즐거운])
To make somebody feel very happy and excited.

unbreakable [ʌ̀nbréikəbəl] a. 부술[깨뜨릴·꺾을] 수 없는
Impossible to break.

halfhearted [hǽfháːrtid] a. 마음이 내키지 않는 (halfheartedly ad. 어쩔 수 없이)
Showing a lack of enthusiasm and interest.

convince [kənvíns] vt. 확신시키다; 설득하다
To persuade someone or make them certain.

torment [tɔ́ːrment] vt. 괴롭히다, 곤란하게 하다; n. 고통
If you torment a person or animal, you annoy them in a playful, rather cruel way for your own amusement.

retain [ritéin] vt. 계속 유지하다, 보유하다, 간직하다
To keep something.

24. VOTE

- **misery** [mízəri] n. 불행, 비참함
Something that causes great suffering of mind or body.

- **floorboard** [flɔ́:rbɔ̀:rd] n. 바닥 널, 바닥; v. 전속력으로 운전하다
Floorboards are the long pieces of wood that a wooden floor is made up of.

- **subconscious** [sʌbkánʃəs] n., a. 잠재의식(의), 어렴풋이 의식(하는)
The mental processes that go on below the level of conscious awareness.

- **flatly** [flǽtli] ad. 단조롭게, 활기 없이
In a way that lacks emotion or interest.

- **pathetic** [pəθétik] a. 가치 없는, (이익이) 매우 적은; 불쌍한, 애처로운
Something or someone that is pathetic is so useless, unsuccessful, or weak that annoy you.

- **inflection** [inflékʃən] n. 소리[음조]의 변화, 억양
A change in how high or low your voice is as you are speaking.

- **brew** [bru:] v. (불쾌한 일이 일어날 움직임이) 태동하다; (커피·차를) 끓이다[만들다]
If an unpleasant or difficult situation is brewing, it is starting to develop.

- **conviction** [kənvíkʃən] n. 신념, 확신; [법] 유죄 판결
A strong belief or opinion.

- **epiphany** [ipífəni] n. 깨달음, 직관, 통찰
An intuitive grasp of reality through something usually simple and striking.

- **delusion** [dilú:ʒən] n. 현혹, 기만, 망상, 착각
The act of believing or making yourself believe something that is not true.

- **bond** [bɑnd] n. (인간관계의) 유대, 연분, 연고, 결속
Something that unites or joins people together.

- **forge** [fɔ:rdʒ] vt. 위조[모조]하다; (거짓말 등을) 꾸며 내다, 날조하다
To make an illegal copy of something in order to cheat people.

Vocabulary in New Moon

irreversible [irivə́:rsəbəl] a. 거꾸로 할[뒤집을] 수 없는; 철회[취소·변경]할 수 없는
(irreversibly ad. 돌이킬 수 없이, 뒤집을 수 없이)
If a change is irreversible, things cannot be changed back to the way they were before.

alter [ɔ́:ltər] v. 변하다, 바꾸다, 변경하다, 고치다
To change something, usually slightly, or to cause the characteristics of something to change.

strain [strein] v. 분투하다; 잡아당기다, 긴장시키다 (strained a. 긴장한)
To try hard to do something, usually to see or hear something.

marvel [má:rvəl] v. …에 놀라다, 경탄하다
To be very surprised or impressed by something.

inflated [infléitid] a. 부풀린, 과장된; 폭등한
Higher than is acceptable or reasonable.

hurdle [hə́:rdl] n. 장애물, 허들; 곤란
A problem or difficulty that must be solved or dealt with before you can achieve something.

dizzy [dízi] a. 현기증 나는, 아찔한
If you feel dizzy, you feel as if everything is spinning round and being unable to balance.

sheepish [ʃí:piʃ] a. 양 같은, 수줍어하는
Slightly uncomfortable or embarrassed because you know that you have done something silly.

at any rate idiom 하여튼, 좌우간에; 적어도
Used to show that you are being more accurate about something that you have just said.

immense [iméns] a. 막대한, 무한한, 광대한
Extremely large in size or degree.

shrug [ʃrʌg] v. (양 손바닥을 내보이면서 어깨를) 으쓱하다; n. 으쓱하기
If you shrug, you raise your shoulders to show that you are not interested in something or that you do not know or care about something.

24. VOTE

indifferent [indífərənt] a. 무관심한; 대수롭지 않은, 중요치 않은
(indifferently ad. 무심하게)
Having or showing no interest in somebody/something.

resign [rizáin] v. 사직하다; 단념하다, 따르다 (resigned a. 받아들이는, 체념한)
To make yourself accept something that you do not like because you cannot change it.

chandelier [ʃæ̀ndəliə́r] n. 샹들리에 (천장에 매달아 드리운 호화로운 장식등)
A chandelier is a large, decorative frame which holds light bulbs or candles and hangs from the ceiling.

polish [páliʃ] v. 닦다, 윤내다; n. 광택; 세련 (polished a. 윤[광]이 나는, 세련된)
If you polish something, you rub it with a cloth to make it shine.

oval [óuvəl] n. 타원체; a. 타원형의, 달걀 모양의
A shape like a circle, but wider in one direction than the other.

prop [prap] n. 소품; 지주, 버팀목; v. 받치다, 버티다; 기대 세우다
The props in a play or film are all the objects or pieces of furniture that are used in it.

tentative [téntətiv] a. 주저하는, 모호한; 시험적인, 임시의
(tentatively ad. 주저하며, 시험적으로)
Not definite or certain because you may want to change it later.

timid [tímid] a. 소심한, 자신이 없는
If you describe someone's attitudes or actions as timid, you are criticizing them for being too cautious or slow to act.

swallow [swálou] vt. 마른침을 삼키다, 들이켜다, 삼키다, 꿀꺽 삼키다
If you swallow, you make a movement in your throat as if you are swallowing something, often because you are nervous or frightened.

peek [pi:k] vi. 살짝 들여다보다, 엿보다; n. 엿봄
If you peek at something or someone, you have a quick look at them.

fierce [fiərs] a. 사나운; 격렬한, 지독한
Physically violent and frightening.

Vocabulary in New Moon

meaningful [míːniŋfəl] a. 의미심장한, 뜻있는
If you describe something as meaningful, you mean that it is useful, serious or important.

crease [kriːs] v. 구기다; 주름이 생기다; 주름투성이로 만들다; n. 주름, 구김살
To make a crease or creases in (paper, fabric, etc.); To develop creases.

growl [graul] n. 으르렁거리는 소리; v. 으르렁거리다, 고함치다
A deep angry sound made when somebody/something growls.

refer [rifə́ːr] vi. 언급하다; 참조하다
To talk or write about someone or something, especially briefly.

animate [ǽnəmèit] vt. 살리다, 활기를 주다; a. 살아 있는, 활기 있는
To make someone seem more happy or active.

clue somebody in phrasal v. …에게 정보를 주다, 가르치다, 설명하다
To give someone information that is necessary or new.

prod [prɑd] vt. 재촉하다, 자극하다; 찌르다, 쑤시다
If you prod someone into doing something, you remind or persuade them to do it.

skeptical [sképtikəl] a. 의심 많은, 회의적인
Having doubts that a claim or statement is true or that something will happen.

overconfident [òuvərkɑ́nfədənt] a. 자신 과잉의, 자만심이 센
Too confident.

haystack [héistæk] n. 건초더미
A large pile of hay, used as a way of storing it until it is needed.

smirk [sməːrk] n. 능글맞은 웃음; vi. 능글맞게 웃다
Smile affectedly or derisively.

★ **appreciative** [əpríːʃətiv] a. 감사의, 감사하는; 감탄하는, 감상을 즐기는
Feeling or showing that you are grateful for something.

24. VOTE

idiot [ídiət] n. 얼간이, 바보
A stupid person or someone who has done something stupid.

alternative [ɔ:ltə́:rnətiv] n. 대안, 선택 가능한 것; a. 하나를 택해야 할, 양자택일의
If one thing is an alternative to another, the first can be found, used, or done instead of the second.

flint [flint] n. 부싯돌(쇠에 대고 치면 불꽃이 생기는 아주 단단한 회색 돌)
Flint is a very hard greyish-black stone that was used in former times for making tools.

grave [greiv] a. 중대한, 근엄한, 엄숙한; n. 무덤, 묘; 묘석
Giving cause for great concern; Very dangerous.

aversion [əvə́:rʒən] n. 혐오, 싫음, 반감
A strong feeling of not liking somebody/something.

earsplitting [íərsplìtiŋ] a. (소리·음성 따위가) 귀청이 떨어질 듯한
Extremely loud.

dearest [dírist] a. 친애하는; n. 여보[당신·그대]
Used when writing to somebody you love.

cringe [krindʒ] vi. (겁이 나서) 움츠리다[움찔하다]
If you cringe at something, you feel embarrassed or disgusted, and making a slight movement.

interject [ìntərdʒékt] vt. (말 따위를) 불쑥 끼워 넣다, 던져 넣다, 사이에 끼우다
To interrupt what somebody is saying with your opinion or a remark.

distort [distɔ́:rt] vt. 비틀다, 뒤틀다; 왜곡[곡해]하다; (얼굴 등을) 찡그리다, 찌푸리다
If something you can see or hear is distorted or distorts, its appearance or sound is changed so that it seems unclear.

proximity [prɑksíməti] n. 근접, 가까움
The state of being near in space or time.

inconspicuous [ìnkənspíkju:əs] a. 눈에 띄지 않는, 주의를 끌지 않는
Not attracting attention.

Vocabulary in New Moon

- **grit** [grit] v. 삐걱거리다, 쓸리다; n. 잔모래 (grit the teeth : 이를 갈다)
  If you grit your teeth, you press your top and bottom teeth together, often in anger.

- **graduation** [græ̀dʒuéiʃən] n. 졸업, 학위 취득
  The successful completion of a course of study at a university, college, or school.

- **unclench** [ʌ̀nkléntʃ] v. 펴다; 억지로 비틀어 열다
  To open (something) that was clenched; To relax, especially one's muscles.

- **triumphant** [traiʌ́mfənt] a. 승리를 한, 의기양양한
  Having achieved a great victory or success.

- **calculate** [kǽlkjəlèit] vt. 계산하다, 추정하다
  To use numbers to find out a total number, amount, distance, etc.

- **ugh** [ux] int. 우!, 악!, 왜!, 캑! (혐오·경멸·공포 또는 기침 소리를 나타냄)
  The way of writing the sound that people make when they think that something is disgusting or unpleasant.

- **flip** [flip] v. 홱 뒤집(히)다, 휙 젖히다; (책장 등을) 넘기다; (너무 흥분하여) 확 돌아 버리다
  To turn over into a different position with a sudden quick movement; To make something do this.

- **skepticism** [sképtəsìzəm] n. 의심, 회의; [철학] 회의론[주의]; 회의적 태도
  The disbelief in any claims of ultimate knowledge.

- **thoughtful** [θɔ́:tfəl] a. 생각이 깊은, 생각에 잠긴
  Thinking deeply, or appearing to think deeply; Reflective.

- **gawk** [gɔ:k] vi. 멍청히 바라보다; n. 둔한 사람, 얼간이
  To gawk at someone or something means to stare at them in a rude, stupid, or unthinking way.

- **blurt** [blə:rt] vt. 불쑥 말하다, 무심결에 말하다; n. 엉겁결에 말함
  To say something suddenly and without thinking carefully.

24. VOTE

purse [pə:rs] v. (불만 등의 표시로 입술을) 오므리다
If you purse your lips, you move them into a small, rounded shape, usually because you disapprove of something or when you are thinking.

chagrin [ʃəgrín] n. 원통함, 억울함, 분함
A feeling of being disappointed or annoyed.

leverage [lévəridʒ] n. 영향력, 수단, 효력; 권력, 세력
Influence that you can use to make people do what you want.

hysteria [histíəriə] n. [병리] 히스테리; (개인이나 집단의) 병적 흥분, 광란
Extreme fear, excitement, anger, etc. which cannot be controlled.

priority [praió(:)rəti] n. 우선, 보다 중요함, 우위, 상위
Something that you think is more important than other things and should be dealt with first.

commitment [kəmítmənt] n. 위탁, 위임; 범행, (범죄의) 실행, 수행; 공약, 약속
Commitment is a strong belief in an idea or system.

hedge [hedʒ] v. 변명의 여지를 남겨두다, 얼버무리다; 울타리를 두르다; n. 울타리; 대비책
If you hedge against something unpleasant or unwanted that might affect you, especially losing money, you do something which will protect you from it.

marital [mǽrətl] a. 결혼의; 결혼 생활의; 부부의
Relating to marriage.

barter [bá:rtər] v. 물물교환하다, 교역하다; n. 물물 교환
To exchange goods, property, services, etc. for other goods, etc. without using money.

eternity [itə́:rnəti] n. 영원, 무궁; 불사, 불멸; 영원성
Eternity is time without an end or a state of existence outside time, especially the state which some people believe they will pass into after they have died.

bluff [blʌf] n. 허세, 엄포, 속임수; v. 허세부리다
An attempt to trick somebody by making them believe that you will do something when you really have no intention of doing it.

Vocabulary in New Moon

angelic [ændʒélik] a. 천사의, 천사 같은; 청아한, 고결한
Angelic means like angels or relating to angels.

chuckle [tʃʌkl] vi. 낄낄 웃다; n. 낄낄 웃음
When you chuckle, you laugh quietly.

smolder [smóuldər] v. (감정이) 사무치다; 울적하다; 그을(리)다, 연기피우다; n. 연기 (남)
To be filled with a strong emotion that you do not fully express.

concentration [kànsəntréiʃən] n. 집결, 집중(력)
The ability to think about something carefully or for a long time.

resignation [rèzignéiʃən] n. 포기, 단념, 체념
The acceptance of an unpleasant situation because you realize that you cannot change it.

★ **gauge** [geidʒ] vt. (사람·행동 등)을 평가[판단]하다
To make a judgement about something, especially people's feelings or attitudes.

★ **seethe** [si:ð] vi. (화가 나서) 속이 부글거리다; 끓어오르다
To feel very angry but to be unable or unwilling to express it clearly.

injure [índʒər] vt. 상처를 입히다, 해치다 (injured a. 상처를 받은, 기분이 상한)
To hurt a person, animal, or part of your body.

ploy [plɔi] n. (구어) (상대를 기만·제압하기 위한) 책략, 계략
A way of behaving that someone plans carefully and secretly in order to gain an advantage for themselves.

crack [kræk] v. 날카로운 소리를 내다; 갈라지다, 금이 가다; 깨지다
To make a sudden, short noise, or to cause something to make this noise.

run off phrasal v. (사람·동물이) 달아나다, 도망치다, (급히) 가다
To leave place or person in a way that people disapprove of.

suck [sʌk] v. 빨다, 흡수하다; (속어) 엉망이다, 형편없다; n. 빨아들임
If you suck something, you hold it in your mouth and pull at it with the muscles in your cheeks and tongue, for example in order to get liquid out of it.

24. VOTE

ship off phrasal v. 쫓아버리다
To send somebody away somewhere, especially when they do not want to go.

quilt [kwilt] n. (솜·털·깃털 따위를 둔) 누비이불; 누비 침대 커버
A thin cover filled with feathers or some other warm, soft material, which you put over your blankets when you are in bed.

chore [tʃɔːr] n. 지루한 일; 잡일, 허드렛일
A task that you do regularly.

laundry [lɔ́ːndri] n. 세탁물, 세탁소
The dirty clothes and sheets which need to be, are being washed.

emergency [imə́ːrdʒənsi] n. 비상사태, 비상시, 위급, 급변
An unexpected and serious happening which calls for immediate and determined action.

expectation [èkspektéiʃən] n. 예상, 기대
A belief that something will happen because it is likely.

distrustful [distrʌ́stfəl] a. 의심 많은, (쉽게) 믿지 않는
If you are distrustful of someone or something, you think that they are not honest, reliable, or safe.

frantic [frǽntik] a. 광란의, 미친 듯 날뛰는
(frantically ad. 미친 듯이, 광포하게, 광란하여)
Behaving in a wild and uncontrolled way.

inability [ìnəbíləti] n. 무능, 무력; …할 수 없음
Something the fact of not being able to do something.

convincing [kənvínsiŋ] a. 설득력 있는, 납득이 가는 (convincingly ad. 설득력 있게)
Making you believe that something is true or right.

undermine [ʌ̀ndərmáin] vt. 약화시키다; 몰래 손상시키다, 모르는 사이에 해치다
If you undermine something such as a feeling or a system, you make it less strong or less secure than it was before, often by a gradual process or by repeated efforts.

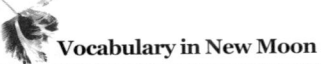

Vocabulary in New Moon

be toast idiom 죽기[끝장나기] 십상이다
Be in very serious trouble.

accidental [æ̀ksidéntl] a. 우연한; 부수적인 (accidentally ad. 우연히)
An accidental event happens by chance or as the result of an accident, and is not deliberately intended.

distract [distrǽkt] vt. (마음·주의를) 흐트러뜨리다, 딴 데로 돌리다
(distracted a. (주의가) 빗나간, 마음이 산란한)
Nervous, anxious or confused because you are worried about something.

dangle [dǽŋɡəl] v. 매달(리)다, 흔들흔들하다; n. 매달린 것
To hang loosely, or to hold something so that it hangs loosely.

rotten [rátn] a. 형편없는, 끔찍한; 썩은, 부패한
If you describe someone as rotten, you are insulting them or criticizing them because you think that they are very unpleasant or unkind.

bulge [bʌldʒ] v. 부풀다, 불룩하(게 하)다; n. 불룩한 것(부분)
To be completely full (of something).

puce [pjuːs] n., a. 암갈색(의)
Reddish-purple in color.

resolve [rizálv] n. 결심[의지]; vt. 해결하다; 결심하다; 의결하다
Resolve is determination to do what you have decided to do.

waver [wéivər] v. 흔들리다, 펄럭이다; 동요하다, 머뭇거리다
To lose strength, determination or purpose, especially temporarily.

conviction [kənvíkʃən] n. 신념, 확신; [법] 유죄 판결
A strong belief or opinion.

ultimatum [ʌ̀ltiméitəm] n. 최후의 말[제언·조건], (특히) 최후통첩; 종국의 결론
A final warning to a person or country that if they do not do what you ask, you will use force or take action against them.

slam [slæm] v. (문 따위를) 탕 닫다, 세게 치다; 털썩 내려놓다; n. 쾅 (하는 소리)
If you slam a door or window or if it slams, it shuts noisily and with great force.

24. VOTE

damnation [dæmnéiʃən] n. 지옥에 떨어뜨림[떨어짐], 천벌; 파멸
The state of being in hell; The act of sending somebody to hell.

speechless [spíːtʃlis] a. 말을 못하는, 말문이 막힌
If you are speechless, you are temporarily unable to speak, usually because something has shocked you.

vow [vau] v. 맹세하다, 서약하다; 단언하다; n. 맹세, 서약
To make a formal and serious promise to do something or a formal statement that is true.

Comprehension Quiz

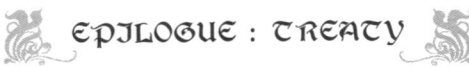

EPILOGUE : TREATY

1. What excuse did Carlisle give for returning to Forks?

   A. Alice and Jasper didn't like school in LA.

   B. Carlisle didn't like his job.

   C. Carlisle missed his home in Forks.

   D. Esme didn't like LA.

2. Why didn't Bella visit Jacob?

   A. She was grounded by Charlie.

   B. Edward wouldn't let her go to La Push.

   C. She didn't want to see him.

   D. The Quileute tribe did not want her on their land.

3. What did Edward say to Jacob?

   A. He said he didn't care about the treaty.

   B. He said Bella wasn't allowed to visit Jacob.

   C. He said Thank you.

   D. He said Jacob wasn't welcome in forks.

EPILOGUE : TREATY

4. What sent Jacob into near convulsions?
- A. Bella was still in love with Edward.
- B. Edward didn't let Bella near Jacob.
- C. Edward said that Jacob was a young and dangerous werewolf.
- D. Bella intended to become a vampire.

5. What was NOT a problem Bella now faced?
- A. Victoria might kill her or someone she loved.
- B. If she didn't become a vampire, the Volturi would kill her.
- C. The werewolves wanted to harm Bella because she hurt Jacob.
- D. Jacob counted Bella with his enemies.

Vocabulary in New Moon

eager [í:gər] a. 열망하는, 간절히 하고 싶어 하는
If you are eager to do or have something, you want to do or have it very much.

conceal [kənsí:l] vt. 숨기다, 감추다; 비밀로 하다, 내색하지 않다
If you conceal something, you cover it or hide it carefully.

calculus [kǽlkjələs] n. 미적분학
Calculus is a branch of advanced mathematics which deals with variable quantities.

sway [swei] v. 흔들(리)다, 동요하다; 설득하다; n. 동요, 지배
If you are swayed by someone or something, you are influenced by them.

procrastination [proukrǽstənéiʃən] n. 미루는 버릇, 꾸물거림; 지연, 연기
The act of procrastinating; Putting off or delaying or deferring an action to a later time.

designate [dézignèit] vt. 지정[지적]하다; 나타내다, 표기하다; 지명하다
If something is designated for a particular purpose, it is set aside for that purpose.

dreary [dríəri] a. 쓸쓸한, 황량한, 음산한, 울적한
Boring and making you feel unhappy.

resume [rizú:m] v. 다시 시작하다, 되찾다
If an activity resumes, or if you resume it, it starts again after a pause.

promptly [prάmptli] ad. 신속히, 재빠르게, 즉석에서, 즉시
Without delay.

gleeful [glí:fəl] a. 매우 기뻐하는, 대단히 기분이 좋은
Someone who is gleeful is happy and excited, often because of someone else's bad luck.

sneak [sni:k] v. (sneaked–sneaked 또는 snuck–snuck) 살금살금 들어오다, 몰래 움직이다; 슬쩍하다; n. 살금살금 몰래 함
To go somewhere secretly, trying to avoid being seen.

EPILOGUE : TREATY

- ★ **fruitless** [frúːtlis] a. 헛된, 보람 없는
  fruit (v. 열매 맺다) +-less (suf. …이 없는)

- 복습 **disapprove** [dìsəprúːv] v. 찬성하지 않다, 안 된다고 하다
  (disapproving a. 못마땅해 하는)
  To feel that something or someone is bad, wrong etc.

- ★ **reciprocal** [risíprəkəl] a. 상호간의(mutual), 호혜적인
  Involving two people or groups who agree to help each other or behave in the same way to each other.

- **prejudice** [prédʒədis] n. 편견; 손해, 침해; vt. 편견을 갖게 하다; 해치다, 손해를 주다
  Prejudice is an unreasonable dislike of a particular group of people or things, or a preference for a one group of people or things over another.

- 복습 **bloodsucker** [blʌ́dsʌ̀kər] n. 흡혈 동물, 흡혈귀; 고리대금업자
  A bloodsucker is any creature that sucks blood from a wound that it has made in an animal or person.

- 복습 **leftover** [léftòuvər] a. 나머지의, 남은; n. 나머지; 남은 음식
  You use leftover to describe an amount of something that remains after the rest of it has been used or eaten.

- **unresolved** [ʌ̀nrizálvd] a. 결심이 서지 않은, 결단을 못 내린; 미해결[미정]의; (소리가) 불협화음인 채로의
  Not yet solved or answered; Not having been resolved.

- 복습 **faucet** [fɔ́ːsit] n. (수도)꼭지, 물 주둥이
  A device that controls the flow of liquid, especially water, from a pipe.

- 복습 **frustration** [frʌstréiʃən] n. 좌절, 실패, 낙담; 장애물
  The feeling of being annoyed, or impatient, because you cannot achieve something.

- 복습 **rude** [ruːd] a. 무례한, 버릇없는
  Having or showing a lack of respect for other people and their feelings.

- 복습 **vent** [vent] vt. (감정 등을) 터뜨리다; (감정 등에) 배출구를 주다; n. 통풍구, 배출구; 구멍
  To express feelings, especially anger, strongly.

Vocabulary in New Moon

복습 downright [dáunràit] ad. 철저하게, 완전히; a. 곧은, 철저한
Completely; Extremely.

복습 insult [ínsʌlt] vt. 모욕하다, …에게 무례한 짓을 하다; n. 모욕
If someone insults you, they say or do something that is rude or offensive.

복습 ooze [u:z] v. 스며 나오다, 새어나오다; n. 보드라운 진흙, 습지
To flow slowly out of something through a small opening, or to slowly produce a thick sticky liquid.

복습 stubborn [stʌ́bərn] a. 완고한, 고집 센
Determined not to change your opinion or attitude.

복습 ascertain [æ̀sərtéin] vt. 알아내다, 확인하다
If you ascertain the truth about something, you find out what it is, especially by making a deliberate effort to do so.

★ enmity [énməti] n. 적의; 증오, 앙심; 적대 감정
The state or quality of being an enemy.

복습 windshield [wíndʃi:ld] n. (자동차 등의) 앞 유리
The windshield of a car or other vehicle is the glass window at the front through which the driver looks.

복습 dispel [dispél] vt. 쫓아 버리다; (공포·불안)을 떨쳐 버리다
To make something, especially a feeling or belief, go away or disappear.

besot [bisát] vt. 술 취하게 하다; 멍하게 만들다, 이성을 잃게 하다
Make dull or stupid or muddle with drunkenness or infatuation.

복습 statue [stǽtʃu:] n. 상(像), 조각상
A statue is a large sculpture of a person or an animal, made of stone or metal.

복습 screech [skri:tʃ] vi. 날카로운[새된] 소리를 내다
To make a unpleasant loud high noise.

복습 cruiser [krú:zər] n. 크라이슬러 PT 크루저(Chrysler PT Cruiser), 스테이션 웨건 콤팩트 카

EPILOGUE : TREATY

- **flaunt** [flɔːnt] vt. 과시하다
  To show something you are proud of to other people, in order to impress them.

- **treachery** [trétʃəri] n. 배반, 위약(違約), 변절, 기만
  Behavior that involves not being loyal to somebody who trusts you; An example of this.

- **sting** [stiŋ] n. 고통; (동물의) 침; 찌르기; 쏘기; vt. 찌르다, 쏘다
  Any sharp pain in your body or mind.

- **betrayal** [bitréiəl] n. 배반, 배신
  The act of betraying somebody/something or the fact of being betrayed.

- **implicit** [implísit] a. 맹목적인, 무조건적인; 함축적인
  (implicitly ad. 맹목적으로, 절대적으로)
  If you say that someone has an implicit belief or faith in something, you mean that they have complete faith in it and no doubts at all.

- **harbor** [háːrbər] n. 피난처; 항구, 항만; v. (계획·생각 등을) 품다; 숨겨주다; 잠복하다
  An area of water on the coast, protected from the open sea by strong walls, where ships can shelter.

- **rely on** phrasal v. …에 의지[의존]하다, …을 필요로 하다
  To trust or depend on someone or something to do what you need or expect them to do.

- **underlying** [ʌ̀ndərláiiŋ] a. (겉으로 잘 드러나지는 않지만) 근본적인[근원적인]
  The underlying features of an object, event, or situation are not obvious, and it may be difficult to discover or reveal them.

- **petty** [péti] a. 사소한, 작은, 마음이 좁은
  Small and unimportant.

- **betray** [bitréi] vt. 배반하다; (남편·아내·여자 등을) 속이다
  To hurt somebody who trusts you, especially by not being loyal or faithful to them.

- **slender** [sléndər] a. 호리호리한, 가느다란; 빈약한
  Thin and delicate.

Vocabulary in New Moon

traitor [tréitər] n. 반역자, 역적, 배신자
Someone have betrayed beliefs that they used to hold by their words or action.

epithet [épəθèt] n. (어떤 사람·집단에 대한) 욕설
An offensive word or phrase that is used about a person or group of people.

instinctive [instíŋktiv] a. 본능적인, 직관적인; 무의식적인
(instinctively ad. 본능적으로)
Instinctive behavior or reactions are not thought about, planned or developed by training.

glossy [glɔ́(:)si] a. 광택[윤]이 나는, 윤기 있는, 반질반질한
Smooth and shiny.

futile [fjú:tl] a. 쓸데없는, 무익한 (futilely ad. 무익하게; 시시하게)
Having no purpose because there is no chance of success.

limp [limp] a. 축 처진[늘어진], 기운이[활기가] 없는
Soft and neither firm nor stiff.

spokesperson [spóukspə:rsn] n. 대변인, 대표자
A person who speaks on behalf of a group or an organization.

lounge [laundʒ] v. 느긋하게 서[앉아·누워] 있다
If you lounge somewhere, you sit or lie there in a relaxed or lazy way.

mossy [mɔ́(:)si] a. 이끼 낀, 이끼 같은
Covered with moss.

trunk [trʌŋk] n. (나무의) 줄기, 몸뚱이; 여행 가방
The trunk of a tree is the large main stem from which the branches grow.

humorless [hjú:mərlis] a. 유머가 없는, 멋없는
Lacking humor or levity; Serious; Not funny, amusing, amused, or lighthearted.

sneer [sniər] n. 비웃음, 냉소; v. 비웃다, 냉소하다
An unpleasant look, smile or comment that shows you do not respect somebody/something.

EPILOGUE : TREATY

tremble [trémbəl] v. 떨다, 떨리다
To shake slightly, usually because you are cold or frightened.

clench [klentʃ] vt. (이를) 악물다, (손을) 꽉 쥐다
To close one's teeth or one's fists tightly, especially in anger.

resentful [rizéntfəl] a. 분개한, 화난
Feeling angry and upset about something that you think is unfair.

cynical [sínikəl] a. 빈정대는, 냉소적인, 비꼬는
Believing that people only do things to help themselves rather than for good or honest reasons.

falter [fɔ́:ltər] vi. 비틀거리다, 말을 더듬다; 머뭇거리다, 움찔[멈칫]하다
To become weaker or less effective.

reunion [ri:jú:niən] n. 재결합, 재회; 화해, 융화
The act of reuniting or state of being reunited.

rigid [rídʒid] a. 굳은, 단단한; 엄격한, 완고한
Stiff or fixed; Not able to be bent, moved, changed or persuaded.

ground [graund] vt. (자녀에 대한 벌로) 나가 놀지[외출하지] 못하게 하다
When parents ground a child, they forbid them to go out and enjoy themselves for a period of time, as a punishment.

glower [gláuər] vi. 상을 찡그리다, 불쾌한 얼굴을 하다; 노려보다; n. 노려봄; 찌푸린 얼굴
To look in an angry, aggressive way.

groan [groun] n. 신음[끙끙거리는] 소리; v. 신음하다, 끙끙거리다
If you groan, you make a long, low sound because you are in pain, or because you are upset or unhappy about something.

butt [bʌt] n. 엉덩이; 굵은 쪽 끝, 밑동
Someone's butt is their bottom.

grit [grit] v. 삐걱거리다, 쓸리다 (**grit the teeth** : 이를 갈다); n. 잔모래
If you grit your teeth, you press your top and bottom teeth together, often in anger.

Vocabulary in New Moon

- **exaggerate** [iɡzǽdʒərèit] vt. 과장하다
  To make something seem larger, better, worse or more important than it really is.

- **shiver** [ʃívər] n. 떨림, 전율; v. (추위·공포로) 후들후들 떨다; 전율하다
  A sudden shaking movement of your body because you are cold, frightened, excited, etc.

- **sincerity** [sinsérəti] n. 성실, 성의
  Honesty.

- **mystify** [místəfài] vt. 혼란스럽게[얼떨떨하게] 만들다 (mystification n. 어리둥절하게 함)
  If you are mystified by something, you find it impossible to explain or understand.

- **fervent** [fə́:rvənt] a. 열렬한; 강렬한; (감정 따위가) 격한; 뜨거운
  Having or showing very strong and sincere feelings about something.

- **gratitude** [ɡrǽtətjùːd] n. 감사, 고마움
  Gratitude is the state of feeling grateful.

- **immerse** [imə́:rs] v. 담그다, 가라앉히다, 적시다; …에 몰두해[게 만들]다
  To put something or someone completely under the surface of a liquid.

- **momentarily** [mòumənté́rəli] ad. 잠시, 잠깐
  Momentarily means for a short time.

- **gag** [ɡaɡ] v. 토할 것 같다; 재갈을 물리다, 말문을 막다; n. 재갈; 보도 금지령; 장난
  To be unable to swallow and feel as if you are about to bring up food from your stomach.

- **treaty** [trí:ti] n. 조약, 협정
  A formal agreement between two or more countries.

- **truce** [truːs] n. 휴전(협정), 정전; v. 휴전하다
  An agreement to stop fighting, usually temporarily.

- **hasty** [héisti] a. 급한, 신속한
  Hurried; Without enough thought or preparation.

EPILOGUE : TREATY

precaution [prikɔ́:ʃən] n. 조심, 경계; 예방책
Something that is done in advance in order to prevent problems or to avoid danger.

temple [témpəl] n. 관자놀이; 신전, 사원
Your temples are the flat parts on each side of the front part of your head, near your forehead.

spasm [spǽzəm] n. 경련, 발작
A sudden and often painful contracting of a muscle, which you cannot control.

sallow [sǽlou] a. (안색이 병적으로) 누르께한, 흙빛의, 혈색이 나쁜
(of a person's skin or face) Having a slightly yellow color that does not look healthy.

russet [rʌ́sət] a. 적[황]갈색의, 팥 빛의
Russet is used to describe things that are reddish-brown in color.

inflection [inflékʃən] n. 소리[음조]의 변화, 억양
A change in how high or low your voice is as you are speaking.

accusation [ækjuzéiʃən] n. 비난, 규탄, 죄, 죄명
The act of accusing someone of having done something wrong.

reflexive [rifléksiv] a. 반응하는, 되돌아오는; 반사성의 (**reflexively** ad. 반사적으로)
Referring back to itself.

tremor [trémər] n. 전율, 떨림; 겁; 떨리는 목소리; 진동
A slight shaking movement in a person's body, especially because of nervousness or excitement.

sarcasm [sáːrkæzəm] n. 빈정거림, 비꼼, 풍자
The use of remarks which clearly mean the opposite of what they say, and which are made in order to hurt someone's feelings or to criticize something in an amusing way.

barrel [bǽrəl] v. (통제가 안 되게) 쏜살같이 달리다[질주하다]
If a vehicle or person is barreling in a particular direction, they are moving very quickly in that direction.

Vocabulary in New Moon

fern [fəːrn] n. [식물] 양치류(의 식물)
A plant with large delicate leaves and no flowers that grows in wet areas or is grown in a pot.

enrage [enréidʒ] vt. 노하게 하다
To cause someone to become very angry.

scenario [sinɛəriòu] n. [연극] 대본; [영화] 시나리오, 영화 각본
A description of how things might happen in the future.

ambush [ǽmbuʃ] v. 매복하다; 매복하여 습격하다; (복병을) 숨겨 두다
To make a surprise attack on somebody/something from a hidden position.

spine [spain] n. 등뼈, 척추
Your spine is the row of bones down your back.

bail [beil] vi. (급히) 떠나다; 보석으로 풀어주다
To escape from a situation that you do not want to be in any more.

turf [təːrf] n. 세력권, 영역; (형사 등의) 담당 구역
The place where somebody lives and/or works, especially when they think of it as their own.

protest [prətést] v. 항의하다, 이의를 제기하다; 주장하다; n. 항의
If you protest against something or about something, you say or show publicly that you object to it.

declaration [dèkləréiʃən] n. 선언, 발표, 포고
An official or formal statement, especially about the plans of a government or an organization; The act of making such a statement.

outstretch [àutstrétʃ] vt. 펴다, 뻗다; 확장하다
To extend by stretching.

restrain [riːstréin] vt. 억제하다, 구속하다
To stop someone doing something by using force.

EPILOGUE : TREATY

- **unreadable** [ʌnríːdəbəl] a. 판독하기 어려운
  If somebody's face or expression is unreadable, you cannot tell what they are thinking or feeling.

- **anticipation** [æntìsəpéiʃən] n. 예상, 기대, 희망
  A feeling of excitement about something that is going to happen.

- **retreat** [riːtríːt] vi. 물러가다, 퇴각하다
  To move away from someone or something.

- **scowl** [skaul] n. 찌푸린 얼굴; vi. 얼굴을 찌푸리다, 싫은 기색을 하다
  An angry look or expression.

- **haunt** [hɔːnt] v. 늘 따라다니다; 자주 가다; (유령이) 출몰하다; n. 자주 가는[나타나는] 곳, 서식지
  If something unpleasant haunts you, it keeps coming to your mind so that you cannot forget it.

- **insignificant** [ìnsignífikənt] a. 무의미한, 하찮은, 사소한
  Not big or valuable enough to be considered important.

- **squeeze** [skwiːz] vt. 꽉 쥐다[죄다], 압착하다; n. 압착, 짜냄
  If you squeeze something, you press it firmly, usually with your hands.

- **fate** [feit] n. 운명, 숙명; 죽음, 최후
  The apparent power that determines the course of events, over which humans have no control.

- **destiny** [déstəni] n. 운명, 숙명
  The things that will happen in the future.

Answers

Comprehension Quiz Answers

1. PARTY	6. FRIENDS	11. CULT
1. C	1. C	1. A
2. B	2. B	2. C
3. C	3. D	3. D
4. A	4. D	4. B
5. D	5. B	5. C

2. STITCHES	7. REPETITION	12. INTRUDER
1. C	1. B	1. B
2. D	2. C	2. A
3. B	3. A	3. C
4. B	4. B	4. A
5. C	5. B	5. B

3. THE END	8. ADRENALINE	13. KILLER
1. A	1. C	1. A
2. D	2. C	2. C
3. B	3. D	3. B
4. A	4. C	4. B
5. B	5. B	5. A

4. WAKING UP	9. THIRD WHEEL	14. FAMILY
1. D	1. D	1. A
2. C	2. C	2. B
3. C	3. C	3. C
4. B	4. B	4. B
5. A	5. A	5. B

5. CHEATER	10. THE MEADOW	15. PRESSURE
1. C	1. C	1. A
2. A	2. B	2. C
3. B	3. D	3. B
4. A	4. A	4. C
5. B	5. D	5. A

16. PARIS
1. B
2. A
3. A
4. B
5. D

17. VISITOR
1. D
2. D
3. A
4. C
5. C

18. THE FUNERAL
1. C
2. D
3. C
4. D
5. A

19. RACE
1. A
2. D
3. B
4. C
5. A

20. VOLTERRA
1. B
2. D
3. A
4. C
5. B

21. VERDICT
1. D
2. B
3. B
4. C
5. D

22. FLIGHT
1. B
2. A
3. D
4. D
5. B

23. THE TRUTH
1. C
2. A
3. C
4. B
5. D

24. VOTE
1. D
2. C
3. A
4. D
5. B

EPILOGUE : TREATY
1. D
2. A
3. C
4. D
5. C

Index

A

aberrant 145
abrupt 22, 165, 233, 322
abruptness 192
absently 99, 181, 303
absentminded 105, 131, 190
absorb 75, 272, 289
abstain 334
abstraction 104
absurd 383, 392
absurdity 207
abuse 84
abyss 194
accelerate 344
accidental 310, 410
accident-prone 28
accomplice 326
accumulate 29
accusation 89, 421
accuse 27, 118, 220, 328
ache 68, 167, 217, 290
achieve 28, 332
acid 76, 247, 316, 397
acquaintance 36
acquisitive 371
addict 276
addiction 143
adjust 245
administrator 27
admirable 72
admiration 366
adolescent 396
adopt 24
adrenaline 99, 189, 282

adulthood 390
affable 117
affectionate 268, 369
afghan 33, 223
afterlife 54
agenda 305
aghast 296
agile 230, 262
aging 258
agitate 391
agonize 293, 371, 391
agonizing 279
agony 85, 163, 222
aimless 147, 277, 347
aisle 91, 332
albino 153
Albuquerque 390
alert 56, 272, 362, 388
alertness 82
alien 367
alienate 318
allegiance 302
alley 350, 361, 381
alleyway 344
allure 345
aloof 68
alter 113, 213, 321, 402
alteration 133
alternative 371, 405
ambush 23, 422
amend 383
amuse 100, 263, 348, 371
amusement 34, 74, 267
analyze 103

ancestor 83, 239
androgynous 352
anesthetic 61, 164
angelic 363, 408
anguish 232, 392
animate 89, 145, 404
ankle 128
annihilate 336
anniversary 175
annoyance 318, 371
annoying 150, 176
antagonism 317
antagonize 334
antechamber 361
anticipate 337
anticipation 175, 207, 423
antisocial 91
apathetic 358
apologetic 51, 73, 98, 294
apology 76, 232
appall 222, 323
apparently 44, 174, 351
appetite 37
appraise 79, 120
appreciate 27, 348
appreciative 404
appropriate 62, 127, 198, 349
approval 199
approximation 252
apricot 20
apt 334
archive 311

archway 380
armed 240
armrest 178
arrangement 72, 293
articulation 26
artificial 361
ascertain 210, 275, 416
ashamed 48, 241
ashen 181, 250
asinine 396
assault 294
assess 261
assessment 358
assumption 212, 272, 309
assurance 102
astonish 195, 362
astonished 84, 370
astonishment 216, 359
astride 151
asylum 311
at any rate 402
athletic 161
atone 146
attendant 332, 381
attractive 362
attune 301, 338
Audi 39
audible 267, 351
aura 129, 275
authoritative 48
autophile 295
avenge 265
aversion 42, 405
aware 55

awareness 76
awe 132
awkward 21, 232, 309, 382
awkwardness 20, 275
axis 239

B

babble 61, 80, 189, 250, 372
backfire 167
baffle 103
bail 422
bail on 176
bait 266, 373
baleful 367
balk 353
ban 390
bandage 58, 172
bane 125
bang 245, 289
banish 192, 291
bankroll 125
banter 71, 129, 264
barefoot 261
barely 30, 161, 265, 368
bark out 222
barn 117
barrel 115, 143, 347, 421
barren 142
barter 407
basilisk 44
batch 265
bathrobe 244
bathtub 184, 312

battering 279
bawl 300
bay 288
beanpole 119
bearable 278
beard 110
beatific 368
beckon 237
bedlam 268
beefy 150
begrudge 294
behead 178
belligerence 317
belligerent 308
bellow 384
bemuse 195, 348
benign 358
bent 20, 371
beseech 333
besot 416
be toast 410
betray 197, 302, 417
betrayal 104, 297, 417
bewilder 324
bewildered 79
bicep 125
billow 344
bitterly 218
bitterness 232
bizarre 53, 212, 338
blacken 121
blade 100
blanch 37, 262
blankly 114, 249, 307
blare 96

Index

blasphemy 393
blast 260
blaze 53, 182, 273
blazer 347
bleach 58
bleak 23, 151
bleary 385
bleed 106, 161, 241, 340
blindly 280
blink 114, 229, 303
blithe 198
blonde 103
bloodbath 174
bloodsucker 219, 263, 317, 415
bloodthirsty 17
bloom 286
blubber 300
bluff 196, 407
blur 98
blurry 229
blurt 323, 406
blush 41
bob 205
bobble 322
boggle 201
bolt 117, 179
bond 391, 401
bonfire 83
bookkeeping 130
boom 347
boredom 304
bottomless 76
boulder 44
bounce 229, 309, 332

bouquet 359
bracken 78
brag 176
brainless 289
brainwash 212
brawny 125
breathtaking 74, 147
breeze 77, 149
brevity 56
brew 401
bribe 119
brilliancy 394
brine 222, 236, 305
brink 147
brisk 98
bristly 28
brittle 218, 246, 367
broach 174
bronze 26, 224
brood 36
brooding 214, 278, 394
bruise 24, 88
brusque 383, 397
brutal 111, 231, 262
brute 110
bubble 91, 192, 378
bubbliness 93
buck 158, 179, 262
bucket 128
buckle 203
budge 231
buffet 268
buffeting 283
bug 152, 263, 316
Buick 333

bulge 274, 410
bunch 173, 308
bundle 119
bunker 278
buoyant 120
burden 249
burly 124
burst 16
bushwhack 192
butt 419
butterscotch 306
buzz 124, 191
by all accounts 54

C

cab 169
cake 162
calculate 406
calculus 91, 190, 275, 414
calf 156, 250
callous 16, 148
Campbell 184
candid 73
canine 201
canister 111
canopy 78
capitulation 175
caption 74
Capulets 32
carcass 240
carefree 71
caress 280
carnage 179
cartwheel 149

carve 40, 223, 304
casserole 306
castanet 247
cataclysmic 172
catatonic 308
catch-22 319
caustic 370
caution 220, 248
cautious 64, 126
cavernous 361
cavity 129
cease 37
cedar 41, 142
ceremonious 144
chafe 355
chafe at 38
chagrin 372, 407
chainsmoker 289
chalky 358
chameleon 133
chandelier 403
chant 377
chaotic 338, 365
chaotically 207
charade 190, 310, 370
chase 203, 221, 268
chastise 264
chat 188
chatter 124, 206, 355, 376
cheekbone 27, 118, 389
cheerful 23, 150
cheery 376
Chevy 25
chide 363

childish 35
chill 63, 147
chime 23, 303, 347
chin 55
chink 78
chirp 191
chisel 344
choke 39, 158, 254, 322, 395
cholesterol 132
chore 312, 409
chortle 174, 248, 369
chorus 41, 126
chromosome 125
chuckle 27, 124, 254, 335, 408
chug 176
chunk 239
churn 234, 288
cinder block 119
cinnamon 345
circumstance 294
citrus 300
civility 350, 388
clamp 348
clang 355
clap 161, 363
clarify 34, 88, 112, 333
clatter 247
claustrophobia 277
claustrophobic 277, 354
claw 84, 94
clench 40, 233, 316, 419
clergyman 53
cliché 283

cliff 82
cling 20, 228, 360, 385
clinical 163, 394
clink 98
clipping 116
cloak-and-dagger 130
closeness 166
clue 93, 234
clue somebody in 404
clump 184
clumsy 112, 228
coalesce 259
coarse 34, 372
coastline 81
coat 32
coax 162
cobble 345, 379
cock 195, 249, 301
cockpit 332
coherent 390
coil 346
coincidental 98
cold shoulder 134
collapse 64, 158, 232
colossal 260
comb through 130
combination 158, 236
Comet 312
comforting 143, 250
commercial 72
commitment 407
communism 91
comparative 338, 360
comparison 95
compartment 273

Index

compassion 254
compatible 395
compel 103, 274, 354
competence 379
complacent 276
complain 26, 129, 261, 339
complaint 43, 166
complicate 37, 159, 272
compliment 168, 199, 373
composition 63
composure 70, 293
comprehend 324, 359
comprehensible 276
comprise 96
compromise 244, 336
compulsion 71, 236
compulsory 211
compunction 195
conceal 43, 119, 318, 414
concede 89
concentration 297, 408
concession 96, 182
concrete 34, 133, 385
concussion 165, 340
condemn 182, 246, 278
condone 244
confess 169
confide 291
confident 103, 167
confirm 135, 307
confirmation 233
conflict 260

confound 369
confront 205
confrontation 213, 328, 335
confusion 201, 273
congeal 296
consciousness 56, 85, 165, 291
consequence 320, 391
consequently 165
considerably 380
conspicuous 42, 334
conspiratorial 197
constantly 393
contemplate 36, 90, 121
contemptuous 360
contentment 275
contingency 34
contour 300
contradiction 76
convalescence 38
convene 361
convenient 268, 364
converge 362
conversational 352
conviction 105, 401, 410
convince 69, 280, 400
convincing 163, 409
convulse 251
convulsion 259
coo 360
coop 42
cooperative 104
coordination 38
copper 131, 264

core 104, 335, 391
corkscrew 239
corny 183
corpse 97
correctly 219
correspond 193
corresponding 118
corrupt 177
cot 56
counterpart 376
coupe 39
coven 195
coward 97
cowardly 244
cower 258, 359
crack 43, 144, 264, 408
cradle 224
cramp 206, 283, 290
crane 153
crap 151, 232, 389
crash down 231
crawl 141, 215
creak 82, 358
crease 20, 166, 303, 404
creativity 114, 166
creep 189
creep somebody out 151
creepy 142
crescent 35, 181, 212, 275
crevice 72
crew 214
crib 71
crimson 224, 344
cringe 59, 180, 308, 405

cripple 105
criticism 258
criticize 391
croak 287, 389
crook 60, 75
crop 216, 258, 359
crouch 48, 161, 259, 281, 353
crucial 156
cruel 272, 286
cruiser 37, 416, 306
crumble 223, 393
crumple 88, 184, 364,
crunch 224
crush 61, 202, 294
crust 111
crutch 183
cub 110
cuff 128
curfew 88
curriculum 91
curse 61
cursive 339
curt 213
curvy 380
cuss 321
cut off 134, 232
cynical 419

D
dagger 201
dammit 295
damn 54, 384
damnation 410
damp 54, 156, 236, 400

dampen 175
dangle 229, 261, 410
Dartmouth 39
dashboard 59, 129, 215, 296, 380
daze 45, 158, 322
dazzle 347, 363
deafen 162
dearest 405
debate 96, 338
decade 57
decent 99
decisive 335, 397
declaration 422
dedicate 110
deer 253
defensive 48, 218, 316
defile 182
deflect 83
deformity 267
dehydrate 306
deity 54
déjà vu 98, 237, 328
deliberate 196, 276
delusion 141, 221, 325, 388, 401
Denali 69, 306
denial 51, 106, 220, 325
dense 90, 168
deprivation 104, 133
deprogram 212
deputy 117
descended 238
description 73, 145, 334
designate 414

desolate 190, 290
desolation 172
despair 23, 381
desperate 35, 96, 198, 354
destiny 423
destructive 102
detach 237, 377
detached 59
detector 382
devastate 292
devoid 53, 145
dew 251, 396
diagnostic 52
diagonal 245
dibs 360
dilapidated 115
dilute 275
dim 79, 132, 337, 383
dime 39
diminish 175
dimly 98, 228, 361
dire 162
disapproval 31, 333, 400
disapprove 148, 280, 415
disapproving 381
disarray 28
disciple 150
discomfort 119
disconnect 163, 183, 383
disgruntled 148
disguise 132, 193, 272
disgust 34, 149, 248, 326
disheveled 360
disjointed 133, 393

Index

dislodge 69
dismiss 92
dismissal 38
dismissive 196
disorient 45, 192, 286
dispel 388, 416
dissolve 30, 246, 273
distinct 75, 201
distinctive 70
distort 80, 199, 214, 405
distract 33, 141, 410, 275
distraction 91, 189, 306
distrustful 409
ditch 205, 272
dither 102, 127, 337
diversion 198
divert 150
divine 48
dizzy 22, 160, 240, 283, 323, 402
don 128
doodle 215
doom 55, 169, 350
doomsday 212
doorjamb 312
doorknob 297
dormant 378
doubtful 84, 183, 353
downpour 116
downright 276, 416
downward 282
drain 127, 249, 353
drawer 327
drawn 273
dread 199, 341

dreary 112, 414
dredge 237
drench 281
driftwood 245
drizzle 20, 114, 222
dryness 99, 191
dubious 102, 218, 301, 392
duck 179, 266, 355
duck out 68
dull 22, 127, 214, 344
dump 90, 128, 289
durable 395
dusk 112, 296
duster 131
dwarf 153
dwindle 96

E

eager 25, 136, 233, 365, 414
eagerness 94
eardrum 112
earsplitting 405
earthbound 129
earthquake 323
easternmost 263
eave 41
eavesdrop 310
ebony 355
eclipse 78
ecstatic 363
eddy 280
edgy 141, 317
edict 165

edifice 348
eerie 277
effectiveness 61
efficient 192
egregious 313
elaborate 379
elate 195, 306
elbow 43, 232
eliminate 191, 326
elusive 64
embarrassing 211
embarrassment 384
embrace 101, 152, 307
emergency 48, 117, 190, 409
emotional 152, 308
emotionless 97, 297, 312
emphasize 144, 174, 326, 373
en masse 231
enchant 320
enclose 21
encounter 280
encourage 41, 157, 338, 397
encouragement 103, 136, 366
encroach 75
end up 59, 90
endanger 210, 334
endure 241, 51, 178
enforce 38, 188, 335
engagement 311
enhanced 52
enigmatic 302

enmity 416
enormous 201, 260
enrage 260, 422
ensue 73
entail 173
enthrall 371
enthuse 161
enthusiastic 29, 153, 273
entitle 181
entourage 368
enunciate 304
envious 133, 161, 364
epiphany 401
epithet 418
equally 194
equation 113
ER 162, 173
errand 141, 317
erratic 228
escort 363
ESPN 70
etch 276
eternity 148, 196, 337, 407
etiquette 321
Etruscan 336
evade 106
evaporate 103
Evel Knievel 292
evident 48, 362, 400
exaggerate 420
exasperation 88
exceedingly 365
exceptional 100, 372
excise 105

exclamation 346
excruciating 22, 114, 392
execute 151
exertion 191, 347
exhale 31, 233, 280, 353
exhaust 64, 204, 290
exhaustion 81, 188, 279, 381
exhaustive 144
exhilarate 400
exhilaration 281
exotic 70, 131
expectation 189, 409
expedition 395
expel 251
experimental 159, 213
expertise 126
exploit 364
explosion 135
exponential 364
exposition 96
exquisite 36, 103, 361
extract 34
extraordinary 16, 203, 397
extreme 30, 311, 352
extremely 230, 373
exuberant 145, 300
exultant 265
eyelash 131
eyelid 22, 383

F
fabricate 102
fabulous 380, 390

façade 379
fad 53
fade 74, 169, 250, 324
fairy 239, 320
fairytale 202
fake 94, 178
falseness 95
falter 200, 295, 419
fan 31, 128
fang 346, 379
fantasize 207, 378
fascinate 149, 366
fascinating 130
fascination 336
fate 266, 423
fated 115
fatigue 381
faucet 309, 415
fauna 205
faux pas 368
feeble 80, 220
fender 151
fern 142, 169, 189, 422
ferocious 190, 278
fervent 54, 205, 290, 420
fester 278
feverish 326
fiancee 262
fib 190
fiber 53
fickle 33, 294
fictional 33
fiend 388
fierce 249, 403
fiercely 205, 307, 382

Index

figment 389
filch 311
filter 78
filthy 219, 321
fingernail 225
firepower 240
fisherman 373
fit as a fiddle 182
fixation 396
flagpole 178
flake 273
flank 202
flare 279
flatly 401
flattered 103
flaunt 417
flawed 199, 348, 382
flawless 192, 283, 390
fleeting 377
flex 125, 252, 325
flick 54, 244, 266
flicker 59, 197
flinch 71, 163, 247, 323, 394
fling 44, 149, 160, 281, 287, 346
flint 405
flip 62, 252, 277, 406
flirt 73, 234
flit 126, 253, 302
floodgate 59
floorboard 264, 401
flora 141, 205
floral 300
flout 336

fluorescent 358
flush 61
flutter 222, 260, 344
flutter down 25
foam 279
foil 175
folklore 83
foray 268
forbid 63
foresight 313
forewarn 246
forfeit 17, 370
forge 327, 401
formidable 335, 368
fraction 202
fracture 194
fragile 56, 351, 382
fragment 51
frail 365
frantic 85, 198, 287, 344, 376, 409
freak 136
freak out 221
freaky 254
frenzied 172, 332
fret 184, 371
friction 355
fringe 178
frosting 57
frown 25, 164, 235, 302
fruitless 415
frustrate 213, 365
frustrating 74
frustration 313, 326, 415
fudge 205

fuel 54
fulfillment 101
fumble 297, 340, 397
fume 157, 220, 370
funeral 80, 143, 310, 392
funnel 351
furious 36, 200, 288
furrow 249, 349
furthest 295
furtive 40, 198
fury 219, 308, 390
fuss 168
futile 418

G

gag 420
gang up 50
gape 325
garbled 383
gargoyle 352
garment 163
gash 50, 106
gasp 22, 193, 250, 288
gauge 408
gauze 53
gawk 303, 359, 406
gear 157
gearshift 156
geese 202
generate 159
generation 131, 277
generous 189, 384
genteel 388
genuine 93
genuine 390

ghastly 388
ghost 368
ghoulish 358
gigantic 201, 238
giggle 73, 126, 348, 360
gimpy 169
gingerly 151
glacial 148
gland 81
glare 42, 166, 261, 369
gleam 50, 337
gleeful 124, 414
glide 362
glint 219, 283, 359
glisten 27, 131, 328
glitter 21
gloom 112, 169, 283, 358
gloomy 245, 348
glorious 42
gloss over something 303
glossy 307, 418
glower 90, 303, 383, 419
glum 25, 176, 308
gnaw 140, 302
goad 221
gonna 174, 293, 389
goodwrench 128
goody-goody 92
gooey 95
goose bumps 33, 149
gore 58
gorgeous 372
grab 45, 148, 236, 345

gradual 136, 332
graduation 406
grainy 287
granite 203, 367
granola 68
grasp 35, 93, 368, 384
gratify 365
gratitude 94, 202, 327, 420
grave 131, 311, 405
gravel 224
gravelly 293
gravitational 129, 396
gravity 172, 281
grease 129
greedy 196, 393
grenade 156, 180
grid 167
grief 293, 304
grieve 194, 294
grille 119, 355
grim 75, 176, 307
grimace 89, 180, 264, 369
grin 27, 148, 261, 397
grind 316
grisly 44, 201
grit 157, 214, 406, 419
grizzled 81
grizzly 110, 135, 166
groan 39, 150, 234, 340, 419
groggy 337
grotesque 97
ground 327, 397, 419

growl 40, 158, 216, 328, 404
grudging 82, 146, 174, 318
gruesome 96, 163, 278, 346
gruff 80, 319
grumble 72, 180, 261, 338
grunt 105, 229, 293
guarantee 266, 334
guffaw 262
gun 296
gush 98, 161, 286, 372
gust 309, 351
gut 180
gutter 103

H
habitual 134
haggard 96
hairsbreadth 206
halfhearted 31, 125, 400
Hallelujah 218
hallucination 102, 158, 292, 348, 388
hallucinatory 389
halt 247
halves 282
hammer 289
harbor 272, 297, 320, 417
Harley Sprint 121
harsh 53, 230, 247
haste 35, 90, 328

Index

hasty 205, 293, 395, 420
hater 220
haul 130, 262
hauler 115
haunt 142, 215, 423
have a lot on one's plate 212
haystack 404
hazardous 30
haze 93, 362
headlong 203, 300
head-up 151
heartless 181
heave 251, 259
hedge 93, 173, 276, 407
helpless 77
hemlock 146, 204
heroine 97
hesitant 135, 168
hideous 68, 143, 360, 377
hindsight 318
hiss 25, 220, 295, 369
hmph 135, 177
hoarse 56, 184, 289
holey 61
hollow 217, 322, 380
honk 94, 268
hoot 267
hop 261
hopelessness 233
hop out 60
Hoquiam 129
horizon 147, 276
hormone 214

horrify 21, 206, 251, 362
horsepower 296
hospitalize 101, 308
hostage 35
hostile 247, 377
hostility 217, 316
hover 159
huddle 164
huff 229, 353
hulk 363
hum 95, 305
humongous 264
humorless 114, 418
humph 105
hunch 111, 189, 288
hurdle 402
hurl 262, 327
hurtle 348
hush 337
hydrate 184
hyperactive 32
hyperventilate 69, 253, 304
hypocrisy 269
hypocrite 247, 269
hypothesis 394
hypothetical 338
hysteria 131, 194, 407
hysteric 238, 376
hysterical 240, 304

I

identifiable 292
idiocy 302
idiot 236, 253, 389, 405

idiotic 157, 393
idly 62, 378
idolize 131
ignition 157, 262, 295
ignorant 254
illogical 246
illuminate 79
illumination 43
illusion 280, 388
imitate 301
imitation 28, 325
immature 391
immense 402
immerse 125, 420
immortal 26, 70, 207, 362
immortality 370
immune 111, 367
impair 115
impasse 26
impassive 58
impatience 73, 325
impatient 68, 165, 269, 365
impend 23, 172
imperfect 68, 302, 378
impish 125
implication 147, 172, 322
implicit 417
implode 216
imply 99, 205
impression 39
impressive 111
improvise 306

impulse 99
impulsive 164, 304
inability 409
inaccurate 125
inaudible 333
incapacitate 113
incisor 201
incline 133, 364
incoherent 83
income 28
incomprehensible 393
incomprehension 235, 339, 392
inconsequential 221, 234, 396
inconspicuous 132, 339, 405
incorrect 101
incredible 175, 221, 235
incredulity 367
incredulous 92
incriminate 164
indecipherable 58
indecision 57, 190, 219, 325
indefinite 99
indestructible 207, 253
indifference 72
indifferent 69, 403
indulge 110
inept 234
inevitable 84, 241, 310
inexcusable 377
inexorable 16
infallible 363

infection 230
infectious 188, 210
infer 116
infiltrate 142
infinitely 16
infinitesimal 350
inflated 168, 402
inflection 401, 421
infuriate 152, 321
infuse 94
ingrained 281
inhale 31, 182, 255, 300, 388
inject 350
injunction 262
injure 64, 408
injury 231
innocence 92, 177
insane 59, 148
insanity 102, 113, 377
insert 136
insignificant 113, 216, 352, 423
inspiration 28, 117, 276
instantaneous 193
instantly 75, 174
instinct 197, 328
instinctive 45, 152, 203, 418
instruct 156, 184, 197
instruction 349
insubstantial 367
insult 230, 254, 416
intact 106, 116
intense 51

intensify 59, 217
intensity 49, 172, 233, 365
intention 235
intentional 192
intently 238, 252
interaction 91
intercede 50
interference 77
interject 405
interlace 355
interminable 70
intermittent 268
interrogation 126
intersperse 126, 146
intervening 57
intimidate 30
intolerable 279
intonation 280
intrigue 338, 366, 391
intruder 40, 111, 228
intrusive 265
investigate 200, 228
investment 183
invitation 188, 318, 350
involuntary 196
inward 106
irate 100, 370
iris 352, 378, 389
ironic 97, 164, 340
irrational 195, 269
irresistible 33, 141
irresponsible 149, 292, 392
irreversible 113, 402

Index

irritate 37, 17, 325
irritated 136
irritation 82, 148, 259, 334
itch 160
Ithaca 310

J
jade 236
jagged 45, 143, 393
jar 287, 337
jawline 31
jaybird 204
jerk 44, 116, 180
jog 204, 279
jolt 22
jostle 346

K
kay 385
kidnap 169, 212
kidney 265
kindergarten 28
kindergartener 132
kismet 115
kitten 196
klutz 28
klutzy 218, 340
kneel 49, 193
knob 244
knuckle 99

L
landmark 167
lane 59, 140, 263, 345
lank 351
lanky 118
lantern 40, 79
lapse 313
lasagna 146
lash 194, 223, 274
latch 85
launch 95, 165, 230, 368
laundry 163, 409
lawn 142
layman 101
leach 224
leafy 132
leak 93, 396
leapt 262
ledge 147
leech 249, 328
leer 350
leftover 88, 292, 415
legitimate 183
let by 48
lethal 210, 277
leverage 407
lick 288
lid 207, 234, 291, 380
lidded 371
lifeless 89
lifelong 378
liftoff 332
light bulb 54
lightheaded 283
lightweight 110
lilt 351
limb 107
limp 80, 219, 291, 418
linger 31, 143, 268, 379
linoleum 38, 134, 224
listlessly 294
literal 134, 263, 312
lithe 200, 400
livid 221
lizard 371
loathsome 371
locale 70
lodge 239
lodge in 23
loiter 91
loll 288
lone 249
loneliness 222
loop 240
lope 69
lounge 61, 72, 418
loyalty 233
lull 88
lullaby 63, 291
lump 69, 218, 329
lung 16, 113, 238, 286
lurch 85, 228, 322
lure 141
lurk 23, 282
lustrous 373
Lutheran 53
luxuriate 394
luxurious 379
lyric 104

M
macabre 58
maiden 175

Makah 149
makeshift 121
malevolent 181
malicious 217
mammoth 202
manageable 107
maneuver 124
mangle 382
marginally 360
marigold 263
Mariners 37
marital 407
marshmallow 179
martyr 43
marvel 144, 318, 402
mash 160, 253
masochistic 50, 140
massacre 207, 390
massive 45, 259, 361
materialize 245
mature 146, 309
maturity 129, 258
maul 269
maverick 336
mayhem 36, 178
maze 112
meadow 142, 238, 339
meaningful 263, 404
meaningless 291
measly 321
meddle 71
medieval 372, 379
meditation 132
melodramatic 60
menace 99, 115, 282

menacing 40, 203, 321, 349
Mercedes 296
merciless 394
merely 55, 236, 349
mesmerize 367
messy 84
metaphorical 319
meteor 281, 394
meth 150
microfiche 311
microscopic 29
microwave 306
midsection 255
midst 268
mileage 92
mill around 347
millennium 335, 364
mimic 22
mingle 300
minimal 93
misadventure 304
misapprehension 392
mischievous 199
miserable 90, 172, 292, 391
misery 401
misty 156, 363
misunderstanding 269, 301
moan 41, 179, 252, 324
mock 42, 120, 173
mockery 220, 230
modest 363
moist 250

moisture 355
moleskin 169
mollify 93
momentarily 24, 213, 293, 420
momentary 101, 191
momentum 229
mono 188
monopolize 152
monotone 90, 352
monstrous 238
Montagues 32
moot 37
mop 58
mope around 88
mopey 190
morgue 57
morose 214, 254
moroseness 88
morph 248
mortality 26, 397
mortify 135
moss 112, 160
mossy 418
motivation 141, 354, 378
mourn 28
mouthwatering 199
muddled 228, 321
muddy 128, 163, 204
muffle 78, 133, 230
mull 52
multihued 239
mumble 25, 124, 214, 316, 394
mundane 320

Index

murmur 48, 158, 255, 304
muscular 201
muse 53, 197, 305, 390
musk 300
mutant 211
mutate 166
mute 78, 234, 333, 381
mutter 41, 126, 213, 317
mutual 95
muzzle 201, 259
mystify 82, 88, 420
mythical 97, 239

N

nagging 112
nape 237
nasty 134, 319
nausea 75, 161, 251
nauseate 181
nauseous 206, 251
nebulous 99
needless 162
negate 392
neglect 312
negotiable 146
nerve 140, 384
neutral 297
nibble 264
no dice 397
Noah and the ark 238
noisy 191
nonchalance 133
nonchalant 312
nondescript 359

nonessential 39
nostril 283
nosy 166
notch 157
nothingness 140, 165, 189
novelty 197
nudge 124, 156
nuisance 210
numb 50, 127, 192, 282
numbness 79, 110, 143
nut 301

O

oath 114
obedient 81
obediently 199
obligate 72
obligation 42, 391
oblivion 308
oblivious 198, 255, 377
obscure 38
obsess 211
obsessive 56, 173, 143
obstinate 90, 180
occasional 191
occasionally 68, 146, 304
ocher 56
oddly 93
odometer 92
offend 33, 120, 151
offense 196
offensive 136
offhand 54
offset 354

ominous 205, 290
on the one hand 319
onionskin 362
onslaught 127
onyx 396
ooze 44, 393, 416
opinionated 397
opposable 206
opulent 376
orbit 172
ordeal 173
organ 106
ornate 360
ostracism 30
ouch 228
outcrop 279
outnumber 99
outrage 103, 259, 395
outrun 213
outshine 365
outstretch 422
oval 403
overboard 61
overcast 22
overconfidence 391
overconfident 404
overestimate 64
overgrown 140, 203
overpower 200, 246, 382
overreact 63
overstate 309
overt 366
overwhelm 56, 102, 195
owe 82, 244

P

pad 201
padded cell 89
pagan 24
pallid 113, 194
pallor 359
palm 32, 173, 320
pang 297
pant 64, 296
papery 364
parade 80
parallel 282
parched 184
parking lot 23, 253
parlor 335
pass out 235
passageway 287
pat 153, 252, 332
pathetic 163, 274, 401
patron 37, 110
pavement 100, 295, 345
paving 353
paw 240
PBS 212
pebble 161
peck 27
peculiar 364
peek 94, 151, 349, 403
peeping tom 294
peer 117, 294, 307
penetrate 323
perceptible 42, 277
perception 254
perceptive 137
perch 33, 168
perforate 189
perimeter 266
peripheral 133, 215
perk 130, 174
permanent 71, 217, 304, 334
perpetual 129
perplex 62, 312
perplexity 302
persistence 176
persistent 180
perspective 153, 292, 394
perverse 366, 381
pessimist 240
petty 417
petulance 177
Peugeot
phase 30, 262
philosophy 310
phony 189
picky 129
piggyback 163
pill 63
pillar 382
pinch 188
pinky 181
piqued 63
pirate 98
pissed off 250
piss somebody off 150
pitcher 264
pitiful 114
pitiless 346
pixie 28, 134
placate 200
placeholder 291
plague 69
playful 40, 168
plea 75
plead 117, 236, 307, 333, 383
plink 51
plop 232
ploy 408
plug into something 49
plug up 223
plunge 35, 194, 281
plunk 235
plural 77, 111
point out 89
pointedly 28
pointless 156, 368
poke 52
polish 24, 403
politeness 366
ponder 88
ponytail 118, 237
pop 22
porcelain 153, 303
porch 40
Porsche 339, 378
portcullis 380
postpone 382
posture 37
potency 165
potent 221
potential 102, 167, 369
pottery 53
powdery 362

Index

preamble 389
precarious 127, 229
precaution 42, 206, 421
precipice 71, 147
precisely 24, 75, 194
precision 130, 305
predawn 245
predict 29
predictable 73
preferable 26
prehistoric 39
prejudice 415
prejudiced 102
preliminary 365
prelude 234
premonition 64
preoccupy 104, 213, 282
pretense 350
preview 95
prickle 247
priority 211, 407
prism 361
probe 81, 318
procrastinate 91
procrastination 414
prod 81, 95, 404
profanity 323
prohibit 165
prohibition 390
prolong 40
prolonged 215
prom 119
prominent 82, 118, 216
promptly 414
prone 302

pronounce 395
pronounced 141
prop 61, 403
propane 79
prophetic 22
proposition 114
pros and cons 110
prospective 369
protective 49, 326, 349
protest 25, 126, 231, 333, 422
protocol 320
provoke 36, 325
prowl 202, 354
proximity 349, 405
pry 385
psychoanalysis 89
psychology 60
psychopath 104, 112
PTA 177
puberty 152
puce 410
pucker 20
puff 301
pulse 32, 106
pulverize 68
puncture 210
pupil 359
purr 198, 296, 350
purse 55, 119, 245, 407
pursue 203
pursuer 97
pushy 188

Q

Q-tip 52
quadruplet 258
qualify 249
quantify 23
quarry 195
quartet 36
queasy 52
quench 279
quicken 177
Quileute 81, 213, 303
quilt 64, 132, 145, 206, 291, 409
quiver 220, 258, 317
quotation 317
quote 301

R

radiance 41, 354
radiate 106, 068
radiator 290
radical 216
rag 282
rage 56, 218, 248, 283
ragged 106, 211
rake 295
ram 260
ramble 61
ramshackle 291
ranger 190, 239
rap 253
rapt 260
rasp 289, 310
rationally 106
rattle 393

rattlesnake 274
ravenous 45
raw 196
razor-sharp 32
reach out 211
realization 240, 279
reappearance 328
rear up 85
rearrange 199, 239
rearview mirror 269
reassemble 311
reassign 389
reassure 309, 353
rebel 168
rebuke 100, 337
reception 31, 376
recipe 131, 160
reciprocal 415
reciprocate with 29
reckless 77, 144, 280
reclaim 104, 113, 142
recliner 312
recognition 79, 193
recoil 84, 267, 320
recreational 301
rectangle 62, 215
rectangular 62, 358
reddish 202
redirect 301
reedy 351
reek 219
reel 217
refer 389, 404
reference 133, 212
reflection 22

reflex 219
reflexive 421
refold 84, 168
regain 56
regardless 54, 71, 183
register 93, 223
regretful 350
regularity 69
reign 120
rein somebody/something in 41
rejection 180, 230
rejoice 363
rejoin 104
rekindle 62, 318
relationship 30, 178, 365
relative 177, 263
release 125, 253, 320
relentless 16
relieve 56, 144, 250, 379
relive 237
relocate 323
reluctance 119, 302
reluctantly 127
rely on 324, 417
remarkable 84
remnant 261
remorse 60, 297, 323
remote 36
remoteness 59
reparable 136
repentant 382
repetition 140
replace 43, 127, 232
repress 189

reputation 117
rescue 211
resemblance 216
resemble 91, 117
resentful 217, 324, 419
resentment 120, 150, 216, 272
reservation 81, 211, 311
residence 321
resign 105, 305, 403
resignation 352, 408
resistant 145
resolve 410
restless 317
restore 310
restrain 367, 422
restraint 366
restriction 117, 197, 336
resume 414
resurface 85
retain 400
retort 219, 247, 323
retreat 200, 423
retrieve 345, 380
reunion 20, 354, 419
rev 159, 295, 329
revenge 199, 210, 278
reverberate 244
reverie 37, 255
revise 393
revisit 111
revive 383
revulsion 246, 319, 396
rez 149
rhetorical 26, 100

Index

ridden 250
riddle 223, 233
ridiculous 29, 150, 221, 289, 364
rigid 49, 392, 419
rim 293, 396
rinse 313
rip 49, 157, 259, 367,
ripple 193, 259, 392
riptide 282
roadblock 340
robotic 223
rooftop 57
Rosaline 33
rosary 372, 377
rot 324
rotate 306
rotten 410
Rotten Tomato 175
routine 400
rowdy 83
rub off (on) 165
rubbish 94
rude 183, 366, 415
rumble 81, 252, 370
rummage 52
run amuck 101
run off 408
ruse 35
russet 118, 202, 260, 421
rusty 202

S
sadistic 35
sag 251
sallow 113, 274, 421
salmon 269
saltine 184
salvage 60
sandy 116
sane 101
sanity 146, 210
sap 204
sarcasm 176, 421
sarcastic 82, 152, 234, 316
sardonic 340
satiny 264
satisfaction 118, 157, 194
saturate 265
scalp 135
scan 200, 295
scan through 94
scant 269
scar 35, 181, 252, 273
scarf 344
scary 30
scatter 44
scavenge 116
scenario 70, 172, 422
scenery 146
scent 42, 200, 300, 389
Scheherazade 382
schmollege 121
schmuck 173
scholarship 151
scoff 366, 370
scold 21, 182, 363, 383
scoop 38

scoot 309
scornful 390
scout 336
scowl 88, 181, 327, 423
scramble 85, 203, 322
scramble for 27
scrawl 74, 115, 215, 339
screech 238, 329, 416
screw 90, 327
screw up 145
scrub 275, 287, 312
scrunch 353
scrutinize 89, 220, 305
scrutiny 128, 164
scuffle 126
sculpture 33, 336
scurry 191
sear 45
seawall 245
seaward 246
seaweed 305
seclude 211
seductive 198
seek 195
seemingly 361
seep 76
seethe 408
seething 366, 400
self-conscious 43
semblance 222
semester 90, 134, 145
semidry 275
senior 25, 173
seraph 36
serene 76, 177, 317

serpentine 59
serrate 198
sew 58, 164
sewer 358
shadowy 57
shaft 20
shale 367
shamble 96
shameful 74
shard 21
sharp 31
shatter 21, 224, 280, 382
shear 224, 235
sheathe 361
shed 124
sheepish 21, 303, 402
sheer 159, 282
sheesh 339
shelter 246
sheriff 80
shimmer 85, 339
shiny 43, 147
ship off 409
shiver 72, 164, 260, 420
shone 20
shortage 115
shortcoming 117
shoulder blade 286
shove 45, 125, 231, 345
shred 278, 325, 260
shrewd 272, 376
shriek 97, 325, 368
shrill 321, 372
shrink 89, 369
shrub 191

shrubbery 119
shrug 51, 143, 252, 402
shudder 55, 183, 259, 377
shuffle 83, 214, 307
shush 30, 96
shy away (from something) 83
sibling 24
sickening 251, 287
sienna 340, 361
sieve 77, 105
sighting 168
significance 179
significant 80
silhouette 246
silvery 181, 313
similarity 24
sincerity 230, 420
sinister 72
sink 324
sink down 193, 250
skeleton 164
skeptical 165, 305, 404
skepticism 393, 406
skid 239
skillet 265
skim 121, 188
skulk 121
skull 160
slack 39
slam 25, 157, 286, 410
slam into 44
slant 222, 245, 354
slap 128, 297, 376

slaughter 241
slave 173
sleek 253
sleep away 104
slender 124, 221, 417
slick 223
slip away 100
slippery 127
slit 252, 304
slosh 21, 115
sloth 68
sluggish 17, 114, 277
slumber 316
slump 69, 215, 251, 318
sly 136
smack 126, 286, 378
smear 115
smirk 231, 352, 404
smolder 31, 320, 408
smug 27, 265, 353
snag 38, 74, 266
snarl 45, 103, 157, 247, 324, 395
sneak 276, 414
sneak up 333
sneaker 261
sneaky 64, 120, 130
sneer 321
sneer 418
snicker 135, 177, 261
sniff 120, 200, 319
sniffle 319
snigger 178
snip 52
snore 230, 291

Index

snort 27, 116, 229, 309, 395
snuffle 79
snuggle 62
soak 53, 223, 290
sob 205, 300
sodden 223
sole 16
solemn 248
solicitous 69
something hack up 33
soothe 65, 150, 291, 344
sophomore 124, 175, 272
sore 230
soreness 310
sour 82, 169, 305
Sox n. 37
sparkle 42, 147, 319
spasm 57, 251, 296, 421
spatter 58, 329
spawn 269
specific 99
speck 25
speculate 218, 334
speculation 159, 376
speculative 55, 339
speechless 411
speedometer 340
spill 62, 145
spill the beans 262
spine 63, 324, 422
spiral 279, 281
spit 215, 247, 324
splash 147, 224, 309

splatter 128, 280, 346
splinter 52
split 141, 266, 295
splutter 83
spokesperson 418
sporadical 326
spot 23
spotless 275, 378
sprawl 33, 145, 167
spree 333
springboard 346
sprint 50, 162, 253, 316
spruce 147, 204, 229
spur-of-the-moment 116
spurt 218, 345
sputter 295
squabble 266
squeak 198, 310
squeaky 236
squeal 134, 225, 295
squeamishness 50
squeeze 25, 127, 248, 305, 423
squelch 204, 292
squint 94, 200, 289
squirrel 204, 277
squirt 178
squish 191, 218
stab 173, 236, 286
stack 41, 190, 392
stagger 80, 182, 228, 305
stagnant 184
stairway 322
stalk 200, 245, 352
stall 159, 244

stammer 27
stamp 167
stance 48, 351
startle 39, 159, 233, 293
startling 24, 79
starve 205
stash 380
static 279
stationary 160
statue 74, 416
statuesque 372
steer 60, 112, 140, 232
stem from 92
stern 60
stewardess 333
sticky 161
stiffen 264, 336, 383
stifle 328
stillness 194
stilted 384
sting 45, 49, 162, 258, 292, 417
stirring 50
stitch 48, 162
stoic 244
stomp 113, 169, 296
straighten 248, 321
strain 82, 301, 402
strangle 111, 238
strategic 267
strategy 51, 177
stray 71, 94, 195
strictly 133
stride 58
strident 134

strike a chord 79
striking 217, 345
stroke 248
stroll 21, 120, 195, 332
stubborn 29, 55, 380, 416
stuffy 215
stumble 77, 181, 249, 338
stun 127, 193, 213, 373
stunt 148
stupidity 159
stupor 78, 140, 337, 384
stutter 26, 135, 288, 395
stymie 206
styrofoam peanut 134
sub 132
subconscious 101, 210, 283, 401
subdue 307, 396
substantial 388
subterranean 354
Suburban 175
suck 179, 255, 408
suicidal 100, 336
suicide 34, 301
sulk 91, 177
sulky 368
sullen 176
sultry 276
sundown 265
superficial 130
superstition 83, 220
superstitious 220
suppress 194, 309
surge 118
surreal 362
surrender 369
surreptitious 81, 166, 254
survivor 97
suspicion 85, 175
suspicious 92, 156, 188, 268, 396
sustain 370
swallow 69, 197, 293, 403
sway 193, 232, 322, 414
swear 149, 222, 250, 294
sweat 62, 245
sweatpants 327
sweaty 252
swerve 348
swift 80, 158, 253, 318, 379
swiftness 203
swing 63, 124, 229, 351
swirl 36, 193, 288, 385
swish 287
swivel 307
syllable 120
symmetrical 192
symmetry 267
sympathetic 184
sympathy 95
symptom 188
synchronize 258

T
taboo 217
tabulate 326
tack 174
tad 92
taint 395
tame 279
tangible 141, 184
tangle 64, 204, 278
tanned 111
tantrum 308
tarmac 332
tasteful 379
tawny 24
tear 43, 198, 327
tear off 327
tease 34, 120, 274, 397
teensy 303
temper 31, 196, 273, 370
temple 31, 248, 336, 421
tempo 152
tempt 51, 92, 144, 174
temptation 51
tenacious 385
tendency 326
tendon 118, 216
tense 58, 152, 233, 287
tension 98, 318, 351
tentacle 246
tentative 93, 136, 403
tenuous 68
terrify 16, 152, 228, 275, 371
theatrical 326
theft 339
thickset 110
third wheel 172

Index

thirst 49, 207
thorough 85
thoroughly 33, 52
thoughtful 52, 176, 317, 406
thrash 292, 345
Thriftway 73
thrill 21, 160, 235, 341
throaty 143, 294
throb 106, 164, 255, 347
throng 346
throttle 156
throw down 34
thrum 329, 384
thrust 157, 182, 258
thud 32, 230, 244
thumb 116, 180, 354
thump 113
thwart 55
tick by 183
tilt 239, 322
timeless 73
timid 263, 403
tingle 44, 62, 160
tinkle 376
tint 339, 373
tiptoe 224, 312, 337
toast 144
token 71
tolerance 334, 381
tolerant 74
toll 16, 347
tomb 349
tombstone 311
toneless 141, 183

topographical 167
torment 400
torrent 286
torso 112, 192, 254
torture 35, 140, 255, 323
tourniquet 49
tousle 26
tow 43, 130, 302
trade-off 102
trail off 51
trailhead 111, 135, 167
traitor 255, 418
tranquil 77, 368
transgress 335
transitory 335
translate 335
translucent 362
trash 261, 325, 381
tray 68, 136
treachery 417
treaty 238, 319, 420
tree-hugger 240
tremble 235, 274, 353, 419
tremor 206, 260, 324, 421
tribe 83, 258
tribute 24
trickle 76
tricky 277
trigger 101, 158, 273
trill 44, 340
trim 352
triumphant 38, 406
trivial 32

truce 30, 420
trudge 72, 183, 278, 385
trunk 142, 221, 251, 418
truthful 180
tuck 60, 43
tug 50, 160, 274, 344
tuition 29
tumble 38
tune 94, 168
tuneless 306
turf 263, 422
turmoil 322
turn away 111
turn down 101
turn into 240, 289
turnoff 38
turret 361, 379
Tuscan 340, 359
twilight 95
twinge 100, 191
twirl 281
twitch 237, 274

U

ugh 70, 248, 406
ultimatum 410
unabashed 266
unamused 229
unattainable 140
unaware 328
unblur 57
unbreakable 48, 400
uncanny 29, 73
uncharacteristic 162, 292
unclench 297, 406

uncomprehending 21, 75, 276
unconcealed 202
unconcerned 267
unconquerable 281
unconsciousness 65, 207, 290
uncontrollable 197
unconvinced 166
uncover 311
undecided 320
undergrowth 77
underlying 267, 351, 417
undermine 409
underpriced 144
undulate 350
unease 50
unendurable 278
unfathomable 29, 54
unforgettable 372
unguarded 142
unimpressive 89
uninhabitable 182
unintelligible 72
uninterrupted 70, 381
unleash 84
unlimited 29
unlit 98
unnerve 218
unorthodox 365
unperturbed 217
unprotected 199
unquestionable 100
unreadable 57, 423
unrecognizable 216

unremarkable 358
unrequited 224, 235
unresolved 415
unseeing 55, 75, 255
unstable 102, 160
unsteady 181, 232
unsuccessful 132
unsupervised 128
unsurprised 175
unthinking 35, 78
untidily 71
unwilling 75, 146, 296, 378
upholster 179
upset 152
upward 32
urge 95
urgency 74, 185
urgent 63, 213, 282, 327, 371
USC 135
utterly 78, 149, 182, 267, 364

V

vacant 143, 222, 288
vague 55, 211, 323
vaguely 70, 190, 290, 380
vainly 281
vanish 24, 225, 354
veer off 237
vehement 30
vein 76, 158, 348
velveteen 179

vengeance 308
venom 32, 231, 274
vent 134, 415
venue 349
verdict 210, 358
vial 34
vibrate 16, 259, 359, 376
vice 248
vicious 194, 231, 346
vine 192
violate 114, 278
violent 204, 296
virtuous 39
vital 105, 234
vitally 390
vivid 36, 118, 279
Volkswagen 119
volley 286
voluntary 235
vomit 51, 179
voucher 62
vow 40, 76, 411
vulnerability 370
vulnerable 246

W

wad 161, 261
waft 130, 146
wallow 60
wary 41, 63, 176, 235
wasteful 338, 377
waver 367, 410
weaken 107
weakly 70, 274
weary 218, 288

Index

wee 345
weird 212, 254
werewolf 239, 353
whim 57, 116
whip 222
whirl 221, 286
whoosh 219, 283, 345
wildlife 166
wimp 145
wince 49, 178, 289, 392
windshield 60, 148, 214, 416
wind up 97
wintry 335, 355
wipe 52, 219, 319
wiry 164
wistful 320
wither 20
wizened 20
wobble 77, 156, 228
wordless 249
wound 49, 162, 231, 346
wrack 107
wrench 144, 159, 194, 388
wretched 265, 384
wrinkle 23, 92, 233, 316
writhe 288
wry 196, 254

Y

yank 90, 158, 237, 266, 349
yawn 82, 290, 310
yearn 210, 236
yell 130, 214, 283, 384
Yellowstone 110
yelp 237, 253

영어원서 읽기 Tips

New Moon을 완독하셨군요! 축하합니다!

원서 읽는 단어장을 활용해보세요!

다양한 원서들을 「원서 읽는 단어장」을 활용해서 읽어보세요. 〈New Moon〉 외에도 〈Charlie and the Chocolate Factory〉를 비롯한 로알드 달의 작품들과 〈Twilight〉, 〈Harry Potter and the Sorcerer's Stone〉 등 여러 영어원서의 단어장이 출간되어 있습니다. 「원서 읽는 단어장」은 시중 서점 및 인터넷 서점에서 구입할 수 있습니다.

「원서 읽는 단어장」 시리즈
- Charlie and the Chocolate Factory
- Matilda
- James and the Giant Peach
- Shopaholic
- Frindle
- The Secret
- Twilight
- Harry Potter and the Sorcerer's Stone
- Charlotte's Web

인터넷 서점에서 '원서 읽는 단어장'을 검색해보세요!

함께 모여 원서 읽는 〈스피드 리딩 카페〉

함께 모여 원서를 읽는 〈스피드 리딩 카페 cafe.naver.com/readingtc〉를 방문해보세요. '수준별 추천 원서 목록', '함께 만든 원서별 단어장', '매월 진행되는 북클럽' 등 원서 읽기에 도움이 되는 자료가 넘쳐납니다. 무엇보다 원서를 함께 읽을 수천 명의 동료들을 만날 수 있는 멋진 곳입니다. 원서 읽기에 관심이 있으시다면 이곳을 방문해서 함께 참여해보세요!

**많은 글을 읽는 것은 영어를 익히는 가장 좋은 방법이 아니다.
그것은 '유일한' 방법이다.** - 세계적인 언어학자 스티븐 크라센 교수

영어원서 읽기는 모두가 인정하는 최고의 영어 공부법입니다. 일상에서 영어를 사용하지 않는 비영어권 국가에서 영어에 가장 쉽고, 편하고, 저렴하게 노출되는 방법이 '원서 읽기'이기 때문입니다. 하지만 영어 구사력이 뛰어나지 않은 한국의 보통 영어 학습자들에게는 선뜻 시작하기 부담스러운 것도 사실입니다.

이런 학습자들을 위하여 영어 초보자들도 쉽게 원서 읽기를 시작하고, 꾸준한 읽기를 통해 '영어원서 읽기 습관'을 만들 수 있도록 고안된 책을 소개합니다.

한국인을 위한 맞춤형 영어원서, '영화로 읽는 영어원서'

「영화로 읽는 영어원서」시리즈는 유명 영화를 기반으로 한 소설판 영어원서로, 내용 이해와 영어 실력 향상을 위한 다양한 콘텐츠가 덧붙여져 있어 보다 쉽고 부담 없이 원서 읽기를 시작할 수 있습니다. 또한 리스닝과 영어 낭독 훈련에 도움이 되는 오디오북까지 함께 제공하여 원서를 부담 없이 읽으면서 자연스럽게 영어 실력이 향상되도록 도와줍니다.

영화로 읽는 영어원서 시리즈 도서 목록

● 각 도서는 해당 영화의 소설판 영어원서입니다

인터넷 서점에서 '영화로 읽는 영서 원서'를 검색 해보세요!

    출간된 본 시리즈 도서들은 독자들의 큰 사랑을 받으며 어학 분야의 베스트셀러를 기록했고, 학원과 학교들에서도 꾸준히 교재로 채택되는 등 영어 학습자들에게 좋은 반응을 얻고 있습니다. (EBS가 운영하는 어학 사이트 EBSlang(www.ebslang.co.kr), 서초·강남 등지 명문 중고교 방과 후 보충 교재 채택 등)

Text copyright ⓒ 2010 Long Tail Books

원서 읽는 단어장
New Moon

초판 인쇄 2010년 10월 4일 ㅣ 초판 발행 2010년 10월 7일

펴낸이 김정순 ㅣ 기획 이수영 ㅣ 책임편집 김수진 유난영
콘텐츠 제작 롱테일북스 편집부

마케팅 한승일 임정진 박정우 이수영 ㅣ 펴낸곳 (주)북하우스 퍼블리셔스
출판등록 1997년 9월 23일 (제406-2003-055호) ㅣ 임프린트 롱테일북스

주소 121-840 서울 특별시 마포구 서교동 395-4 선진빌딩 4층
전자메일 helper@longtailbooks.co.kr ㅣ 전화번호 02-3144-2708 ㅣ 팩스 02-3144-3121

ISBN 978-89-5605-481-0 14740   978-89-5605-319-6 (세트)

롱테일북스는 (주)북하우스 퍼블리셔스의 임프린트입니다.

이 도서의 국립중앙도서관 출판도서목록(CIP)은 e-CIP 홈페이지(http://www.nl.go.kr/cip.php)에서
이용하실 수 있습니다. (CIP제어번호 : CIP 2010003407)